your own business

A PRACTICAL GUIDE TO SUCCESS

2nd edition

To Eamon
in appreciation
of your support
[illegible] 1/9/99

your own business

A PRACTICAL GUIDE TO SUCCESS

2nd edition

Wal Reynolds
Warwick Savage
Alan Williams

Nelson ITP®
102 Dodds Street
South Melbourne 3205

Email nelsonitp@nelson.com.au
Website http://www.nelsonitp.com

Nelson ITP® ***an International Thomson Publishing company***

First published 1994
10 9 8 7 6
99 98

National Library of Australia
Cataloguing-in-Publication data

Reynolds, Wal, 1942– .

Your own business: a practical guide to success
2nd ed.
ISBN 0 17 008934 7.
1. Small business - Australia - Management. I. Savage, Warwick, 1935– . II. Williams, Alan J. (Alan John), 1937– .
III. Title.
658.0220994

Cover designed by Cristina Neri
Cover illustration by Gené Klutke
Illustrations by Gene Bawden
Printed by McPherson's Printing Group

Nelson Australia Pty Limited ACN 058 280 149 (incorporated in Victoria) trading as Nelson ITP.

PREFACE TO THE THE SECOND EDITION

Most books which are used by teachers and students, as either text books or references, inevitably and necessarily go through a process of change and improvement if they are to survive. Since the first publication of *Your own business: A practical guide to success* in 1989, we have been delighted by its reception by users of all kinds, and have been heartened by so much favourable and constructive comment.

Although it was written mainly for small business management students in Institute of Technology (TAFE) courses, and for general readership, *Your own business* has become the staple diet of students in many other courses of study. It has found its way into courses of agricultural enterprises, into numerous industry-specific training programmes, NIES courses, and undergraduate business courses at university level. The book has proved to be flexible — challenging for students, while providing an understanding of the basics.

In deciding what improvements to make for this new edition, we have been pleased to have the comments and suggestions from a number of users. We have tried to incorporate as many of these as possible.

New chapters have been added. Chapter 2 discusses some of the recent and exciting trends in small business in Australia and overseas. Chapter 8 introduces a new approach to undertaking a feasibility study, while Chapter 13 explores in more detail the task of financing the business. All original chapters have been thoroughly reviewed and many changes have been made to enhance the practical application of this book. We hope this second edition will prove to be even more valuable to the users than its predecessor.

Wal Reynolds
Warwick Savage
Alan Williams

CONTENTS

Background

CHAPTER 1

Small business in Australia

There is a great deal of interest in small business in Australia. Nevertheless, there are two matters on which opinons differ widely. First, there is no single, satisfactory definition of a 'small business' which suits all needs. Secondly, and partly because of the first issue, we do not know exactly how many small business enterprises exist in Australia.

The aims of this chapter are to:

- enable you to understand the nature of small firms and their owner/managers, and
- make you aware of the vital contributions that your business can make to the economic health of your country and state and other aspects of life in your local community.

WHAT IS A SMALL BUSINESS?

It is important that we know, or can agree on, what constitutes a small business. Is size the only difference between small firms and larger ones? If so, how are we to measure this size difference? If not, how else do they differ?

The first efforts to define a small business, made in the United States of America about fifty years ago, were based on size and have caused much confusion. Some firms — for instance, manufacturers — use a lot more equipment than others (they are said to be more capital intensive), while others rely less on equipment and more on employees (making them labour-intensive firms.) Defining small business solely in terms of capital investment or the number of staff employed can produce odd and misleading results. So, too, can using sales volume, profits earned or market share. In short, no single numerical measure is satisfactory.

Are there any clear differences between small firms and large or medium-sized ones that can be built into a useful definition?

In addition to the fact that small firms are normally considered independent of any external managerial and financial control, two other major features distinguish them from larger ones:

- their size
- the fact that they are owner managed.

The size of small firms and the fact that they are owner managed dramatically affect their performance.

In 1971 the Wiltshire Committee, which was set up by the Australian Government to enquire into small business problems, defined a small firm as one

in which one or two persons are required to make all of the critical management decisions — finance, accounting, personnel, purchasing, processing or servicing, marketing, selling — without the aid of internal specialists, and with specific knowledge in only one or two functional areas . . .

and added that

normally the conditions defined will be found in the majority of enterprises having less than 100 employees.

In Australia, this is the most widely used definition of a small firm, except that the maximum number of employees is 100 for manufacturing firms and 20 for all others. (It is usual to include owner/managers, who play an active role in managing, in the count of employees.)

From his study of 33 624 new small firms in Australia, Alan Williams (1991) reported the average size of those new firms, at startup, to be:

2.2 Owner/ Managers	+	2.5 Full-time-equivalent employees	=	4.7 Persons

It is now widely agreed that small firms are not just small-scale versions of large companies. They have many features (and, therefore, problems) that are not found in large organisations. They have to be managed quite differently!

Small firms are not simply small-scale versions of large companies.

FEATURES OF SMALL FIRMS

Small firms have the following features, which are generally not shared by larger companies:

- small management team
- strong owner influence
- centralised power and control
- lack of specialist staff
- multi-functional management roles
- a close and loyal work team
- informal and inadequate planning and control systems
- lack of promotable staff
- lack of control over the business environment
- limited ability to obtain finance
- labour-intensive nature of work
- limited process and product technology
- narrow product/service range
- limited market share and heavy reliance on few customers
- decisions — intuitive rather than rational
- responses — reactive rather than innovative
- leadership — personal but task-oriented
- education, experience and skills — practical but narrow
- low employee turnover
- product dedication rather than customer orientation
- the owner's personal idiosyncrasies
- reluctance to take risks
- strong desire for independence
- intrusion of family interests
- the owner's health and age.

Small management team

Overall responsibility for management is in the hands of one owner/manager or several of these, and control is closely guarded. As the firm grows, this concentration of power can create many problems and stress, and lead to a shortage of expertise in the firm.

Strong owner influence

An owner/manager with a strong personality or radical views can have a great influence within a small firm. His or her skills, knowledge and overall competence therefore directly affect the firm's survival. The situation can be made worse if the owner/manager is not willing to delegate vital decision-making responsibility to employees unless forced to do so by heavy workloads.

In any complex task such as owning and running one's own business, advice from others provides valuable checks and balances, and owner/managers should seek and use this readily available help.

Centralised power and control

Linked with strong owner influence, there is in many small firms a fiercely defensive attitude in owners about their proprietorial rights. This often leads to an excessive and stifling concentration of power and control at the top. Refusal to delegate can have one of two effects:

1. growth is prevented beyond a size that can be handled by the owner/manager, or
2. growth occurs but work overload aggravates owner/manager stress to the point where the firm is out of control and a total shambles.

Lack of specialist staff

One of the most serious problems facing small firms is a lack of specialist staff. This again means that owner/managers often have to carry heavy workloads and muddle through in areas of management where they lack experience and knowledge; both problems endanger the survival of small firms.

The problems resulting from this lack of specialised skills in various areas of management point to the need to seek expert advice and guidance from external professionals such as accountants, bankers or government advisers.

Multi-functional management roles

Because small firms lack the funds to employ specialised managers, owner/managers and senior employees are often required to carry out several jobs at once, and tend to become generalists, or jacks of all trades. Staff must be flexible and willing to co-operate for the good of the firm.

A close and loyal work team

Because of its need to pull together and co-operate fully, a small firm usually comprises a close and loyal team, especially if the business is successful. This loyalty tends to persist even in the face of low wages, especially within a new firm.

Employees of small firms often willingly identify with the firm, talking in terms of ‘our’ company, ‘we’ and ‘us’.

Informal and inadequate planning and control

Most small firms lack proper planning and control procedures and do not have good accounting books and records, partly because of the owner’s ignorance about their importance, and partly because of a shortage of specialised staff and expertise. This causes many financial and managerial difficulties.

Lack of promotable staff

Poor personnel planning often leads to poor staff training and thus to a lack of promotable staff. However, many such employees do get promoted. Nepotism (favouring family members) is fairly common. Promoting staff who cannot handle the extra responsibility only creates more problems at the top.

Lack of environmental control

Small firms are often squeezed, bullied, delayed and ignored by the environment in which they operate — by customers, suppliers, banks, unions, government departments and others — because of their size and lack of bargaining power.

These difficulties are worsened by many owner/managers' general ignorance about how to reduce the effects of inflation, recession and adverse government regulations, or how to beat major competitors in getting a larger share of the market.

Limited ability to obtain finance

When seeking funds, whether by borrowing (debt) or from investors (equity), small firms often face relatively unfavourable and even harsh treatment in comparison with larger firms. This is due in part to the greater risk in lending to and investing in smaller ventures, and in part to the limited ability of owner/managers to prepare and present persuasive funding applications and credible business plans.

Labour-intensive work

Most small firms use 'low' rather than 'high' technology, and most are found in labour-intensive industries — retailing and personal and professional services. The reasons for this include difficulty in raising the funds needed for heavy investment in capital equipment, and the limited technical expertise of many owner/managers.

Limited process and product technology

Many small firms, especially those in manufacturing and related industries, suffer from limited knowledge about new production methods and/or new products available. These limitations are often the result of reluctance or inability of owner/managers to try new methods or get involved with new products or technology.

Narrow product/service range

Many small firms tend to be started and built on a single product, or on a narrow range of similar products or services. Such specialisation might give the firm a competitive advantage, but if the need to change is ignored or rejected (for whatever reason) the firm might become dangerously vulnerable, depending for its life on a product that will not sell and therefore has no future in the marketplace.

Limited market share and heavy reliance on few customers

By definition a small firm has many competitors, and when it depends on a local market (as most do) it will usually have only a fairly small share of that market. Also, many small firms follow the dangerous practice of relying on too few customers.

From a study of 213 small manufacturers, service firms and retailers in Newcastle (New South Wales), Williams (1981) found that 134 (63%) made at least half of their 1980–81 sales to five or fewer customers, and 26 (12%) made at least three-quarters of their sales to five or fewer customers.

This problem is linked with the issue of limited process and product technology. When another product range is added, the opportunity arises to satisfy more needs in the firm's market segment (market penetration) or to attract wide or different market segments. Either way, more customers might be gained and vulnerability reduced.

Decisions — intuitive rather than rational

Many owner/managers lack the ability to solve problems and cannot approach management decisions rationally. Rather, they avoid analysis and tackle issues with their intuition and 'gut feeling'. A more balanced approach is needed: one of analysis supported by intuition based on experience.

Responses — reactive rather than innovative

Too many owner/managers react hastily to problems and difficulties as they arise rather than look ahead and plan new ways of avoiding them in the future. Responding innovatively — doing things in new and better ways — is an entrepreneurial skill.

Leadership — personal but task-oriented

Most small business owner/managers prefer to work on a personal basis with employees, especially when the firm is quite small. They avoid elaborate and formal organisation; rigid job descriptions are rare. Nevertheless, they are very much concerned with getting work done and sales closed. On the 'managerial grid' they tend to be more task-oriented than people-oriented.

Education, experience and skills — practical but narrow

Owner/managers in 'craft-type' firms (as opposed to 'high-tech' ones), tend to have limited education and training. As a result their skills and knowledge are fairly narrow and gained from practical experience. They have a low regard for formal training, and will not attend training courses except when they provide directly and immediately useful skills — they prefer to learn by doing! The 'school of hard knocks' can be a long and painful experience.

Such attitudes create obstacles for a firm. Every firm needs sound practical skills. But it also needs broad thinking, open minds, innovative solutions to slippery and persistent problems, an ability to think and plan ahead and a willingness to see the firm as a whole. All these come more easily to owners who have a broader and more challenging education.

Low employee turnover

Small firms have a lower rate of employee turnover than larger firms and therefore they have a more stable workforce, despite generally lower wages and salaries in smaller firms. Strikes and other types of industrial unrest and action are less common. All this means that labour costs may be lower.

Williams (1986) found that loyalty and job satisfaction are higher among employees of small firms than in larger companies.

Product dedication rather than customer orientation

For various reasons smaller firms tend to be product-oriented and not sufficiently alert to, or aware of, market factors that might indicate a need for some change in the firm's overall image, or a need to change the product or service.

Owner/managers from technical backgrounds who are craft-oriented often become obsessed with the beauty and quality of their handicraft, and gain more satisfaction from producing something than from selling it for a profit. Business survival is highly dependent upon building a competitive advantage, and this can only come from providing what buyers want at an acceptable price.

The owner's personal idiosyncrasies

It is well known to those who are called to help small firms in difficulty that problems are sometimes caused or worsened by the owner's idiosyncrasies. Personal habits such as laziness, lack of attention to detail, uncontrolled spending, bad temper, alcoholism, lack of promptness, discourtesy and many others can seriously affect the way the firm is managed.

Reluctance to take risks

For many owner/managers, the decision to go into business for themselves is a major one. Not only is it traumatic and frightening; it also represents a huge personal risk. The startup experience, together with the realisation that failure might be as close as a single bad decision, creates in many owners a strong fear of change which results in complete avoidance of risk.

This attitude can harm a small firm, because there are times when the firm must take a risk that it cannot afford *not* to take. In other words, doing nothing is sometimes more dangerous than taking some action that is viewed as rather risky. An excessive fear of, and aversion to, risk can freeze a manager's thoughts and actions to the point where decisions cannot be made and nothing can be done. Careful study of the advantages and disadvantages of taking some step 'in faith' is desirable at all times, especially since 'paralysis from analysis' is too common a complaint.

Strong desire for independence

Studying the personal histories of owner/managers and identifying their reasons for having started in their own businesses reveal in most cases a strong and persistent desire for independence. This is widely recognised as the personality trait common to most entrepreneurial individuals, but it can cause problems. People with a strong streak of independence tend to reject advice from others, regarding it as criticism and interference, and therefore often refuse to seek help until it is too late.

Intrusion of family interests

The effects of intrusion by family members into the affairs of small firms can be both pervasive and destructive. Also, the employment and promotion of family members can prevent or delay the promotion of loyal and worthy employees and place incompetent people in senior management positions. The financial interests of the owner's family (for instance, their wanting dividends and profits) can work to disadvantage severely a small firm with cash flow problems. In short, family members can become defensive and ultra-conservative managers, and difficult employees.

The owner's health and age

If the owner/manager's age and physical and psychological health adversely affect his or her skills and motivation, the firm's performance can be seriously undermined.

Most of the above features of smaller firms stem from their smallness and the fact that they are owner managed. They reinforce the statement made earlier that small firms cannot, and in fact should not, be run as though they were scaled-down versions of corporate giants.

HOW MANY SMALL ENTERPRISES ARE THERE IN AUSTRALIA?

Getting an accurate count of small firms is not easy! Estimates from available studies vary widely. In 1980, Enterprise Australia reported a total of some 750 000 small firms in Australia, but other studies suggest a lesser figure.

A reasonable total in 1993 is between 750 000 and 800 000, with about 100 000 in primary industries and at least 650 000 in non-rural business activities. These figures are really only estimates because the size and composition of the small business population is always changing. It varies daily in total and in its mix of different types of firms.

In most years there would be a net increase of about 5000 to 6000 enterprises — maybe 35 000/36 000 startups and 30 000 closures (most, but not all of which would be failures). However, in times of economic recession, such as 1982–83 and 1989–93, there are likely to be net decreases in the small business population, and some distinct variations in the mix of firms (for example, between industries). It has been estimated that in the 1982–83 recession there was a net decrease of some 4000/5000 small enterprises; in the current recession it is expected that Australia's small business population will decrease by not less than 10 000/12 000 enterprises.

Figure 1.1 shows the proportion of all Australian firms in various size groupings, measured by numbers of employees.

> Over 98% of all Australian enterprises are small.

Small firms are most numerous in service industries, with 99.7% of all service firms employing fewer than 100 persons, followed by retailing with 99.3%, wholesaling with 97.0% and manufacturing with 96.9% (Williams, 1975, p 412).

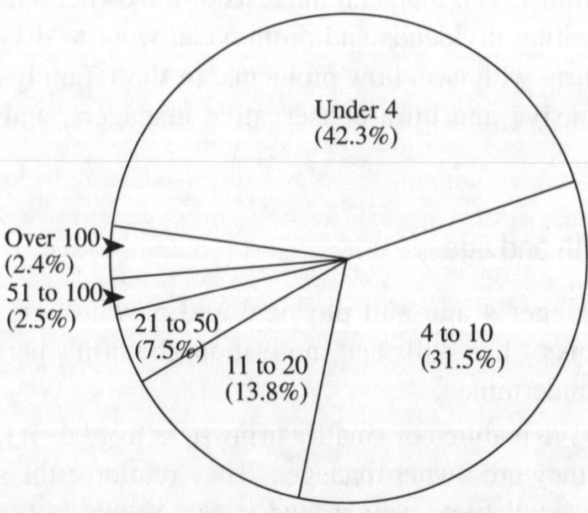

FIGURE 1.1 Small businesses in Australia, by size (number of employees)
Source: adapted from Williams, 1991

The following data were gathered by Williams in his study of 33 624 small firms in Australia during the years 1973 to 1990, using four classifications:

- legal form (that is, formal structure)
- business location
- industry classification
- startup method.

Legal form

Small firms can be sole proprietorships (with a single owner), partnerships (having between two and twenty partners) or private (proprietary) companies with up to fifty shareholders. Williams broke down the 33 624 small firms according to their legal form. His findings are shown in Figure 1.2.

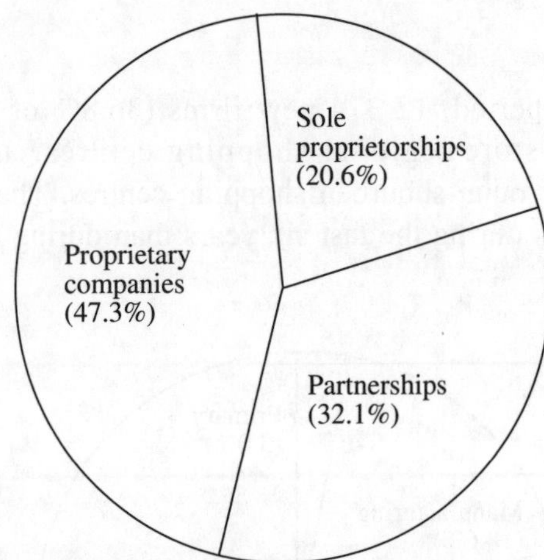

FIGURE 1.2 Small businesses in Australia, by legal form
Source: Williams, 1991

There were 12 972 family-run firms, making up 38.6% of the total or 48.4% of all partnerships and private companies in the study. The most popular mix of relatives was husband and wife — 56% of partnerships and 53% of private companies. The next most frequent ownership grouping was husband and/or wife and adult children, followed by siblings and/or in-laws.

Business location

The 33 624 small firms were located as shown in Figure 1.3. Of new firms, 46% preferred outer suburban locations. During the 17 years of the study, there was a marked increase in the proportion of firms starting in outer-suburban locations, and a substantial decrease in the proportion choosing central business district locations.

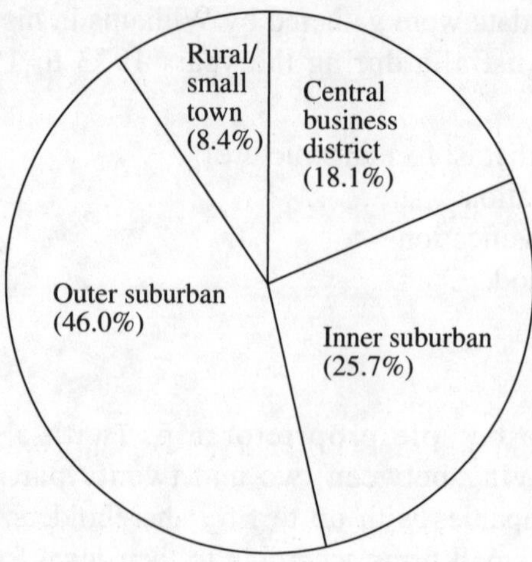

FIGURE 1.3 Small businesses in Australia, by location
Source: Williams, 1991

During the study period, 12 374 new firms (36.8% of those studied) located in multi-store regional shopping centres, and the strong preference was for outer-suburban shopping centres. These preferences were more obvious during the last six years than during the earlier part of the study.

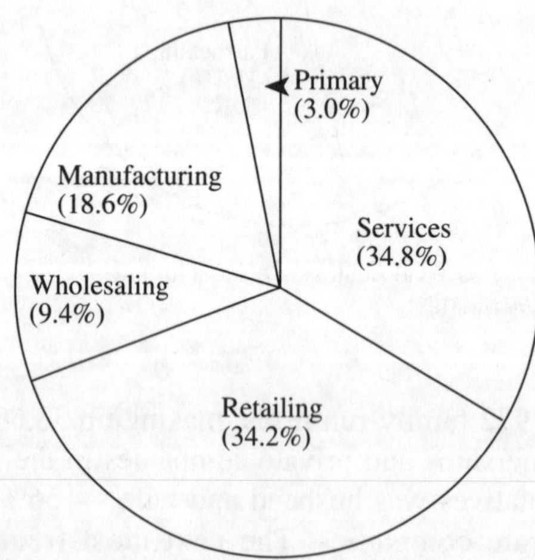

FIGURE 1.4 Small businesses in Australia, by industry
Source: Williams, 1991

Industry classification

Figure 1.4 shows how the small firms were distributed among the various industries. Retailing and services were the two most popular industries. During the study period, the proportion of new firms in the services industry increased markedly, with small decreases in all other industries.

Startup method

As Figure 1.5 shows, over two-thirds of the new firms in Australia are started from scratch, and most of the others result from the purchase of an existing firm.

Franchised firms accounted for 2140 — 6.4% of the total. There were clear signs that franchising was increasing in popularity towards the later years of the study.

In 1990, more than 10% of new small firms in Australia were franchised, with the proportions of franchisees in retailing and some services sectors being over 20%.

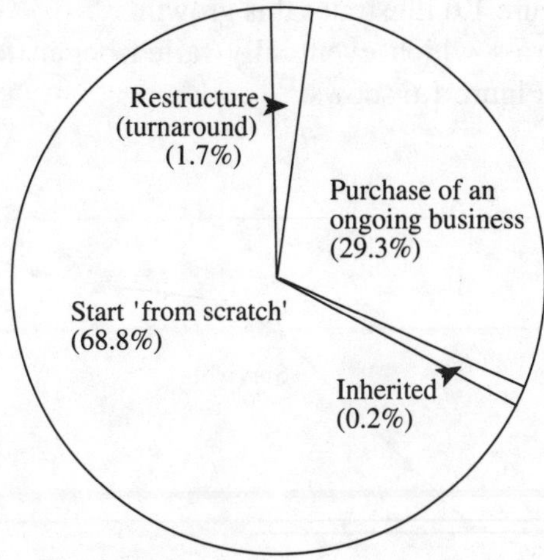

FIGURE 1.5 Small businesses in Australia, by startup method
Source: Williams, 1991

THE SOCIAL AND ECONOMIC ROLE OF SMALL BUSINESS

It is truly impossible to judge the importance of the small business sector just by the number of small firms it comprises. Small firms, and their owners and employees, make varied and vital contributions to the economic and social wellbeing of our nation that cannot be expressed in, or properly appreciated from, figures such as those above.

Contribution to employment

It is estimated that the small business sector employs at least 60% of the total Australian workforce of 8.5 million — about five million people. This represents an average of almost 6.8 persons in every business enterprise, including full-time-equivalent employees and owner/managers. This average figure compares with the startup average of 4.7 owner/managers and employees in the firms studied by Williams.

> Australia's small firms employ more people than large companies do.

Studies in the United States indicate that, over the past 20 years, new small business ventures have accounted for at least 70% of the many millions of new jobs created. Williams has reported that Australian small firms that survive are job creators: for example, in surviving firms, average employment (including owner/managers and full-time-equivalent employees) grew each year, doubling after four years and trebling after nine. By the end of 12 years, average employment in the surviving firms had reached 17.6 persons — 332% above the average startup figure. Figure 1.6 illustrates this growth.

In contrast, firms which eventually failed began to shed workers before failing, as Figure 1.6 shows.

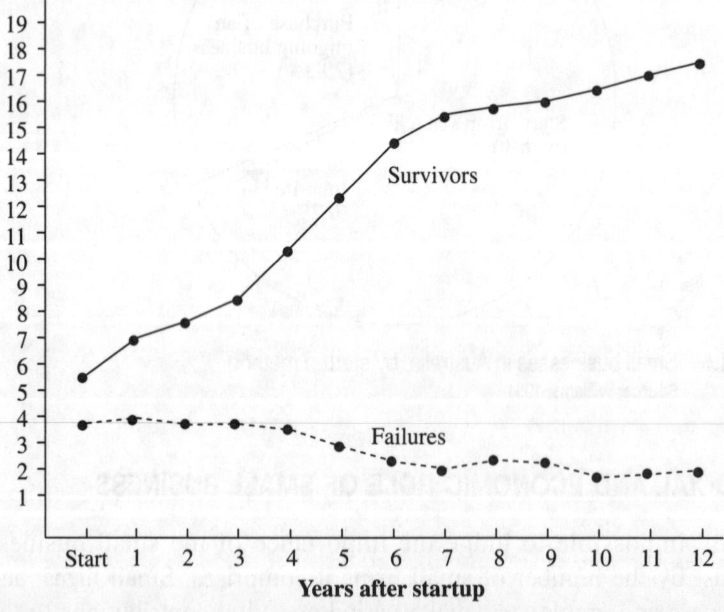

FIGURE 1.6 Average numbers of owner/managers and full-time-equivalent employees for surviving and failed companies, at end of each year after startup

Contribution to gross national product

The total value of all goods and services produced in Australia for any year is the gross national product (GNP). From the information available, it is estimated that small firms contribute about 40% of our GNP. In retailing, the motor trades and other service industries, the contribution is over half; in manufacturing and wholesaling it is about 25% each.

It is now widely believed that small firms make a very significant contribution to our economic growth and development.

Other contributions

Other valuable contributions made by our small firms include:

- providing a breeding ground for new industries and for new entrepreneurs and, in so doing, assisting innovation
- providing greater competition, and thereby acting as a check on monopoly
- acting as the foundation of free enterprise
- adding greatly to the rich variety of goods and services available to consumers
- providing employment and productive outlets for people who are unwilling or unsuitable for employment in larger organisations
- providing a wider range of choice and high standards of personal service to consumers
- acting as a seed bed from which large companies will grow
- acting as specialist suppliers of parts and components to large companies
- being a rich source of new ideas, inventions and innovation in products, services and technology, and
- contributing to society's values and stability, especially in rural areas.

Another significant contribution of small business is in providing worthwhile and meaningful employment for women, immigrants and other groups in society for whom 'traditional' employment opportunities are often hard to come by. This matter is discussed in more detail in Chapter 2.

Small enterprises, given their high numbers, make very significant contributions to the economic welfare of Australia and the quality of life in every community across the nation. Their vital role in society can be enhanced, and their owner/managers can reap satisfying rewards, as long as these firms can find ways to survive in a fiercely competitive economic environment. This book is intended to help these things be achieved.

There is clear evidence that the role of small business as a driving force in our economy is being recognised increasingly by governments.

During the 1980s there were a number of enquiries into various aspects of the efficiency and economic performance of the small business sector, the most significant being that chaired by Mr David Beddall, MP, the Minister for Small Business and Customs from 1990 to 1993. Arising from the 'Beddall Report' recommendations were a number of detailed enquiries and policy initiatives designed to remove some of the more obvious and serious impediments to the efficient economic performance of our small business sector.

Summary

A small business is one that is relatively small in its particular industry, is independent of any external controls and is owner-managed. Small firms differ from larger enterprises in many ways that go well beyond variations in size. Many of these features mean that they cannot and should not be managed like large companies.

Although exact counting is impossible, it is estimated that there are 750 000 small firms in Australia — about 98% of all firms. They are most numerous in services and retailing. Most are unincorporated, being sole proprietorships (21%) and partnerships (32%). Franchised firms are rapidly growing in number, and nearly half of all multi-owned firms are family run. Small ventures are tending to locate away from central business districts, and over one-third have chosen regional shopping centre locations. More than two-thirds of small firms in Australia are started from scratch, and another 30% are formed by the purchase of an existing business. At startup small firms employ an average of 4.7 persons (2.2 owner/managers and 2.5 full-time-equivalent employees). Small businesses in Australia make vital contributions to job creation and overall employment opportunities, and to many other aspects of our nation's economic health and quality of life.

Key words

family-run business	retailer
location	service firm
manufacturer	small business
owner/manager	sole proprietorship
partnership	wholesaler
proprietary limited company	

Review exercises

Circle the appropriate letter (A, B, C or D) to complete each of the statements following.

1 The first major study of small business in Australia was carried out by the:
A Bolton Committee
B New South Wales Government
C Wiltshire Committee
D Commonwealth Department of Labour and Industry.

2 The most widely used 'official' definition of small business in Australia includes a maximum of:
A 100 employees for all types of firms
B 20 employees for manufacturers, 100 for all others
C 20 employees for all types of firms
D 100 employees for manufacturers, 20 for all others.

3 In Australia, the average size of small firms, at startup (including owner/managers and full-time-equivalent employees), is:
A fewer than two persons
B between two and four persons
C between four and six persons
D more than six persons.

4 The total number of small enterprises in Australia is approximately:
A 625 000
B 700 000
C 750 000
D 890 000.

5 Small firms are most predominant in:
A retailing
B manufacturing
C wholesaling
D services.

6 Most small businesses in Australia are:
A sole proprietorships
B partnerships
C proprietary companies
D family firms.

7 The most popular location for small firms is:
A inner suburbs
B small towns
C central business districts
D outer suburbs.

8 The most popular startup method is:
A starting from scratch
B buying an existing business
C franchising
D inheriting a business.

9 Of the total Australian workforce, small firms employ about:
A 35%
B 48%
C 60%
D 70%.

10 Small firms are characterised mostly by their:
A small size and owner management
B serious inefficiency
C flexibility and adaptability to meet changes
D major contributions to Australia's export income.

REFERENCES

Williams, A J 1975, A Study of the Characteristics and Performance of Small Business Owner/Managers in Western Australia, unpublished doctoral thesis, University of Western Australia

Williams, A J 1981, Aspects of Environmental Vulnerability as Correlates of Small Business Performance, unpublished paper

Williams, A J 1986, 'The Discretionary Component of Work: A Comparative Study of Work Discretion and Job Satisfaction in Large and Small Enterprises', in Renfrew, K M & Back, R D *Australian Small Business and Entrepreneurship Research*, Institute of Industrial Economics, Newcastle, pp 23–42

Williams, A J 1991, 'Small business survival: The role of formal education, management training and advisory services', *Small Business Review 1990–1991*, Bureau of Industry Economics, Small Business Research Unit, Australian Government Publishing Service, Canberra, pp 43–82

Wiltshire Committee 1971 (Chairman: F M Wiltshire), *Report of the Committee on Small Business*, Australian Government Publishing Service, Canberra

CHAPTER 2

Current trends in small business ownership and management

During the 1980s and continuing into the present decade, there are a number of significant trends in the patterns of ownership and management of small enterprises in Australia. Although these trends are not unique to Australia, most of the facts and figures presented in this chapter are based on Australian research.

The purpose of this chapter is to help you understand the growing role of:

- women as small business owner/managers
- foreign-born owner/managers, in what is usually known as ethnic business, and
- part-time and casual/temporary employees in small firms.

WOMEN IN SMALL BUSINESS

In North America and Europe, it has been observed for at least a decade that growing numbers of women are owning and managing their own small firms. This trend has become very notable during the 1980s. Research by Williams shows that Australian women are also entering small business ownership in large and increasing numbers.

Historically, small business ownership has been an area of economic activity which has been dominated by men. However the situation is changing, rapidly and persistently.

In the early to mid-1970s males outnumbered females as small business owner/managers by about four or five to one. For example, in a study of small business in Western Australia, Williams (1975) found that only 45 (or 18%) of 250 owner/managers were females. In a later study covering the period 1973 to 1984, Williams (1987) reported that only 19.1% of 22 034 owner/managers throughout Australia were females. Furthermore, the vast majority (90.5%) of these female owner/managers were involved in partnerships or proprietary companies, some with other women, but most — about 80% — with male co-proprietors. During the period 1973–1984 very few Australian women were in business as sole proprietors or in partnership with other women.

In 1993 the picture is very different. During the past decade male domination of small business came under serious challenge, as increasing numbers of women sought careers as owners or employees of small businesses. In large measure this trend is a consequence of a significant shift in female values and roles in modern society. In the 1990s more women are seeking professional careers, both before and outside marriage, than ever before. Many regard small business as a preferred place of work. Many women have found that working under male managers and experiencing sexual and other forms of harassment and discrimination is increasingly intolerable. In short, many women are finding work satisfaction in small business, as an alternative to being fully committed to domestic responsibilities or being in employment in male-dominated and male-controlled work situations. Many have gone into business as a means of escaping a situation known as 'social marginality' — in which one's employment does not match one's perceived abilities, skills and ambitions.

Despite strong motivation to start their own businesses, or to seek employment in small firms, the transition to this new work role has not been easy for many women. Many have been out of the workforce for as long as 20 years while raising their children, and their job skills are rusty, if not obsolete. In juggling domestic and other work responsibilities, they have needed understanding and support from their husband and children. Of those women who have entered business ownership, over half have reported confronting serious and persistent discrimination in trying to procure start-up funding and other resources. More than a few have been insulted and abused when they demanded to be treated on the same basis as males who start their own businesses.

Notwithstanding such obstacles, the growing numbers of women in small business demonstrate the ability to persevere and succeed in the face of difficulty — whatever their motivations to do so! For reasons which will be obvious from the discussion above, Williams has found that, on average, Australian women starting in business are somewhat older than men — about 35 years for males and over 40 years for females.

Female owner/managers are more likely to be found in the retailing and services sectors, in which the required skills match the prior training and work experience of most females. Nevertheless, in manufacturing nearly 5% of sole proprietorships are operated by women, and more than 35% of multiple-owner firms have at least one female owner/manager.

Figure 2.1 shows the proportions of small enterprises which were owned and managed by males, by females, and by males and females jointly during the period 1978–92. It can be noted that of all the firms surveyed, the proportion of male-owned small firms, and those owned or operated jointly by males and females steadily decreased since 1978, while the proportion of female-owned firms increased from 19% to 34% during the 14-year period.

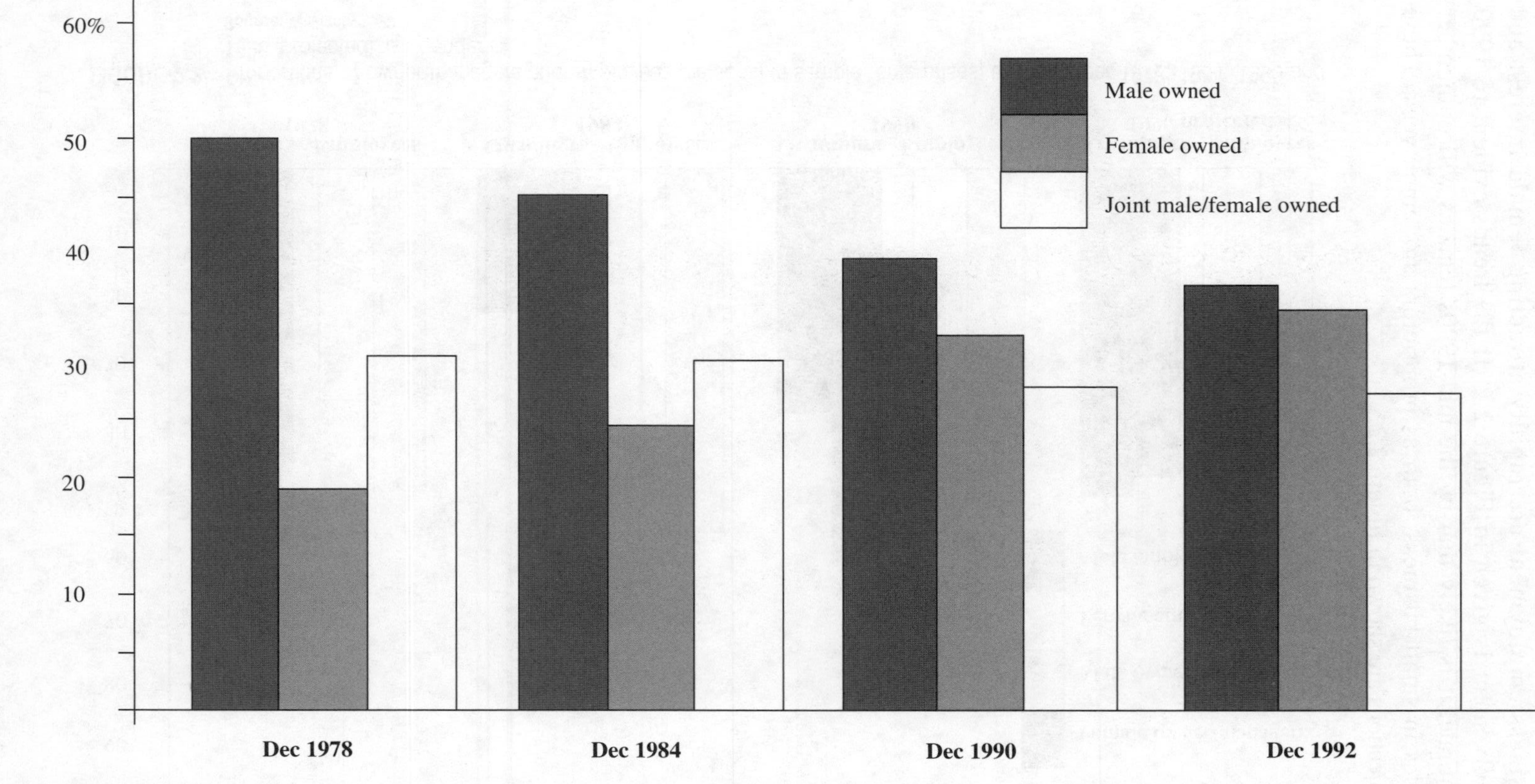

FIGURE 2.1 Surviving sample enterprises at December 1978, 1984, 1990 and 1992, by gender of owner/managers
Source: Williams, 1992

Further evidence of the fact that entrepreneurial careers and small business employment are rapidly attracting female interest and involvement is given in Figure 2.2. If the trends evident to 1990 continue, it is likely that by the mid-1990s females will outnumber males in small business, both as proprietors and employees. These projections are shown in Figure 2.2.

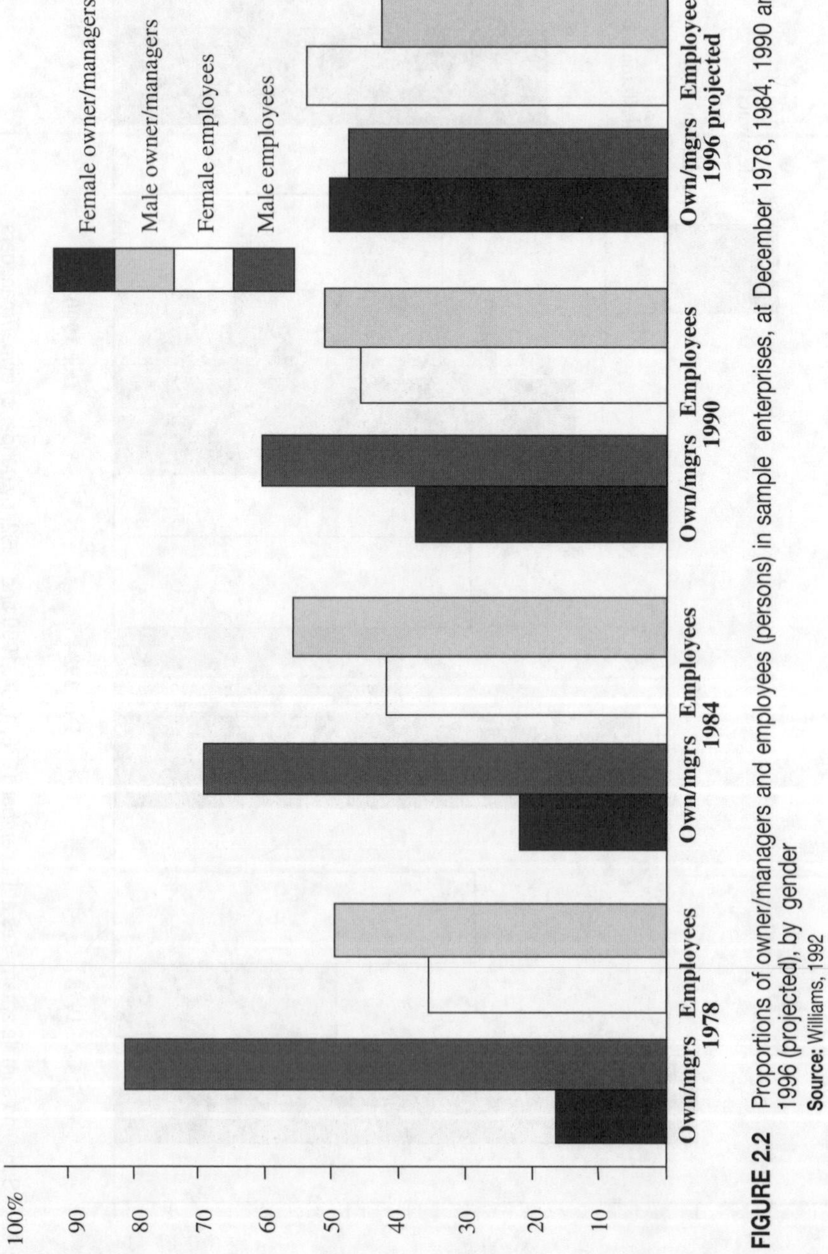

FIGURE 2.2 Proportions of owner/managers and employees (persons) in sample enterprises, at December 1978, 1984, 1990 and 1996 (projected), by gender

Source: Williams, 1992

Several reasons have been given above for women's growing interest in small business careers. There is, however, another reason for the rapid increase in female employment in small enterprise. Female proprietors in small firms are showing a strong preference for hiring female employees. In female-owned small firms, female employees average 86% of all employees with males very much in the minority (see Figure 2.3), whereas in male-owned enterprises female employees comprise only 37% and males 63%. Hence, as the number of female-owned firms increases, their staff hiring preferences are ensuring increasingly large numbers of female employees.

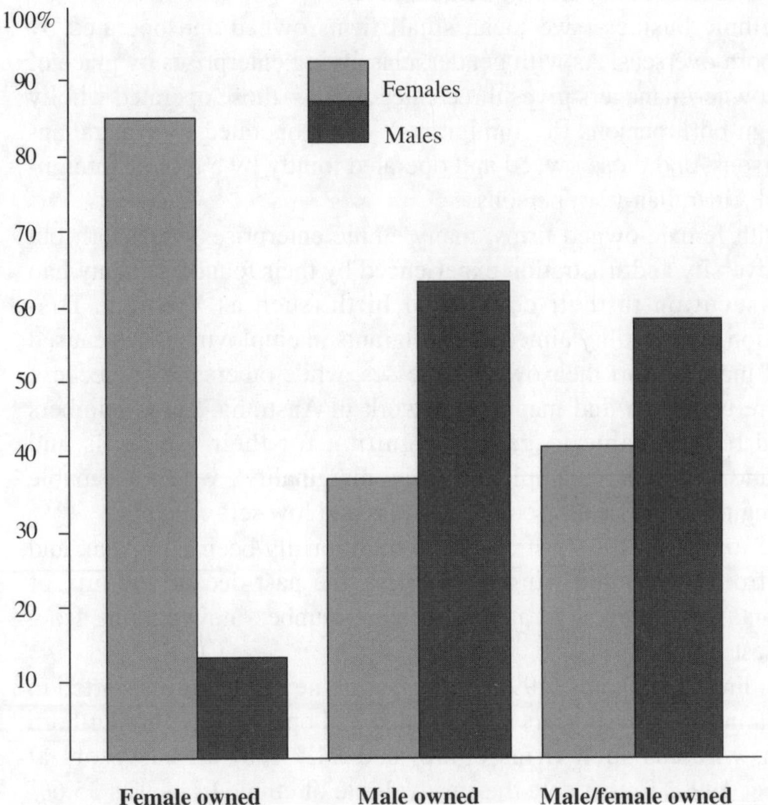

FIGURE 2.3 Proportions of female and male employees, by gender of owner/managers
Source: Williams, 1992

In summary, the evidence clearly shows a rapid and sustained growth in female entrepreneurship in Australia, as elsewhere. By about 1996 females are likely to outnumber males as owner/managers and as employees in small enterprises, particularly in the retailing and services sectors. Research data suggest that female-owned small firms are as likely to be successful as those owned and operated by males. Small firms operated jointly by male and female proprietors tend to perform a little better.

THE ETHNIC BUSINESS

There can be little doubt that the ethnic business community in Australia is making, and will continue to make, unique and vital contributions to the nation's economic and social welfare. Such firms not only serve the needs of their associated ethnic groups, but increasingly attract custom from Australian-born people, as any ample number of clients at the average Chinese restaurant will demonstrate.

By 'ethnic business' we mean small firms owned and operated by people born overseas. As with gender, classifying enterprises by place of birth of owner/managers gives three categories — those operated wholly by foreign-born persons (ie immigrants), those operated by Australian-born persons, and those owned and operated jointly by a mix of foreign-born and Australian-born persons.

As with female-owned firms, many ethnic enterprises were born out of the adversity and frustration experienced by their founders. Many had fled persecution in their country of birth, such as Vietnam. Discrimination and hostility aimed at immigrants in employment has caused many of them to start their own businesses, while others did so because they were unable to find meaningful work in Australia. Large numbers reported being unable to gain recognition for their job skills and qualifications, another example of 'social marginality', which is capable of causing psychological discomfort, stress and low self-esteem.

While immigrants to Australia have traditionally been European, and mainly from the United Kingdom, during the past decade the mix of immigrants has changed greatly, with large numbers now coming from South-East Asia.

According to Williams (1992), 22.6% of all new small firms started in Australia in the past 20 years were owned and operated by foreign-born persons, whereas such firms comprised 24.1% of all survivors at December 1990. To that date the survival rate of ethnic firms was 35.6% compared with 33.4% for all types of small firms. Small enterprises operated wholly by foreign-born persons therefore have a somewhat better survival rate than those run by Australian-born.

Ethnic firms tend to be dominated by males, contrary to the trend toward female involvement in small business generally. The 2702 ethnic firms in existence at December 1990 (Williams, 1992) had 13 096 proprietors, of whom 95.5% were males, and almost 80% of those were in firms operated by males only. Of these ethnic firms only 127 (4.7%) were owned by women, compared with over 30% for small firms generally.

It was noted above that in small firms owned by women there is a strong preference for hiring female employees. Similarly, in ethnic business there was found to be a strong preference for hiring employees with the same ethnic background as the proprietor(s), (see Figure 2.4). Furthermore, all employees were of the same nationality as the owner/managers in 84.3% of firms operated by foreign-born males; in female-owned ethnic firms that proportion was 93.2%. In addition, the proportion of female employees in female-owned ethnic firms was 96.1% on average.

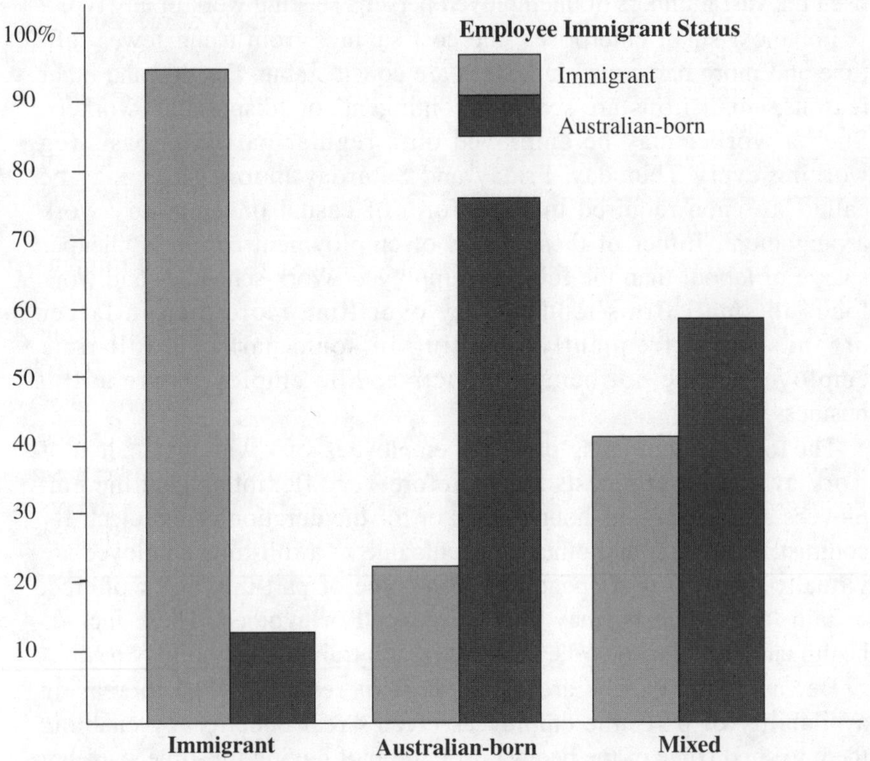

FIGURE 2.4 Proportions of immigrant and non-immigrant employees, by immigrant status of owner/managers
Source: Williams, 1992

More than 92% of all the ethnic firms studied made much use of family members. The most popular combinations were husband and wife (28.6%), one or both parents with adult children (36.4%) and siblings and/or in-laws (16.3%). Husband and wife were both proprietors in 33.1% of the firms studied, and one or more siblings had proprietorial interests in 34.4%.

Ethnic businesses comprise about one-quarter of all small firms in Australia, and are more likely to survive than firms operated by Australian-born people. Ethnic businesses commonly employ people from the same ethnic and national background as the proprietor(s), and are dominated by men — both as owner/managers and employees.

Trends in types of employment

During the past 20 years, and especially in the 1980s, there have been major changes throughout the workforce in the mix of full-time and various types of part-time employment. This trend has been very noticeable among smaller enterprises. Some of these changes have been associated with the growing trend towards female involvement in small business ownership and employment. Another factor, in recent years, has been the vast numbers of unemployed persons seeking work of any type.

For most small enterprises, the cost savings from using fewer full-time and more part-time employees are considerable. For this and other reasons, small firms are seeking 'contingent' or 'disposable' workers. Such a worker may be employed on a regular part-time basis (eg working every Thursday, Friday and Saturday morning), or may be called in when required in some form of casual or temporary work arrangement. Either of these forms of employment can be a cheaper source of labour than the full-time employee. Work schedules and work loads in small firms tend to vary over time more than in larger organisations, frequently resulting in some part of a full-time employee's time not being productive. Idle employees are still a business cost!

The total costs of using part-time employees vary with the amount of work available. The costs are therefore very flexible, since the employees are paid by the hour or day, or for the duration of a project. By contrast, the wages and other payments due to a full-time employee are virtually fixed costs. Depending on the type of part-time work offered, certain 'add-on costs' may also be reduced or avoided. These include health care, severance costs, payroll tax, job training and holiday pay.

Because small firms are often short of resources, the increasing availability of part-time employees creates real benefits by enabling them to shed some of the heavy cost burden of having full-time staff, but there are some disadvantages which need to be noted. Employee loyalty, reliability and quality of work performed may be eroded by using casual fill-ins, especially in times when finding another job is easy. A business with fewer full-time (ie permanent) employees may also offer less customer satisfaction for those who seek highly personalised service and who like being served by the same person. Sometimes highly technical and specialised job skills are not readily available in part-time, casual or temporary staff. Despite such disadvantages small firms are obviously placing more importance on the cost benefits to be gained from reducing their reliance on full-time employees.

Obviously, any business over a particular size needs a core of full-time employees. These individuals are those whose skills and knowledge are vital for the firm's survival, and whom owner/managers thereby regard as necessary to retain, despite the heavy costs of doing so. It is in the 'non-essential' types of work that part-time employees are likely to be used — clerical, secretarial, bookkeeping, sales and security, to list only a few.

Many firms, for similar reasons, are turning to sub-contracting as a means of controlling labour costs and increasing their flexibility in employment. Small building firms, for example, are able to exercise more control over work quality and costs of specialist sub-contractors (by threatening not to use them in the future) than may be the case with employees.

The following figures, based on research by Williams (1992), give an indication of how small enterprises in Australia are becoming increasingly reliant on non-full-time employees. From a study of 16 086 small enterprises in existence at 31 December 1992, it was found that there were:

- owner/managers (all full-time): 77 411
- full-time employees: 171 925
- part-time, casual and temporary employees: 265 069
- total employees: 436 994
- total persons involved: 514 405.

The 265 069 people employed in regular part-time, casual or temporary work in the small firms in this study represented 71 569 full-time-equivalent employees. (Five persons each working one day weekly, or two working for half a week represent one full-time-equivalent employee.) On average, each of these firms had 4.8 owner/managers, all of whom were working full-time. On average there were 10.7 full-time employees and 16.5 non-full-time employees. Obviously some firms in the study had grown to be quite large enterprises. These were the long-term survivors!

KEY WORDS

casual/temporary employment	immigrant
ethnic business	part-time employment
full-time employment	social marginality

REVIEW EXERCISES

1 What are the major reasons why increasing numbers of women are entering small business ownership?

2 What does this chapter indicate about employee hiring practices in small enterprises?

3 What are some of the serious difficulties facing women who seek to make a career in small business ownership?

4 Why are such large numbers of immigrants entering small business ownership?

REFERENCES

Williams, A J 1975, A Study of the Characteristics and Performance of Small Business Owner/Managers in Western Australia, unpublished doctoral thesis, University of Western Australia

Williams, A J 1987, *The Characteristics and Performance of Small Business in Australia (1983 to 1985): A Study of the Characteristics of Small Australian Business Ventures and their Owner/Managers, and a Longitudinal Investigation of their Economic Performance*, monograph, University of Newcastle

Williams, A J 1992, 'Employment patterns and practices in small firms in Australia: An assessment of skill deficiencies and training needs', *Small Business Review 1992*, Australian Government Publishing Service, Canberra

CHAPTER 3

Small business success and failure

As with most things we do in the hope of achieving success, running a small business effectively depends very much on *knowing the basics and doing them well.*

The purpose of this chapter is to help you to:

- understand the basic requirements for success in your small business
- recognise the risk of going into your own small business
- understand the major causes of small business success and failure, and
- make better decisions based on the guidelines for success in a small firm.

THE ESSENTIALS FOR SUCCESS IN A SMALL FIRM

This section briefly outlines the essentials for small business survival and success and as such is an overview of the rest of the book in which these basics are discussed in more detail.

It will be obvious, even to a casual observer, that small firms that can survive, grow and thrive are very different from those that fail outright or eke out a marginal hand-to-mouth existence. For the small operator, getting into business is fairly easy. However, survival depends on due care in planning, startup and running. While no single formula can guarantee that a small firm will survive, *success comes from doing the basics well.* The list that follows describes the necessary ingredients for successfully starting and managing a small enterprise. It is based on studies into the main reasons for small business failure in Australia. The list may be used for looking at existing firms, or as an action checklist when creating a new business or buying an existing firm.

Small business owner/managers must work hard at the basics.

To build a thriving, healthy and successful business, owner/managers should do the following:

1 Create and build the business on a real market opportunity. Find an opening with as many customers and as few competitors as possible.

Every business *must sell its products or services to survive*. What is more, it must sell enough to cover all costs and earn profits. A vital part of the startup process is the feasibility study, which must be carried out to answer the question: is there a market for the product or service on which to build the business?

In any attempt to answer this question, two aspects of that market must be looked at very carefully:

- Is the market big enough?
- Will it last for a reasonable time?

If there is doubt in either case, the viability (capability of survival) of the proposed business must be in doubt.

2 Identify or create some distinctive competence (being different, better or unique in some way), and convert this into a sustainable competitive advantage.

To survive, every firm must be better than all its competitors at something. This distinctive competence must be converted into a feature of the product or service that attracts buyers, thereby making sales and giving the firm an advantage over its competitors.

The longer that advantage can be sustained (that is, not copied by rival firms) the better.

3 Realise that:

- unless steps are taken to prevent it, competitive advantage is temporary because of the actions of competitors (Rubik's Cube is an example), and
- the firm will be either extinct or different in (say) five years' time, therefore
- forward planning and the search for new opportunities (products, ideas, customers) must go on continually, and
- change must be welcomed, not rejected or ignored.

4 Continually work to create and improve the firm's image (reputation or goodwill). On this you will build a strong sales base and healthy growth.

Most buyers do not consider only price in deciding where to buy. They look for features they like, including price and details such as courtesy, service, convenience of location, range and depth of merchandise, and overall shopping enjoyment.

5 Strive to be the best rather than the biggest.

Pushing for size and rapid growth can undermine the health (the critical resources) of the firm, so growth must be controlled.

When growth allows resources to be weakened, the firm will almost certainly meet a crisis point (see Chapter 25). It is better to push for moderate sales growth and to properly manage the business so that cash flow and profits are assured.

6 Success comes more from finding and/or creating opportunities and exploiting them than from solving problems, although this is necessary for survival.

Problems must not be ignored, but a positive approach to finding and/or creating business opportunities is the basis of healthy sales growth.

7 Build on strengths, and concentrate effort and resources.

Concentrate effort and resources on doing one or several things very well, rather than dilute effort and resources by trying to do everything.

The so-called '80/20 rule' says that 80% of what we do leads to 20% of the results (see Figure 3.1). This means that most people waste most of their time and effort on activities that produce few worthwhile results. Work out your priorities (the important things that need to be done) and plan activities to achieve them.

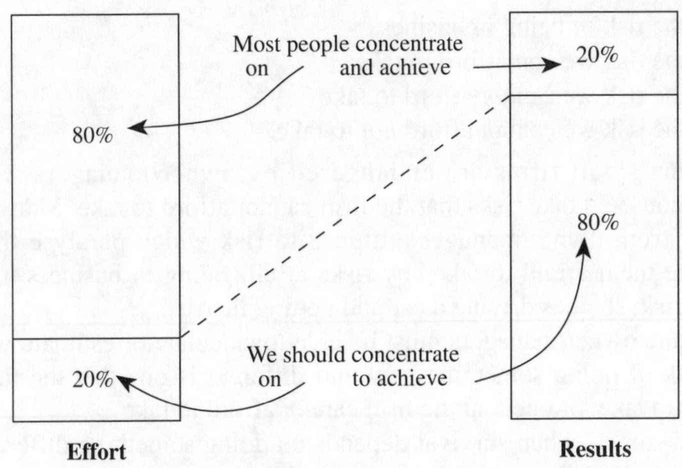

Three basic applications:

80% of your sales come from 20% of your customers

80% of your sales come from 20% of your products

80% of your time is spent on 20% of your jobs

FIGURE 3.1 Pareto or the 80/20 rule

8 Recognise the difference between efficiency (doing things right) and effectiveness (doing the right things).

There is little point in doing the wrong things the right way! Selling the right product or service to the right customers, from the right location and at the right price is being effective — success is created in the marketplace. Producing a profit is evidence of being efficient.

Good time management also means doing the *right* things (being effective, and not taking 80% of our time to do 20% of our work) and getting more done in each day (being more efficient).

9 Be innovative.

Look for new and better ways of running the business — be a leader, not a follower. Change is nearly always accompanied by some *risk* — often the risk one cannot afford *not* to take (see point 11). Many smaller changes are often easier to implement, easier to live with, and just as effective as trying to make larger scale, sweeping changes.

10 Seek and use expert advice. This is an investment, not an expense.

A great deal of technical, business and management help is now available from professional experts and advisers in most functional areas of business. Australian research by Williams (1991) shows that the ability of small firms to survive is greatly improved when their owner/managers seek and use advice from external specialists, such as accountants, solicitors and consultants, and undertake business/management training programmes.

11 Recognise the following types of risk:

- the risk of being in business
- the risk we *can* afford to take
- the risk we can*not* afford to take
- the risk we cannot afford *not* to take.

Some small firms are endangered by owner/managers who are impetuous and take risks that the firm cannot afford to take. Many others suffer from owner/manager attitudes to risk which paralyse them by making them afraid to take any risks at all. Being in business involves some risk; so does driving a car and getting married.

Astute owner/managers must be able to calculate or estimate whether the risk of doing something new and different is one that the firm *can* afford to take, or one that the firm can*not* afford to take.

Sometimes, when survival depends on doing something different (for instance, changing to a new location, adding a new branch, or taking on a new product), that risk might be one that the firm cannot afford *not* to take! Doing nothing is often more risky than doing something new and different.

12 Avoid being over-dependent on others.

Being heavily dependent on too few customers for a large proportion of total sales, or on a single supplier for critical materials or stock, can mean that the firm is vulnerable to the decisions of one party or several parties outside the firm.

It is very important to:

- widen the sales base to have as many customers as possible, and
- have alternative or back-up suppliers.

13 Get rid of unprofitable and/or unsaleable products and services.

The product on which the firm was founded may now sell only if heavily advertised at much cost, or only at a greatly reduced price. In either case, that product can hardly be said to be the basis of the firm's competitive advantage.

It is a fact of business life that products and services have 'lifecycles'. As they become obsolete, unfashionable, out-of-date, superseded, or for any reasons impossible (or even very difficult) to sell, it may be time to get rid of them. With good planning and an entrepreneurial approach new products and services are ideally available in anticipation of the discarding of old ones.

14 Manage the firm's resources efficiently and effectively.

The five basic resources in every business are

- cash and funds
- people (both customers and employees)
- physical assets (such as plant and equipment)
- time, and
- information (for decisions and management).

15 Realise that every business/management decision and action (and every 'non-decision' and 'non-action') will affect the firm's survival ability.

Owner/managers of small firms must always be aware of, and alert to, all factors that might reduce the firm's ability to survive. In running the firm, it is important that they realise that every managerial decision they make, and every managerial action they take will either enhance or reduce the firm's survival ability.

In every decision and action, survival of the business must therefore be the foremost goal. It must also be realised that inability to make decisions relating to the firm's survival can reduce survival ability.

No firm can survive if it is leaderless. Strong, effective and skilled leadership is therefore a critical factor in small business success. This is due to the popular (and justified) view that poor management kills small firms, most of which depend on one or two owners to provide the necessary managerial and entrepreneurial input.

16 Use time efficiently and effectively.

Time is the only one of the five critical resources (see point 14) that is totally limited in supply. It must be used efficiently (getting more done in each day) and effectively (getting done those things that are most important — the top-priority activities).

For owner/managers and employees alike, time is money. Wasting time is therefore wasting money!

17 Regard cash flow as the lifeblood of the business, and maintain strong liquidity by:

- using *budgets*
- watching *profitability*, through adequate margins
- controlling *credit sales* and accounts receivable
- carefully managing *inventory levels*, and
- operating with lean *overhead costs*;

all of which require *good records*.

18 Keep good records and realise that, to be useful as a business resource, information must be:

- appropriate to the user's needs
- understandable to the user
- concise yet meaningful
- accurate within reason
- economically produced, and (of greatest importance)
- up to date.

19 Hire the right people for your team, use them and involve them in the business, motivate them by rewarding them wisely (thus reducing staff turnover) and get rid of all 'dead wood'.

Because of the high cost of having employees, choose them carefully, using a job description, and measure their individual productivity, and thereby their individual worth, to your firm.

20 Continually update product knowledge and technical skills throughout all levels and parts of the firm.

An essential part of creating and maintaining a strong competitive advantage is having up-to-date product knowledge and technical competence. Buyers of products want those products only because of the services they provide — a drill is bought because the buyer needs holes in a piece of timber.

Most buyers therefore expect firms to have and provide information about what their products will and will not do, how they should be used, and other user-related matters.

Your ability to provide such information will require your attendance at product launching activities, subscribing to and reading technical journals and product manuals, keeping in touch with manufacturers and suppliers, and employee training.

21 Regularly review the suitability of the firm's location.

A firm's location is a critical factor in its ability to attract buyers and make sales, particularly for retailers and some service firms. For manufacturers a good location is also important, but more for cost reasons.

A good location usually incurs higher occupancy costs, but a poor location, even with low rental, leasing or ownership cost, is a handicap. A particular business location might change from being excellent to being poor in a short time, as road systems and resultant traffic patterns change, the mix of neighbouring firms varies, and other changes affect the flow of potential buyers to the business.

22 Learn from errors made, and do not repeat them.

Mistakes are made in every small firm, particularly in the early stages, and particularly if owner/managers are lacking technical, management or entrepreneurial experience and expertise. In some cases the errors will be so serious as to bring about failure, in others inexperience and ignorance will lead to problems that might not be 'fatal' but from which owner/managers should learn and which they should not repeat. With this, external advice and/or management training can help greatly.

23 Watch for signs of mental stress and, if you find them, decide on the cause and deal with it.

Excessive and lengthy periods of stress prevent individuals from performing their work efficiently and effectively, and commonly lead to serious illness. There are many aspects of owning and operating a small firm that can be very stressful, and studies show that the probability of failure is increased when owner/managers are highly stressed (see Chapter 23), simply because they cannot manage properly and they lose control of the business.

Some common outward signs of stress are excessive smoking, alcohol and drug abuse, accidents on the job, depression and inability to concentrate. In order to find the cause of the stress and do something about it, you might consider getting a partner or more staff to relieve work overload, or taking a training course to learn how to supervise employees or to manage the firm's finances. In extreme cases, stress might require you to quit the business.

24 Be decisive and assertive — decide on the best course of action, and follow it!

Major problems rarely go away if ignored. Successful owner/managers can quickly size up situations requiring action, collect the information needed, decide on the best course of action and take it. Putting off making decisions is really only loading oneself with unfinished jobs and more worry, and this creates more stress.

Be an action person, but a thinking one! You must be able to make tough decisions and take tough actions when needed.

25 Believe in yourself and your business.

As a final and most important consideration, if you are not totally committed to succeeding in what you are doing, you are probably better off out of it!

Your commitment to succeeding must, at certain times, become an obsession. The stakes are usually very high; the rewards for those who succeed are great, but the penalties for failing are painful.

Owning and running your own business is more than a job. It is a way of life that has no room for lukewarm enthusiasm or a half-hearted desire to win.

Aim to be a winner, or get out!

FAILURE AND ITS CAUSES

What is business failure?

A business fails when it stops trading for either of the following reasons:

- it becomes bankrupt (a legal process to distribute among the creditors the property of a person or firm who will not or cannot pay their debts); or
- it voluntarily closes down because it is insolvent (unable to pay its debts when they are due), unable to trade profitably, or facing financial difficulties.

If a firm ceases to operate because of death, ill health or any other personal reason not directly associated with trading or financial problems, it is not classed as a failure.

About 30 000 small firms fail in Australia every year — 100 every work day.

Only about one failure in every six or seven is a bankruptcy. In most failures the decision to close down is made by the owner(s), and stocks and assets are sold and debts paid off as far as possible. If all debts cannot be paid in full, all creditors must agree to partial payment (eg, 85¢ in the dollar), or the firm might be forced into bankruptcy because one or more creditors decide(s) to take legal action to recover this money.

Inventory trouble

It is estimated that up to 30 000 businesses fail in Australia annually — about 100 every working day! Because most failures are voluntary closures, the accurate number of failures is virtually impossible to count. This figure is nearly 5% of the nation's estimated small business population and indicates a huge waste of human and economic resources.

More than three new firms in every ten fail within one year of starting.

When do small businesses fail?

Almost every study of the age of small business failures shows that most failed firms are fairly young. For example, Williams (1975, p 70) found that 28% of 863 bankrupt small Australian firms had been in business for less than one year, 41% less than two years, and 69% less than five years.

Studies of the survival and failure rates of new small firms over time have given similar results. Williams studied 33 624 small business startups in Australia for the years 1973 to 1990 and recorded failure rates as shown in Figure 3.2.

The increasing proportion of women in small business in Australia (as in other countries) has been discussed in Chapter 2. It should be noted that the failure and survival rates of small enterprises which are owned and operated by women does not differ greatly from those which are operated by men. The survival rate is slightly better for small firms operated jointly by men and women.

About 32% of new small firms failed within the first year, 16.5% in the second year, 13% in the third, 7% in the fourth and about 5% during the fifth year. When these yearly failure rates (the broken line in Figure 3.2) are added, we find that nearly 50% failed within two years, over 60% within three years and 73% within five years; after five years only one-quarter of starters were still in business! There is also evidence that early failures are increasing.

While this huge failure rate is cause for concern, it must be noted that not all small firms fail. When we look at why some firms can survive and others cannot, in most cases the causes are fairly obvious. Can these causes be remedied? Can many small business failures be avoided?

Why do small businesses fail?

It is said that some of the causes of business failure are related to how well the firm is managed (and this includes personal areas such as motivation, self-discipline, and so on), while other causes come from outside the firm (for example, economic conditions such as the inflation rate and rapid economic, political and social changes).

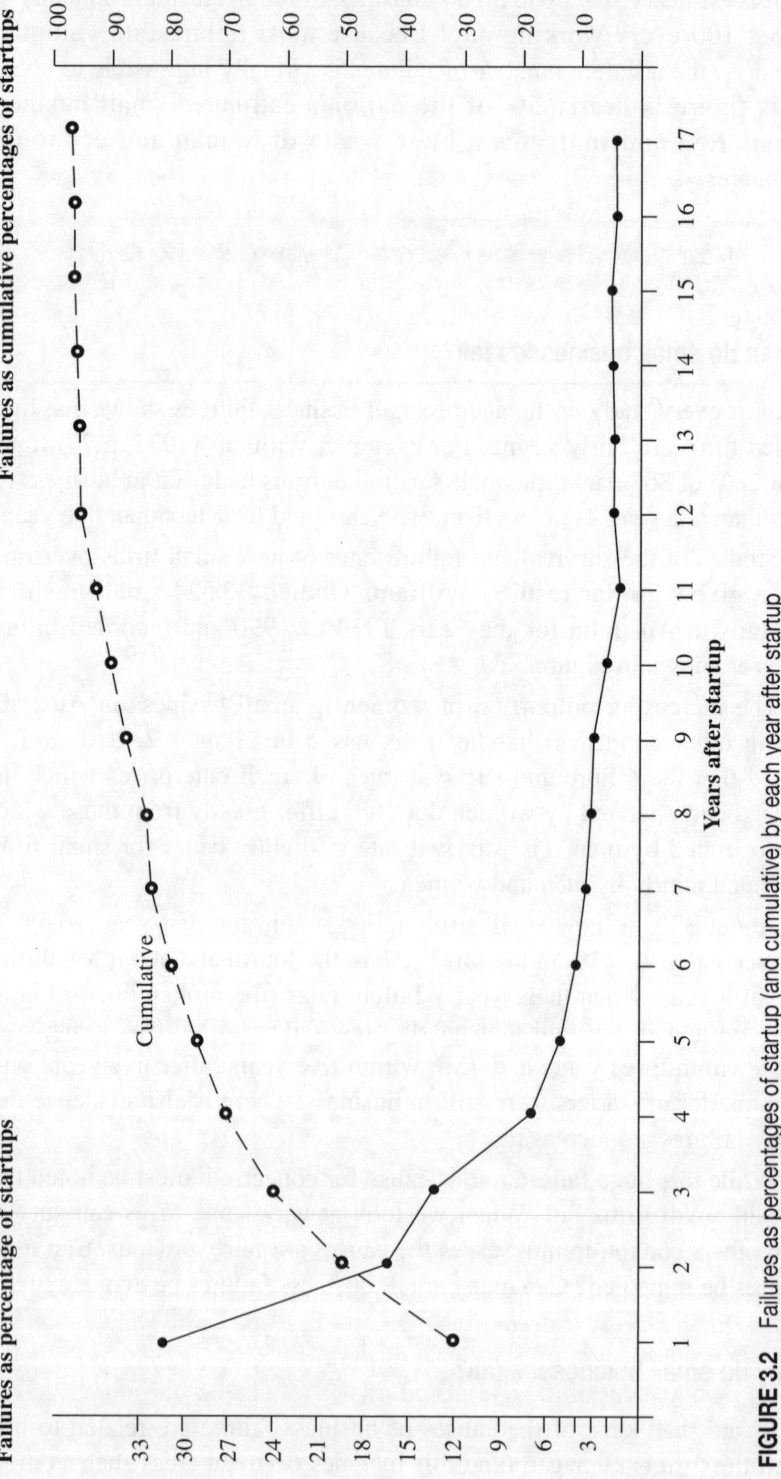

FIGURE 3.2 Failures as percentages of startup (and cumulative) by each year after startup

Source: adapted from Williams, 1991

Poor management is the major factor in business failure.

Most studies link internal problems such as management incompetence or inefficiency with most failures. For example, Dun & Bradstreet consistently state that over 90% of all business failures are associated with 'managerial inexperience and incompetence'.

If we know which management skills, knowledge and techniques are vital for successfully starting and running a small firm, and if these can be taught and learned, the overall quality of management, and therefore the general level of small business survival, can be improved.

Deciding exactly what has caused a small firm to fail is not easy! In most cases several serious problems are working together, each affecting the other, eroding resources and reducing the firm's ability to survive. Often, the inability of management to cope with difficult external conditions is a cause.

Poor collections

It is not simply that bad debts, or slow-selling stock, or excess costs, or lack of sales are — alone or collectively — the cause of failure. These problems are only the *symptoms* of poor management, and it is this poor management that is behind almost all small business failures.

In a small firm, the personal qualities and managerial skills of the owner/manager(s) (one or two persons in most cases) have a direct effect on the success or otherwise of the firm. The destructive influence of an incompetent or inexperienced owner/manager is far more likely to harm a small enterprise than is any single executive in a large corporation. Linked with skills in management are various personal attitudes, values and motivations which affect how owner/managers go about their work.

TABLE 3.1 Reasons for business failure, by percentage of firms affected by each reason

	Reasons	Percentage of failed firms
1	Lack of business/management experience, skill and ability	60.50
2	Inadequate, inaccurate or non-existent books and records	55.35
3	Inflation and inability to operate with fluctuating costs and prices of:	
	(a) wages	
	(b) interest rates	
	(c) services (telephone, power, etc)	
	(d) pricing difficulties	38.79
4	Union 'interference' and problems	27.93
5	Excessive private drawings	22.33
6	Under-capitalisation (particularly at startup)	21.38
7	Over-use of credit (bad debts and slow collections)	20.60
8	Inventory problems (slow stock turnover and dead stock, records, ordering, etc)	20.36
9	Inability to use/understand financial reports and statements	17.78
10	Inadequate sales (too few customers for too many competitors)	17.50
11	Rapid rate of technological change (affecting product knowledge, skill requirements, staff training, work quality, etc)	17.06
12	Lack of financial planning (no budgets, inadequate cash reserves, tax payout problems, etc)	16.63
13	Industry-wide downturns	14.40
14	Problems with staff supervision, motivation and productivity	12.63
15	Failure to seek and use external advice	12.12
16	Inability to get and keep good staff	11.05
17	Lack of product development and market analysis	9.10
18	Inability to borrow needed funds	8.34
19	Insufficient knowledge of competition (affecting pricing/selling decision)	7.39
20	Unproductive use of assets (over-capitalisation)	7.28
21	Poor promotion and dubious image	6.75
22	Premature expansion (pushing volume and creating cashflow problems)	4.89
23	Reliance on too few customers/suppliers	4.78
24	Poor location	3.01
25	Inability to cope with seasonal fluctuations	2.89
26	Poor time management	2.80
27	Acting without adequate risk assessment (ie gambling)	2.68
28	Over-reliance on gearing (funding operations at 'excessive' interest rates)	2.13
29	Interpersonal problems among owner/managers	2.02
30	Inability to assess risk associated with expansion, new investment, etc	1.47
31	Uninsured disasters (fire, partner death, embezzlement, loss of profits, etc)	0.67

Source: Williams, 1991

As part of his studies on small firms in Australia, Williams investigated the reasons for failure during the years 1973 to 1990 of 22 408 small firms (66.6% of the 33 624 firms studied). As expected, there was no simple answer. Owner/managers of each of these failed firms were asked to give up to five reasons for their failure. The result was 69 210 responses covering over thirty major reasons. The owner/managers were also interviewed so that their responses could be checked and verified. Table 3.1 shows these failure reasons in order of importance, and the percentage of firms whose failure was affected by each reason.

Almost three-quarters of new firms fail within five years of starting.

Neglect

It is noteworthy that in nearly two-thirds of the failed firms the owner/managers admitted that 'lack of business and management experience, skill and ability' was a key factor leading to failure — clearly an internal problem which, in many cases, could have been remedied. Well over half the failed firms had inadequate or inaccurate books and records, or had none at all. This, too, could have been remedied.

Problems associated with difficult economic conditions were seen as significant by nearly four out of ten failed firms. Most of these difficulties were to do with increasing operating costs, and with problems in pricing goods and services in times of inflation. From their responses it is clear that many small business operators are at a complete loss to know what to do in the face of economic (external) problems, and many take protective measures. At the same time, of course, and under the same economic conditions, many small firms thrive and grow. So even if external conditions do not make business life easy, greater management skill could enable more firms to cope.

Difficulties involving unions and industrial relations seriously affected nearly 30% of the failed firms. This issue is very hard to solve. The best advice would seem to be to treat employees in a fair and open manner.

About one failed firm in every five thought a group of factors to be important. All of these, and most of the others listed in Table 3.1, indicate poor management by, or personal problems of, owner/managers.

When these 31 reasons are grouped, the major reasons for failure of small firms in Australia are, in order:

1 financial management and liquidity problems
2 management inexperience and incompetence
3 problems coping with inflation and other economic conditions external to the firm
4 poor or non-existent books and records
5 sales and marketing problems
6 staffing
7 difficulties with unions
8 failure to seek and use expert advice.

Internal and therefore 'controllable' factors resulting from management deficiencies (that is, all except point 7 in the above list) were seen as major contributors to failure in about 95% of the failed firms studied. If coping with difficult economic conditions is also assumed to be an 'uncontrollable' factor, the 'controllables' still contributed to 80% of the failures.

From all of the evidence, we must conclude that inability to manage is the underlying reason for most small business failures. Too many people go into business for themselves without any realistic understanding of the skills and knowledge needed to survive. Too many lack the experience as an employee which would have given them the necessary expertise. Many have personal weaknesses and bad habits which make the situation worse. Most need help but are not willing to admit the fact and seek out people who can help. Most will not take up any opportunities to improve themselves by training in business methods.

Avoiding failure

> Most failures can be avoided.

Obviously it is better to recognise your managerial and other deficiencies *before* starting in business, and to take steps to remedy them. However, even if you have already 'taken the plunge', it is not too late. Most gaps in management knowledge and skills can be filled. Help is even available to managers whose performance at work is affected by personal problems.

In most small firms, improved management is possible and the probability of failure can be greatly reduced.

In the next three chapters we will look more closely at the kinds of personal skills, knowledge, commitment and motivation needed for success in owning and running a small firm.

SUMMARY

Most failures of small firms occur in the first months or years. It is during this time that lack of knowledge, skills, management experience, technical proficiency and entrepreneurial drive really take their toll on new and struggling small ventures.

Good management entails giving attention to the basics — the 80/20 rule again! Many managers get bogged down in trivial detail and lose sight of the few really important matters. To summarise, the rules for success in small business are:

1 Create and build the business on a real market opportunity (find a niche).
2 Identify or create some distinctive competence and convert this into a sustainable competitive advantage.
3 Realise that:
   - competitive advantage is temporary
   - the firm will be either extinct or different in five years' time, therefore
   - planning ahead and searching for new opportunities must go on continually and
   - change must be welcomed.
4 Create and improve the firm's image.
5 Strive to be the best rather than the biggest.
6 Remember that success comes from finding and/or creating opportunities.
7 Build on strengths and concentrate effort and resources.
8 Recognise the difference between efficiency and effectiveness.
9 Be innovative.
10 Seek and use expert advice.
11 Recognise the various types of risk.
12 Avoid being over-dependent on others.
13 Get rid of unprofitable and/or unsaleable products and services.
14 Manage the firm's resources efficiently and effectively.
15 Realise that every business/management decision and action will affect the firm's survival ability.
16 Use time efficiently and effectively.
17 Regard cash flow as the lifeblood of the business.
18 Keep good records.

19 Hire the right people, use them and involve them in the business, reward them wisely and get rid of all 'dead wood'.
20 Continually update product knowledge and technical skills.
21 Regularly review the suitability of the firm's location.
22 Learn from errors made and do not repeat them.
23 Watch for signs of mental stress and, if these are found, decide on the cause and deal with it.
24 Be decisive and assertive — decide on the best course of action and follow it.
25 Believe in yourself and your business!

KEY WORDS

bankrupt	effectiveness
business failure	efficiency
cash flow	image
competitive advantage	innovation
distinctive competence	insolvent

REVIEW EXERCISES

Circle the appropriate letter in each case.

1 Moving a business from a poor location to a better one is an example of a risk the owner(s):
A can afford to take
B cannot afford to take
C cannot afford not to take
D should not have to take.

2 A business is generally said to have failed when:
A it is unable to trade profitably
B it becomes insolvent
C it is declared bankrupt
D any of the above occur.

3 Estimates indicate that the number of business failures in Australia every year is about:
A 15 000
B 20 000
C 30 000
D 50 000.

4 Business failures are more likely to occur among:
A older firms in which owners lose interest
B firms that grow too big too fast
C newer and smaller firms
D small firms in manufacturing.

5 Which of the following is the more common 'cause' of small business failure?
   A Inability to get and keep good staff
   B Under-capitalisation, especially at startup
   C Reliance on too few customers and/or suppliers
   D Poor location

6 In general, business failure is caused by:
   A factors which are controllable
   B uncontrollable problems
   C controllable factors plus some uncontrollable ones
   D none of these sorts of problems.

7 Most business failures occur among firms in which age group?
   A Under one year
   B 1 to 3 years
   C 3 to 5 years
   D Over 5 years

8 Of all the major causes of business failure, the most important is:
   A fraud
   B lack of managerial skill
   C neglect
   D disasters and other external causes.

References

Williams, A J 1975, A Study of the Characteristics and Performance of Small Business Owner/Managers in Western Australia, unpublished doctoral thesis, University of Western Australia

Williams, A J 1991, 'Small business survival: The role of formal education, management training and advisory services', *Small Business Review 1990-1991*, Bureau of Industry Economics, Small Business Research Unit, Australian Government Publishing Service, Canberra, pp 43–82

1

Thinking

Thinking about your own business is a personal activity. It involves considering what having a business means to you and which type of business appeals to you. So one of the first things to consider is what you want from your business. What you can achieve depends to a large extent on what you bring to your business – in terms of your background, experience, knowledge and personal characteristics, and also your own level of commitment to the business.

This section is designed to help you identify what you need in order to start a small business, and how your personal attributes will affect your choice of business and your chances of starting a successful business. It describes the major factors involved and provides, in Chapter 6, a detailed self-evaluation. Completing the evaluation will allow you to measure your strengths in each factor and identify specific areas in which you might need to develop yourself. This knowledge can be very valuable because it can make the difference between a successful start and an unsuccessful one.

Take the time to read this section thoroughly and do all the exercises carefully. Your attention to this section is the first indication you will have of your level of commitment to your own business.

CHAPTER 4

Owner/manager commitment and responsibilities

So far we have looked at the nature of small business. We have examined an overview of small business in Australia and discussed the factors leading to success or failure of small business operations. At this stage it is important to realise that going into business means taking risks, accepting rewards and responsibilities and working with other people.

By the end of this chapter, you should be able to:

- decide whether you are willing to take the necessary risk
- assess the level of personal involvement which your own business will demand, and
- identify the responsibilities of going into your own business.

PUTTING EVERYTHING AT RISK

It is often said that most Australians, at some stage of their lives, dream of having their own small business. This dream is almost as strong as the dream to have their own home, and in fact both dreams share four common factors:

- independence
- money
- planning, and
- security.

The first common factor is gaining *independence*. Australian's crave independence in wanting their own home — to be free from paying rent and be able to 'do their own thing' in their own home. A big attraction of small business is the dream of being your own boss and making your own decisions — in other words, of doing it your way!

The second factor is money, or, put another way, costs. Costs can be broken down into three common parts:

- establishment or purchase costs
- running costs, and
- expansion costs.

Establishment or purchase costs are the total of all costs needed to build or purchase the house or business. These include legal fees, consultation fees, licences, search fees and goodwill. Such fees are usually much higher than most people expect, often leaving the new owner short of money and borrowing capacity. It is a common mistake for people buying or establishing a business to see these costs as total costs and forget about running costs and expansion costs.

Running costs are the costs of day-to-day running and maintenance such as electricity, wages, vehicle expenses, repairs and loan repayments. Failure to provide for these expenses can spell disaster for a small business and turn the dream into a nightmare.

Expansion costs are the costs of developing or expanding. If no provision has been made for these, there can be no growth or improvement. In turn, the business might lose opportunities — which, in a changing world, could be fatal.

The third common factor is the need for planning.

Things don't just happen.

In building or purchasing a business, as in acquiring a home, legal restraints have to be considered and approvals have to be sought and given. A goal has to be set, to be achieved within a time frame, and a plan has to be made and implemented.

The fourth common factor is security. A good business is a source of psychological and physical security, as is a good home. However, this security will disappear if the business fails or the house collapses; and while it is not a daily occurrence for houses to collapse, it *is* very common for businesses to fail, as we have seen in the previous chapter.

The risk involved in owning a business is far greater than that in owning a home. Should a business fail, the owner risks not only the money invested, but also, in many cases, much else, including:

- borrowed money
- assets
- health
- family and friends, and
- self-esteem.

If your business fails you could lose everything.

People going into business also risk their health due to the long hours and continuous pressures of their work. Should the business start to fail, these work hours and pressures usually increase, resulting in very high stress on the owners. This often leads to physical and mental deterioration. The effects of stress are more fully covered in Chapter 23.

These factors also have an effect on family life, and unfortunately marriage break-ups are common with business failure. The loss of assets (including the house), income and lifestyle cannot be ignored. It is also common at this stage to find that there is no time or money for social life, and friends disappear. As well as this, the owners of a failing business usually do not want to discuss their problems with friends or outsiders, thus placing more strain on themselves, their marriages and their families.

The family unit is often placed under great stress when the decision is made to go into business using the family home as security for a loan. Conflict arises where at least one family member sees the threat to the family home as totally negating the goal of owning a business. Such conflict *has* to be resolved to give the new business a normal chance of success and to reduce the tension at home. Studies by Alan Williams have shown a much higher chance of failure in businesses where family support is lacking.

One of the most tragic results that can come from a business failure is the loss of self-esteem due to the blame which many people put on themselves. This stigma of 'shame' can completely erode the person's pride and destroy their self-respect and self-confidence, making the return to 'normal' life even more difficult. Without self-respect and confidence, it is much more difficult to find alternative employment.

Thus a person going into business must recognise the chances and the realities of failure, and hence the risk of losing everything — not just the money invested in the business. *The risk is real.* There is no proposition that is a 'sure thing' and the risk of failure will be ever present with any small business. If there were no risk in small business everyone would have one, as the rewards can be great.

One of the measures of the degree of risk is the level of profit. Usually, the higher the risk the greater the profit and the lower the risk the lower the profit. This is so because if people are prepared to put everything at high risk, they should expect a higher return for the taking of that risk. Conversely, if they are not prepared to take a risk they should not go into business on their own.

THE NEED FOR PERSONAL INVOLVEMENT

So far in this chapter we have seen that going into business means putting everything at risk; not only the money invested in the business, but also the owner's assets, health, personal relationships, way of life and self-respect. There is only one way to avoid this risk: not to go into business.

With such a high risk it is important that the owner be prepared to commit a full-time effort, not just part-time or casual involvement. Neglect, as we saw in Chapter 3, is one of the prime causes of business failure. With so much at risk, the owner should see the business as a business and not as a substitute for a job — full- or part-time. Small business can be, and should be, fun — but it is also hard work; just ask any small business person.

If you look carefully at any small business you will see a host of reasons why owners must be totally involved, such as:

- customer expectations
- decision-making
- planning
- image
- staff
- cost, and
- income.

Customer expectations

The customers of a small business expect to see the owner actually present and involved in the business, believing they will get better service or value if the owner attends to them. As a case in point, the owner of a supermarket noticed that his sales fell when he was not working 'on the floor'. As an experiment, he spent a week in full contact with his customers and sales rose. The logical extension of this discovery was to ensure that he was 'on the floor' during the key trading periods each day; and he claims that this factor was the main reason he doubled his sales in 12 months.

Decision-making

By being in constant touch with the customers, owners can recognise shifts in demand and expectations, and pick up warning signs such as returns, complaints, slow-moving stock and low staff morale, which would not otherwise be easy to detect. They can then decide promptly what action can be taken to rectify emerging problems.

Planning

In most small businesses, the staff do not have access to key sources of information such as bank balances, market plans, product development, expansion plans, and so on. It is therefore not reasonable to expect them to make non-routine decisions — or key decisions which will affect the future of the business.

The planning process in a small business is not an isolated activity which can be done for, say, one hour each night; rather, it is a continuing process interwoven with the daily activity of the business. The owner must be present and involved in order to implement that process.

Although the owner can certainly delegate particular areas of responsibility, the total responsibility for the success of the business cannot be delegated and ultimately rests with the owner.

> It is your business — your money — your income — your risk —your life! You can't delegate it to anyone else!

Image

The image of any small business is the picture that other people have of it. Every business has an image in the minds of each of its customers and this image can make it or break it. The personal involvement of the owner usually means higher standards and a personal pride in the business and its ability to satisfy customers. This type of involvement must generate a better image than does a business in which the operators or staff do not care.

Staff

There is a very big difference between working for an employer and working for yourself. When you work for yourself and have staff, you must demonstrate leadership, set an example, train and motivate staff, and plan for development. A small business owner must have, and show, a commitment to these things if the business is to survive. A situation must be created in which the staff want to work *with* the owner rather than *for* him or her. This necessitates building a good staff team and training employees on a continuing basis. It is not hard to imagine what happens if staff perceive the owner to be uninterested and uninvolved in the business to which they are committing their efforts.

Cost

Have you ever wondered why small business owners work such long hours? Most small business owners cannot afford all the staff they would like to employ and the only way for them to get the work done is to do it themselves. To be competitive you cannot afford to have spare staff.

The main reason for the total involvement of the owner, especially in the initial stages of the business, is therefore cost. Only when the staff are trained can delegation increase and the owner afford to spend more time managing the business. A small business owner can rarely enjoy the luxury of sick leave or even holidays. People going into small business are often given the following advice by experts and colleagues:

> 'Take a good holiday before you start, as it will be a long time before you can take another.'

Despite the obvious logic of this advice, many small business people refuse to accept it — and wonder why their staff and customers leave them. To the small business owner holidays are a luxury, not a condition of service, especially in the early stages of the business. In many cases if the owner goes on holidays the business must shut down, leaving the customers to decide whether to wait or go elsewhere. In other words, the real cost of a holiday could be the loss of the business.

Income

The driving force in a business is profit. The owner of a small business therefore cannot afford to regard the business as a part-time occupation, an easy job, or a mere hobby. Hobbies and small businesses are often confused, but there are big differences between the two; namely

- a hobby does not usually require total commitment with total risk
- a hobby is usually engaged in for enjoyment or therapy
- a hobby, unlike a small business, is not seen by the taxation department as an income producer, and
- finally, it is important to remember that . . .

> Hobbies can, and often do, grow into small businesses — but small businesses should never be allowed to become hobbies.

The key to any small business is the small business owner — the person with the total commitment and the driving force that makes that business better than all the others.

The responsibilities of the small business person

So far we have seen that anyone going into small business puts everything at risk and must be personally involved. They must also know the responsibilities they are accepting. These fall into two categories:

- responsibilities to people
- responsibilities under law.

Responsibilities to people

The small business operator is responsible to four groups of people:

- self and family
- staff
- customers
- the community.

Self and family

Small business cannot exist without people, and that includes yourself and your family.

For most small business operators, the business is the major source of income. Therefore, they have a responsibility to themselves and to any dependants to ensure the survival of the business. To do this, profits must be made and a positive cash flow generated. Without profits and a positive cash flow the business will fail, and if this happens the family could lose everything. No business is worth more than your family; if a business threatens to cause family breakdown, then it is time to take a step back and have a long, hard look at the situation.

Staff

Any small business person employing staff should see them as people who depend upon the continuation of the business. This does not mean that owners should bow to the dictates of the staff, but they should certainly see them as more than mere units of production or sales.

Customers

Customers are also people and must be treated as such. They want satisfaction and the fulfilment of promises concerning matters such as delivery, quality and service. However, this does not mean that small business owners should submit to unreasonable customer demands. Remember: you are going into business to make money, not friends.

The community

The wider community expects small business people to share their concern for social issues such as waste disposal, pollution and fair trading.

Responsibilities under law

The second area of responsibility for small business operators is the legal one. This includes:

- taxation
- government acts and regulations
- awards
- legal agreements.

Taxation

The responsibilities laid down in the Taxation Act are law and neglect or abuse of them carries heavy penalties. These responsibilities are constantly changing, but the small business person cannot claim ignorance as a defence.

> The best advice you can be given on taxation is 'Have a good accountant!'

(Taxation is discussed in more detail in Chapter 22.)

Government acts and regulations

All three levels of government in Australia have rules and regulations designed to impose order and control on the business world and to protect the community and the public.

These rules and regulations are subject to a continual review process, which doubles the difficulty for small business owner/managers: they must not only be aware of the regulations but also keep themselves up to date with the changes.

The small business person should be familiar with all laws governing their operation, including those in areas such as:

- contract law
- negotiable instruments
- discrimination
- fair trading
- legislation
- local government by-laws
- credit
- equal opportunity
- trade practices
- superannuation
- taxation
- staff.

Many of these laws and regulations are highlighted in the checklist in Chapter 12.

Awards

Both federal and state awards dictate the responsibilities for essential working conditions and minimum payments to employees. Chapters 12 and 20 cover some of these responsibilities; but, once again, obtaining professional advice is essential in this area.

Legal agreements

Any small business person who enters a valid legal agreement such as a contract or a lease has the same responsibilities under law as any other person.

Not all of the responsibilities discussed above are equal in rank. Some, for example those relating to taxation and awards, are legally enforceable. Others, such as those concerned with staff welfare, are desirable; but they all come back to the owner's ultimate responsibility to self and family: that is, the need to make a profit. Without profit, there can be no staff, no customers — in other words, no business.

Summary

Small business is not a simple way of making money. Anyone going into business must accept three hard facts:

- that they put everything at risk
- that they commit themselves to total personal involvement, and
- that they assume responsibilities both to people and under law.

If all of this might seem daunting, take heart! There are now about 750 000 small businesses in Australia and, while many fail, many others succeed. If your business develops as planned it will give you rewards you can gain nowhere else.

> Small business is a way of life and is one of the great Australian dreams — just don't be caught napping.

Key words

commitment	responsibility
image	risk
independence	security
planning	stress

Review exercises

1 What five things could you lose, in addition to the money you invested, if your business fails?

2 List seven reasons why you should be totally involved in your own business.

3 What is the difference between a small business and a hobby?

4 What two responsibilities do you accept when you decide to go into business?

CHAPTER 5

Basic skills for small business operators

The driving force and key decision-maker in every small firm is its owner/manager. This individual or this small team (usually two or three people at the most), exerts power and influence over the firm that are far greater than the power and influence of any salaried executive in a large company. Because of this, the managerial ability, other skills and personal qualities of owner/managers determine to a great extent whether their firms fail or survive.

> Managing a small firm means being a jack of all trades.

The aim of this chapter is to help you to:

- appreciate the importance to your business of your experience, knowledge and personal qualities, and
- identify the major skills, attitudes and drives necessary for successfully starting and running your own business.

In Williams' study of small business in Australia, the management practices used in 33 624 small firms were investigated. It was found that their chances of surviving were related to the following evidence of good management:

- well-planned and accurate accounting books and records
- frequent accounting reports
- thorough startup preparation
- wide sales base (large number of major customers)
- growth in sales volume
- growth in profits earned
- growth in positive cash flow
- less dependence on borrowed funds
- use of cash budgeting
- use of written long-range (up to two years) planning
- use of time management methods
- regular review of location suitability
- review of sales/marketing effectiveness and business image
- use of financial data for management

- skill in hiring and motivating employees
- skill in financial management, and
- skill in overall managerial performance.

Those firms that showed clear signs of being well managed tended to earn larger profits and have better cashflow, and were more likely to survive.

TECHNICAL SKILLS

Every small firm sells products (goods or merchandise) and/or services (work, advice, knowledge or expertise). The mechanic who is unable to tune vehicles properly, handle automatic transmissions or solve electronic fuel injection problems, or the doctor who is unable to diagnose illnesses accurately, will not survive for long in business.

Technical, professional, trade and occupational skills must be carefully learned and diligently kept up to date. The overall quality of the product or service offered, which is an essential element in giving the firm a 'head start' (competitive advantage) over its rivals, and in getting and keeping its desired market share, depends largely on three factors:

1 the availability of high-quality merchandise at a competitive cost;
2 the product and technical knowledge of staff and their ability to
    - give potential buyers greater appreciation of the benefits and advantages of a particular product or service, and
    - explain or show how the product works, its safety features, convenience and operating features, both of which will help buyers to make informed comparisons and properly judge the likely usefulness and value of a particular product or service; and
3 up-to-date technology and know-how, which ensure that the quality of service, and the skill used in repairs and maintenance, are second to none.

In industries where technology is complex and rapidly changing (particularly in 'high-tech' industries), updating technical know-how and product knowledge is essential if a firm is to keep or improve its competitive position. In industries where technology is fairly basic, where product changes are minor and where new products are infrequent, the need for updating is less but never absent. Sales growth could benefit considerably, for instance, if a small food store were able to advise buyers about the nutritional advantages of a new type of bread; a health food shop could acquaint customers about possible side-effects associated with new dietary supplements; or a furniture retailer could provide informed guidance to buyers on the flammability dangers of different types of cushion inserts.

Basic skill No 1 = High-quality technical and product knowledge.

Updating methods, products and relevant industry know-how can be achieved by various means, including:

- attending manufacturers' presentations and new product launchings
- reading technical magazines and journals
- studying product manuals
- attending training courses, and
- communicating with manufacturers and suppliers.

Selective training of staff will spread new and improved techniques and knowledge throughout the firm and probably increase the employees' interest, motivation and self-respect, as well as their skill levels. Research by Williams has shown business survival to be related to how well, and how often, firms update their technical and product knowledge.

MANAGING VITAL RESOURCES

As we have already seen, every business needs certain resources to be able to function. Owner/managers and their senior employees are responsible for the efficient and effective use of these resources so that the firm's goals can be reached. While specialised managers in large companies might have primary responsibility in one or two resource areas (for example, for finance managers, information and cash), in fact all managers need to use time and people resources as well. The owner/manager of a small venture must be aware of the importance of all five resources (see page 33), and ensure that all are properly managed and kept in balance.

Basic skill No 2 = Efficient management of resources.

Management is often defined as getting things done through other people, namely employees or subordinates, but this is a rather cynical, if not simplistic, definition. Rather, management is the process by which the resources of organisations (including small business ventures) are brought together and used in working towards predetermined goals. Management is a complex task, which few people do really well.

Early management writers of the 1920s listed the following functions as part of the work of managers:

- planning the path to a healthy future (see Chapter 8)
- organising (setting up a workable organisation)
- obtaining the resources needed

- directing and supervising these resources
- co-ordinating (getting all the parts to work together), and
- controlling (measuring progress and correcting faults).

Personal skills

To perform all the above functions effectively and efficiently, the manager must develop and use certain personal skills. These include:

- communicating
- leadership
- problem-solving and decision-making
- handling information.

Communicating

Effective communication involves sending clear messages from one person to another. In business, communication is used to inform or advise, instruct and persuade. Managers, on average, use about 75% of their working time communicating by one means or another. Careful use of feedback improves the accuracy of communications.

Leadership

Managers lead other people — their employees and subordinates. Good leaders have the ability to persuade others to direct their efforts towards a shared goal. Some lead by authority; others use threats (fear), personal influence (charisma), bribes, or knowledge and expertise.

Managers, in their role as leaders, can be classed either as people-oriented (concerned mainly about the feelings and welfare of their employees) or task-oriented (concerned mainly about getting the job done). Most managers are in fact concerned about both, but tend to lean more one way than the other. Successful entrepreneurs are usually more task- than people-oriented in their dealings with employees. (See the later part of this chapter.)

In their role as leaders, managers are often called upon to:

- resolve conflicts and disputes, and
- bargain and negotiate with various parties.

Problem-solving and decision-making

These activities usually go together. Problems are obstacles which, unless overcome, will prevent goals being reached. Solutions to problems are achieved by means of good decisions, and these come from taking the following steps:

1 Identify and define the problem. Get to the problem itself and do not be side-tracked into chasing symptoms.

2 Gather any information that might have a bearing on the problem. Be open-minded and avoid 'stacking the evidence'. Organise the information into facts, hearsay, advice or reliable opinions.
3 List all possible solutions. Using the information you have collected, think out every workable course of action.
4 Test each possible solution and look at the effects of any likely decision. Will it work? What will it cost? Will there be any adverse side-effects?
5 Choose the best solution. This should be the most workable option from the list you have made.
6 Put your chosen solution into action.
7 Check whether the solution works. Solutions to problems are not always perfect, so you might need to make some adjustments.

Making decisions means choosing between alternatives. Since there is rarely a clear choice between a completely right solution and a completely wrong one, this usually requires making a judgement between one that is 'almost right' and one that is 'probably wrong' — a compromise. There is always some level of risk in implementing solutions, and managers must learn to live with the results of their decisions. Making a good decision to solve a problem or resolve a difficulty will bring the firm's activities back onto the planned course. Good decisions need good information, and much of this will have to come from the firm's records.

Handling information

Information is a business resource, necessary for making decisions. Managers must receive and send large quantities of information in the form of facts and figures, and must develop skills in sifting, summarising, interpreting and analysing large amounts of other information. Some information handled in the day-to-day running of a small business will be useful; much of it not.

ENTREPRENEURIAL SPIRIT AND DRIVE

The popular view is that anyone who starts, owns and operates a small business automatically qualifies as an 'entrepreneur'. This might be true in some cases, but it is certainly not in many others. There is much more to it. Some people who start a small business might be seriously short on entrepreneurial drive and spirit and their firms can fail as a result. Conversely, some people who are indeed entrepreneurial choose to remain within existing large companies (although the way they manage is often not appreciated), and do not start their own ventures.

True entrepreneurs are people who have a particular style of management. In running their own business ventures, they are free to apply their entrepreneurial tendencies.

Since the term *entrepreneur* was first listed in a French commercial dictionary in 1723 it has been written about in much detail, but after 270 years there is still less-than-complete agreement about its definition. The term comes from the French word *entreprendre*, meaning to undertake (a project), or be enterprising. If someone is described as 'entrepreneurial' it means they have a number of personal characteristics that cause them to seek out and undertake certain kinds of work-related activities. In other words, the behaviour of people who are highly entrepreneurial is somewhat different from that of people who are not. They have different attitudes and values, and manage in ways that are not always acceptable in larger and older companies. Nevertheless, an entrepreneurial approach to management is vital for business growth and survival.

In the popular conception, the entrepreneur is one who is daring, innovative, aggressive and willing to take risks to reach some goal. Entrepreneurs typify the 'rags to riches' theme. To some (Collins, Moore and Unwalla, 1964, p 19), the entrepreneur (who might just as easily be female as male):

rises on his own by solid achievement, not by social climbing. He gets there by what he knows, not who he knows. His resources are all inside, not outside . . . He is resolute, disciplined, and utterly devoted.

Entrepreneurs are people who have both the will (in other words, desire or motivation) and the skill to project an idea or scheme into the future and, by backing their judgement with innovative action and persistence, turn that idea into a reality.

Basic skill No 3 = Entrepreneurial spirit and drive.

They have also been described as 'maniacs with a mission', and as people who 'light fires' under a business.

The typical drives and motivations of successful entrepreneurial managers come under the label of 'achievement motivation' or 'need for achievement'. Studies have shown that successful entrepreneurs, or 'high achievers', have most if not all of the following characteristics:

Ambition and future orientation

Entrepreneurs are seen to be strongly committed to clear, challenging and realistic future goals — often long-term ones. They not only set goals but also work hard and persistently towards them — they are very strong-willed. They tend not to dwell on past mistakes, but see the past and present as a 'launching pad' from which to reach the future. The successful building of a healthy and growing business enterprise needs a vision — and long-term commitment and involvement.

Innovativeness

Effective entrepreneurs continually seek new and better ways of doing their work and pursuing their goals. In a small business the entrepreneur, being future-oriented and motivated by the desire to succeed, will look to doing what is obvious for business survival and success and will search for better ways of making sales. In most cases, this will mean searching for new and better products and services.

Confident assertiveness

Entrepreneurs have a strong need to take the initiative and to seek to influence others — they want to be in control. They tend to be strong, self-confident leaders who know where they are going (towards their goals), and how to get there (in a straight line). Studies have shown that they are assertive rather than submissive in their dealings with others.

Readiness to take moderate risks

Entrepreneurs have a marked preference for tasks of moderate difficulty, and for taking moderate risks. They tend to be neither gamblers (in high-risk undertakings the chances of succeeding are slim, and skill cannot affect the outcome) nor risk-averse (in low-risk undertakings success is almost a certainty, there being little or no challenge in achieving it). It is the prospect of achieving success by using their ability, knowledge, specific skills and effort that motivates entrepreneurs.

Alertness to change and opportunity

Because they are innovative and future-oriented, entrepreneurs have a strong desire for change (new and better ways to do things) and opportunities to achieve their goals. The future is important because it is where opportunities lie. Entrepreneurs are often called 'change-makers'.

Search for excellence

Entrepreneurs are motivated to seek excellence in all they do. Their goals are high but realistic and reachable. Once a certain goal is reached, another and more demanding one is set and the search for excellence goes on.

Strong competitive spirit

Proven entrepreneurs are highly competitive individuals who aggressively pursue their goals. Competition takes two forms. The more usual form is that in which someone strives to compete against others, and this means using better strategies and tactics to win. In such situations the external standard is the ability of the competitor. The other form of competition is that in which someone competes against self-imposed (internal) standards. Here, the standard of performance required to better the previous performance (in other words, to win) becomes higher and higher. Successful entrepreneurs have been shown to prefer this internal competition — to reach ever higher and continually become better.

Self-reliance and independence

Entrepreneurs are known to be individualists with a preference for being independent. From their upbringing they develop a strong need to be self-reliant, and dislike being under the control of others. This is one of the main reasons why they leave the security of paid employment to set out by themselves, often in the company of a like-minded individual, to embark on a new and probably dangerous career in small business.

This streak of independence should not be assumed to mean that entrepreneurs will not seek help when it is needed. Many owner/managers of small firms (not necessarily entrepreneurs) will not seek help from external experts, but most successful entrepreneurs are willing to do so.

Energy and drive

Successful entrepreneurs work hard and with great enthusiasm. This is particularly so when they are involved in a task of moderate difficulty, in which their skill will affect the outcome.

Practicality and action orientation

Entrepreneurs are not impractical dreamers. They certainly dream dreams, but they also have the desire to turn them into realities. Entrepreneurs have the will and skill to change their dreams into ideas, schemes and goals, and then make them happen.

Preference for broad direction rather than detail

Because of their future orientation, and their desire to provide the broad overall momentum of their business, many entrepreneurs have little interest in detail. This means that they tend to be more concerned with effectiveness (doing the right things for success) than with efficiency (doing things the right way). This should not be taken to mean that the details necessary for managing the business efficiently can be ignored! If the entrepreneur cannot or will not give the details the attention they deserve, someone else must do so: a partner or trusted employee.

Resourcefulness and shrewdness

Entrepreneurs are known for their resourcefulness — the ability to work out ways of getting things done. In their bargaining and negotiating, they are sharp-witted and able to distinguish good deals from bad.

A thick skin

Effective entrepreneurs are able to withstand the many stresses encountered when running a business. They are not so hurt by criticism, so defeated by problems and setbacks, or so despondent when let down by those they trust that they cannot control the situation. In other words: they cope!

Tolerance of uncertainty and ambiguity

Many aspects of the entrepreneurial undertaking (such as being a 'change-maker' and getting a new business up and running) are uncertain and ambiguous. In these situations managers meet new, complex and often insoluble problems and they might be unsure or totally ignorant of how to go about the job. Successful entrepreneurs handle such situations without getting stressed — they tolerate (and work well despite) high levels of uncertainty and ambiguity.

Motivation by money

Entrepreneurs see profit as an important measure of success, but they are not 'turned on' by money for its own sake. Entrepreneurs do not see money as a goal in itself; rather they use it as a means of bringing ideas into reality — as a means of becoming successful.

Determination and persistence

Most entrepreneurs are strongly determined to succeed at whatever they undertake, sometimes to the exclusion of all else. In solving problems and working to reach goals, their determination can be a near-fanatical persistence and no hurdle or problem is allowed to beat them. These characteristics are more obvious when they are working on tasks that interest them — usually tasks of moderate difficulty.

Dislike of wasted time

Because they are future-oriented action people — doers — entrepreneurs are aware of the value of time without being 'clock-watchers'. They find that time goes quickly when they are working with intense determination on a challenging task. They have been known to work around the clock on a vital job, virtually without realising it.

Work orientation rather than people orientation

Because of the importance to entrepreneurs of goals and achieving success, they tend to be concerned more with getting a job done than with other people's feelings. They are assertive, like being in control and evaluate all things in terms of whether it will help them succeed. Studies have shown that successful entrepreneurs choose experts rather than friends or family members as employees.

High level of realistic optimism

Far from fearing failure, entrepreneurs see mistakes as a chance to learn, improve and go on to success. They are not defeated by setbacks or problems, but are willing to try again and again. They believe in themselves and their ability to achieve the goals they have set.

Internal driving force

One of the features of effective entrepreneurs is that they are driven by their own internal motivation and the strong belief that their success will be due to their own efforts and skills, and not a result of other people's actions, lucky breaks or chance events.

Openness to feedback

Entrepreneurs seek feedback, because they want very much to know how well they are doing in achieving goals and competing against self-imposed standards. They use this information to improve their performance.

Personal responsibility

Since entrepreneurs actively seek and take initiative, they naturally prefer to be in control of, and personally responsible for, the results of whatever they undertake. They also prefer situations in which their personal contribution can be measured — this feedback is important in providing satisfaction from their success.

Drive for status improvement

Entrepreneurs tend to come from working-class (or 'blue-collar') backgrounds, and generally have a desire to improve their socio-economic status. Like the ability to make money, they regard this as a measure of how successful they are.

Dislike of interruptions

Because they enjoy work and become so involved in it, entrepreneurs dislike interruptions.

Preference for challenging work

Most highly entrepreneurial individuals prefer challenging work (that is, activity with a goal) to leisure time. They get bored 'doing nothing'; even when they are physically inactive their minds are at work. People with entrepreneurial drive will seek out and get involved in work which helps to satisfy their general need to achieve. They have a preference for work that provides:

- variety
- scope for initiative
- freedom to make their own decisions
- scope for independent action
- personal responsibility
- opportunities to achieve and create
- a challenge
- opportunities for self-development
- opportunities to perform better than others (and be seen to do so)
- mental and physical demands
- opportunities to be innovative
- recognition of high-quality work, and
- moderate risk of success or failure.

This rather long list of characteristics indicates that entrepreneurial behaviour is complex. Any person with high levels of all or most of the attitudes, values and behaviour patterns described would be a highly entrepreneurial individual. Some people have such traits in plenty, and others have considerably fewer of them. In fact, if a large number of people were picked at random and measured for these characteristics, the resulting spread of scores would look something like that shown in Figure 5.1.

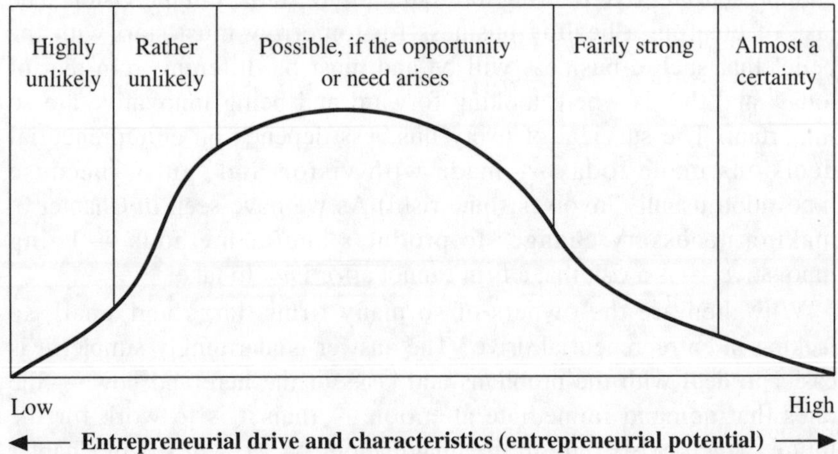

FIGURE 5.1 Distribution of entrepreneurial drive and characteristics, and probability of undertaking an 'entrepreneurial career', among a random sample

Australians tend to have lower entrepreneurial potential than other nationalities because of the effects of our child-rearing, educational and general work practices, which emphasise conformity rather than individualism.

It would not be surprising if you saw most of the entrepreneurial characteristics listed above as qualities which would be necessary, or at least useful, for setting up and running a new business successfully. It is often argued that the primary and most valuable entrepreneurial quality is the ability to be creative or innovative.

Given the complex ingredients that go to make up entrepreneurial spirit and drive, it is not surprising to find that few entrepreneurial managers also have superior administrative skills. When two or more individuals combining entrepreneurial drive and administrative skills form a partnership or private company, that firm has a great advantage over one that is lacking in either.

Whether managed by an individual or a team, no business can afford to bask in the glory of its past success, or wallow in the misery of yesterday's mistakes. The past and the present are a springboard for leaping into the future, and the entrepreneur's role is to create a successful tomorrow — with ample markets and customers — for the firm. This depends on decisions made today. The need to plan ahead, to grow at a sensible and healthy rate and in the right direction, and to realise that the future is the only 'place' where opportunities exist, are dealt with in Chapters 8 and 25. Past opportunities should be today's sales and profits. Will the same be true of future opportunities?

Any small firm wanting a healthy future must have a clear vision of this future. It takes an entrepreneurial outlook, entrepreneurial spirit and entrepreneurial drive to bring to life the future framed in the vision. The task of creating a healthy business for tomorrow must start with the belief that such a business will be and must be different from that of today, and this is where looking forward and being innovative are so important. The survival of every business depends on entrepreneurial decisions made today — made with vision and 'guts' (because innovation usually involves some risk!) As we have seen in Chapter 3, making necessary changes to products and/or methods — being innovative — is a risk that a firm cannot afford *not* to take!

Why then are the owners of so many firms, large and small, so lacking in entrepreneurial drive? The answer is alarmingly simple: it is easier to deal with the problems and tasks of the here and now — the ones that demand immediate attention — than it is to work for the future, which exists only in the imagination. As we will see in Chapter 21, on time management, the 'tyranny of the urgent' is a major reason why managers act on immediate issues but leave undone the less urgent ones. Yet what can be more important than the firm's future?

People can be trained in technical skills and some aspects of management but they cannot be trained to be entrepreneurs. However, since entrepreneurial behaviour is largely determined by attitudes, values and personality traits (as we have seen), which can be changed if a person sees the need to change and is willing to do so, entrepreneurial drive and motivation can be increased. The starting point is to measure, and thereby become aware of, the level of your own personal entrepreneurial characteristics and behaviour. You can do this in Chapter 6.

SUMMARY

Before making any moves to get into a small business, all intending owner/managers should clearly understand that, to a great extent, their success will depend on up-to-date technical know-how, wide-ranging managerial skills, and a large measure of entrepreneurial drive. All of these are difficult to find in one owner/manager; multi-owned and managed enterprises are more likely to have these inputs and are recommended.

All intending owner/managers should assess their personal skills, knowledge and entrepreneurial drive before committing funds to a small business. It is important that gaps and weaknesses are identified and remedied.

Entrepreneur's Credo

I do not choose to be a common man.
It is my right to be uncommon — if I can.
I seek opportunity — not security.
I do not wish to be a kept citizen, humbled and dulled by having
the state look after me.

I want to take the calculated risk;
to dream and to build,
to fail and to succeed.

I refuse to barter incentive for a dole;
I prefer the challenges of life to the guaranteed existence;
the thrill of fulfilment to the stale calm of Utopia.

I will not trade freedom for beneficence
nor my dignity for a handout.
I will never cower before any master nor bend to any threat.

It is my heritage to stand erect, proud and unafraid; to think
and act for myself, to enjoy the benefit of my creations and
to face the world boldly and say:
This, with God's help, I have done.
All this is what it means to be an Entrepreneur.

Source: American Entrepreneurs' Association

KEY WORDS

competitive advantage
entrepreneur
entrepreneurial drive
'high-tech' industries
managerial skills
technical skills
technology

REVIEW EXERCISES

Circle the appropriate letter in each case.

1 A major motivation for becoming an entrepreneur is often:
   A the lack of a college or university degree
   B being the son or daughter of an entrepreneur
   C an ability to be a planner
   D an inability to work for someone else.

2 Management can best be described as:
   A supervision of employees and subordinates
   B making decisions about the firm's resources and taking follow-up actions
   C maximising the firm's financial returns
   D organising the firm's employees.

3 The number of people a manager is directly responsible for is known as his or her:
   A division of labour
   B organisation structure
   C management function
   D span of control.

4 Employees' productivity and job satisfaction are:
   A usually related
   B negatively related
   C not related at all
   D rarely related.

5 Which of the following is least likely to be an entrepreneur's motivation?
   A Strong desire to compete and excel
   B Desire for economic security
   C Readiness to face new challenges
   D Ability to accept the new and unusual

6 In giving instructions to an employee an owner/manager is:
   A controlling
   B planning

C directing
D organising.

7 In deciding on a new product, an owner/manager is:
A innovating
B planning
C directing
D organising.

8 Control is:
A determining whether or not plans are being followed
B making sure that employees follow the rules
C keeping records
D all of the above.

9 An owner/manager can be innovative by:
A making use of information which has not been used before
B thinking of a new idea and then using it
C adapting an idea to enable it to be used in some new way
D doing all the above.

10 Of the following features of good management, the most difficult for many entrepreneurs in small firms is:
A effective delegation of authority
B a simple business structure
C good control over the firm's operations
D a narrow span of control.

REFERENCES

American Entrepreneurs' Association, 'Entrepreneur's Credo'

Collins, O F, Moore, D G & Unwalla, D B 1964, 'The enterprising man and the business executive', *Michigan State University Business Topics*, vol 12, no 1, Winter, pp19–33

CHAPTER 6

Owner/manager self-evaluation

Chapter 5 outlined the major skills, areas of knowledge, types of experience and personal qualities necessary for successfully starting and managing your own small business venture. It stressed that you (and your co-owners, if any) are the most important ingredient in the success of your business. Upon your shoulders the future of the whole venture rests, and the quality of your decisions, your overall level of technical, managerial and entrepreneurial capability and your attitudes, values and enthusiasm for the venture are all crucial for its success!

> Measuring your personal skills and motivations is the first step into your own business.

There is little point in conducting market studies, assessing the firm's likely financial viability, or doing anything else unless you are able and willing to do the job for which you are employing yourself. Like any job, but to a greater extent, owning and managing a small firm takes a heavy toll on those who try it without the necessary skills, knowledge, experience and personal qualities to make it succeed. The end results in such cases very often include financial failure, loss of self-respect, marriage breakdown, family problems and serious stress with its many associated medical problems. Merely thinking you have all the necessary personal capabilities, and being excited and enthusiastic, are not enough. Having confidence in yourself is better than having none, but you must be sure that this confidence is justified. Testing this before you make any financial commitment to the proposed business may save you from a major disaster.

If you are wondering how on earth you can assess your own suitability, do not despair. There *are* measures available and many of them are provided here.

The purpose of this chapter is to give you the opportunity to measure:

- your general readiness for getting involved in an 'entrepreneurial career' (in other words, starting and running your own business), including your entrepreneurial potential
- how well your education, training and work experience are suited to

setting up and running the *business you have chosen*, and

- how well you are prepared for the actual startup.

The questions that follow are drafted on the assumption that you, as a reader of this book, are either: thinking of going into business; actually planning and preparing to do so; or in business already. You should answer according to your own situation. We have tried to take into account the fact that individual lifestyles vary widely and are subject to much change. Please do not take offence if we have unwittingly omitted or misrepresented your particular lifestyle or set of values in any of the questions in this chapter.

On aspects of your managerial and entrepreneurial potential for success in your business venture you will be able to compare your scores with the scores of many thousands of successful and unsuccessful owner/managers in Australia. Do not jump to a conclusion from looking at your total score in any single section of this assessment. Complete all sections first, then note your most serious weaknesses and your strengths.

For all questions, simply tick the correct or most appropriate box.

AM I READY TO GO INTO MY OWN BUSINESS?

This section will enable you to find out how ready and suited you are to going into business — *any business*. Scoring methods are given on pages 79–81, 89–91, 98–101, 103–4, 106–7, 109–10.

A Age when starting business

What was (or will be) your age when starting this business?

Under 20 years	☐	20 to 24 years	☐
25 to 29 years	☐	30 to 34 years	☐
35 to 39 years	☐	40 to 44 years	☐
45 to 49 years	☐	50 to 54 years	☐
55 to 59 years	☐	60 years or over	☐

B Health

1 How often do you suffer from illness that prevents you from being at work?

Frequently	Sometimes	Occasionally	Rarely	Never
☐	☐	☐	☐	☐

2 Describe your general physical health.

Always excellent	Usually good	Average	Varies	Not good
☐	☐	☐	☐	☐

3 Do you have regular (annual, at least) medical check-ups?

Yes ☐ No ☐

4 Are you a moderate to heavy smoker (at least one packet daily)?

Yes ☐ No ☐

5 Have you had any serious illness in the past two years that needed an operation and/or hospitalisation?

Yes ☐ No ☐

6 Do you often (say at least weekly) take analgesics or tranquilisers for nerves, inability to sleep, or any other similar problem?

Yes ☐ No ☐

7 Is there any history of illness in your family that may have an adverse effect on your ability to lead an active working life (such as asthma or a heart problem)?

Yes ☐ No ☐

C Reasons for wanting to go into my own business

Tick the most appropriate box to show the importance (or otherwise) of each of the following reasons for deciding to go into your own business. Read through the whole list before ticking any boxes.

	A very strong reason				Not a strong reason
1 My life is (was) being wasted — there is (was) no real future as an employee.	☐	☐	☐	☐	☐
2 To provide extra income (ie wage/salary not adequate).	☐	☐	☐	☐	☐
3 I intend to build a solid future investment for myself and my family.	☐	☐	☐	☐	☐
4 I wish to be independent and in control of my own future.	☐	☐	☐	☐	☐
5 The influence of others, such as family, relations and/or friends.	☐	☐	☐	☐	☐

6 I wish to prove to myself and others that I can make a success of something difficult and important, like having my own business. ☐ ☐ ☐ ☐ ☐

7 I dislike working for a boss. ☐ ☐ ☐ ☐ ☐

8 To make a success of my life by making a better living from my own ideas and abilities. ☐ ☐ ☐ ☐ ☐

9 I worry about future financial security for myself and my family. ☐ ☐ ☐ ☐ ☐

10 I need(ed) work, because of unemployment. ☐ ☐ ☐ ☐ ☐

11 I am (was) frustrated in my present (previous) job. ☐ ☐ ☐ ☐ ☐

12 I just want to try something different. ☐ ☐ ☐ ☐ ☐

D Family support and encouragement

1 Is your home/family life happy?

Very	Fairly	Average	Below average	No
☐	☐	☐	☐	☐

2 What is your family's attitude to your being in business?

Strong/active support ☐

Fairly enthusiastic ☐

Some interest ☐

No interest ☐

Opposed ☐

Strongly opposed ☐

3 Do (or will) you get strong support and encouragement from your family in your small business efforts?

Yes	Some	Not sure	A little	No
☐	☐	☐	☐	☐

4 Are any of your family members willing to work in the business, either regularly or when needed?

Yes ☐ No ☐

5 Do you have a home/marital partner?
(If 'No' do not answer Question 6.)

Yes ☐ No ☐

6 What are your home partner's work obligations?

Home duties only ☐
Home duties and family business, part-time ☐
Home duties and family business, full-time ☐
Home duties and outside job, part-time ☐
Home duties and outside job, full-time ☐
In full-time job ☐

E Other obligations

1 Do you have (or do you intend to have) any other job as well as your work in this business?

Yes ☐ No ☐
(If 'No' do not answer Question 2.)

2 About how many hours each week (on average) are (or will be) involved in that other job?

Under 4 hours ☐ 12 to 16 hours ☐
4 to 8 hours ☐ 16 to 20 hours ☐
8 to 12 hours ☐ over 20 hours ☐

3 Are you usually an active member of any club, society or association?

Yes ☐ No ☐
(If 'No' do not answer Question 4.)

4 About how many hours each week (on average) do (or will) your club or association activities take up?

Under 2 hours ☐ 6 to 8 hours ☐
2 to 4 hours ☐ 8 to 10 hours ☐
4 to 6 hours ☐ Over 10 hours ☐

F Family background

These questions, unless otherwise stated, relate to your childhood and adolescent years, generally while you were living at home and in the care of your parents and close family. If applicable, for 'parents' read 'guardians', and for 'father' read 'mother'.

1 During most of your childhood adolescent years, what type of work did your father mainly do?

Employee — professional ☐

— clerical/administrative ☐

— manual/technical ☐

Self-employed ☐

2 Describe your parents' general financial condition.

Wealthy ☐

Average ☐

Fairly poor ☐

3 Where were you born?

Overseas ☐

In another Australian state ☐

In this state ☐

4 How many major moves (changes of jobs and homes) did your parents have during your time of living with them?

None ☐ 5 or 6 ☐

1 or 2 ☐ More than 6 ☐

3 or 4 ☐

5 How many job changes (changes of employer) have you had?

None ☐ 7 or 8 ☐

1 or 2 ☐ 9 or 10 ☐

3 or 4 ☐ More than 10 ☐

5 or 6 ☐

6 What was your birth order?

Only/eldest ☐ Fourth born ☐

Second born ☐ Fifth or later ☐

Third born ☐

7 Are (or were) any of your brothers, sisters or other close relatives (not parents) in business for themselves?

Yes ☐ No ☐

8 At about what age (if at all) do you recall your parents showing you to do things without their help, being concerned with your attitude towards work and success, and encouraging you to become independent and ambitious and to do well in all you do?

Under 8 years ☐ 16 to 20 years ☐

8 to 12 years ☐ Over 20 years ☐

12 to 16 years ☐ Not at all ☐

9 How well did you get on with your father?

Very well ☐ Not very well ☐

Quite well ☐ Very poorly ☐

Indifferently ☐

10 Did you respect your parents enough to want to achieve something worthwhile with your own life, to make them proud of you, or to copy their example?

Yes ☐ No ☐

G Relevant education

1 How much time have you spent studying any business-related subjects or courses (eg supervision, finance, selling, management, bookkeeping) at *any level* of your education?

None ☐ 1 to 2 years ☐

Under 6 months ☐ 2 to 3 years ☐

6 to 12 months ☐ Over 3 years ☐

(If you answered 'None', do not answer Question 2.)

2 To what level of education did you study these business-type subjects or courses?

High/secondary school ☐

College/university ☐

Scoring methods

A Age when starting business

1	3
5	9
10	9
7	5
3	2

Your scores

A	

B Health

1 [1] [2] [3] [4] [5]

2 [5] [4] [3] [2] [1]

3 Yes [2] No [–]

4 Yes [–] No [1]

5 Yes [–] No [3]

6 Yes [–] No [3]

7 Yes [–] No [1]

B	

C Reasons for wanting to go into my own business

For each item, score:

[5] [4] [3] [2] [1]

Multiply each of your 12 scores by the number given. Add the 'products' column.

Item	Scores		Products
1		× 2 =	
2		× 1 =	
3		× 3 =	
4		× 2 =	
5		× 1 =	
6		× 4 =	
7		× 1 =	
8		× 4 =	
9		× 2 =	
10		× 1 =	
11		× 2 =	
12		× 2 =	

C	

D Family support and encouragement

1 [5] [4] [3] [2] [1]

3 [5] [4] [3] [2] [1]

4 Yes [2] No [1]

5 Yes [2] No [1]

2 [6] [5] [4] [3] [2] [1]

6 [5] [4] [3] [2] [1] [1]

D [ ]

E Other obligations

1 Yes [1] No [2]

3 Yes [1] No [2]

2 [8] [3] [6] [2] [4] [1]

4 [8] [3] [6] [2] [4] [1]

E [ ]

F Family background

1 [1] [2] [3] [4]

2 [1] [2] [3]

3 [3] [2] [1]

4 [1] [4] [2] [5] [3]

5 [1] [5] [2] [6] [3] [7] [4]

6 [3] [2] [2] [3] [1]

7 Yes [2] No [1]

8 [6] [3] [5] [2] [4] [1]

9 [5] [2] [4] [1] [3]

10 Yes [2] No [1]

F [ ]

G Relevant education

1	1	4	2	1
	2	5		2
	3	6		

G	

Total scores

	Your scores	Maximum scores
A		10
B		20
C		125
D		25
E		20
F		42
G		8
		250

Summary	
High	Above 205
Above average	166–205
Medium	126–165
Below average	86–125
Low	Below 86

Interpretation

Are you ready to go into your own business? You should take note of those parts of this section where you got less than half of the maximum scores. They might suggest reasons for not going into your own business — yet, or ever!

A total score below 125 suggests that you are better suited to a career other than owning and running your own business. If your total score falls in the 'medium' range, take much care, and make a move to go into business only if your scores in other sections of this personal assessment are 'above average' or 'high'. If you scored above 165 your prospects look encouraging, but see how you score on later sections. A score above 205 makes you admirably suited to running your own business.

AM I PREPARED FOR GOING INTO *THIS* BUSINESS?

In this section you will be measuring your knowledge, experience and preparation for going into *this* business — that is, the particular business you are thinking of entering, or actually planning to enter.

All scoring is shown at the end of this section, after 'E — Startup preparation'. For all questions tick the appropriate box.

A Job-related education

1 How much time have you spent studying any subjects or courses (at any level of your education) relating to the *type of work* you are (or will be) doing in *this* business (eg hairdressing, building, plumbing, law, accounting, design, or any other technical or professional training)? (Do not include apprenticeship or on-the-job training in your answer.)

None	☐	1 to 2 years	☐
Under 6 months	☐	2 to 3 years	☐
6 to 12 months	☐	Over 3 years	☐

(If you answered 'None', do not answer Question 2.)

2 To which level of education did you study these work-related (ie technical or professional) subjects or courses?

High/secondary school	☐
College/university	☐

B Work (occupational) experience

The questions in this part of the survey relate to your trade, occupational or professional experience *as an employee*. If you are at present in a business of your own, these questions relate to *work experience prior to starting your business*.

1 How many years' experience have you had in the *same kind of work* (ie the same trade or line of business) as your proposed or existing business?

None	☐	5 to 10 years	☐
Under 2 years	☐	10 to 20 years	☐
2 to 5 years	☐	Over 20 years	☐

(If you answered 'None', do not answer Question 2.)

2 Has your occupational trade or professional experience been mainly the same as or different from the work of your planned or existing business?

Always the same	☐	Mostly different	☐
Mostly the same	☐	Always different	☐
Some of each	☐		

3 Have you undertaken any type of formal job training (eg apprenticeship, professional year, course of study, etc) *appropriate to the type of work* in your proposed or existing business?

None ☐ 1 to 2 years ☐

Under 6 months ☐ 2 to 3 years ☐

6 to 12 months ☐ Over 3 years ☐

4 How wide/narrow has your work experience as an employee been within the same trade, line of business or profession as your proposed or existing business?

Very wide ☐ A little narrow ☐

Fairly wide ☐ Fairly narrow ☐

Wider than average ☐ Very narrow ☐

C Managerial experience

The questions in this part of the survey relate to your experience as an *employee manager*. Once again, if you are at present a business owner, these questions relate to *management experience before starting this business*. Management means work involving planning, organising, staffing, controlling and (in particular) supervising or directing the work of other people.

1 How many years' management experience have you had in the *same type of firm* (ie the same trade or line of business) as your proposed or existing business?

None ☐ 5 to 10 years ☐

Under 2 years ☐ 10 to 20 years ☐

2 to 5 years ☐ Over 20 years ☐

(If 'None', do not answer Question 2.)

2 How has the work in your management experience compared with the work of your planned or existing business?

Always the same ☐ Mostly different ☐

Mostly the same ☐ Always different ☐

Some of each ☐

3 In which aspects of business have you had management experience? (More than one answer is possible.)

Sales/marketing ☐ Office/accounting ☐ Production ☐

Finance ☐ Purchasing stores ☐ Other ☐

Personnel ☐

4 If the levels of management can generally be described as:
lower (eg leading hand; section foreman),
middle (eg supervisor/manager of large section),
upper (eg manager of large department),
top (eg general management, on board of management),
which level of management responsibility did you reach?

Lower	☐	Upper	☐
Middle	☐	Top	☐

5 How much training/education have you undertaken through courses of study in any aspect of management (eg supervision, selling, accounting, etc)?

None	☐	1 to 2 years	☐
Under 6 months	☐	2 to 3 years	☐
6 to 12 months	☐	Over 3 years	☐

D Ownership experience

The questions in this part relate to your *experience* (if any) *as the owner/manager of a business*. If you are currently in business, these questions refer to your *previous business*, if any. If you have never previously owned a business, answer Question 1 as 'None', and go straight to Part E.

1 How many years' experience have you had as an owner/manager (in a previous business)?

None	☐	5 to 10 years	☐
Under 2 years	☐	10 to 20 years	☐
2 to 5 years	☐	Over 20 years	☐

(If you answered 'None' to Question 1, answer no further questions in Part D.)

2 How does your previous business (if any) compare with the present or proposed business?

Quite different	☐	Fairly similar	☐
Somewhat different	☐	Very much the same	☐
Similar in some ways	☐		

3 How recently were you in your previous business?

Within the last 6 months	☐	2 to 5 years ago	☐
6 to 12 months ago	☐	5 to 10 years ago	☐
1 to 2 years ago	☐	Over 10 years ago	☐

4 What was your *main* reason for leaving the previous business?

Bankrupt/insolvent ☐ Health problems ☐

Unprofitable* ☐ Lost interest+ ☐

Personal problems/reasons ☐ Good offer to sell out++ ☐

* You realised that it was probably impossible to stay in business profitably and got out before 'going broke'.

\+ Could include the fact that something else became more important in life, even though the business was financially sound.

++ In this case you were persuaded to sell out at a profit — a successful business.

5 Ignoring the reason you have given for not still being in your previous business (Question 4), how would you rate your performance as an owner/manager? (Give yourself an *honest score* according to how well you think you handled the job of owning and managing the business!)

Excellent ☐ Average or unsure ☐ Not very well ☐

Quite good ☐ Below average ☐ Poor ☐

Fair ☐

E Startup preparation

Questions in Part E relate to fact-finding activities and other preparations for starting *this* business. They are therefore relevant only to those people who are *already in business, or fairly close to starting*. For others, the questions should provide a worthwhile checklist of what should be done and known before starting.

1 How long after your *definite* decision to start or buy *this* business did (or will) you actually open for business?

Under 3 months ☐ 1 to 2 years ☐

3 to 6 months ☐ 2 to 5 years ☐

6 to 12 months ☐ Over 5 years ☐

2 After you made the decision to go into business, how many knowledgeable people did you talk with about matters relating to buying or starting *this* business?

None ☐ 7 to 9 ☐

1 to 3 ☐ 10 or more ☐

4 to 6 ☐

(If 'None', do not answer Question 3.)

3 If you did seek expert advice, which people did you talk with? (More than one answer is possible.)

Trade association	☐	Bank manager	☐
Management consultant	☐	Solicitor/lawyer	☐
Someone in business	☐	Accountant	☐
Government small business help*	☐	Employer	☐
Trade supplier (wholesaler)	☐	Other	☐

* eg in New South Wales: Office of Small Business; in Victoria: Small Business Development Corporation

4 Have you calculated the **net profit** you will need in order to gain a *reasonable* reward for your:

(a) time, effort, experience, etc? Yes ☐ No ☐

(b) financial investment? Yes ☐ No ☐

5 Have you calculated the **gross sales income** you will need to achieve in order to earn the profit you feel you want?

Yes ☐ No ☐

6 Have you done a **market survey** (or any kind of study) to find out whether there is any chance of reaching the sales figure you need, with *this* business, in *this* locality?

Yes ☐ No ☐

7 Have you calculated how much **capital** you have available and how much you will need to borrow?

Yes ☐ No ☐

8 Are (were) you sure of being able to borrow the funds you need?

Yes ☐ No ☐

9 What proportion of the total capital you need(ed) will (did) you have to borrow (from *any* source)?

Under 20%	☐	60% to 80%	☐
20% to 40%	☐	Over 80%	☐
40% to 60%	☐		

10 Do you *know* (for your chosen line of business) roughly how much from each dollar of sales income you can reasonably expect to keep as **net profit**?

Yes ☐ No ☐

11 Do you *know* (for your chosen line of business) what the typical/average **mark-up** is?

Yes ☐ No ☐

12 Do you *know* anything about your likely **competitors** (eg location, tactics, strengths, etc)?

Yes ☐ No ☐

13 Do you *know* whether *this* business has any real chance of **growing**?

Yes ☐ No ☐

14 Do you *know* how much **stock/materials/supplies** you need to keep the business moving?

Yes ☐ No ☐

15 Do you *know* what is the average **stockturn** for firms in your line of business?

Yes ☐ No ☐

16 Does (or will) your mark-up take account of **inflation**? (If you do not know how inflation will affect your business, answer No'!)

Yes ☐ No ☐

17 Do you *know* the difference between **profit** and **cash flow**?

Yes ☐ No ☐

18 Have you prepared a **cash budget**?

Yes ☐ No ☐

19 Do you *know* how to get a **selling price** for each article or product you sell?

Yes ☐ No ☐

20 Have you planned a system of **record-keeping** for:

(a) debtors (accounts receivable)? Yes ☐ No ☐

(b) creditors (accounts payable)? Yes ☐ No ☐

(c) stock (including materials, etc)? Yes ☐ No ☐

(d) assets? Yes ☐ No ☐

(e) cash receipts and payments? Yes ☐ No ☐

(f) wages and salaries, and the deductions from these (eg taxation)? Yes ☐ No ☐

21 Do you *know* how to calculate your **profit** or **loss** without the help of an accountant?

Yes ☐ No ☐

22 Have you considered carefully the advantages and disadvantages of operating as a sole trader, partnership, company or (maybe) trust?

Yes ☐ No ☐

23 Do you understand the **taxation** aspects of each of these business structures?

Yes ☐ No ☐

24 Have you considered carefully the most suitable **location** or site for *your* business?

Yes ☐ No ☐

25 Have you planned the **layout** of your shop, office or factory with care, thought and advice?

Yes ☐ No ☐

26 Do you *know* (even approximately) what your **break-even** sales figure is (will be)?

Yes ☐ No ☐

27 Have you planned to hire **staff** based on carefully prepared job descriptions?

Yes ☐ No ☐

28 Have you considered the possibility of **buying a franchise**?

Yes ☐ No ☐

29 Have you given serious thought to **credit control** and its importance?

Yes ☐ No ☐

30 Have you considered how you will **divide** the work and **delegate** responsibility to employees?

Yes ☐ No ☐

31 Are you honestly prepared to make do with an income a lot lower than you could have earned as an employee, if necessary, during the first few months of the new business?

Yes ☐ No ☐

32 Have you investigated the advantages and disadvantages of leasing (some of) the assets you need, or buying second-hand items, rather than buying all new assets?

Yes ☐ No ☐

33 Do you plan to make and/or market a second line (or more lines) of product or service?

Yes ☐ No ☐

34 Are you aware that you need more than technical/trade/professional skill to have a successful business?

Yes ☐ No ☐

35 Do you believe that the success or failure of your business will depend to a very large extent on *you*?

Yes ☐ No ☐

36 If you are buying (or intend to buy) an existing business, have you taken (or are you taking) every possible step to make sure that you are getting what you pay for? (For instance, do you understand what you are getting when you pay for 'goodwill'? Are the assets in good order? Is the lease satisfactory? Why is the business for sale? etc.)

Yes ☐ No ☐

Scoring methods

A Job-related education **Your scores**

1 [1] [4] [2] [5] [3] [6]

2 [1] [2]

A ☐

B Work (occupational) experience

1 [1] [4] [2] [5] [3] [6]

2 [5] [2] [4] [1] [3]

3 [1] [4] [2] [5] [3] [6]

4 [6] [3] [5] [2] [4] [1]

B ☐

C Managerial experience

1
1	4
2	5
3	6

3
2	1	1
2	1	1
1		

5
1	4
2	5
3	6

2
5	2
4	1
3	

4
1	5
3	7

C	

D Ownership experience

1
1	4
2	5
3	6

3
6	3
5	2
4	1

4
1	4
2	5
3	6

2
1	4
2	5
3	

5
7	4	2
6	3	1
5		

D	

E Startup preparation

1
1	4
2	5
3	6

3
1	1
1	1
1	1
1	1
1	1

2
1	4
2	5
3	

9
5	2
4	1
3	

E	

For Questions 4 to 8 and 10 to 36, score 1 for Yes, nil for No.

Interpretation

Are you ready to start *this* business? Check on any parts where you gained less than half the maximum score. If weaknesses are obvious, you can do something about it — for example, become better prepared, or get more management experience.

If you scored below about 75, postpone starting until you have remedied your weaknesses, especially if your scores in other sections of this personal assessment tend to be below average. A 'high' or 'above average' score indicates that you are fairly well prepared to get into this kind of business.

Do I have enough entrepreneurial drive?

To assess properly the level of your entrepreneurial drive you have to measure the following four broad characteristics:

A Task and achievement motivation
This is a major area of entrepreneurial motivation, made up of a general desire to succeed, improve and meet (mainly) self-imposed standards of excellence and be innovative.

B Locus of control
These questions measure the extent to which you believe that your success is due to your own personal effort and skill (internal locus of control), and how much you believe it to be the result of luck, chance, fate or the influence of other people (external locus of control with aspects of both chance and powerful others).

C Tolerance of ambiguity
This is your ability to work effectively in situations of much uncertainty and ambiguity without experiencing discomfort or stress. Ambiguity occurs when people face new or complex situations and do not know what to do. Such work situations are difficult for many people when the information needed for doing the work is 'vague, incomplete, fragmented, . . . uncertain, inconsistent, contrary, contradictory, or unclear' (Norton, 1975, p 608).

D Role perception
This investigates how you see the kinds of skills necessary for doing the work of a small business owner/manager — how you define that work role. Your role perception will indicate the *direction* of your efforts in aiming for success.

A Task and achievement motivation

This part is based on questions developed in Singapore by Technonet Asia (UP Institute of Small-Scale Industries), which are used here with kind permission.

For each statement, ask yourself: *'How strongly do I feel and think this way?'* Indicate how strongly you agree or disagree with each statement by ticking the appropriate box. Do not miss any items. There are no right or wrong answers — what is important is how you actually think and feel. Answer fairly quickly, without considering how you 'ought to' act.

The boxes are labelled as follows:

SDA = strongly disagree
DA = disagree
UPD = unsure, probably disagree
UPA = unsure, probably agree
A = agree
SA = strongly agree

	SA	A	UPA	UPD	DA	SDA
1 When a special problem arises at the end of a hard day's work I still find myself with a reserve supply of energy.	☐	☐	☐	☐	☐	☐
2 Mistakes and failures overwhelm me so much that I can't learn from them.	☐	☐	☐	☐	☐	☐
3 I find it hard to beg — that is, to ask favours from other people.	☐	☐	☐	☐	☐	☐
4 I want to earn only as much as I need to enjoy a comfortable way of life.	☐	☐	☐	☐	☐	☐
5 The knowledge, experience and training I have for my (proposed) business are insufficient.	☐	☐	☐	☐	☐	☐
6 While my product/service may not be entirely new, I am thinking of new and better ways to make it competitive.	☐	☐	☐	☐	☐	☐
7 It is not necessary to be scientific and rational about management, as long as I have the will to do what I want done.	☐	☐	☐	☐	☐	☐
8 I don't find it hard to persuade other people to trust my ability to succeed.	☐	☐	☐	☐	☐	☐
9 I prefer not to work with unlovable, unpopular people, even if this means that I might not reach my goals.	☐	☐	☐	☐	☐	☐

	SA	A	UPA	UPD	DA	SDA
10 I don't need to waste time and money on 'market research'. If my product sells, I will go on producing it.	☐	☐	☐	☐	☐	☐
11 I work just as hard as most people I know.	☐	☐	☐	☐	☐	☐
12 I don't see any need to read the newspaper every day.	☐	☐	☐	☐	☐	☐
13 I don't fear investing my money in a venture whose dividends I have calculated.	☐	☐	☐	☐	☐	☐
14 I believe that problems and barriers can be turned into opportunities to be exploited.	☐	☐	☐	☐	☐	☐
15 The health and vigour I have motivates others.	☐	☐	☐	☐	☐	☐
16 I can't be away from my business too long because no one else can manage it properly.	☐	☐	☐	☐	☐	☐
17 I don't get upset when I am given negative feedback about the way I perform.	☐	☐	☐	☐	☐	☐
18 I have weaknesses and fears that are very hard to resolve.	☐	☐	☐	☐	☐	☐
19 When I do something, I always make sure that it is done with excellence.	☐	☐	☐	☐	☐	☐
20 I accomplish most when I work alone, under no one's direct supervision.	☐	☐	☐	☐	☐	☐
21 I don't enjoy working in a team as its leader. I would rather just be a member.	☐	☐	☐	☐	☐	☐
22 I doubt my ability to do my work properly when I must do it under new, unfamiliar and difficult conditions.	☐	☐	☐	☐	☐	☐
23 It is I who influences the outcome of events in my life, not luck or fate.	☐	☐	☐	☐	☐	☐
24 I am frequently ill.	☐	☐	☐	☐	☐	☐

	SA	A	UPA	UPD	DA	SDA
25 I don't enjoy results, no matter how good, unless they come from my own efforts.	☐	☐	☐	☐	☐	☐
26 I wait for other people to come up with new ideas and start the action.	☐	☐	☐	☐	☐	☐
27 I find nothing wrong in seeking expert advice about how I should run my business.	☐	☐	☐	☐	☐	☐
28 A risk is worth taking if the probability of success is 20–40%.	☐	☐	☐	☐	☐	☐
29 I consider a customer who complains about my product or service a troublemaker.	☐	☐	☐	☐	☐	☐
30 I will consider a risk worth taking if the probability of success is 70–100%.	☐	☐	☐	☐	☐	☐
31 Stress and tension reduce my efficiency.	☐	☐	☐	☐	☐	☐
32 I am unprepared for the results of my actions.	☐	☐	☐	☐	☐	☐
33 I can be a strong leader, but in a way that makes others willing to follow me.	☐	☐	☐	☐	☐	☐
34 I don't allow failures to discourage me.	☐	☐	☐	☐	☐	☐
35 I don't mind routine, unchallenging work if the pay is good.	☐	☐	☐	☐	☐	☐
36 I am unwilling to work any more than eight hours a day.	☐	☐	☐	☐	☐	☐
37 I enjoy doing things best when I get information on how well or how poorly I am doing.	☐	☐	☐	☐	☐	☐
38 I would get frustrated if my business or some other important project were to fail.	☐	☐	☐	☐	☐	☐
39 I get pleasure in responding to challenges, so competition makes me work harder.	☐	☐	☐	☐	☐	☐
40 I like change because I get restless and discontented with familiar tasks.	☐	☐	☐	☐	☐	☐

	SA	A	UPA	UPD	DA	SDA
41 I consider a risk worth taking if the probability of success is 40–60%.	☐	☐	☐	☐	☐	☐
42 I am unwilling to change my mind once it is made up, even if new facts suggest I am wrong.	☐	☐	☐	☐	☐	☐
43 I often feel weary and sometimes unwell after a day's work.	☐	☐	☐	☐	☐	☐
44 Success is the result more of good luck than of personal effort.	☐	☐	☐	☐	☐	☐
45 Sole proprietorship is the best form of ownership for a business to succeed.	☐	☐	☐	☐	☐	☐
46 I avoid changing the way things are done.	☐	☐	☐	☐	☐	☐
47 I have more abilities than most people.	☐	☐	☐	☐	☐	☐
48 If my business fails, I won't take it as a personal defeat.	☐	☐	☐	☐	☐	☐
49 I can turn my dream into a common goal by talking about it in a way that inspires other people to help me make it happen.	☐	☐	☐	☐	☐	☐
50 I find it hard to win friends and influence other people.	☐	☐	☐	☐	☐	☐
51 While others may see nothing unusual in a certain situation, I am often able to notice in it new opportunities for business.	☐	☐	☐	☐	☐	☐
52 In view of my overall business competence, I will have difficulty achieving my goals.	☐	☐	☐	☐	☐	☐
53 The business I am in (or planning for) is not very unusual.	☐	☐	☐	☐	☐	☐
54 I have trouble obtaining loans from people.	☐	☐	☐	☐	☐	☐
55 I can't wait and watch things happen — I prefer to make them happen.	☐	☐	☐	☐	☐	☐
56 I don't give up easily, even in the face of severe difficulties.	☐	☐	☐	☐	☐	☐
57 I am willing to take substantial risks for substantial returns.	☐	☐	☐	☐	☐	☐

	SA	A	UPA	UPD	DA	SDA
58 People should be hired on the basis of friendship and loyalty, rather than for their competence.	☐	☐	☐	☐	☐	☐
59 I am willing to accept both positive and negative results from my decisions and actions.	☐	☐	☐	☐	☐	☐
60 The knowledge, experience and training I have for my work are good enough.	☐	☐	☐	☐	☐	☐
61 I don't think too much about the negative consequences of my decisions and acts.	☐	☐	☐	☐	☐	☐
62 I don't care if the profit is small, so long as I am certain to get it.	☐	☐	☐	☐	☐	☐
63 I often lack vigour and vitality.	☐	☐	☐	☐	☐	☐
64 There is no reason to consult other people about how to run my business better, because I am satisfied with the way I do it.	☐	☐	☐	☐	☐	☐
65 My business competence is better than that of the 'ordinary person' in the community.	☐	☐	☐	☐	☐	☐
66 I have difficulty in asserting myself or going against the majority opinion.	☐	☐	☐	☐	☐	☐
67 Even if I am capable, hard-working and ambitious, I can't start a business if I can't get the money.	☐	☐	☐	☐	☐	☐
68 I don't get discouraged by an initial 'No!' from a buyer, because I am usually able to persuade him or her to buy my product.	☐	☐	☐	☐	☐	☐
69 I am able to succeed (in spite of severe difficulties) because I am very resourceful.	☐	☐	☐	☐	☐	☐
70 When I fail with one thing, I immediately turn my attention to another goal.	☐	☐	☐	☐	☐	☐
71 I rarely see the future as bright and promising.	☐	☐	☐	☐	☐	☐

	SA	A	UPA	UPD	DA	SDA
72 I don't allow myself to think of the future as dim and gloomy.	☐	☐	☐	☐	☐	☐
73 I tend to over-estimate my capabilities for succeeding in any venture.	☐	☐	☐	☐	☐	☐
74 As an entrepreneur, I need to adopt sound managerial skills so that my business need not be a 'one-man show' but can be a co-operative effort between me and my employees.	☐	☐	☐	☐	☐	☐
75 People around me seem to doubt my ability to start and run a business successfully.	☐	☐	☐	☐	☐	☐
76 Once I start on some task, I usually finish it properly.	☐	☐	☐	☐	☐	☐
77 I try to find out as much as possible about the methods used by successful business people (by reading their life stories).	☐	☐	☐	☐	☐	☐
78 If necessary, I would give up full control over my business to bring in a new partner whose funds, skill and knowledge would be beneficial to the business.	☐	☐	☐	☐	☐	☐
79 In business, I am more concerned with long-term growth than short-term profits.	☐	☐	☐	☐	☐	☐
80 I find it hard to come up with ideas for doing new things or for doing things better.	☐	☐	☐	☐	☐	☐
81 I value a job for the satisfaction and sense of achieving something worthwhile that it brings, rather than for the good pay.	☐	☐	☐	☐	☐	☐
82 I fear moving into a new undertaking I know nothing about.	☐	☐	☐	☐	☐	☐
83 I find it hard to go on working towards a goal when I meet obstacles.	☐	☐	☐	☐	☐	☐
84 I can work better under stress.	☐	☐	☐	☐	☐	☐
85 I can motivate and lead others.	☐	☐	☐	☐	☐	☐

	SA	A	UPA	UPD	DA	SDA
86 I believe there are always new and better ways of doing things.	☐	☐	☐	☐	☐	☐
87 I prepare for trouble before it comes.	☐	☐	☐	☐	☐	☐
88 I use records, books and reports when setting business goals.	☐	☐	☐	☐	☐	☐
89 It is not easy for me to get other people to do what I want them to do.	☐	☐	☐	☐	☐	☐
90 Careful planning, based on getting as much information as possible, is desirable before getting started on any project, and does not take away the fun of adventure.	☐	☐	☐	☐	☐	☐
91 I've never tried to introduce new products to a market, and I do not think I want to.	☐	☐	☐	☐	☐	☐
92 I have confidence in my ability to be successful in almost everything I try.	☐	☐	☐	☐	☐	☐
93 I don't mind working in conditions of uncertainty as long as the probability of gain or success is 'reasonable'.	☐	☐	☐	☐	☐	☐
94 I should be an expert in the product or service I wish to sell.	☐	☐	☐	☐	☐	☐
95 I am healthy and fit for stressful work.	☐	☐	☐	☐	☐	☐
96 I face and solve problems as they arise.	☐	☐	☐	☐	☐	☐

Scoring methods

Look carefully at the scoring table on page 99. Of the 96 items, half are scored 'positively', ie:

SA	A	UPA	UPD	DA	SDA
6	5	4	3	2	1

The numbers of the 48 items that are scored 'positively' are shown on the left side of the scoring table, and the others 'negatively', ie:

SA	A	UPA	UPD	DA	SDA
1	2	3	4	5	6

The numbers of the items scored 'negatively' are shown on the right side of the scoring table.

Scoring table

		Items with positive scores	Items with negative scores	Total scores
Row 1 Risk-taking	Item no : Rating score :	13 41 57 93	28 30 62 82	
Row 2 Hope of success and fear of failure	Item no : Rating score :	14 38 72 87	32 61 71 96	
Row 3 Persistence and hard work	Item no : Rating score :	34 56 76 84	11 36 70 83	
Row 4 Energy and mobility	Item no : Rating score :	1 15 40 95	24 31 43 63	
Row 5 Use of feedback	Item no : Rating score :	17 37 77 88	2 29 42 64	
Row 6 Personal responsibility	Item no : Rating score :	23 25 55 59	21 26 44 48	
Row 7 Self-confidence and self-reliance	Item no : Rating score :	20 47 73 92	18 22 66 67	
Row 8 Knowledgeability	Item no : Rating score :	60 65 90 94	5 10 12 52	
Row 9 Persuasive ability	Item no : Rating score :	8 49 68 85	3 54 75 89	
Row 10 Managerial ability	Item no : Rating score :	27 33 74 78	7 16 45 50	
Row 11 Innovativeness	Item no : Rating score :	6 51 69 86	46 53 80 91	
Row 12 Achievement-orientation	Item no : Rating score :	19 39 79 81	4 9 35 58	
			Grand total	

Transfer your rating (SDA or A, etc) for each item to the appropriate place on the scoring table, and use the above scoring method to write in the actual score for each item rating. For example, if you ticked Item 1 as follows:

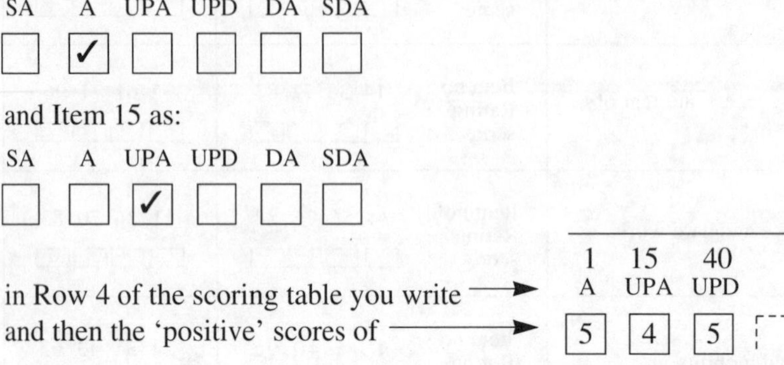

Score all 48 'positive' and all 48 'negative' items on the scoring table as shown above. Then add your scores across each row, and put that total in the 'total scores' column. Add these twelve totals to get your grand total.

Interpretation

Each of the twelve rows in the scoring table is labelled with a characteristic associated with successful entrepreneurship. All are associated with task and achievement motivation.

For each row (ie each characteristic) in the scoring table you could score between 8 and 48. These scores are grouped and interpreted as follows:

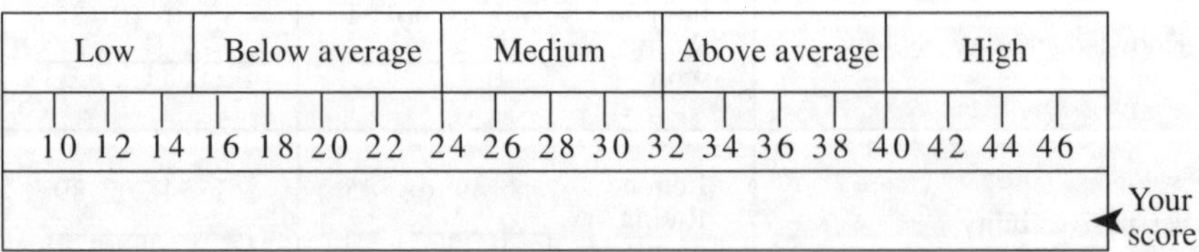

Low scores indicate weaknesses; high scores show strengths.

On your scoring table you have a grand total, which can be interpreted as follows:

Low	Below average	Medium	Above average	High
150	200 250	300 350	400 450	500 550
				Your score

To give yourself an indication of your strengths and weaknesses in the various aspects of task and achievement motivation, draw a line on the following graph to connect your total scores for each of the twelve characteristics from the scoring table.

A total score of 485 or more indicates a high level of task and achievement motivation, and suggests strong entrepreneurial drive. A score between 390 and 485 is above average. A score below 280 suggests that you should carefully weigh up the risks of going into your own business; a very low score (under 180) casts serious doubts on the wisdom of undertaking an entrepreneurial career. A 'medium' score (between 280 and 390) suggests that you should look carefully at your scores on other aspects of entrepreneurship, before making any move.

	Low	Below average	Medium	Above average	High
Risk-taking	•	•	•	•	•
Hope of success and fear of failure	•	•	•	•	•
Persistence and hard work	•	•	•	•	•
Energy and mobility	•	•	•	•	•
Use of feedback	•	•	•	•	•
Personal responsibility	•	•	•	•	•
Self-confidence and self-reliance	•	•	•	•	•
Knowledgeability	•	•	•	•	•
Persuasive ability	•	•	•	•	•
Managerial ability	•	•	•	•	•
Innovativeness	•	•	•	•	•
Achievement-orientation	•	•	•	•	•

Look at the above graph to see whether your low score was due to very low scores on several of the twelve characteristics, or due to overall low scores.

B Locus of control

These questions were developed by Levenson (1972, 1973) and used with permission.

For each of the 24 statements that follow, tick the appropriate box to indicate how much you agree or disagree. There are no correct or incorrect answers.

The five columns are labelled as follows:
SDA = strongly disagree
DA = disagree
NAD = neither agree nor disagree
A = agree
SA = strongly agree

	SA	A	NAD	DA	SDA
1 Whether or not I get to be leader depends mostly on my ability.	☐	☐	☐	☐	☐
2 To a great extent my life is controlled by accidental happenings.	☐	☐	☐	☐	☐
3 I feel as though what happens in my life is mostly determined by powerful people.	☐	☐	☐	☐	☐
4 Whether or not I ever cause a car accident will depend on my skill as a driver.	☐	☐	☐	☐	☐
5 When I make plans, I am almost certain to make them work.	☐	☐	☐	☐	☐
6 Often there is no chance of protecting my personal interests from bad luck.	☐	☐	☐	☐	☐
7 When I get what I want, it's usually because I'm lucky.	☐	☐	☐	☐	☐
8 Even if I were a good leader, I would not be made a leader unless I played up to people in positions of power.	☐	☐	☐	☐	☐
9 How many friends I have depends on how nice a person I am.	☐	☐	☐	☐	☐
10 I have often found that what I think will happen does happen.	☐	☐	☐	☐	☐
11 My life is chiefly controlled by powerful others.	☐	☐	☐	☐	☐
12 Whether or not I will be responsible for causing a car accident will be a matter of chance or fate.	☐	☐	☐	☐	☐
13 People like myself have very little chance of protecting our personal interests when they conflict with those of powerful people.	☐	☐	☐	☐	☐

	SA	A	NAD	DA	SDA
14 It's not always wise for me to plan too far ahead because many things turn out to be a matter of good or bad fortune.	☐	☐	☐	☐	☐
15 Getting what I want means I have to please those people above me.	☐	☐	☐	☐	☐
16 Whether or not I get to be a leader depends on whether I'm lucky enough to be in the right place at the right time.	☐	☐	☐	☐	☐
17 If important people were to decide they didn't like me, I probably wouldn't make many friends.	☐	☐	☐	☐	☐
18 I can pretty much determine what will happen in my life.	☐	☐	☐	☐	☐
19 I am usually able to protect my personal interests.	☐	☐	☐	☐	☐
20 Whether or not I am involved in a car accident will depend on other drivers.	☐	☐	☐	☐	☐
21 When I get what I want, it's usually because I worked hard for it.	☐	☐	☐	☐	☐
22 In order to have my plans work, I make sure that they fit in with the desires of people who have power over me.	☐	☐	☐	☐	☐
23 My life is determined by my own actions.	☐	☐	☐	☐	☐
24 It's chiefly a matter of fate whether or not I have a few friends or many friends.	☐	☐	☐	☐	☐

Scoring methods

For each item, score your responses as follows:

SA	A	NAD	DA	SDA
5	4	3	2	1

Internal		**Powerful others**		**Chance**	
Item 1	☐	Item 3	☐	Item 2	☐
4	☐	8	☐	6	☐
5	☐	11	☐	7	☐

Internal		**Powerful others**		**Chance**	
Item 9	☐	Item 13	☐	Item 10	☐
18	☐	15	☐	12	☐
19	☐	17	☐	14	☐
21	☐	20	☐	16	☐
23	☐	22	☐	24	☐
Total	☐	Total	☐	Total	☐

For each of the three aspects of locus of control (internal, powerful others and chance) your score should be between 8 and 40.

High:	above 34	Below average:	14–20
Above average:	28–34	Low:	below 14
Medium:	21–27		

On the graph below draw three columns to show your score on each of the three aspects of locus of control.

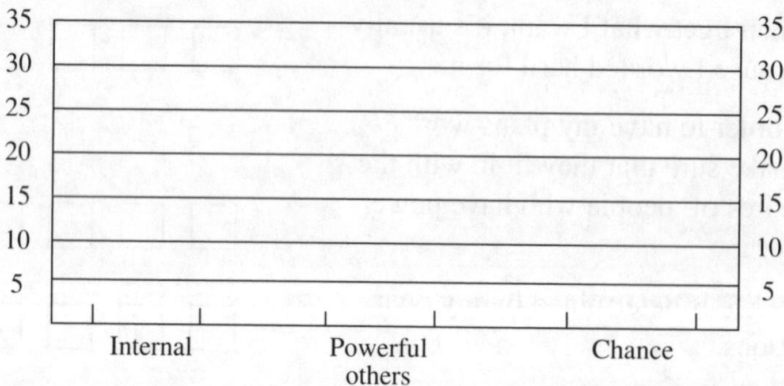

Interpretation

Strongly entrepreneurial people believe that success in whatever they do will be the result of their own skill and ability, and that luck or the influence of other people plays very little part. If your score for 'Internal' was 30 or more, and scores on 'Powerful others' and 'Chance' were much lower, you have an appropriate locus of control to be an entrepreneur. If either or both your 'external' scores were about the same as or higher than your 'internal' score, this suggests that you are not committed to the belief that you can determine your own future.

C Tolerance of ambiguity

This section of the personal assessment examines how well you can tolerate uncertain and ambiguous situations, of which there are many in running a business. The questions used here were designed by Budner (1962).

For each of the 16 statements given below, you are asked to indicate how strongly you agree or disagree. There are no 'right' or 'wrong' answers. Indicate your answers by ticking the most appropriate box alongside each statement.

The abbreviated headings for the boxes are:

STA = strongly agree
MOA = moderately agree
SLA = slightly agree
SLD = slightly disagree
MOD = moderately disagree
STD = strongly disagree

	STD	MOD	SLD	SLA	MOA	STA
1 An expert who doesn't come up with a definite answer probably doesn't know too much.	☐	☐	☐	☐	☐	☐
2 There is really no such thing as a problem that can't be solved.	☐	☐	☐	☐	☐	☐
3 Many of our most important decisions are based upon insufficient information.	☐	☐	☐	☐	☐	☐
4 A good job is one where what is to be done and how it is to be done are always clear.	☐	☐	☐	☐	☐	☐
5 In the long run it is possible to get more done by tackling small, simple problems rather than large and complicated ones.	☐	☐	☐	☐	☐	☐
6 The sooner we all acquire similar values and ideals the better.	☐	☐	☐	☐	☐	☐
7 People who fit their lives into a schedule miss most of the joys of living.	☐	☐	☐	☐	☐	☐
8 It is more fun to tackle a complicated problem than to solve a simple one.	☐	☐	☐	☐	☐	☐
9 Often the most interesting and stimulating people are those who don't mind being different and original.	☐	☐	☐	☐	☐	☐
10 People who insist upon a 'yes' or 'no' answer just don't know how complicated things really are.	☐	☐	☐	☐	☐	☐

	STD	MOD	SLD	SLA	MOA	STA
11 Teachers or supervisors who hand out vague assignments give students a chance to show initiative and originality.	☐	☐	☐	☐	☐	☐
12 A good teacher is one who makes you wonder about your way of looking at things.	☐	☐	☐	☐	☐	☐
13 What we are used to is always preferable to what is unfamiliar.	☐	☐	☐	☐	☐	☐
14 A person who leads an even, regular life in which few surprises or unexpected happenings arise really has a lot to be grateful for.	☐	☐	☐	☐	☐	☐
15 I like parties where I know most of the people more than ones where all or most of the people are complete strangers.	☐	☐	☐	☐	☐	☐
16 I would like to live in a foreign country for a while.	☐	☐	☐	☐	☐	☐

Scoring methods

For items 1, 2, 4, 5, 6, 13, 14 and 15 score as follows:

STD	MOD	SLD	SLA	MOA	STA
6	5	4	3	2	1

and for items 3, 7, 8, 9, 10, 11, 12 and 16:

STD	MOD	SLD	SLA	MOA	STA
1	2	3	4	5	6

Your scores

1	2	3	4	5	6	7	8	9	10	11	12	13	14	15	16	Total

Scores between 16 and 96 are possible. Enter your total score below, and note the interpretation.

Low	Below average	Medium	Above average	High
20 24 28	32 36 40 44	48 52 56 60	64 68 72 76	80 84 88 92

Your score

Interpretation

A score of 64 or better suggests that you can work well in conditions of some uncertainty — where there are no clear instructions or methods for you to follow, and where you will face new and often complex tasks in which you will have to use your judgement in deciding what to do, and how.

A score of 80 or more suggests that you enjoy such situations and excel in them.

A score below about 32 would indicate that you get very uncomfortable, highly stressed and frustrated when you have to work in such conditions — you would do well to avoid them.

D Role perception

In other parts of this personal assessment you were asked to say how much you agreed or disagreed with particular ideas. You were urged not to judge the rightness or wrongness of your responses. In this section you are asked to say how important each of 50 personal characteristics is (or should be) for success in starting and running a small business.

For each characteristic place a tick in the appropriate box.

	Vitally important					Not very important
1 Obliging	☐	☐	☐	☐	☐	☐
2 Rational	☐	☐	☐	☐	☐	☐
3 Tenacious	☐	☐	☐	☐	☐	☐
4 Tactful	☐	☐	☐	☐	☐	☐
5 Conventional	☐	☐	☐	☐	☐	☐
6 Competitive	☐	☐	☐	☐	☐	☐
7 Casual	☐	☐	☐	☐	☐	☐
8 Conformist	☐	☐	☐	☐	☐	☐
9 Enterprising	☐	☐	☐	☐	☐	☐
10 Extroverted	☐	☐	☐	☐	☐	☐
11 Independent	☐	☐	☐	☐	☐	☐
12 Considerate	☐	☐	☐	☐	☐	☐
13 Authoritarian	☐	☐	☐	☐	☐	☐
14 Apprehensive	☐	☐	☐	☐	☐	☐
15 Shrewd	☐	☐	☐	☐	☐	☐

	Vitally important					Not very important
16 Conservative						
17 Forceful						
18 Reserved						
19 Generous						
20 Imaginative						
21 Unemotional						
22 Self-reliant						
23 Spontaneous						
24 Innovative (original)						
25 Agreeable						
26 Sensitive						
27 Assertive						
28 Dogmatic						
29 Co-operative						
30 Ambitious						
31 Relaxed						
32 Sociable						
33 Decisive						
34 Self-confident						
35 Aggressive						
36 Adaptable						
37 Placid						
38 Strict						
39 Defensive						
40 Introverted						
41 Cautious						
42 Dependent						
43 Self-centred						
44 Restrained						

45 Analytical

46 Initiating

47 Unimposing

48 Sympathetic

49 Dominant

50 Submissive

Scoring methods

Score

Vitally important			Not very important		
6	5	4	3	2	1

for items

2	11	21	28	38
3	13	22	30	43
6	15	23	33	45
9	17	24	34	46
10	20	27	35	49

and score

Vitally important			Not very important		
1	2	3	4	5	6

for items

1	12	25	36	42
4	14	26	37	44
5	16	29	39	47
7	18	31	40	48
8	19	32	41	50

Interpretation

Total scores will fall between 50 and 300. People with high scores (over about 225) see a need for small business owner/managers to be ambitious, energetic, self-reliant and goal directed — all features of doers and entrepreneurial individuals. Low scores indicate a belief that successful owner/managers should let things happen as they will, and be unimposing and 'laid back' — not at all entrepreneurial.

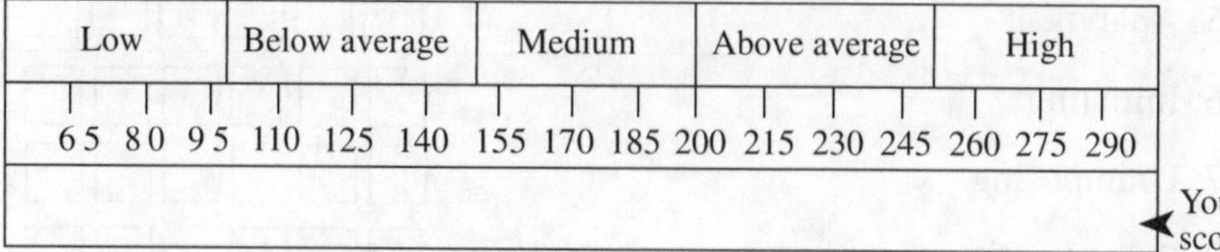

If you scored below 100 you have an incorrect understanding of how owner/managers should perform to be successful. A score of over about 225 indicates a more accurate understanding of how successful small business people go about their work. The characteristics which show up as more appropriate for successful management of small firms are those scoring 6 for 'vitally important' (see scoring method above).

Obviously extremes at either end of the scale are not desirable, but highly successful owner/managers tend to be aggressively self-confident and self-reliant rather than casual or introverted. Williams (1991) found that owner/managers of surviving firms had an average score of 195 on role perception, while those of failed firms averaged only 138.

Conclusion

Do you have enough entrepreneurial drive and initiative to be a success in owning and running your own small business?

If you scored below average (or worse) on three of the four sections of the personal assessment, there must be real doubt as to whether you have enough entrepreneurial drive to be successful. Our advice is that you should take a course in entrepreneurship development, read more about it, or team up with someone who has a high level of entrepreneurial characteristics and behaviour. Better still — do all these things!

References

Budner, S 1962, 'Intolerance of ambiguity as a personality variable', *Journal of Personality*, vol 30, no 1, March, pp 29–50

Levenson, H 1972, 'Distinctions within the concept of internal-external control: Development of a new scale', *Proceedings of the 80th Annual Convention of the American Psychological Association*, vol 7, pp 259–60 (Summary)

Levenson, H 1973, 'Multidimensional locus of control in psychiatric patients', *Journal of Consulting and Clinical Psychology*, vol 41, no 3, pp 397–404

Norton, R W 1975, 'Measurement of ambiguity tolerance', *Journal of Personality Assessment*, vol 39, no 6, pp 607–19

Williams, A J 1991, 'Small business survival: The role of formal education, management training and advisory services', *Small Business Review 1990–1991*, Bureau of Industry Economics, Small Business Research Unit, Australian Government Publishing Service, Canberra, pp 43–82

Technonet Asia (UP Institute of Small-Scale Industries) 1981, *Entrepreneurs Handbook*, Singapore

CHAPTER 7

What are your chances of starting?

In Chapter 4 we saw that going into your own business is one of the great Australian dreams. Many people have this dream, but only a small percentage actually transform their dream into reality. This chapter looks at this low conversion rate. After reading it you should be able to:

- identify the main reasons why many small business ideas are never put into practice
- summarise the main questions to be asked before going into business, and
- start the planning process for your own business.

THE SORTING-OUT PERIOD

How many times have you heard people say:

'Why don't we go into business?' or
'There is a fortune to be made if only . . . Why don't we . . .?' or
'You are a great cook . . . Why don't you open a restaurant?'

Have you noticed that, in the majority of cases where you have heard people talk like this, they did *not* continue with the idea and actually start their own business? The reasons why so many 'good' ideas are never put into practice are shown in Figure 7.1.

This curve shows a typical pattern of activity from the expression of the original idea to the actual start of the business based on that idea. Looking at the curve you will notice that more and more people drop their idea of going into business as they progress along the typical pre-start path. It is important to remember that:

- some proposals take years to evaluate while others will take only hours or minutes; and
- the steps highlighted are meant to be general steps only, and the order of the steps might vary. Let us look at each step.

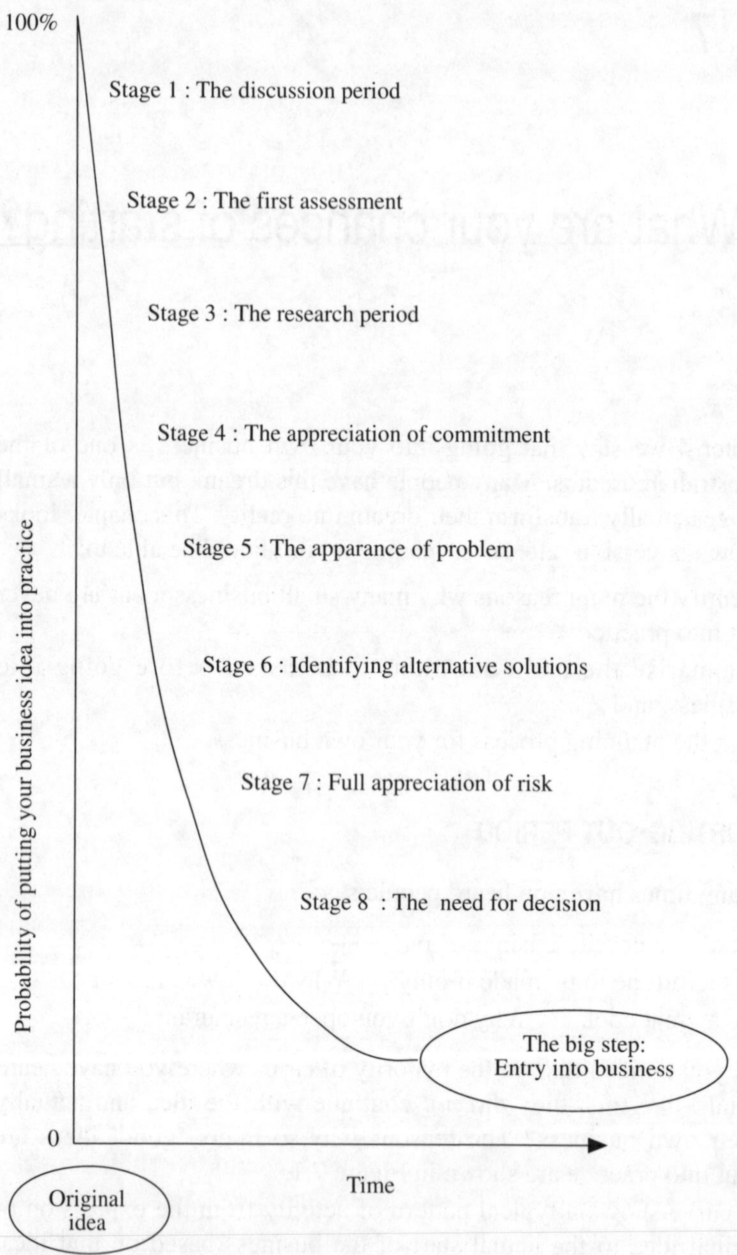

FIGURE 7.1 The 'sorting-out' curve

Stage 1: The discussion period

After the original idea has been formed the most common pattern is to talk about the proposal and its implications. At this stage the idea is usually a concept only, as there has been no time to gather information. It is not surprising to see many ideas 'die' at this stage due to lack of commitment, or poor motivation or support, or maybe a realisation that the idea itself is impractical or too difficult.

Stage 2: The first assessment

At this stage the idea of going into business is usually very strong and there is a desire to investigate the practical aspects such as where the business will operate from, how it will be staffed, how much it will cost (as a guide) and a whole host of operating details. A lot of people lose their drive at this point as they begin to appreciate that going into business requires planning, money and a commitment of both time and effort.

Stage 3: The research period

Having realised the need for planning and money, it is normal for the potential small business person to look for more facts and details. The aim of this research is to give a clearer picture of the proposed business, the methods of operation and the possible market — in other words, a realistic understanding of the proposed business. It is common during this period for many ideas of starting a business to be dropped, as the research has shown the idea to be, say, impractical, too complicated, already in existence, or maybe not what was originally expected. Many people also do not know how to start their research. Some sources of information for this research are shown in the appendix at the end of this book.

Stage 4: The appreciation of commitment

Having done the initial research, the next step is to say 'What must be done, and how will it affect me (or us)?' Starting a business will usually require the involvement of money, labour, time and other resources. When many people realise the need to commit *their* time, money, labour and other resources, they often decide that starting a business is not for them.

Stage 5: The appearance of problems

Once the commitment has been appreciated and accepted, further research usually takes place and obstacles or problems appear as the idea is pursued. The need for experience is often paramount, as is the question of money. The idea of a partnership seems excellent at first, but then come the problems of sharing authority, money, time, effort, trust, and often family life. As the study continues, government regulations, legal restrictions, lack of knowledge, competitors' activities and often the need for secrecy can make the idea of starting a business impractical or undesirable, and still more business proposals die at this stage.

> Small business is not for the faint-hearted, it is for those who believe that nothing is impossible.

Stage 6: The identification of alternative solutions

Many business proposals are abandoned at this stage because there appear to be no solutions to the problems that have arisen. At this point many people fail to look for alternative solutions, ie another way around the problem. Typical examples are to consider:

- leasing v buying
- renting v owning
- alternative processes
- different suppliers
- sub-contracting v manufacture
- new distributors
- different packaging.

And so the list goes on . . .

This stage is really an exercise in lateral thinking, in looking for other answers to the problems being faced. To help yourself in this process, make sure you talk to your professionals — accountant, solicitor, banker, small business counsellor, consultants, etc. Surviving and growing in small business is all about identifying and solving problems.

Stage 7: The appreciation of risk

At this stage people usually become aware of the risk they face and the fact that the risk is unavoidable if they want to go into business. In earlier chapters we discussed the fact that you can risk everything (not just your money) when you go into business.

If you need to borrow money you have to offer the lender some acceptable security, and this usually means mortgaging your home. If the property is jointly owned, your home partner might flatly refuse to do this. In such cases, however, lenders simply take the view: 'If you won't risk your assets — why should we?' Consequently, many business proposals are abandoned at this stage.

Stage 8: The need for decision

Somewhere in the whole process of looking at starting a business the question that has to be confronted is 'Yes or no?' Many people cannot make that final decision to proceed — even though it is what they desperately want. The reasons for such last-minute hesitation are numerous but usually come back to factors such as:

- they are secure with what they have
- they are not prepared to back their judgement
- they are unable to adjust to change
- they consider the risk too big
- they consider the challenge too difficult
- their friends have told them not to.

Whatever the reason, many business ideas are dropped at this stage simply for the want of someone to say 'yes'.

In summary, from the moment of having the original idea of starting a business to the time of actually going into business, there is a massive sorting-out process. It is estimated that a mere 2% to 3% of initial ideas are actually put into practice. In other words, an estimated 97% to 98% of all business ideas that are considered are *never* put into practice.

The big step: Entry into business

Having decided to go into business, many people do not know where to begin. The second section of this book is devoted entirely to the process of getting started in your own business. In fact, Chapter 8 is designed to help you create a written feasibility study for your own business idea. The following five chapters provide a hands-on approach to show you how to take the big step, ie how to join the ranks of the small business people in Australia.

Meanwhile, you are invited to consider some key issues you should look at before you actually go into business.

QUESTIONS TO ASK

The main questions that you should ask before you go into business can be summarised into four areas:

- you and your family
- your money
- your business idea, and
- your operations.

An honest self-evaluation in these four areas is essential.

If you have been reading from Chapter 1 to this point, you should now have a better understanding of all that you need to do, and seriously consider *before* getting involved in the actual startup process and investing money in a new business venture.

From reading Chapter 3 in particular you should be aware of the causes of most small business failure, and of the vital ingredients for survival and success! You will realise that total dedication and commitment to the venture are essential, and that you will be putting a great deal at risk. Furthermore, by going into your own business, you will be taking on a number of major responsibilities. In short, owning and running a small business is not easy, and should not be undertaken without fully appreciating what will be required of you! The obvious question is: Are you willing and able to accept the responsibility and the necessary level of commitment to hard work and dedicated effort?

With your own business idea in mind follow through the sorting-out process outlined in this chapter and do not be tempted to hurry and cut corners. Give every aspect and every angle of going into your own business serious and careful thought. Talk with as many other people as possible, get their advice and weigh up the idea. If and when you make the move, be '110 per cent' sure you are doing the right thing, and equally determined to make it a winner!

> You will be the major factor and driving force in your business.

From what has been discussed in previous chapters, you will realise that you are going to be *the* major factor in whether your business is a success or a failure. Your business outcome will reflect your knowledge, your training, your business ability, your management style, your administration and your entrepreneurial flair.

In short, your business is you! If you decide to extend yourself and your ability by taking on a partner, make sure your choice is the right one. Ask yourself:

- Can you work with someone else — sharing the responsibility and the authority as well as the effort and the resource?
- Can the partner also work with someone else?
- Is the partner similarly committed to succeeding and also willing to be actively involved in running the business?
- Can you and the partner work together in this business proposal?

If you are considering taking on a partner, don't be tempted to avoid these questions. Partnerships can and do work, BUT the wrong partner can destroy you and the business faster than any other factor!

> Having a business partner means that the business is no longer exclusively yours!

Being the major driving force in the business means more than being committed to its success, important though that is. It also requires that *you* (and your colleagues, if any) must be able to give the business all or most of what it needs in order to be successful. A lot of special advice and guidance is available from experts and professionals outside your business, and their wisdom and expertise should be regularly sought. However, *the buck stops with you!* Your contributions are indispensable. While these experts or professionals can offer advice and guidance, you are the one who makes the decisions!

Your personal experience, knowledge and overall skill in doing the work of the business — whether it be bricklaying, cake decorating, accounting, engineering, or running a petrol station or milk bar or whatever — will determine the quality of the goods and services you will be selling. This, in turn, will affect your ability to attract customers and make sales, which you must do to survive in business.

In addition, the business must be operated in such a way that it is successful in gaining a sufficient share of the market and also becomes profitable. Your experience in management (perhaps as a leading hand, supervisor or department manager, etc), or in previously running a business of your own, should have provided you with understanding and expertise in managing people, working with the other resources of the firm, making decisions to solve the many problems you will face, and doing the other 101 things required. If this experience is lacking, you should perhaps pause — and ask yourself:

'Am I ready yet?'

Much help and training is available and you should use it to add to whatever managerial and entrepreneurial experience you might already have.

It is hoped that you have taken the opportunity in Chapter 6 to measure yourself in the many areas of experience, skill, knowledge and personal qualities which studies have shown to be so vital in owner/managers. If you find you are weak or 'below par' in any areas of skill or knowledge, pay special attention to the appropriate chapters in the remainder of the book and seek help.

Summary

Most people at some time in their lives think of starting a business of their own, but very few actually do so. Getting started in a new business needs excitement and plenty of enthusiasm but, because the consequences of failing are so drastic, starting should come only after much serious thought, discussion and a period of sorting out all the 'ifs' and 'buts'.

If at any time there is any major doubt about the wisdom of taking this step, if you feel that your commitment is less than total, if you are put off by the emerging problems and responsibilities, or if you are unsure of making the final decision, these should be taken as warnings: don't do it — yet!

To those who would say that such advice takes all the enjoyment out of getting started in business, we urge you to find a business (perhaps through an accountant) which has recently failed and talk with its owner/s about the 'fun' of 'going broke'.

Key words

commitment	research
planning	risk

Review exercise

Draw your own 'sorting out' curve showing the eight stages of going into business. On this curve indicate the stage of development you believe your business proposal has now reached.

CHAPTER 8

Establishing alternatives — your feasibility study

Deciding whether or not to go into business is very similar to considering marriage. It is a major step, with far-reaching commitments and responsibilities — and not something to be treated lightly or without serious consideration.

You must not only decide 'How should I begin to consider the alternatives?' but you should also take a step backwards and ask 'What are the alternatives?', and 'Are they what I really want?'

This chapter is designed to assist any person who is contemplating making a major business investment — that is, anyone who is going into business for the first time, diversifying, or simply expanding an existing business.

After reading this chapter, you should be able to:

- prepare a set of personal objectives
- define your business idea
- describe the contents of a feasibility study
- identify the key areas which need to be researched
- organise the content and presentation of your feasibility study.

THE PLANNING PROCESS

The first step in any planning process is deciding what you really want to do or achieve. This seems so obvious, yet it is amazing how few business people take the trouble to do it. What is not surprising is that those who do are the successful ones.

Planning is a simple process that starts with a broad goal which is a statement describing in general terms a desired outcome. A goal can be linked to a dream, a vision, or even a way of life. It is usually not specific and may be likened to a mental picture painted with a very broad brush.

When you ask yourself the question 'How will I achieve this goal?', the answer is in fact an aim. This aim gives you direction by being more specific than a goal and by providing a means of achieving the goal. Again, an aim is still very broad, but, by asking the question 'What am I

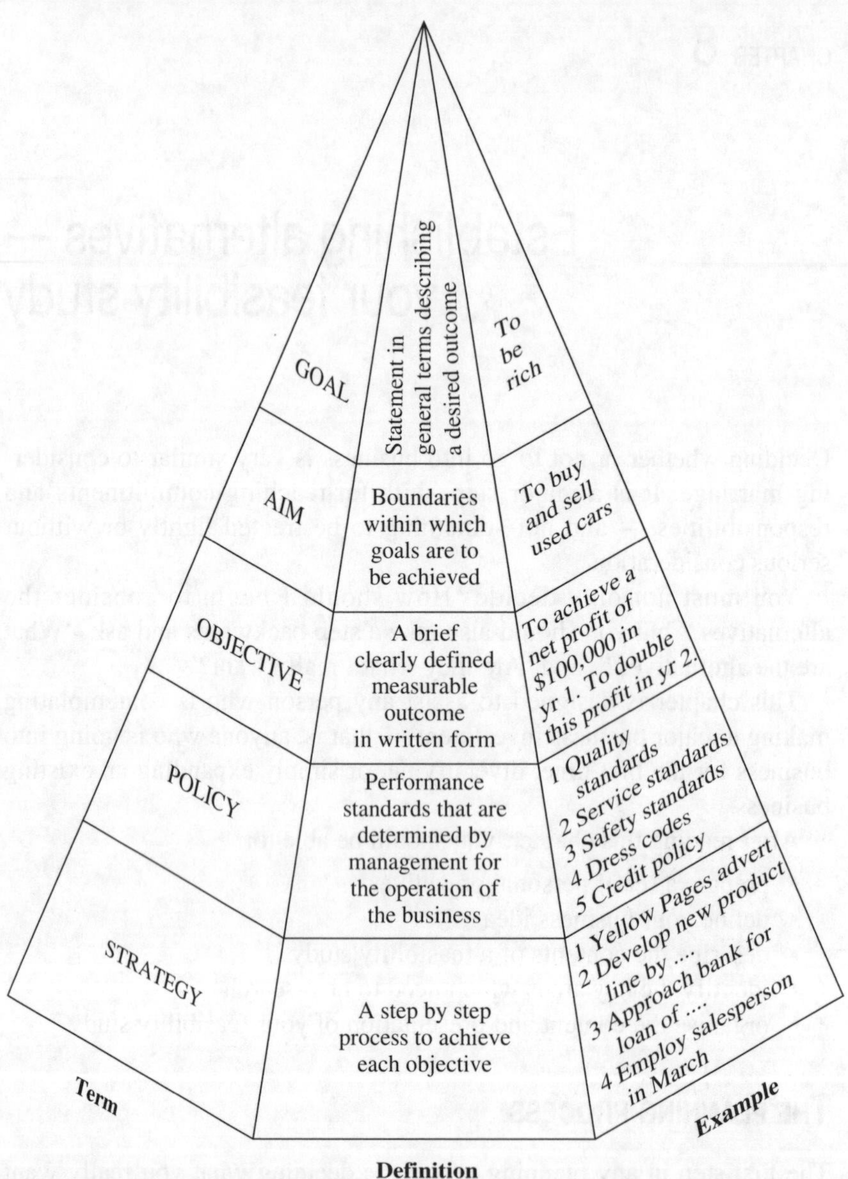

FIGURE 8.1 The planning process

really trying to achieve?' we at last find both direction and motivation as our answers form objectives.

Objectives are clearly defined and measurable outcomes in written form. They are the key to any plan, as the success of the plan can be directly related to the quality of the objectives upon which it is based. The planning process we have discussed so far is shown in Figure 8.1.

We have just seen that the motivation and direction of any plan comes from the objectives. Developing a good set of objectives takes practice, and you should ensure that each objective is workable.

Characteristics of objectives

Every objective has to be:

- clearly defined
- measurable
- achievable
- challenging
- brief
- written.

Clearly defined

Your objectives should be written in such a way that there is no doubt or confusion about your intentions. If you ask yourself 'What do I mean by this objective?' and your answer is different from your written words, then you have not defined your objective clearly enough. Your wording must be precise; otherwise it remains an aim rather than an objective.

Measurable

The only way to test the effectiveness of an objective is to measure actual outcomes against the objective. Most people have trouble with the measurability requirement, but it is vital. If an objective is not measurable, then it is more a wish than an objective. Gaining direction and motivation depends on your being able to see your progress towards the objective. If you have written down an objective that is not measurable, keep thinking about it. How will you know how far you are from achieving it? How will you know if you exceed it? When you can answer these questions, rewrite the objective.

The main measure is time: set a date by which you want the objective to be achieved. A simple way of doing this is to start your objective with: By . . . (insert date of completion of your objective), I will . . .

There are two major time frames used in setting objectives. The first is short term — up to 12 months. The other is long term — that is, one to five years into the future. Other measures that can be used are numbers or units such as dollars, kilograms, etc.

Achievable

When setting your objectives, make sure they are achievable. You are only human, and nothing demoralises more than failure at what you are trying to achieve, especially when you have given a 100% effort to the project. Some things are impossible, even for you!

Challenging

If there is no challenge in an objective it is probably of little value, as you will not be extending yourself to achieve it. Without a challenge we tend to drift; and the setting of objectives, as we said earlier, is to give us both direction and motivation. The bigger the challenge the bigger the reward. (But remember that your objectives must also be achievable.)

Brief

A good objective can be expressed in fewer than 20 words. If you have used more than 20 words you will probably find you have:

- included more than one objective in your statement
- not clearly identified what you are trying to say, or
- included your rationale, background or support material in the statement.

Be brief — it pays!

Written

Until your objective is in writing, it is simply a wish that is easily forgotten, readily changed or modified. In reality, an objective is far less effective or believable while it remains unwritten.

When you are writing your objectives make sure that the language you use is positive. Use phrases such as *I will* rather than *I would like to*, and *I shall* rather than *It would be nice if*. This use of positive language will separate the achievers from the 'gunnas' — people who are 'gunna' do this and 'gunna' do that.

> Business objectives must be in harmony with personal objectives.

Kinds of objectives

To be successful, people in small business need two sets of objectives: one for their personal life and one for their business. Only when these are in harmony will there be enough energy and motivation for the business to succeed. Personal objectives are most important because they are the source of energy and drive needed in business. Successful people are aware of this, and make sure that their success in business will help them to achieve their personal objectives.

Setting and writing objectives is a major breakthrough for most people. If you have trouble starting or writing your objectives, don't despair. It is like any other skill — it requires an introduction to the concept, a starting point, and a lot of practice. We have introduced the concept to you, and now is the best starting point. Let us start with your practice.

The first objectives to define are those for your personal life. Only you can do this.

Personal objectives

A set of personal (or life) objectives should include:

Emotional	life companion family friends
Material	finance status house and contents car
Physical and mental	health education recreation hobbies
Spiritual objectives	values beliefs purpose

To start setting your personal objectives try building a mental picture, then write down a description of it, in the following way:

1 Sit in a quiet place and choose a particular date some three years in the future.
2 Picture in your mind what you would like to be doing at that time. Keep looking for details in your picture. Where are you? How many people are with you? Who are they? What are you and they doing, saying, wearing? What are the surroundings — furniture (if indoors), plants and scenery (if outdoors)? Why are you and the other people there?
3 Add more detail until you have a very clear mental picture of how you would like things to be in three years' time.
4 From your mental picture, identify the various factors to be included in your personal objectives.
5 Write notes to describe your picture.
6 Spend a few minutes each day for a week recalling your picture, adding details and making alterations where necessary.
7 After this time, look at your description and identify a set of objectives for your personal life. Make sure that the way you write each one meets the requirements for setting of objectives as already outlined.
8 Consider obtaining a drawing, a picture or a visual reminder of your mental picture to reinforce your personal motivation. When you obtain this visual reminder, display it in a strategic spot where you cannot miss seeing it continuously.

> Planning is essential to reach objectives.

When you have arrived at a set of personal objectives, make some notes about how owning and running a small business will help you achieve them. Also note the areas of your life where your business will conflict with your personal objectives. This is important. When personal and business objectives are in harmony, mutual benefit is derived. When they conflict, you will need to identify the cost — what you are prepared to give up, or pay, in terms of one or more of your objectives. Benefits and costs will both affect the energy and drive you can bring to your business.

An example of this process concerned a woman who enrolled in a bookkeeping course so that she could help her husband (a tradesman) in their business. She hated the idea of bookkeeping, being more interested in dressmaking, at which she was very competent. It seemed to her that the marriage depended to some extent on her doing the bookkeeping for the business. To achieve her personal goal of still being happily married in three years' time, she decided to sacrifice her dressmaking until she had developed the skills needed to do the bookkeeping for the business. You will see that personal objectives are just that — very personal! There is no 'right' or 'wrong'; they are *your* objectives.

Another example of the value of setting personal objectives is that of the electronics manufacturer who was asked the question: 'What do you want to achieve in your personal life?' After being led through the eight-point exercise described above, he saw himself flying a helicopter over mountains with a friend in three years' time. It was discovered that he had never been in a helicopter, let alone flown one. He set a plan, which started with a joy flight and led him to obtain his pilot's licence and finally to buy his own helicopter — all within eighteen months! The planning system works — try it!

Figure 8.2 provides a worksheet that might be of use in writing personal objectives.

Business objectives

Setting business objectives is very similar to setting your own personal objectives. However, at this stage of the planning process, you do not have a business. In Chapter 14 we discuss the actual business plan process, and setting business objectives is a key point at that stage.

However, at the feasibility stage the key objectives you are setting are personal rather than business. The only business objective you can have at this stage is to write your feasibility study.

By . . /. . /. . . I will . . . .
. . . .

By . . /. . /. . . I will . . . .
. . . .

By . . /. . /. . . I will . . . .
. . . .

By . . /. . /. . . I will . . . .
. . . .

By . . /. . /. . . I will . . . .
. . . .

By . . /. . /. . . I will . . . .
. . . .

By . . /. . /. . . I will . . . .
. . . .

By . . /. . /. . . I will . . . .
. . . .

By . . /. . /. . . I will . . . .
. . . .

By . . /. . /. . . I will . . . .
. . . .

FIGURE 8.2 Personal objectives

THE FEASIBILITY STUDY

Note that the feasibility study is not a plan for how to run a business. It is a systematic analysis of the possibility of putting a business idea into practice. It leads the writer of the study through the sorting-out curve described in Chapter 7.

Ingredients

Each feasibility study is unique and personally tailored to an individual idea. Businesses are just as unique as people; so, while a feasibility study can follow general guidelines, it should not follow a rigid pro forma approach. There are, however, six key sections that should be included in all feasibility studies:

- the business idea being considered
- the key people involved
- the market available
- the proposed operational structure
- finance and viability, and
- the recommendations of the study.

The business idea

What business are you really trying to enter? You should try out a few words to describe the real nature of your proposed business. Using a maximum of one typed page, describe the proposed business in terms of a broad description of the idea, the product/services, the general location, and who will be operating the business. Highlight why your idea would be different from those behind existing businesses. Even at this early stage, you should be able to state:

Why will your business be successful?

This summary should also include any relevant points — eg that the business is a franchise arrangement, or that you hold a patent, or that you are aware of a new development providing the opening for such a business. This page should simply outline the business idea you are considering, and give a self-contained general overview. At this stage you should resist the temptation to expand in detail.

The key people

Any business is only as good as the people involved in it.

This section of the feasibility study looks first at the key people (eg partners) who are involved in the proposal. A profile of these people should be created, showing their strengths and skills, their backgrounds and their experience. These profiles are not simply a chronological employment history; rather, they show the contribution each of the key people can make to the proposed business, as well as highlighting any need for additional skills or partners. Figure 8.3 shows a standard model that could be used for profiling key people.

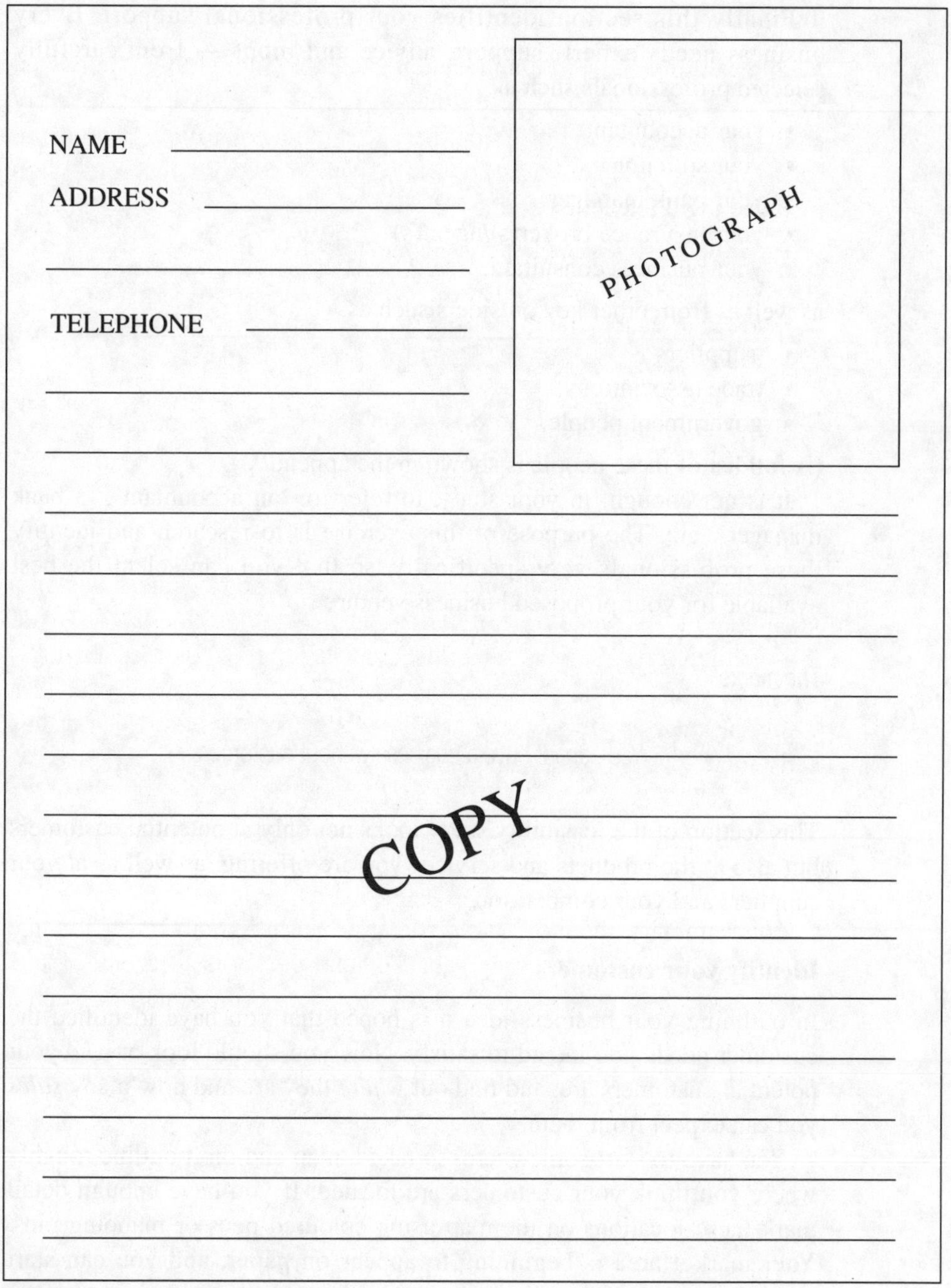

NAME ______
ADDRESS ______
______
TELEPHONE ______

PHOTOGRAPH

COPY

FIGURE 8.3 A standard profile

The personal objectives of the key people should also be listed in this section. Ideally you should consider a minimum of 10 personal objectives for each partner. As stated earlier, these objectives should be a mixture of both short- and long-term time frames. The outlining of personal objectives at this stage identifies any potential conflict and gives a more positive direction to the team.

Finally this section identifies your professional support. Every business needs expert support, advice and input — from carefully selected professionals such as:

- your accountant
- your solicitor
- your bank manager
- your insurance broker(s)/agent(s)
- your business consultant,

as well as from other key outsiders such as:

- suppliers
- trade associations
- government people.

(A full list of these people is shown in the appendix.)

It is not enough, in your study, to refer to: 'an accountant', 'a bank manager', etc. The purpose of this exercise is to research and identify these professionals very specifically, so that you can select the best available for your proposed business venture.

The market

You cannot have a business without customers.

This section of the feasibility study looks not only at potential customers but also at the products and services you are offering, as well as at your suppliers and your competition.

Identify your customers

In outlining your business idea it is hoped that you have identified the customer needs you intend to satisfy. Now you should look at *who* your potential customers are, and find out *where* they are and how many *sales* you can expect from them.

You have to start somewhere, so take a map and on it outline roughly where you think your customers are located. If you have enough detail mark these locations on the map using coloured pens or mapping pins. Your market area is beginning to appear on paper, and you can start making more decisions about your probable market boundaries.

What type of people will want to buy (and be able to buy) your products or services? Where are they? Again, put them on your map by highlighting their locations. Indeed, in any business proposal you have already made the assumption that you will locate in a particular area. By looking at your potential market with a customer map you may decide to alter your original idea or location.

This step of defining your market needs to be based on accurate research so it will answer some of your basic questions, such as:

'Where is the market?'

'Is the market big enough?'

'Do I have to re-think the whole exercise?'

(A guide to sources of information required to carry out this research is shown in the appendix.)

This exercise of defining your market is an ongoing one as markets, like everything else, change. A toy store, for example, may operate well in an area of young families, but in 10 to 15 years' time the market will change drastically as the population ages

It is important in this section that your research allows you to quantify the size of the market: that is, how big it is in terms of total dollar sales, number of customers and potential customers, etc. You need to establish whether or not your proposed market is growing or contracting in size. You need accurate information on the size and composition of the market you are considering. You need *figures* for your study.

In looking at your potential customers, try to break them into groups or segments. Customers in these groups should have a common factor and can be more easily identified and planned for as a group rather than individually. (Chapter 17 — Marketing strategy and management — can help you in this area.)

Define your products and services

Make a detailed list of the products and services you plan to offer. It may help to group your customers into segments. You might try listing the products and services by segment, or you might simply decide to list them as a whole.

This list of products and services can be (and should be) supported by brochures, pictures and drawings. If this support is substantial, don't hesitate to include it in appendix form rather than disrupt the flow of the main story.

Identify your suppliers

If you are producing products/services, you need to purchase the materials or products somewhere. This section of the study is geared towards identifying not only key suppliers but also data such as:

- their addresses and contacts
- their product range
- their services
- their prices and conditions.

If brochures/catalogues etc are available, include them as part of the appendix to your study.

Define your competition

When you go into business you will have competition. This competition will be both *direct* (other firms trying to sell their goods and services to your customers) and *indirect* (you will be competing with everyone else for those limited consumer dollars).

Most people are aware of direct competition. It may be very obvious in say, industries such as the computer software field, or less apparent — for instance, a French restaurant might compete with a pizzeria, a fish-and-chips shop and a snack bar at the local hotel. They are all competing for the chance to satisfy the customer's need to eat away from home.

The concept of indirect competition, however, is less familiar. It recognises that most people have a limited income, so there is a limit to how much they can spend. This means that the firm selling computer software is in fact competing indirectly with the French restaurant. If people spend money on computer software it might mean that they decide not to eat out for a period until their budget returns to normal.

One of the purposes of your feasibility study is to decide how you could match and beat your competitors. To beat the indirect competitor you have to be good — you have to persuade potential customers that they can't do without your product or service. (This method is outlined in more detail in Chapter 17.) With your direct competitors, make a list of them using such sources as:

- your own knowledge
- telephone and trade directories
- suppliers' knowledge, and
- professional advice.

Be aware that there may be firms that are not yet competitors but could have the ability to enter the market quickly. These also include competitors from outside your market area who could easily begin operations in that area.

When you have made up this list, try to estimate the size of the market each competitor is serving. In some industries, such as car sales, this is fairly easy. In others, for instance toy manufacturing, it is almost impossible. However, you should try to work out each competitor's share of the market (remember the 80/20 rule) and see where your share can be expected to come from. As a guide, go back to your list of competitors and get to know them all — perhaps even better than they know themselves. First check their good points and their strengths, then check their weaknesses. See what they are *not* offering the customers and how they are *not* satisfying customer demands. This will show you your opening.

Remember that it is *not* enough for you to add up all the market share estimates (the total must be 100%) and see whether there is room for your business in that market. You must be aggressive: aim at taking your desired market share from your competitors. If you give them a chance, they will certainly take your share.

> You are not going into business to make friends — you are going there to make money, and your business will survive only if you are prepared to be aggressive.

In this section of your feasibility study, include:

1 your main competitors'
   - names
   - addresses
   - contact details
   - market share (estimated);

and,

2 for each competitor, at least two good points and two bad points.

This will help you to capitalise on your competitors' experience, avoid their mistakes and plan your entry into the market.

The final parts of this section are your maps and the introduction. We have mentioned the maps earlier. You should have a map or maps showing geographical boundaries or groupings, and also your key customers and/or your competition and/or suppliers.

You finish the marketing section of your feasibility study by writing the introduction. Although this begins the section, it is in reality a summary of the market — an overview — and is therefore written in hindsight. Write your introduction only after you have:

- identified and evaluated your potential customers
- identified your products and services
- identified your suppliers
- analysed your competition.

The operational structure

There are numerous decisions that you have to make whenever you consider putting a business proposal into practice. It would be nice if you could make these decisions in a standard, logical order, but this is never the case in practice. As you progress along the sorting-out curve (Chapter 7) you will find yourself looking for answers to questions such as:

- Where do I set up?
- What will I call the business?
- Do I form a company?
- How much money will I need?
- Which equipment will I need?
- How much stock will I need?
- Will I need staff?
- Will I lease or buy?
- Which licences will I require?

and so on. The list of questions is endless!

One way of approaching this situation is to use your feasibility study to divide your analysis of the business into key groupings, namely:

- location
- site plan
- equipment & stock
- legal structure
- legal checklist and
- staffing.

Location

Your choice of location and layout is a critical factor and Chapters 10 and 11 are devoted entirely to these physical considerations. At this stage, simply remember that your choice of location (general area) and site (actual address) are dependent upon and subsequent to your analysis of your customers. Do not fall into the trap of picking a site simply because it is convenient to *you* rather than your potential market.

Site plan

Once you have established a location/site, put your ideas for the business on paper by constructing a site plan. This plan will allow you to visualise your operation; list your space, equipment and stock needs; and identify problems and solutions. It will also give you information and answers you need for legal requirements and your financial considerations.

You do not need a draftsperson to draw up your site plan. Simply draw your building(s) to scale and show where you expect everything to fit in. One easy approach to this task is to start with a scaled outline of the building and fill it with scaled cardboard cut-outs of the equipment and fittings you are considering. The use of cut-outs enables you to play 'What if?' as you explore alternative layout proposals. When you have found what you consider to be the 'best solution', put it on paper in a form similar to that used for the example in Figure 8.4.

You can include on the site plan numbers linked with a legend or an index to the various assets required in the business. The site plan legend shown in Figure 8.5 is a simple way of listing all equipment and also establishing what you own and what you would need to acquire.

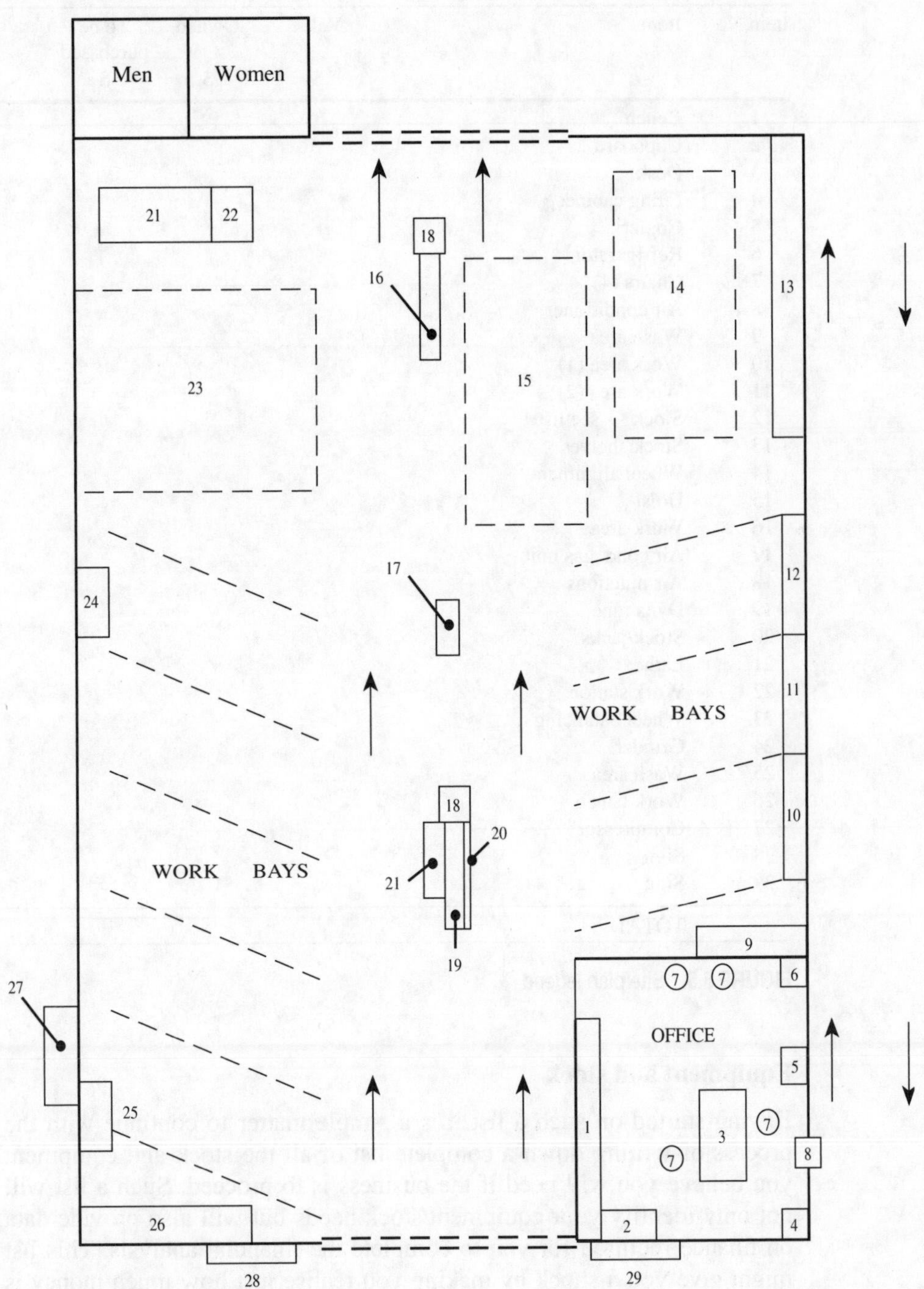

FIGURE 8.4 Site plan

Item No	Item	Value $	Owned $	To be purchased $
1	Bench			
2	Cupboard			
3	Desk			
4	Filing cabinet			
5	Copier			
6	Refrigerator			
7	Chairs (4)			
8	Air conditioner			
9	Wash area			
10	Work area (1)			
11	Work area (2)			
12	Stock — see list			
13	Stock shelves			
14	Wheel alignment			
15	Hoist			
16	Work area			
17	Air cond. gas unit			
18	Air junctions			
19	Dyna tune			
20	Stock/jacks			
21	Lathe			
22	Work station			
23	Wheel balancing			
24	Grinder			
25	Wash area			
26	Work bench			
27	Compressor			
28	Sign			
29	Sign			
	TOTAL			

FIGURE 8.5 Site plan legend

Equipment and stock

Having started on such a list it is a simple matter to continue with the process of writing down a complete list of all the stock and equipment you believe you will need if the business is to proceed. Such a list will not only identify your equipment/stock needs but will also provide data on finance required for you to complete the financial analysis. This list might give you a shock by making you realise just how much money is involved.

Legal structure

Your choice of legal structures is usually between a sole trader, a partnership and a proprietary limited company. A detailed outline of these legal structures, together with a direct comparison between them, outlining both advantages and disadvantages, is given in Chapter 12.

Legal checklist

Ascertaining what regulations, laws and licences will affect your proposed business idea is a complex question which you should have checked by your advisers. However, you can do most of the preliminary investigation by simply working through your own legal checklist, an example of which is shown in Chapter 12. Insurance is also covered in Chapter 12.

Staffing

The only other major area to be considered in this operational section of the feasibility study is the question of who will do the work. You and your partners are only human and you cannot work 24 hours a day, seven days a week. In considering whether or not your business idea will mean employing staff, you might care to refer to Chapter 20, which looks at the staffing requirements of small business.

Finance and viability

The ultimate decision facing anyone going into business is largely determined by two key financial considerations:

- How much money do I need?
  and
- Will the business be financially worthwhile?

Capital requirements and sources

To give your business proposal any serious chance of succeeding you must have sufficient funding. One of the major startup problems, as seen in Chapter 3, is under-capitalisation, which is trying to get a new business going (or keep a newly purchased business ongoing) with insufficient funds.

To avoid this problem, we suggest that you:

1 Gain as much knowledge as possible of the type of business you are starting — before you start. This can come from working in the industry, trade or profession, or from work experience, research, discussions or study. The more you know, the greater the range of alternatives you will be able to identify and evaluate.
2 Continually seek expert advice. A comprehensive list of people and organisations available to help you is given in the appendix.
3 Decide on the assets you need and calculate their cost. It is in this area that expert help is invaluable. You should remember that there are alternatives to buying — for example, leasing, hiring, subcontracting — and maybe even different approaches to manufacturing or processing. You may also consider the possibility of second-hand rather than new equipment as a means of conserving your available funds.

One useful way of estimating your asset requirements is to look at your site plan (Figure 8.4) and use your site plan legend (Figure 8.5) as a very effective working tool. Make sure you include a realistic level of stock in this evaluation.

4 Allow for working capital. Working capital, in practical terms, is the value of the funds necessary to run the business actively on a day-to-day basis. To establish how much working capital you will need to provide for your proposal, you need to identify the major cost areas and estimate the period of time involved. For most new ventures an acceptable period of time is three to six months — but you would be wise to check with your financial adviser on this point.

For identifying and estimating major cost areas, the worksheet shown in Figure 8.6 will be of some assistance.

ITEM	MONTH1	MONTH 2	MONTH 3	MONTH 4	MONTH 5	MONTH 6	TOTAL
Accountancy							
Advertising							
Bank charges & interest							
Electricity							
Insurance							
Printing, postage etc.							
Rent							
Repairs, maintenance							
Telephone							
Travelling							
Vehicle costs							
Wages, salaries							
Other —							
—							
—							
Miscellaneous							
Total Running costs							
***add* Purchases**							
Total working capital							

FIGURE 8.6 Working capital worksheet

5 Determine your startup capital. By adding together the value of the assets you need (Step 3, above) and your estimated working capital (Step 4), you can evaluate your total setup costs.

Once you have this figure you can then start to look at your need for borrowed money. Remember that funds are available from two sources: your own investment (equity capital) and lenders such as banks, etc (debt capital). Most lenders are reluctant to lend 100% of the capital required and you will find that they have strict lending guidelines.

They will want to know the level of your family or personal net worth. This is simply a listing of all your assets and all your liabilities. Every lending authority has its own easy-to-use Net Worth worksheet to assist you in your calculations. It is just a matter of asking you for a copy of their forms. (This topic is covered in more detail in Chapter 13 — Financing your business.)

The second question to be considered in this section is

Will the business be financially worthwhile?

Financial viability

There is only one reason, as we have said earlier, for going into business, and that is to make a profit. Unless you make a profit, you cannot stay in business for any length of time. Sooner or later you will run out of money! The profit you make will have to be sufficient to pay for your drawings, your loan repayments, and further investment in the business.

To determine the level of profit you need to make, you need to estimate:

- your living costs
- your desired 'wage' or drawings, and
- your expected return on investment.

To estimate your own living costs, it is generally agreed that the best approach is to look at your outgoings over a reasonable period — say, one year. In any yearly period, you will have some expenses that are fixed and cannot be altered or deferred. These are called fixed costs and include such items as loan repayments, car registration, council rates, etc. They are called fixed because the dates and amounts of payment are, in reality, fixed. Variable costs are those that can be varied in relation to their amount or date of payment. Examples of variable living costs are food, clothing, maintenance, etc.

Discretionary living costs are expenditures over which you have total control, whether they are incurred or not, ie gifts, entertainment, holidays, etc.

The worksheet shown in Figure 8.7 is designed to assist you in calculating your living costs.

ITEM	JUL	AUG	SEP	OCT	NOV	DEC	JAN	FEB	MAR	APR	MAY	JUN	TOTAL
Expenditure													
Fixed expenses													
House													
— council rates													
— water rates													
— loan repayment													
— gas													
— electricity													
Insurance													
— medical													
— building													
— contents													
— life													
— car													
— other													
Loan repayments													
—													
—													
School fees													
Superannuation													
Taxation													
Telephone													
Vehicle													
— licence													
— registration													
— repayments													
Other													
—													
—													
Total fixed Expendture													

FIGURE 8.7 Yearly living costs worksheet

ITEM	JUL	AUG	SEP	OCT	NOV	DEC	JAN	FEB	MAR	APR	MAY	JUN	TOTAL
EXPENDITURE													
Variable													
Fares													
Maintenance													
— car													
— house													
Petrol													
Shopping													
— chemist													
— clothing													
— food													
— other													
Store accounts													
—													
Other													
—													
—													
Total variable													
Discretionary													
Entertainment													
Gambling													
Gifts													
Holiday													
Other													
—													
Savings													
Sport													
Total discretionary													
Total expenditure													

FIGURE 8.7 cont'd

Once you have calculated your monthly living costs it is easy to set a desired wage or level of drawings. If you go into business, you will need to cover your monthly living costs with a sufficient level of personal drawings. You will work harder in your own business than you would for an employer — so allow for a satisfactory level of reward for your efforts.

The final factor to be considered in looking at your return is to recognise that you will have funds tied up in the business and that you are entitled to have a return (ie interest) on your investment. If you had the money invested elsewhere, eg in a bank, you would expect a return, so allow for it.

You now have all the information required to establish both your capital requirements and the viability of your business proposal. It is a simple process to arrange this information in a logical seven-step format. The following example, using simplified figures, is presented to you as a model for your feasibility study.

Step 1 Calculate family/personal net worth.

Value all assets and total	$190 000
Identify all liabilities and total	$40 000
NET WORTH (assets less liabilities)	$150 000

Step 2 Determine total funds available for equity investment.

Decide which assets will be used to invest in the proposed business, and total them. This would include funds available from taking out loans using items of property as security (eg second mortgage)	$50 000

Step 3 Calculate total living costs (per month).

Total fixed costs (eg rates, car registration)	$700
Total variable costs (eg food, petrol)	$500
Total discretionary costs (eg holidays, gifts)	$300
Total savings	$400
TOTAL MONTHLY COSTS	$1900

Step 4 Calculate borrowed funds needed to start new business.

For assets needed	$80 000
For working capital available (first three months)	$40 000
Total funds needed	$120 000
less equity funds available (from Step 2)	$50 000
TOTAL TO BE BORROWED	$70 000

Step 5 Calculate profits needed (per year).

(a) 'Wages' for time, effort and skill
- must exceed (12 x $1900 = $22 800 as in Step 3)
- based on 'reasonable' annual wage for senior staff with required skill, experience,

knowledge, qualifications, responsibility, working hours, etc, adjusted for taxation and other non-employee benefits: say, $25 000

(b) Return on investment
- 'reasonable' annual return on owner equity compared with returns on other 'safer' investments, say, 10% on $50 000 (from Step 2) $ 5 000

TOTAL OF PROFITS NEEDED (per year, before tax) $30 000

Step 6 Calculate sales level needed to earn this profit.

If forecast total costs (including interest on borrowed funds — see Step 4) are about average, use the industry average for 'net profit on sales', say 10% per year:

$30 000 x 100/10 = $300 000

Step 7 Ask: 'Can this sales level be reached?'

This means referring to the market study discussed above. If the market share that is considered to be possible will produce sales of $300 000 yearly, the proposed business seems to be viable.

Note that your firm's profitability on sales is likely to be less than the industry average of 10% (and this is probable in a new business), larger sales will be needed to earn the $30 000 profit being looked for — if profit on sales is only 8%, for example, sales of $375 000 will be needed. If there is good reason to believe that the new firm will be more profitable than the 'average', a smaller sales total will be needed. If profit on sales can be lifted to 12%, annual sales of only $250 000 will be needed to give the profit desired.

To gain a more realistic appreciation of your yearly sales figure, look at it as a monthly, weekly or even daily sales figure. Thus $300 000 per annum may be seen as:

- $25 000 per month (12 months per year)
- or $6250 per week (48 working weeks per year)
- or $1040 per day (6 days per week)
- or $1250 per day (5 days per week).

By expressing the sales figures in this fashion it is often easier to answer the question 'Can this sales level be achieved?'

If the required sales figure seems impossible to reach, operating procedure and costs might be reviewed or expected profits reduced. There are limits to both actions, and the end result might have to be that plans to go into this business, at this time, are dropped.

Too many people, excited by the prospect of proudly operating their own business, become totally unrealistic about the sales volume they will reach. Enthusiasm is necessary, and wishful thinking has its place, but they should not outweigh sense and logic. All of the above estimates and figures should be checked by your accountant and banker. It is better to be brought down to reality by the cold, hard facts of life before your funds are committed and money is borrowed.

Recommendations of the study

At the start of this chapter we said that a feasibility study is a systematic analysis of the possibility of putting a business idea into practice.

The final part of the study to be written, therefore, is a summary of the decisions that have evolved from this systematic analysis of:

- the business idea
- the key people
- the market available
- the proposed operational structure, and
- finance and viability.

The recommendations section should be short, truthful and direct. It is not usually a straight 'yes' or 'no' answer on whether to go ahead; rather, it is a qualified recommendation based upon a set of conditions and assumptions that have been outlined in the study. Very often the recommendation is simply: 'Under these conditions the proposal appears (or does not appear) to be viable, but . . .'

The study can only provide a recommendation. It cannot make a decision — only you can do that — but the study will give you the information you need to make that decision.

Good luck with your study!

Writing and presenting your study

The main purpose of your feasibility study is to provide a tool to assist you in making a major business decision. It also provides you with a formalised analysis that encourages meaningful discussions with your family, your advisers, potential partners and lenders; and it is an excellent tool to assist you in negotiating with potential suppliers and customers.

You can produce a professional feasibility study by following a few simple guidelines.

- Your study should be produced and presented in a professional manner. It is written by you and should be in your language, using your terms and your own style. It is tailor-made for your business proposal.
- Create a simple filing system to store the material you collect in your research. Organise your filing system so that the material you collect can be easily found and used.
- Make sure that you carry a diary with you at all times, so that you are aware of commitments and your ideas are not lost. If you visit

your future competitors, write down (after you leave their premises) at least two good points and two bad points about their business. The heart of any data system should be your diary.

- It is just as easy to present your study professionally as it is in any other way. Start by having it wordprocessed or typewritten. This makes for easier reading, and it gives your study more credibility and authority.
- Organise your study in a folder, preferably one with clear plastic inserts which allow for ease of entry and adjustment. A study in a folder or a cover looks professional. Folders are not expensive and they will protect the study from the effects of constant handling.
- The suggested layout for your study could be:

  Cover sheet
  Contents list
  1 The business idea
  2 The key people
    2.1 Profiles
    2.2 Personal objectives
    2.3 Professional support
  3 The market
    3.1 Introduction
    3.2 Customers and segments
    3.3 Products and services
    3.4 Suppliers
    3.5 Competition
    3.6 Maps
  4 The business
    4.1 Location
    4.2 Site plan
    4.3 Equipment and stock
    4.4 Staffing
    4.5 Legal checklist
  5 Finance and viability
    5.1 Capital requirements and sources
    5.2 Financial viability
  6 Recommendations
  Appendices

- Present support material and working papers for your study in appendix form. This allows for easy reference to the data and provides a logical storage point that does not disrupt the flow of the story itself.
- Remember that your study is written by you for you. The study will contain confidential information which you may not want everyone to read. If you are presenting the study to anyone, simply censor your study by taking out the sections you do not want them to see.

Information sources

The information you need to write your study is available if you know where to look. Much of it will be contained in your own background experience and records and also in data you can gain by:

- visiting competitors
- talking and listening to relevant people
- attending workshops, seminars and courses
- asking other small business people
- joining small business groups and associations, and
- talking to previous owner(s) if you are buying a business.

Never be afraid to ask questions or to ask for help. At the very worst, people can only say 'No!' but most people are only too happy to assist when approached correctly. If you don't know where to start, ask one of your professional advisers to point you in the right direction. Once you have made the first step in researching your business, the rest seems to follow naturally.

When you are doing your own research, remember a few key rules:

- Check your facts and if you don't know something, find out — the information is available somewhere.
- Use your professional advisers — for input and also to check your proposals.
- Be practical — don't try to be 100% accurate when in many cases a guide is sufficient.

A research directory showing sources of information and help available is included for your assistance in the appendix.

Perhaps now you can understand the saying:

> Most businesses don't plan to fail — they simply fail to plan!

SUMMARY

You have now been introduced to the concept of a feasibility study, ie a planned approach to the evaluation of a business idea.

The approach starts with an overview of the planning process which enables you to establish, very clearly, exactly what you want to achieve in your personal life. Once this is established it is a simple process to research and develop your business idea, with special emphasis on:

- the idea itself
- the key people involved
- the market to be approached
- the proposed operational structure
- finance and viability

and finally,

- the recommendations of the study.

Writing the feasibility study is not a difficult task, but it does involve a lot of work. It needs commitment and it needs a plan!

We believe that this chapter provides all the guidelines, references and worksheets to enable you to write your own feasibility study. Only you can provide the commitment. It is your business idea; it should be evaluated with your feasibility study, written by you, for your benefit, in your own style and words.

We wish you well!

Key words

aim
drawings
feasibility study
financial viability
goal
objective
partnership
planning
policy
profile
proprietary limited company
site plan
sole trader
strategy
working capital

Review exercises

1. What is a feasibility study?
2. What are the key parts of any feasibility study?
3. Good objectives have six characteristics. What are they?
4. Which aspects of your life should be included in your personal objectives?
5. Which business objective should you include in your feasibility study?
6. List the seven steps needed to evaluate the financial viability of your business idea.
7. Using the format outlined in Figure 8.2, construct ten personal objectives.
8. Using the format outlined in Figure 8.3, write your own profile.
9. Using a form provided by your bank, construct a list of your assets and liabilities, to establish your net worth.
10. Draw a site plan for your proposed business, using guides shown in Figures 8.4 and 8.5.
11. Estimate your own monthly living costs, using the format shown in Figure 8.7

2

Starting

CHAPTER 9

Ways of going into business

Many people going into business for the first time want to know whether it is better to buy an existing business as a going concern or to start one from scratch.

After reading this chapter you should:

- be aware of possible ways of getting into your own business, and
- be able to decide which startup method is most suited to your business idea.

There are two main ways of starting in small business. According to research by Williams (1991), the most common method used in Australia is starting from scratch (see Table 9.1). The next most common is buying an existing business as a going concern. In both cases you can 'go it alone' or you can take out a franchise, which means buying the right to use someone else's business idea, strategy and format.

Three less common methods are to inherit a business (usually as a going concern); to restructure or restart a failed business; and for employees (usually senior managers) to buy a firm from its owner(s). Only the last of these rarer methods is discussed here.

TABLE 9.1 Startup methods used in Australia 1973–1990

Startup Method	Number	Percentage
Starting 'from scratch'	23 291	69.27
Purchase of existing firm	8 676	25.80
Inherited business	71	0.21
Buy-ins and buy-outs	424	1.26
Other restructuring/new ownership of previously failed business	1 162	3.46
Total	33 624	100.00%

Retailing was the industry in which starting from scratch was most prevalent — 84%. Of the 33 624 firms studied by Williams, 2140 (6.36%) were franchised ventures but the number was growing rapidly towards the later years of the 17-year study. By the year 2000, franchising is expected to be the most popular method of getting into business in Australia. This is probably because the survival rate of franchised firms is far superior to that of small firms generally.

Starting from scratch

Probably the most challenging way to get into business is to start from scratch — to plan and create a business venture where none existed previously, from the idea stage through to actually owning and operating a new venture — having done a market study, assessed the financial viability of the firm, chosen a good location, and planned every aspect of the project along the way.

It is widely thought that this startup method is the one most likely to fail, but an Australian study (Williams, 1991) does not support this (see Table 9.2).

> In Australia over two-thirds of new firms are started from scratch.

Should I start from scratch?

Creating your own business from nothing is the logical choice if:

- no worthwhile business of the type proposed and in the location desired is available for purchase, or
- the market which the new business is to enter is not being fully catered for by existing firms and a new competitor will not overcrowd the market.

Starting from scratch is usually thought to be riskier than all other ways of getting into business. There is likely to be uncertainty about many factors in the process of this method of startup, especially about whether the market is big enough for the product or service to be sold. Even if a market study shows a sufficiently large market, it can be wrong — particularly if the product or service is new. Two ways to avoid this uncertainty are:

1 to buy an existing business with a proven sales record (its market does exist but will it last?) or
2 to buy a franchise.

Both options are discussed in this chapter.

Compared with other means, there is clearly more to do in setting up a new business from scratch, there is more scope for errors, and it takes longer to plan, organise, start and make financially viable. However, the rewards might be much greater if the product or service is right and if the market exists.

Despite the difficulties listed above, in Australia, firms started from scratch seem more likely to survive than firms purchased as going concerns (Williams, 1991).

Over the whole period of Williams's study, of 33 624 startups 22 408 (66.6%) failed and 11 216 (33.4%) survived. The survival and failure patterns for those firms according to startup method are shown in Table 9.2.

TABLE 9.2 Survivors and failures by startup method

Startup Method	Failures	Survivors	Totals
Starting 'from scratch'	15 116 (64.9%)	8 175 (35.1%)	23 291
Purchase of existing firm	6 171 (71.1%)	2 505 (28.9%)	8 676
Inherited business	54 (76.1%)	17 (23.9%)	71
Buy-ins and buy-outs	277 (65.3%0	147 (34.7%)	424
Other restructuring/ new ownership of previously failed business	790 (68.0%)	372 (32.0%)	1 162
Totals	22 408 (66.6%)	11 216 (33.4%)	33 624

Advantages and disadvantages

Starting from scratch has certain advantages:

- You do not have to pay for goodwill (as you do when buying a business as a going concern).
- You can avoid the 'unseen' problems of many firms for sale, such as poor location, and poor reputation among customers, suppliers or employees.
- You have more freedom to use your own ideas in creating the kind of business *you* want it to be — *your* product or service, *your* choice of location, *your* staff and *your* methods.

However, as is to be expected, there are some disadvantages:

- Some intending owners cannot handle the greater uncertainty about how to put it all together and whether it will become a viable enterprise.
- It is usually quicker, and can be easier, to purchase an existing firm than setting up a new firm from scratch.
- Positive cashflow (where cash receipts exceed cash payments) usually takes much longer than when one buys an existing business.
- It is often harder to persuade a financier to lend to, or invest in, a new business with no proven track record than to do so for an existing business, even with new management.

How to start from scratch

It is not really possible to list in sequence the steps for starting a new business, as the order may differ in each case. However, the following stages are common to most startups:

1 Decide whether you are personally prepared for, and suited to, owning and running your own business. (Chapter 5 outlines the important areas of skill, knowledge and experience needed, and the kinds of personality characteristics desirable for success as a small business owner/manager. In Chapter 6 you can find out how you match up in personal readiness.)

You are the key to your firm's survival and success. Nothing else matters unless your firm has high-quality technical, managerial and entrepreneurial inputs. No matter how good the product, or how large the market, studies show very clearly that, for a poorly managed firm, the odds are against survival.

2 Decide on the type of business you want, then do the following:

(a) Assess its probable survival ability, particularly in the market place.

This means deciding:

- which product(s)/service(s) your firm will sell,
- whether you will enter manufacturing, retailing, services or wholesaling, and
- the market segment (or 'target') you wish to reach.

(b) Identify the special strength, unique feature or distinctive competence that will become the basis of your firm's competitive advantage.

(c) Decide whether a sufficiently large market exists for your proposed product or service. Will that market last a reasonable time?

(d) Identify and locate that market segment (see Chapters 8 and 17).

(e) Measure or estimate the size of the target market. Then assess the nature and strength of the competition, to decide whether the proposed business has enough sales potential to make it viable.

3 Study the firm's financial viability. Look at its chances of earning enough profit to give its owner(s) an acceptable living. Doing this ties in with measuring the size of the firm's sales potential as indicated in 2(e) above and in Chapter 8.

4 Select a suitable location, using the target market as a guide (see Chapter 10).

5 Consider how the business might be funded — from

(a) equity funds (that is, capital invested by owner(s)) and

(b) funds to be borrowed,

then look at the advantages and disadvantages of the various alternative sources of startup capital.

6 Prepare the feasibility study (see Chapter 8) using information obtained about, and decisions made on, the matters listed above. Present the feasibility study to potential lenders as a basis for arranging finance to start the business.

7 Buy, rent or lease the physical facilities needed (premises, equipment and so on).

8 Make arrangements for supplies (inventories, raw materials, spare parts) and services (electricity, water, gas, telephone).

9 Determine staffing needs in accordance with the administration plan(see Chapters 8 and 20). Select, hire and train employees as needed.

10 Develop methods and procedures to enable the business to function as outlined in the operational plan.

11 Complete all legal requirements such as:
 (a) the legal form of the business
 (b) registration of the business name
 (c) insurances
 (d) lease(s)
 (e) taxation requirements
 (f) shops and factories regulations
 (g) contracts for hiring staff, equipment, etc.

12 Set up the required accounting books and records.

Buying an Existing Business

If you buy an existing business as a going concern (which means that it is in working order) you will usually purchase or take over the firm's:

- physical facilities (such as premises, equipment and furniture)
- inventories of various kinds
- customers and amounts owned by them
- contractual rights and legal rights (such as patents)
- employees, and
- goodwill.

Exactly what is purchased in the deal will be negotiated by the buyer and seller, as will the values of each item.

> Buying a going concern might seem the easy way into business — but it is easy to buy a 'lemon'.

Many people choose to buy an existing firm because they consider it easier than starting from scratch, then fail to carry out all the necessary checks and finish up paying for someone else's disaster. As shown in Table 9.2, buying a business as a going concern by no means guarantees success. The great Australian dream of having your own business (see Chapter 4) can quickly turn into a nightmare which might go on for a long time! However, sometimes a business in trouble is sold to new owners who are then able to make it profitable — this is known as a 'turnaround'.

Advantages and disadvantages

Compared with starting 'from scratch', buying a business has the following advantages:

- You might have less trouble obtaining finance, particularly if the existing business has a profitable history and a promising future.
- It is generally quicker and easier to buy a business as a total package than to put one together by starting from scratch.
- Total cost is agreed and certain, whereas when you start from scratch, startup costs and capital needs for the first six months or so are often hard to estimate and usually more than expected.

Among the more obvious disadvantages and dangers are:

- There is always the risk of buying a 'lemon' in a poor location, with slow-paying customers, obsolete equipment, unskilled or indifferent employees and/or poor credit ratings among suppliers.
- There can be problems with valuing goodwill as a fair measure of the firm's ability to make sales and earn profits, because of its image or reputation among its customers.
- There is a need to value fairly the physical facilities and assets being purchased as part of the going concern. Debtors with a book value of $18 000 might not really be worth that amount. If they are not, what will they be worth to the buyer?
- There is a risk that, despite all investigations, the business is going downhill for reasons that cannot be remedied (such as a baby wear shop for sale in a suburb of mainly retired older people).
- There is the problem of reaching a negotiated selling price, and payment arrangements which are acceptable to both buyer and seller. To avoid these difficulties you should engage a professional adviser.
- The costs of using a business broker and an accountant and/or solicitor to carry out the necessary investigations can be heavy.

How to buy an existing business

When you set out to buy an existing small business, most of the considerations relating to how to start from scratch still apply. In particular, questions about the firm's competitive advantage, likely market share and viability of market share will need careful study — there is little point in buying into a firm which is suffering from a severe case of 'hardening of the markets' (a condition in which a firm operates with a seriously declining market share).

Also, for a purchase to take place it is essential that the intending buyer arranges:

- independent and expert checks on the value of every item to be included in the purchase, including goodwill

- verification of the actual existence, and proof of ownership, of every such item
- close scrutiny of financial reports, taxation returns and assessments, banking records, all other relevant books and records for about the past five years, and trading figures up to the current month
- calculation of all relevant ratios to assess the firm's past financial performance in terms, for example, of return on owner's equity, profit on sales and so forth
- independent assessments of the financial health of the business from suppliers and the bank, and of the sales/marketing performance from customers
- careful scrutiny of all legal obligations (for example, lease conditions)
- having the seller terminate all employment contracts to allow the buyer freedom to avoid past obligations to all staff (such as long service leave and accumulated sick leave)
- a check on the seller's rights to start another business in direct competition with this one.

No stone should be left unturned in coming to an informed and verifiable evaluation of the present value of the business, and of its future prospects. Your accountant and solicitor will need to complete their investigations and report to you before you can properly consider the seller's asking price. Only then can negotiations take place.

Although the asking and offered prices are usually the major issues, other matters might affect the outcome of the negotiations. These could include:

- the seller's urgency in selling, and reasons for doing so
- the buyer's available funds
- payment terms (one lump sum or instalments)
- restrictions on the seller's right to open a competing business
- remedies for fraud (for instance, seller not disclosing all liabilities, and including assets in the sale which are not owned by the seller)
- incorrect and/or false figures.

Of Australian firms that change hands as going concerns, 71% eventually fail (see Table 9.2). From this evidence it is obvious that many purchase deals are carried out hurriedly and without careful and expert verification of values, or checks of all kinds.

FRANCHISING

An intending owner/manager might either buy a franchised business as a going concern (subject to conditions in the franchise agreement) or might start one from scratch. There are widespread indications of a growing boom in franchising in Australia and very real advantages in taking this path.

The basis of franchising is that the owner or supplier of a product, service, process or trade name (the franchisor) enters into agreement with a business (the franchisee) to give that business the right to sell the product or service or use the process or trade name. The franchise agreement outlines the rights and obligations of both parties and, in particular, gives the franchisee a specified (and usually exclusive) right to operate in a particular trading area. In return for this right to sell or use, and for other assistance, the franchisee agrees to pay a sum of money which may include an initial (up-front) fee, royalties on sales, and a charge for shared advertising and promotion campaigns.

Depending on the specific terms of the agreement, the franchisor might also provide (and be paid for) startup assistance, technical training and on-going management advice.

Since a franchised firm has the support and backing of the franchisor, including name and logo (McDonald's, Angus and Robertson, and Pizza Hut, for example), much of the risk associated with starting a totally independent business is removed. Williams (1991) has reported a 77% survival rate (1637 from 2140) among franchised firms in Australia, compared with about 30% among non-franchised firms.

Because the franchisor is clearly interested in the success of each associated franchisee, close attention is paid to the approval of franchisees, the selection of location, staff and management training, business methods, product/service quality and all aspects of the setting up and conduct of the business.

There are five main types of franchises:

1 Fast-food outlets — These are probably the most successful and best known of all franchised activities. Standardised food lines are sold, with heavy emphasis on efficiency leading to rapid service and cleanliness.

2 Other retailing — Virtually every shopping centre contains further examples of retailing franchises — bookshops, pharmacies, and shops selling vehicle spare parts and accessories, clothing, hardware and electrical appliances.

3 Service industry — Many branches of the service industry involve franchises — motel chains, taxation services, pest control firms, health studios and many others selling business, personal and professional services.

4 Manufacturing — The franchisor supplies essential formulae, know-how or ingredients for manufacturing a product. An example is soft drinks.

5 Dealerships — These are widespread, especially in the distribution of motor vehicles, petrol and related products, and many household lines.

Another arrangement, not strictly franchising but often confused with it, is one in which small firms join a 'buying group' and benefit from cheaper (bulk) purchasing, use of a common name and logo and shared advertising spending.

Advantages and disadvantages

For franchisees, the advantages are:

- The franchisee gets the backing and support of the professional marketing and management expertise of the franchisor, this being more than a totally independent small firm could afford to buy.
- Proven products and services that have extensive buyer awareness and market acceptance lead to more rapid sales growth.
- The probability of survival is higher, since many basic and fatal errors are avoided.
- Cost savings can be made if stock and materials are available through bulk buying by the franchisor.
- Access to startup finance is easier because of the link with a nationally known franchisor.
- Technical and management training and guidance are available.

Franchising improves your chances of success.

For franchisors the advantages are:

- Businesses grow rapidly (by attracting more franchisees), at lower cost and less risk, than if they expanded by starting their own branches.
- The franchise agreement provides a measure of control over the quality and efficiency of franchised operations, thereby improving the probability of their being successful and, in turn, more profitable for the franchisor.

For the franchisee there are several disadvantages:

- There is a risk that the franchisor might fail.
- Close outside control over your business and lack of real independence might prevent you from using your own initiative and ideas (the franchisor makes the 'rules') and impose rigid rules and conditions (such as specified opening hours, restrictions on terminating the franchise arrangement, limits on sources of merchandise or on the products or services sold).
- Franchise costs might be heavy, especially as the royalty fee is a percentage of sales and will increase as your sales efforts are successful.
- The product might be a poor seller — for example, a fad whose day is gone.

For the franchisor, the main task is selecting from among many applicants those who have the potential to succeed as franchisees.

How to enter a franchise arrangement

As with any investment of a large sum of money (in many cases, one's life savings), going into a franchise deserves much careful investigation. Once signed, the franchise agreement can be a legally binding contract, impossible to escape from without severe financial penalties. A breach of any of the terms of the contract could result in court action by the franchisor and you might lose your investment. Go in with your eyes open, and only after getting expert advice. The Australian Franchisors' Association is a reputable body which is making efforts to assist anyone wishing to enter franchising, either as a franchisor or a franchisee.

In particular, the following are worth checking very carefully:

- the credibility of the franchisor
- the acceptability to you of specific clauses in the agreement about matters such as cancellation, transfer or renewal of the franchise, the grounds for terminating the franchise and so forth
- prospects for increasing sales of the products or service.

Inheriting a Business

This method of getting into business might appeal to people without funds of their own to invest. However, the law frowns very sternly on taking steps to facilitate an inheritance. As often as not, beneficiaries of a will who find themselves owning a business are totally unprepared for the experience and are most reluctant to keep it.

If inheriting an ongoing business through the death of a relative or friend, the beneficiary clearly has no choice about what kind of firm he or she is entering, and might lack experience in business management or have no interest in learning. A further problem would arise if the business were badly run down or if the deceased were ill for some time and lost interest in the firm. There is also the difficulty of trying to revitalise a firm by breaking traditions and habits maintained by the deceased owner.

In view of the potential pitfalls, it is not at all surprising to note that the survival rate of inherited businesses is only 24% — well below the rates for other startup methods, as shown in Table 9.2.

The best advice for a beneficiary with a business which he or she cannot handle is to get some training urgently or hire a good manager, and don't interfere. If there is no desire to get involved, it is better to sell the firm.

MANAGEMENT BUY-OUT

A method of getting into business which is attracting much interest in recent years is when the employees of a firm purchase that firm from its owner(s). This can be done at any time, but is more common if the owner is planning to retire or has put the business up for sale for any other reason.

Seek professional and independent advice, no matter how you plan to start out.

SUMMARY

The choice of a way of going into business for yourself will depend largely on circumstances. Starting from scratch means putting the whole thing together from virtually nothing, and plenty of time and patience are needed to do that properly. The main thing to investigate is whether or not there is a sufficiently large market to sustain the new business.

Buying a business as a going concern has advantages if its viability is assured and thorough checking precludes the purchase of a 'lemon'. Franchising is an option, whether you wish to start from scratch or to buy. A great deal of the uncertainty is removed by having a franchisor provide (at a cost) valuable help, advice and guidance in setting up and running the business. There is evidence that being franchised very much improves the firm's survival ability. Other methods of going into business are to inherit the firm, or to be involved in a management buy-out.

In all cases, much care and thorough investigation of all aspects of the proposed venture are essential.

KEY WORDS

beneficiary
business plan
competitive advantage
distinctive competence
equity
franchise
franchisee
franchisor
going concern
goodwill
management buy-out
market segment
operational plan
starting from scratch
viability

Review exercises

Circle the appropriate letter in each case.

1 The startup method least likely to be successful is:
- A buying an existing business
- B starting from scratch
- C franchising
- D inheriting a business.

2 Which of these statements is correct?
- A Franchising is declining in importance in Australia.
- B Starting from scratch is the startup method most likely to be successful.
- C Starting from scratch is the easiest way to get into business.
- D A market study is not necessary when buying a business as a going concern.

3 Franchising is most popular in:
- A retailing
- B manufacturing
- C wholesaling
- D service firms.

4 The first step to take in starting a business from scratch is to:
- A arrange finance
- B choose the best possible location
- C assess your own technical, managerial and entrepreneurial abilities
- D do a market study.

5 A major cost usually involved when buying a business, but not appropriate when starting from scratch, is/are:
- A the services of an accountant or financial consultant
- B legal fees
- C registration of the business name
- D goodwill.

6 In franchising, the supplier of the product, process or trade name is called the:
- A franchisee
- B distributor
- C franchisor
- D dealer.

7 A new business can be funded from:
   A trade creditors
   B equity funds
   C long-term borrowing
   D all of these sources.

8 Retired people and ethnic groups are examples of:
   A economically deprived groups
   B market segments
   C target markets
   D both B and C.

9 An intending small business owner who is trying to decide whether or not to open a hairdressing salon, and who has no experience in that type of business or any relevant market data to guide the selection of a location or startup method, is facing:
   A certainty
   B risk
   C uncertainty
   D none of the above.

10 A market segment is:
   A a firm's share of the total market
   B that part of the total market likely to need and buy the product or service you are selling
   C all potential buyers of your product or service
   D all of the above.

Reference

Williams, A J 1991, 'Small business survival: The role of formal education, management training and advisory services', *Small Business Review 1990–1991*, Bureau of Industry Economics, Small Business Research Unit, Australian Government Publishing Service, Canberra, pp 43–82

CHAPTER 10

Choosing the best location

As indicated in Chapter 9, one of the more important tasks in getting a new business started from scratch is to find and obtain the best possible location. When a business is being considered for purchase as a going concern, the suitability of its location should be checked. This chapter should help you to:

- appreciate the importance of a good location
- identify the factors that influence the choice of a business location
- select the best location for your business, and
- evaluate the advantages and disadvantages of leasing and buying a location (the premises) for your business.

As we saw in Chapter 8, a thorough market study must be carried out as the means of deciding whether a proposed business has an adequate market for its product or service. The basic question is: 'Is there a big enough market to justify starting *this* business?' The potential market, which *might* enable the creation of a new venture or the continuation (by purchase) of an existing one, will be in a particular area (for example, a suburb or a town). Answering the above question is therefore possible only with reference to a particular business location.

A good location is vital for success — a poor one is a liability.

A firm's location acts as a bridge or link between the demand for the goods or services it offers (its customers) and the supply of essential resources such as materials, merchandise and labour (its suppliers). If it is in the wrong place, either the expected market will not exist, or its resource supplies will not be available, or both. Choice of a location, and site, is not a once-only task. Finding a good one is important; moving is costly, often impractical and sometimes impossible. Nevertheless, reviewing the suitability of the firm's location might show that, over time, a good choice could become a poor one. If that happens, a move at the first opportunity is desirable. Reviews should be done regularly, especially when a lease is up for renewal and when a new branch is being considered. Williams (1991) has found that regular reviews of location suitability improve the chances of business survival.

It is well known that the main consideration in locating many small firms is convenience, usually expressed as closeness to the owner's home and availability of vacant premises at low rental. However, relying on these two reasons without further investigation can be disastrous. If premises are vacant, ask questions. Why did the previous tenant move out? Did that business fail? Why? How many previous failures have been located there?

LOCATION AND SITE

The process of choosing a place to do business should be one of narrowing down the options. For some people, the choice of *state or region* is the starting point. Then follows a decision on a *city or town*; then a *suburb or section* of that city or town; and finally a specific *site*.

> Location analysis means making good use of readily available information.

A site is a specific address within a location. Sites in regional and neighbourhood shopping centres are usually allocated to certain types of business, so that the mix of firms maximises customer traffic and sales for the whole centre. In other words, if you intend to situate your business in such a centre, you might have little or no choice about the site you will get.

If you are considering a non-shopping centre location, you might need to give particular thought to the better side of the street, whether to be on a corner site or in a walk-through mall, and so on. Studies have shown that, in general, preferred sites are those that:

- are shaded from the afternoon sun
- give customers shelter from poor weather
- are nearest to large department stores which 'pull' many customers
- are nearest to major population growth areas
- are nearest to areas with the highest pedestrian traffic flow
- fit with the direction of vehicle and pedestrian traffic flow
- are away from breaks in pedestrian traffic such as taxi and bus zones, alleys and loading bays, and
- are on the left side of the street (going towards town) if the business caters for customers who buy while travelling from home to town, and on the right side if it caters for home-bound traffic.

> Different types of firms have different location needs.

By way of example: (1) A drive-in liquor store is situated on the left side of a major road linking an outer suburb with the city centre, as shown in Figure 10.1. Is this site a good one? Why? (2) Why should/should not a butcher have premises on the east side of the street?

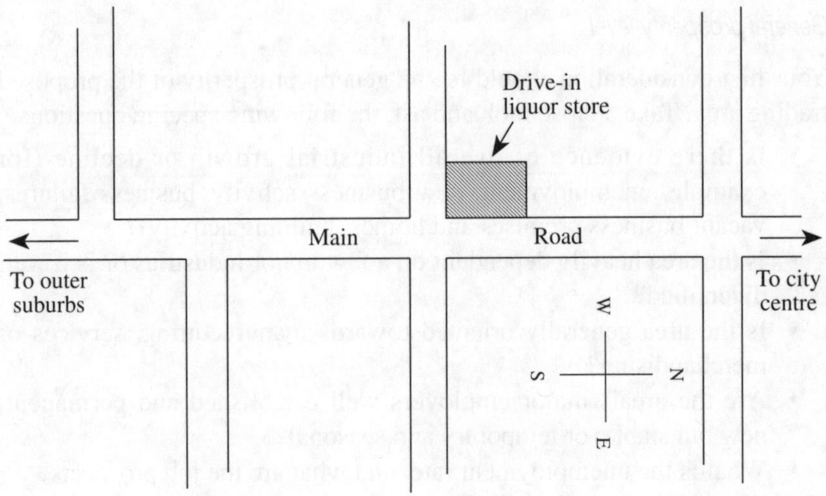

FIGURE 10.1 A problem location?

GENERAL LOCATION FACTORS

Although different types of firms, even within the same industry, have to consider different issues in selecting a good location, some concerns apply to all. These include personal, economic and various other sorts of factors.

Personal factors

Nearness to home and family (which affects travel time) and similar factors can be used in picking a location, but they should not be the only considerations. A smaller town may be preferred over a city location for reasons labelled as 'quality of life'.

Economic factors

Examination of the economic base of a likely trading area and a study of its population (demography) are an essential part of location analysis. Vital economic factors include:

- general prosperity level
- population patterns and trends
- purchasing power
- competition

- geographic and climatic conditions
- site history
- occupancy costs
- location affinity and complementarity.

General prosperity level

Your first consideration should be the general prosperity of the proposed trading area. Take a close look and ask the following specific questions:

- Is there evidence of overall industrial growth or decline (for example, unemployment, new business activity, business failures, vacant business premises and homes, building activity)?
- Is the area heavily dependent on a few major industries or is it well diversified?
- Is the area generally oriented towards manufacturing, services or merchandising?
- Are the area's major employers well established and permanent, new but stable, or temporary and seasonal?
- What is the unemployment rate, and what are the job prospects?
- What is the growth in bank savings?

Population patterns and trends

This is a most essential aspect of location analysis. You should ask:

- What is the area's total population?
- How many of that population are potential customers?
- What are the ages, ethnic groups and ratio of sexes in the area?
- Is there population growth or decline? What are the future trends?
- Is the population settled and stable, or moving?
- What is the ratio of family to one-person households?
- What is the ratio of rental to owned accommodation?
- In which industries are potential customers employed?
- What are the education levels among potential customers?
- Are the likely customers professional or blue-collar workers?

Rapid increases in numbers of young married couples with small children will indicate good prospects for sales of new homes; household fittings, equipment and appliances; clothing; and all food lines, including fast food. The existence of a sizeable ethnic population might show a need for a restaurant specialising in the relevant cuisine. Setting up business to retail high-quality, top-price men's wear will not be recommended in a low-income working-class area. A baby-wear business in a suburb with an average age of over 50 years will hardly be a winner. And so on.

Poor location

Purchasing power

By asking the questions listed above about the area's general economic condition, its future prospects and its population patterns, you can estimate the purchasing power in that area for your product or service.

Example: The proposed business is in footwear retailing.

1 Calculate the number of family units in the area.
2 Multiply this by the average take-home income. (This is total disposable income per family unit.)
3 Multiply this by the proportion spent on footwear yearly. (This is the total annual purchasing power for footwear.)

Information needed for these calculations is available from industry associations, local councils and libraries. The higher the disposable income, the more likely buyers are to spend on non-essential goods and services.

Competition

Unless there is no competition for that part of the area's disposable income that is to be spent on footwear (a highly unlikely situation!), you will need to think carefully about your rivals for a share of the market. Ask:

- How many are there? Where are they located? Why?
- How well are they doing?
- Are any new shopping centres planned for the area? If so, where are these to be located?
- Are existing firms new or well established?
- What are their strengths (competitive advantage) and weaknesses?
- Are any gaps in the footwear market not being filled?
- Can the area support another footwear retailer?

The last question is one of great importance: are there already enough footwear retailers for the purchasing power of this area? If it is unlikely that the area can support another, you might have trouble reaching break-even sales volume. A valuable piece of information to help you answer this question is the number of people needed (on average) to support a store of this type. Table 10.1 shows that, in the United States, about 9350 people are needed to make a footwear store viable. No such detailed figures are available for Australia, but the situation is probably similar.

TABLE 10.1 Number of inhabitants per store by selected kind of business (US national average)

Kind of business	Number of inhabitants per store	Kind of business	Number of inhabitants per store
Food stores		*Automotive dealers*	
Grocery stores	1 534	Motor vehicle dealers — new and used cars	6 000
Meat and fish (seafood) markets	17 876	Motor vehicle dealers — used cars only	17 160
Candy, nut and confectionery stores	31 409	Tyre, battery and accessory dealers	8 764
Retail bakeries	12 563	Boat dealers	61 526
Dairy products stores	41 587	Household trailer dealers	44 746
		Gasoline service stations	1 195
Eating, drinking places			
Restaurants, lunchrooms, caterers	1 583	*Miscellaneous*	
Cafeterias	19 341	Antique and second-hand stores	17 169
Refreshment places	3 622	Book and stationery stores	28 584
Drinking places (alcoholic beverages)	2 414	Drug stores	4 268
		Florists	13 531
General merchandise		Fuel oil dealers	25 425
Variety stores	10 373	Garden supply stores	65 118
General merchandise stores	9 837	Gift, novelty and souvenir shops	26 313
		Hay, grain and feed stores	16 978
Apparel and accessory stores		Hobby, toy and game shops	61 340
Women's ready-to-wear stores	7 102	Jewellery stores	13 495
Women's accessory and specialty stores	25 824	Liquefied petroleum gas (bottled gas) dealers	32 803
Men's and boys' clothing and furnishing stores	11 832	Liquor stores	6 359
Family clothing stores	16 890	Mail-order houses	44 554
Shoe stores	9 350	Merchandising machine operators	44 067
		Optical goods stores	62 878
Building material, hardware and farm equipment dealers		Sporting goods stores	27 063
Lumber and other building materials dealers	8 124	*Furniture, home furnishings and equipment*	
Paint, glass and wallpaper stores	22 454	Furniture stores	7 210
Hardware stores	10 206	Floor-covering stores	29 543
Farm equipment dealers	14 793	Drapery, curtain and upholstery stores	62 460
		Household appliance stores	12 585
		Radio and television stores	20 346
		Record shops	112 144
		Musical instruments stores	46 332

Source: Small Business Administration, 1981, p 27

Geographic and climatic conditions

These will determine, or at least influence, the location of certain types of firms. A store specialising in winter sports equipment will gain an advantage by locating reasonably close to skiing areas.

Site history

Excellent locations are rarely vacant. Vacant premises often have a history of business failure, and very careful investigation of these is recommended.

Occupancy costs

Rental or leasing expenses are a fixed cost, and can be a large proportion of the total operating expenses for a small firm. The best sites will attract high rentals, but not every high-cost site is necessarily a good one. As a rule of thumb, the factors in Table 10.2 can guide your choice of high- or low-rent sites.

TABLE 10.2 Characteristics of stores appropriate for high- and low-rent sites

	Hight-rent area	Low-rent area
1	High value of merchandise in proportion to bulk	Low value of merchandise in proportion to bulk
2	Window display highly important	Large amount of floor space for interior display
3	High rate of turnover	Low rate of turnover
4	Low gross margin per item	High gross margin per item
5	Impulse or convenience goods sold	Shopping lines sold in addition
6	Appeal to transient trade	Established clientele
7	Relatively little advertising	Much advertising
8	Price and convenience stressed	Use of features of various kinds to attract customers
9	Low overhead	High overhead

Source: Small Business Administration, 1965, p 18

Location affinity and complementarity

Studying the other firms near your proposed business site, whether they will be competitors or not, might give you some further guidance on where to locate.

Grouping together firms of the same or similar type often benefits all. There are many examples of clothing stores, professional services (such as architects and doctors) and vehicle retailers (on Parramatta Road in Sydney's west, for instance) operating within the same area. Rubbing shoulders with the competition in this way encourages easier 'comparative shopping' by customers, and overall sales are often increased.

Some businesses complement others and should be located near them. Florists often operate near undertakers; confectionery shops and restaurants are often located near theatres. The mix of shops in well-planned shopping centres is aimed at maximising sales for all (and rental income for the shopping centre) through the complementarity of tenant business activities.

Other factors

A number of other types of factors have a role to play in the complex matter of location of small businesses. These include:

- availability of resources
- support from the local community
- access, visibility and aesthetics
- zoning regulations
- reputation
- room for expansion.

Availability of resources

Ready access to supplies of materials and/or merchandise might affect choice of location. Availability of employees with appropriate skills is a major consideration for some types of business.

Support from the local community

An active chamber of commerce and supportive local council are indicators of a healthy and progressive community attitude towards commercial growth and development.

Access, visibility and aesthetics

Increased preference for one-stop shopping and the widespread use of motor vehicles have tended to favour regional shopping centres over central business districts during the past 20 years. These are certainly visible, and are placed with accessibility (in driving time) and parking in mind.

It should not be assumed that all sites within a regional shopping centre have equal accessibility and are equally visible. Within many shopping centres, especially if they are poorly designed, some shops will be placed in 'dead-end' corridors and quiet corners and so lack both ready access and high visibility.

The general aesthetic impression of the street, mall, shopping centre or other location might either help your business or detract from your ability to draw customers. Poor sites are those where bad lighting, noise, dirt and dust, offensive odours and lack of space cause reductions in passing traffic and decrease sales.

Zoning regulations

Careful checks should be made of any government regulations and zoning restrictions that could limit your choice of location.

Reputation

Localities with high crime rates and a reputation for vandalism are not likely to be good shopping areas, and probably should be avoided.

Room for expansion

Failing to consider the likely need to expand the premises might later necessitate a move to a completely new location; whereas, with a little forethought, a site could have been chosen that would have lent itself to expansion — which would have been easier and cheaper.

OPTIONS WITHIN LOCATIONS

Once a particular geographical or population region has been decided on (for example, the northern suburbs of Sydney, the Hunter Valley, Albury/Wodonga or Geelong, to name some widely different areas), various options within each choice must be considered.

Small-town 'main street'

Prime positions in small towns are usually those in the main street and those adjacent to a hotel, post office or supermarket. Locations around the corner from the main street normally have lower occupancy costs and might be attractive to customers who need vehicle parking space.

> A good location will attract customers.

Central business districts

In large towns and cities the original town and commercial centre is now referred to as the 'central business district' (CBD). Buildings are often older, but extensive rebuilding, renovating and remodelling are transforming more and more previously run-down areas into attractive shopping malls and arcades. Some very large cities have several CBDs. Many of the older inner-city suburbs have their own CBDs.

Although CBDs draw buyers from far and wide, they present the small business operator with several serious problems such as parking and traffic congestion and high rental.

Suburban (neighbourhood) shopping centres

Most suburbs have their 'centre' where retail and service firms have congregated over the years. Sometimes a major development has replaced older buildings with a mall or a shopping centre that accommodates about 8 to 12 small shops in association with a supermarket of moderate size. Except for such developments, there is usually no attempt to create a sensible mix of shops, and direct competition is widespread. (For instance, several coffee shops can operate almost side by side.)

Neighbourhood shopping centres rely heavily on the local trading area, and have to compete with the greater drawing power of the larger regional shopping malls and centres.

Regional multi-store shopping centres

Regional shopping centres are usually large commercial developments, controlled by professional property managers, often containing 50 to 100 stores that offer variety, depth and range in goods and services and having several 'anchor' department or variety stores as the major tenants. The hallmarks of the regional shopping centre are convenience (in terms of parking, air-conditioning, accessibility and services such as rest rooms, child-care centres and parcel pick-up) and variety. They are placed mainly in outer suburbs and near housing estates.

To the naive small business owner/manager, a site in a major shopping centre might seem ideal, but careful checking could prove otherwise. Developers of large shopping centres often attract major retail chains by offering large floor space for low unit (per square metre) rental, and then charge the smaller tenants much higher unit rental. Typically, small firms might occupy 20% to 25% of the total floor space of a large shopping centre but pay up to half of all the rent.

Williams (1991) compared the costs and benefits experienced by small retailers in New South Wales who located in regional shopping centres with those of small retailers located elsewhere. Some of his findings are:

- Occupancy costs for small retailers in regional shopping centres represent a much larger proportion of total operating costs (34%) than they do for non-shopping-centre retailers (27%).
- Small retailers in shopping centres generally rate their occupancy costs as much higher in relation to occupancy benefits than do non-shopping-centre retailers.
- Owner/managers of small retail firms in regional shopping centres regard the terms and conditions of their rental/leasing agreements as very much less favourable than do owner/managers of similar firms operating from non-shopping-centre locations.
- The survival rate among small retail firms in regional shopping centres was significantly lower (36%) than that among small retailers located elsewhere (43%).

Clearly, it must not be assumed that shopping centre locations are always superior to non-shopping-centre locations.

Highway strips or ribbon shopping zones

These follow major roads and highways in and near metropolitan areas. With the growth of multi-store shopping centres, shops on traffic routes are increasingly dependent on through traffic. Parking, noise and access are major problems.

Small shopping malls

In many small towns, upgrading the local shopping centre has resulted in a variety of location patterns. One style of development has been the shopping mall, adjacent to a council or private car park, which gives shops the added benefit of improved access (see Figure 10.2).

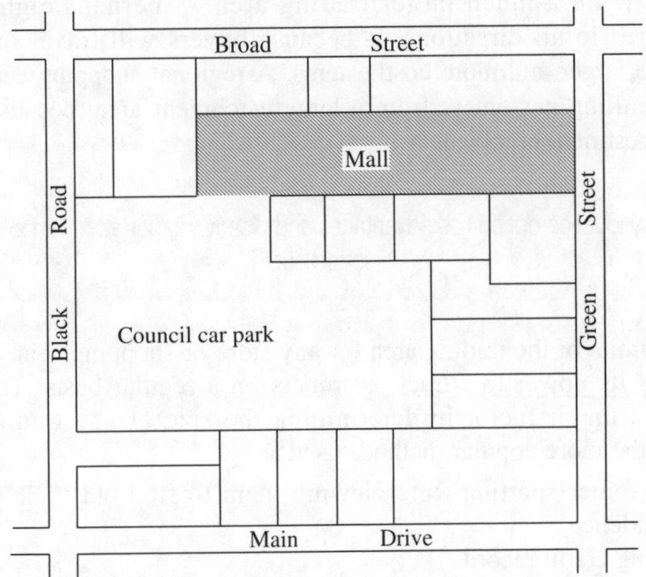

FIGURE 10.2 Small shopping mall (associated with car park)

Industrial parks and estates

In most population centres, areas specially zoned as light industrial are set aside. Many small manufacturers, fabrication plants, machine shops, repair firms and similar businesses are concentrated in these areas.

Isolated sites

There are countless thousands of small shops in isolated locations. These are usually suburban convenience shops, run by a family, unable to compete on price, but open 'at all hours'.

TRADING AREA ANALYSIS

A way to assess more accurately the size of the firm's potential market (and, therefore, the suitability or otherwise of a potential location) is to gauge the size of the likely trading (or catchment) area (see 'Economic factors', page 163).

The size of the likely trading area will determine the size of the population whose purchasing power is to be calculated. Purchasing power also depends on other matters, such as the average income in the area. A suburban convenience shop selling groceries might have a trading area covering several blocks in each direction and including some 300 to 500 households. A store selling durable consumer goods (such as domestic appliances, major furniture lines or motor vehicles) will draw on a much larger trading area — perhaps eight to ten kilometres in all directions — because buyers will travel further to purchase larger and more costly items. A regional shopping centre will aim at pulling customers from a large catchment area, because of the huge investment involved.

> Every location option has advantages and disadvantages which should be sorted out.

The limits of the trading area for any store or shopping centre are the limits of its power to attract customers on a regular basis. Travelling time is a major factor in determining the size of any trading area. Among the more popular methods used are:

- customer spotting (interviewing them to find out their place of residence)
- using credit records
- carrying out a telephone survey.

Using these methods, you can determine the primary trading area — or the area from which about 60% or more of your customers come. The secondary trading area will bring another 25% of customers, and the fringe will bring the remainder (see Figure 10.3).

Several other factors modify the size and shape of any trading area. Man-made barriers to travel (such as major highways and railways to be crossed) and natural barriers, like rivers and steep hills, can restrict customers' willingness to travel in certain directions to shop. Figure 10.3 illustrates this effect.

Another (more complex) method is Reilly's Law of Retail Gravitation, which estimates the break-even point between any two shops, shopping centres or towns. It finds the distance from a business location at which residents are indifferent as to whether they drive to shop A or shop B — and it is not necessarily the half-way point in travel time or distance. Other methods use computers to carry out complex data analysis.

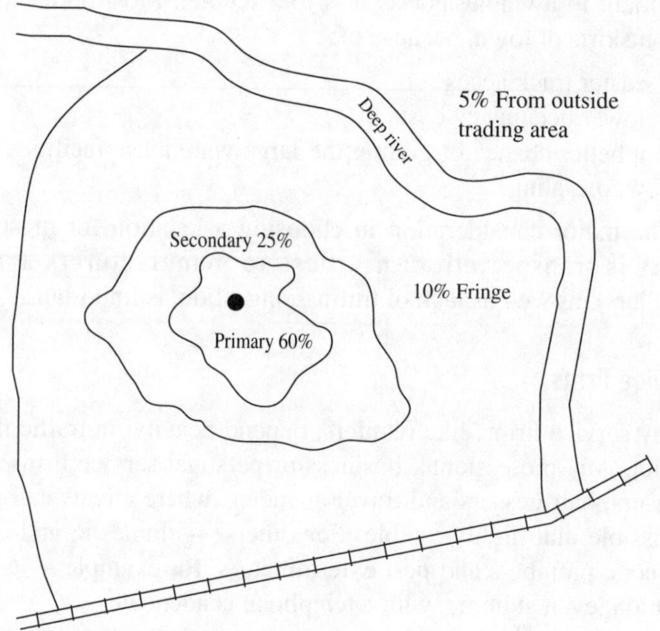

FIGURE 10.3 Trading area

LOCATION ANALYSIS FOR DIFFERENT INDUSTRIES

The general locational factors outlined above apply to all types of firms. In addition, in choosing a good location, small manufacturers will have some problems that differ from those faced by retail shops.

Retailers

Retailers are 'revenue-dependent' firms. Their main purpose in choosing a good location is to maximise sales, and for this they depend on passing vehicle and pedestrian traffic. Sites with heavy traffic flow usually have high occupancy costs. Some types of retail firms will suit high-rental sites, and others will not (see Table 10.2).

When calculating pedestrian traffic at a potential site, only the relevant customers should be counted (for instance women, if a ladies' wear shop is being planned). Seasonal patterns should also be noted.

Wholesalers

Wholesalers who sell to retailers will usually make deliveries to their buyers; others (such as plumbing and electrical wholesalers selling to tradespeople) have their buyers call to select their requirements. This will have a bearing on location. So, too, will the need for large-vehicle access to deliver merchandise. Customer traffic flow is not nearly as important to a wholesaler as it is to a retailer. Most prefer locations on the outskirts of town, because of:

- easier truck access
- lower occupancy costs
- a better chance of getting the large warehouse facilities needed for wholesaling.

The major consideration in choosing a location for most wholesale firms is transportation: nearness to manufacturers and markets (retailers), as well as lack of traffic congestion, is important.

Service firms

Many service firms, like retailers, depend heavily on traffic flow; others do not. Any professional, business or personal service firms such as tax advisers, hairdressers and travel agencies, where clients call in, must be accessible and highly visible. For others — domestic and commercial cleaners, plumbers and pest exterminators, for example — a convenient location, even at home, with a telephone is adequate.

Manufacturers

Unlike retailers, firms involved in manufacturing tend to be more 'cost dependent' than revenue dependent, and therefore efforts to minimise production and distribution costs affect their choice of location. Because of special needs in machinery, equipment, storage and work flow, it is usually difficult and expensive to move a factory.

The main location matters to be considered are:

- availability of raw materials and nearness to suppliers
- nearness to markets
- transport facilities (road, rail, air and sea)
- availability of skilled employees
- access to essential services (power, water, gas, waste disposal and fire protection)
- zoning regulations limiting effluent, pollution and noise
- potential for expansion if and when needed
- special needs such as clean air.

The importance of each of these factors to any one firm will depend on the manufacturing process and the type of raw materials needed. If raw materials are more bulky and costly to transport than the finished product, nearness to suppliers will be more important than nearness to markets.

To buy or lease premises?

Leasing business premises (and any other asset) is one way of preserving much-needed funds and working capital, especially at startup, and more especially if the new firm is under-capitalised. Leasing and rental costs are tax deductible.

In deciding whether or not to enter a leasing or rental agreement the following questions are among the more important:

- What is the rental or leasing cost? How often are increases likely, and by how much?
- Is the lessor (the landlord) to be responsible for normal maintenance and all property costs such as rates and insurance?
- Can the lease be assigned? (That is, can the premises be sublet?)
- Exactly which costs are involved (water, rates, power, etc)?
- Who will be responsible for repairs and modifications to the premises? (If I install an air-conditioner can I take it with me when I leave?)
- Are there any expenses to be shared with other tenants or with the landlord?
- Are there any restrictions on my use of the premises?
- Is the lease renewable when it expires?

Buying business premises requires the outlay of a large sum of money, and payment in instalments might be possible. There are tax deductions for expenses associated with the upkeep of owned business premises, including depreciation. A major advantage of owning premises is that you are free to modify the building and use it as you wish (subject to regulations).

If the business fails, the premises can be disposed of, whereas in a leasing situation you might be locked in, unless the agreement allows for subletting or otherwise quitting the lease under such circumstances. The same applies, but with less urgency, if the business expands and needs larger premises.

All advantages and disadvantages, and the relative costs of buying (including interest on funds borrowed) and leasing (including taxation benefits) need to be carefully examined before the decision is made.

SUMMARY

Careful choice of the best possible business location is vital to success. Proper placement of your business can be done only after you have evaluated the advantages and disadvantages of all available premises, using the guidelines in this chapter.

Many location options are available to most small firms. These might range from central business districts to suburban and regional shopping centres, shopping strips on highways, shopping malls and 'isolated' neighbourhood sites.

A business must be located so as to minimise its operating costs and/or maximise its sales potential from the trading area it will serve. Careful investigation of the area's general economic condition, its population patterns, trends and purchasing power, and the competition, are vital.

Selection of a suitable site should only follow adequate study of the site history, occupancy costs, effects of location affinity and complementarity, access, zoning regulations and the general attractiveness of the particular area.

It should be noted that different considerations apply to location selection for firms from different industries. In addition, all owner/managers have a choice between owning business premises and leasing or renting them.

TABLE 10.3 Checklist for locating a store

I City or town

A Economic consideration

1 Industry
- (a) farming
- (b) manufacturing
- (c) trading

2 Trend
- (a) highly satisfactory
- (b) growing
- (c) stationary
- (d) declining

3 Permanency
- (a) old and well-established
- (b) old and reviving
- (c) new and promising
- (d) recent and uncertain

4 Diversification
- (a) many and varied lines
- (b) many of the same type
- (c) few varied lines
- (d) dependent on one industry

5 Stability
- (a) constant
- (b) satisfactory
- (c) average
- (d) subject to wide fluctuations

6 Seasonality
- (a) little or no seasonal change
- (b) mild seasonal change
- (c) periodical — every few years
- (d) highly seasonal in nature

7 Future
- (a) most promising
- (b) satisfactory
- (c) uncertain
- (d) poor outlook

B Population

1 Income distribution
- (a) mostly wealthy
- (b) well distributed
- (c) mostly middle-income
- (d) poor

2 Trend
- (a) growing
- (b) large and stable
- (c) small and stable
- (d) declining

3 Living status
- (a) own homes
- (b) pay substantial rent
- (c) pay moderate rent
- (d) pay low rent

C Competition

1 Number of competing stores
- (a) few
- (b) average
- (c) many
- (d) too many

2 Type of management
- (a) not progressive
- (b) average
- (c) above average
- (d) alert and progressive

3 Presence of chains
- (a) no chains
- (b) few chains
- (c) average number
- (d) many well-established

4 Type of competing stores
- (a) unattractive
- (b) average

TABLE 10.3 contd

(c) old and well-established
(d) Are many people buying out of the community?

D The town as a place to live

1 Character of the city
(a) Are homes neat and clean or run-down and shabby?
(b) Are lawns, parks, streets, etc neat, modern, attractive?
(c) adequate facilities available

(i) banking
(ii) transportation
(iii) professional service
(iv) utilities

2 Facilities and climate
(a) schools
(b) churches
(c) amusement centres
(d) medical and dental services
(e) climate

II The actual site

A Competition

1 Number of independent stores of the same kind as yours
(a) same block
(b) same side of street
(c) across street
2 Number of chain stores
(a) same block
(b) same side of street
(c) across street
3 Kind of stores next door
4 Number of vacancies
(a) same side of street
(b) across street
(c) next door
5 Dollar sales of nearest competitor

B Traffic flow

1 Gender of pedestrians
2 Age of pedestrians
3 Destination of pedestrians
4 Number of passers-by
5 Automobile traffic count
6 Peak hours of traffic flow
7 Per cent location of site

C Transportation

1 Transfer points
2 Highway
3 Kind (bus, tram, automobile, railway)

D Parking facilities

1 Large and convenient
2 Large enough but not convenient
3 Convenient but too small
4 Completely inadequate

E Side of street

F Plant

1 Frontage — in metres
2 Depth — in metres
3 Shape of building
4 Condition
5 Heat — type; air-conditioning
6 Light
7 Display space
8 Back entrance
9 Front entrance
10 Display windows

G Corner location — if not, what is it?

H Unfavourable characteristics

1 Fire hazards
2 Cemetery
3 Hospital
4 Industry
5 Employment office
6 Undertaker
7 Vacant lot — no parking possibilities
8 Garages
9 Playground
10 Smoke, dust, odours
11 Poor sidewalks and pavement
12 Unsightly neighbourhood buildings

I Professionals in block

1 Medical doctors
2 Dentists
3 Lawyers
4 Veterinarians
5 Others

J History of the site

Source: Small Business Administration, 1965, pp 29–30

Key words

aesthetics
central business district (CBD)
disposable income
lessee
lessor
location
location affinity
location complementarity
neighbourhood shopping centre
occupancy costs
purchasing power
regional shopping centre
shopping mall
site
trading area

Review exercises

Circle the appropriate letter in each case.

1 A logical business reason for locating a firm in one's home town area would be:
A closeness to supplies
B desire to help develop one's home community
C availability of employees
D established reputation with the bank, suppliers and potential customers.

2 On which of the following should a small manufacturer place the highest priority when choosing a business site?
A customer accessibility
B relative cost of operating the business from that site
C employee convenience
D closeness to banks and other services

3 On which of the following should a small retailer place the highest priority when choosing a business site?
A customer accessibility
B relative cost of operating the business from that site
C employee convenience
D closeness to banks and other services

4 In evaluating a particular service-business location, careful attention must be given to:
A traffic flow
B the site's past business history
C customer parking accessibility
D all of the above.

5 Poor retail locations lead to:
A lower sales
B poor business image
C high staff turnover
D excessive occupancy costs.

6 The problem of where to locate a business concerns:
   A new firms
   B expanding firms
   C older firms
   D all types of firms.

7 High-rent locations are most suitable for businesses that:
   A have a low merchandise turnover rate
   B need space to expand
   C have high overhead costs
   D have low gross margins on their merchandise lines.

8 Low-rent locations are more appropriate for firms that:
   A have well established and loyal customers
   B appeal to passing traffic
   C stress price and convenience
   D need attractive window displays.

9 The practice of locating competing firms near each other is known as:
   A decentralisation
   B location affinity
   C location complementarity
   D market orientation.

10 One advantage of owning (rather than leasing) the business premises is:
   A less risk due to falling property values
   B avoidance of loss due to fire or other disasters
   C the business cannot be forced to move
   D lower maintenance costs.

References

Small Business Administration 1965, *Small Business Location and Layout*, US Government Printing Office, Washington, DC

Small Business Administration 1981, *Starting and Managing a Small Business of Your Own*, US Government Printing Office, Washington, DC

Williams, A J 1991, 'Small business survival: The role of formal education, management training and advisory services', *Small Business Review 1990–1991*, Bureau of Industry Economics, Small Business Research Unit, Australian Government Publishing Service, Canberra pp 43–82

CHAPTER 11

Setting up your premises: Internal layout and design

Layout concerns the placement of fixtures, equipment, machinery and merchandise within business premises so that maximum benefit can be obtained from the available floor space.

In evaluating a business site for rental, lease or purchase, or in planning and building new premises, small business managers often fail to give layout the attention it deserves. For retailers and many service firms, customer flow, without crowding, is more important. In wholesale warehouses, both these requirements can be relevant. For manufacturers, work flow is the major factor in determining layout.

After reading this chapter you should:

- understand the factors that might influence the choice of layout and design of premises for your business, and
- be able to choose an appropriate layout for your firm.

The major guidelines for designing and arranging layout of equipment, fixtures, merchandise or materials, customer or work flow routes and all other facilities in business premises vary from one type of business to another. However, in all cases either one of two considerations will be of primary concern:

- the most efficient flow of work (as in production and manufacturing), or
- maximising the flow of customer traffic through the store.

> Good internal layout and design will encourage buying in retail stores.

Several other factors will also affect layout. The size and shape of the business premises (including placement of lighting, air-conditioning, stairs, lifts and escalators) will either help or hinder your operations. In addition, the need for visual control over an area of activity (from the manager's office, for instance) can influence the design of those areas.

Let us now look at layout considerations for the various industry sectors.

RETAILING

Retail store layout and design must maximise sales volume by attracting buyers and encouraging their movement through the store. A good location might have little effect on sales unless passing traffic is persuaded to at least enter the shop. All entrances should invite passers-by to come inside. The quality of window dressing and the overall visual impact will both play a large part in this.

The basics of layout

Depending on the size and shape of your premises, the type of merchandise you are selling and customer buying patterns, there are various layouts to choose from:

- the grid (see Figure 11.1)
- open-plan or free-form (see Figure 11.2)
- the shop or boutique (see Figure 11.3).

The grid plan suits self-service shops, moves traffic in certain directions and is efficient for handling large numbers of customers. The open-plan or free-form layout (as used by K Mart, for example) aims at more relaxed shopping, but can create security problems. In the shop or boutique arrangement, each major type of merchandise is placed in a particular area or 'shop'. Many variations on these three basic layouts are possible.

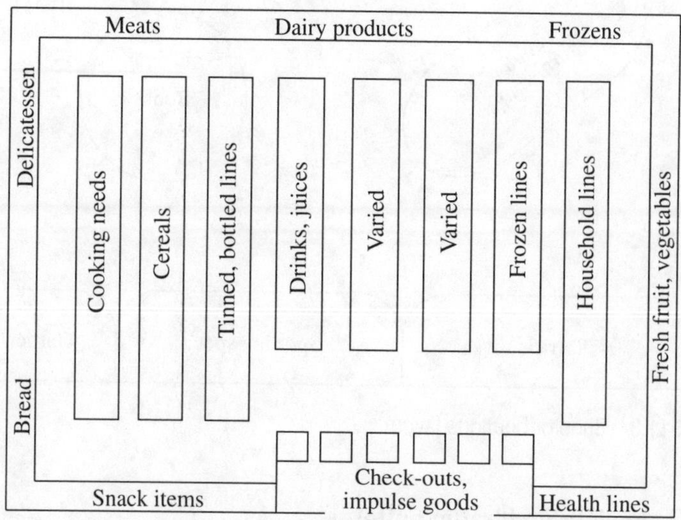

FIGURE 11.1 Grid layout

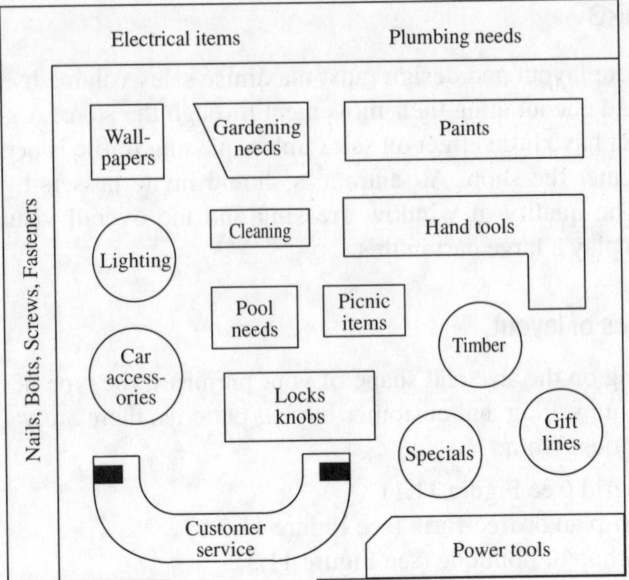

FIGURE 11.2 Open-plan or free-form layout

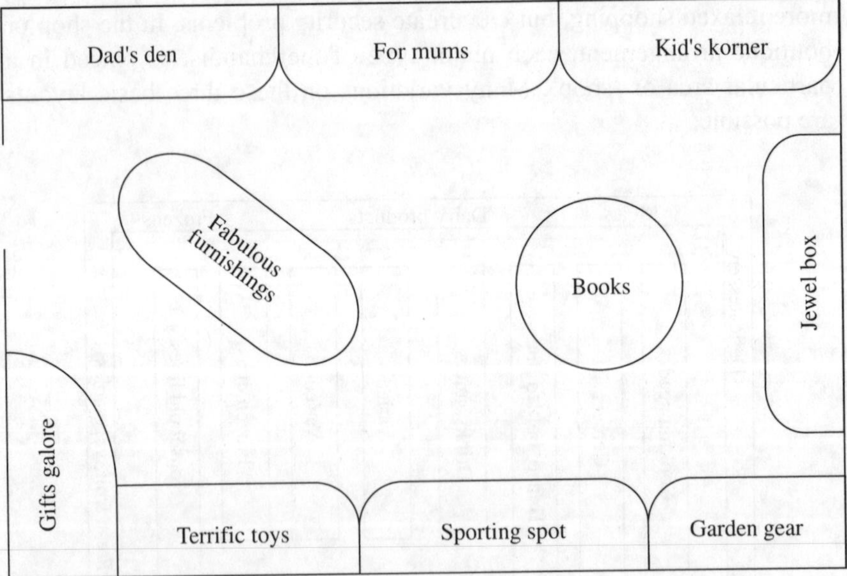

FIGURE 11.3 Shop or boutique layout

Buyer behaviour and traffic patterns

Choice of layout and the actual placement of types of merchandise within the shop should take into account the behaviour of buyers, especially their patterns of movement around the store. Retailers should be aware of the following points:

1 Customers enter a shop either

(a) knowing what they intend to buy (called *destination traffic*); or
(b) wishing to browse before deciding whether and what to buy (*shopping traffic*).

2 If possible, shopping traffic tends to move to the right after entering and circulates, generally in an anticlockwise direction. Destination shoppers, trying to avoid the congestion caused by slower and less predictable browsers, head to the left if possible and travel clockwise.

3 Goods with high gross margins (more profitable goods) should be placed to the right of the main entrance to attract the attention of browsers. Goods with low margins (the faster moving basics or staple lines) should be placed to the left since they will be sought by most destination shoppers.

Place your merchandise according to customer traffic movements.

4 All customers will move through the front part of the store, but not all will go to the back. Those parts of the shop with the most traffic flow will have the greatest sales, so it is common to find the more profitable lines towards the front and the basics towards the rear of the shop (thus forcing destination shoppers to move past slower selling and high-margin lines). Impulse goods are also usually placed nearest the traffic flow — at the front or on the main aisles. It should be noted that some customers dislike these practices.

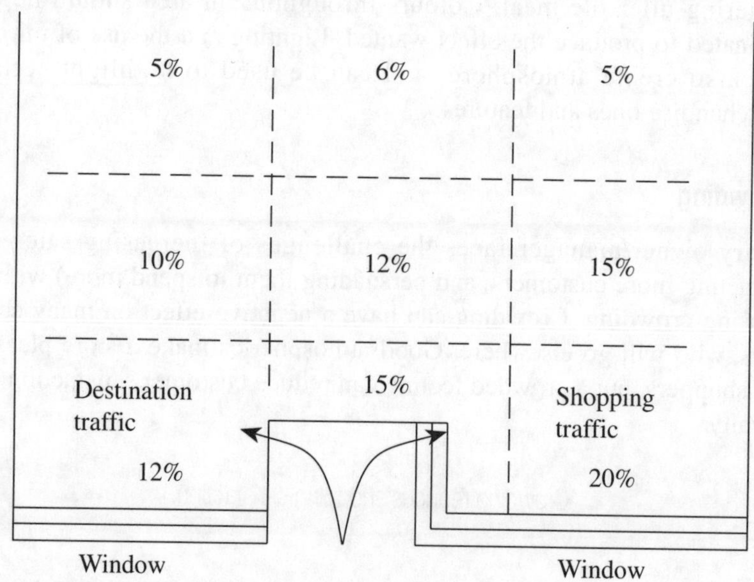

FIGURE 11.4 Retail store layout with percentage of sales by areas

5 Figure 11.4 shows the approximate proportions of total sales which should come from each section of the store. The value of floor space decreases from the front to the back. If there is a rear or a side entrance these guidelines need adjusting.

6 In the placement of merchandise on shelves, customer buying behaviour should be borne in mind. Stock items placed near floor level and above head height do not sell as well as those closer to eye level.

7 Since the front part of a store has more customer traffic, it should produce most of the sales and it is therefore more valuable. Another widely used method of estimating the placement of merchandise is the '4-3-2-1 rule'. This method requires 40% of sales to come from merchandise placed in the front quarter of the store, 30% from the next, 20% from the third and 10% from the rear quarter.

Atmospherics

Customer satisfaction with a particular shop is also influenced by its interior decor. Lighting, colour and style of presentation all influence customer attitudes to the shop, which in turn affect buying behaviour.

Careful use of colour can create certain moods and impressions. Soft pastels are peaceful; light colours make a small shop 'feel spacious'. Bright colours can overpower and detract from the merchandise. Fast-food shops often use red and other bright colours to generate faster customer turnover, since such colours are not 'soothers' and discourage lingering after the meal. Colours throughout an area should be co-ordinated to produce the effect wanted. Lighting and the use of mirrors can also create atmosphere, and can be used to highlight certain merchandise lines and features.

Crowding

Every owner/manager faces the challenges of increasing sales (by attracting more customers, and persuading them to spend more) without causing crowding. Crowding can have a negative effect on many shoppers, who will go elsewhere. Good atmospherics make a store pleasant for shoppers, but a crowded feeling can reduce customer satisfaction and loyalty.

> Crowding reduces shopping satisfaction.

Crowding might be experienced if there are 'too many' other shoppers in the store, and if bad placement of merchandise, signposts and advertising placards, narrow aisles or too few check-outs restrict movement through the shop. These restrictions will be felt more acutely by destination shoppers. Personal factors can affect an individual's level of discomfort or distress from crowding — previous experience with crowds, time pressure or traits such as impatience and aggressiveness, which are found in type-A personalities (see Chapter 23).

The effects of crowding can include anxiety, confusion, frustration, anger, difficulty in making choices and poor buying decisions (from an excess of information and pressure). An absence of crowding encourages a more relaxed approach to shopping, and leads to better comparison of merchandise, more impulse buying, more satisfaction with the shopping trip and the store, and the intention to come back.

Awareness of the possibility of crowding and of its consequences, and attention to customer buying behaviour, atmospherics and the basics of good layout, can all greatly improve the sales performance of retail shops.

WHOLESALING

The main requirement in planning the layout of a wholesale warehouse is quick and easy access to fast-moving merchandise. This will speed up order filling and reduce employee travelling time. The aisles should be in a direction which gives ready access to the delivery counters and to truck loading areas.

SERVICE FIRMS

Layout guidelines for small service firms will usually be similar to those used for retail shops, but must be adjusted to suit the particular needs of the kinds of service sold. A restaurant will need to design the kitchen with work flow in mind, and the eating space with customer comfort as the main consideration.

MANUFACTURING

For manufacturing and assembly operations the movement of raw materials through the various processes until they become finished goods is the most important requirement in designing the plant layout. The objective is smooth and efficient work flow.

Product layout

> Good internal layout and design will improve work flow and reduce manufacturing costs.

Product layout is suitable when the operations to be performed are standard in their nature (for example, drilling six holes in pre-set places) and their order. The raw materials are moved along a fixed route to each work station in turn, and the required operations are carried out. The placement of each machine or work station can be done so as to avoid backtracking, and there are many possible variations, such as straight line, L flow, U flow, circular flow, and S flow. This layout is best used when the firm is involved in continuous production of a standardised product. Figure 11.5 illustrates product layout.

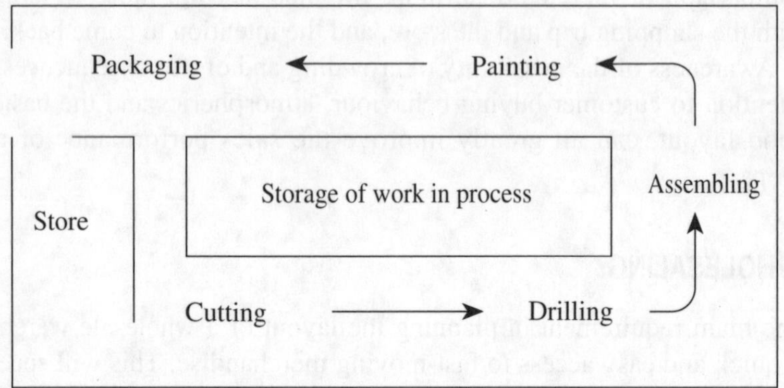

FIGURE 11.5 Product layout

Process layout

When the firm's work is mainly job order or customised (where each job is completed to customer requirements, and most are different) process layout is more appropriate. Vehicle repair shops are usually arranged in this way. Each job is moved through its various operations by being sent to the next machine or work station as necessary. There is no set pattern or sequence for every individual job (see Figure 11.6).

A vehicle repair shop would usually be arranged in this way. Each car could need a full tune-up, or brake adjustment, or suspension check-up, or towbar fitting, or any combination of these.

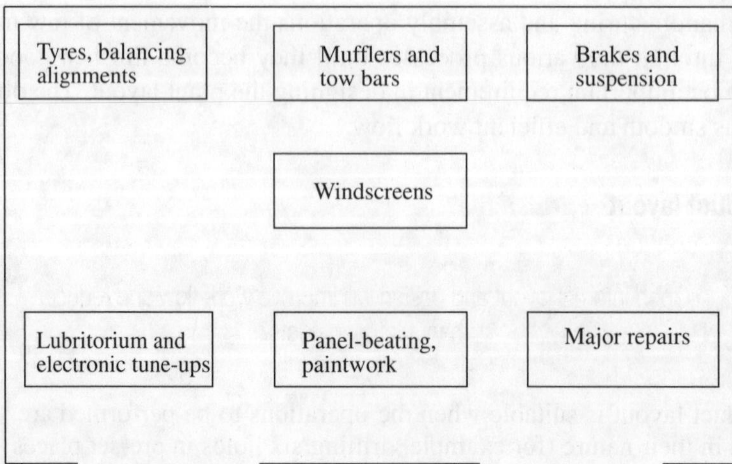

FIGURE 11.6 Process layout

SUMMARY

A firm's internal design and layout should be aimed at helping the flow of work or the flow of customers or both. In the one, costs are saved; in the other, sales are increased.

For retail shops, buyer behaviour and traffic patterns are major considerations. The satisfaction of buyers is increased if they do not experience crowding and find the shop's decor, colouring and lighting (atmospherics) pleasing. For wholesalers, speedy access to merchandise is a major requirement in designing warehouses.

Most service firms need to consider both customer flow and work flow. Design of factories for manufacturers has to assist smooth and efficient work flow of materials to finished goods. Various types of manufacturing operations require quite different layout considerations.

KEY WORDS

atmospherics
crowding
destination traffic
layout
shopping traffic
staples

REVIEW EXERCISES

Circle the appropriate letter in each case.

1 A store's image or reputation is created by:
  A its prices
  B its range and quality of merchandise
  C its location
  D all the above.

2 Which of the following retailers would be most likely to use the grid layout pattern?
  A high-fashion ladies' wear shop
  B supermarket
  C footwear retailer
  D none of the above.

3 In a retail store the goods which customers usually seek out and purchase are best placed:
  A towards the rear of the store
  B in the front half of the store
  C along the side walls
  D throughout the whole store.

4 In planning factory layout, a manufacturer should be concerned mainly about:
A aesthetics
B efficient use of space
C ease of customer traffic flow
D all of the above.

5 The type of factory or workshop layout in which similar machines are placed together is known as:
A process layout
B product layout
C work flow layout
D circular flow layout.

6 Self-service food supermarkets generally have a:
A box layout
B open-plan layout
C grid layout
D shop layout.

7 Destination traffic in a store tends to move:
A anticlockwise
B clockwise
C in no set pattern
D to the specials.

8 Merchandise lines should be placed to the right of the store entrance if they:
A are staple lines
B are hard to sell
C have low gross margins
D have high gross margins.

9 According to the '4-3-2-1 rule', a retailer with gross sales of $586 000 per annum should produce, from the merchandise placed in the front half of the store, sales income of:
A $527 400
B $410 200
C $234 400
D $175 800.

10 The effects of crowding on shoppers:
A depend on individual experience and personality
B can be eliminated by good layout
C are eliminated by good atmospherics
D can be reduced by appropriate advertising and fair prices.

CHAPTER 12

Legal matters

By now you will appreciate that there is more to going into business than just putting up a sign. In fact, it might be illegal for you to put up that sign! There are many legal constraints on small firms and ignorance of the law is no excuse or defence. To assist you in the complex legal areas affecting small business, this chapter has been designed as a lay person's guide. It should give you a better understanding of the law and enable you to communicate better with your accountant and solicitor.

After reading this chapter you should be able to:

- decide which type of business structure would best suit your business
- register a business name
- list the main types of insurance applicable to your business
- adopt an effective method of buying insurance, and
- discuss in general terms key points involved in
  - choosing a solicitor
  - buying or renting premises
  - employing staff
  - granting credit, and
  - consumer protection.

In this chapter we seek to outline the key areas of the law that will affect your business operation. Because the law is constantly changing, you must be aware of the law and you must keep up to date with changes. It is useless to argue that 'you just did not know'. It is your business and you are responsible for it.

BUSINESS STRUCTURES

One of the first key questions the intending small business operator must ask is: 'Which legal form of organisation, or structure, is best for my business?'

The types of business structure available in Australia are:

Most common forms	*Other forms*
Sole traders	Public companies
Partnerships	Companies limited by guarantee
Proprietary limited companies (ie private companies)	Co-operatives
	Close corporations
Trusts	Limited partnerships

The sole trader

The sole trader is the easiest and cheapest form of business to go into. It is ideal where there is one owner who makes all the decisions and runs the business (either with or without staff). The sole trader can trade under his or her own name, or register a business name. Registration of a business name does not make the sole trader a separate legal entity — he or she is still responsible for any actions of the business. The law makes no distinction between the sole trader as a business and the sole trader as a person. The sole trader's business and private assets are seen as being common — and totally at risk (as outlined in Chapter 4) for any action taken against the business.

Partnership

The partnership is the second easiest organisation to establish. Designed for structures which have more than one owner, partnership laws in each state allow 2 to 20 people to come together and carry on business in common with the intention of making a profit. Each state has its own Partnership Act and most states require written evidence of a partnership if it is expected to last more than one year. Such written evidence is usually a partnership agreement, which should cover points such as:

- details of the partners
- nature of the business
- managerial responsibilities and limitations
- capital investments
- division of profits (and losses)
- drawings and loans
- termination clauses
- new partners
- dispute settlement, and
- dissolution and distribution.

Many partnerships consist of a husband and wife team. It is strongly recommended that even these partnerships have written agreements, even though this is not compulsory in some states. The two main reasons for this are:

- taxation, and
- the possibility of a marriage break-up.

The agreement does not make a partnership a separate legal entity. Like the sole trader, the partners are responsible for all debts incurred by the partnership and any actions taken against it. Furthermore, each partner is not only jointly responsible for all debts, but also individually responsible. This means that, if you have a partner who has no assets and the partnership is sued, you could have to pay everything if you are the only partner with assets. This frightening fact makes it even more desirable to have a written partnership agreement that has been drawn by a competent legal adviser.

Proprietary limited company

A company is a radical departure from the two types of legal structure so far discussed — the sole trader and the partnership.

A company is formed when a group of people (or firms) combine as shareholders and incorporate under the provisions of the Companies Act. As shareholders they own the company, which is a separate legal entity. The company:

- can own property in its own name (and not its members' names)
- is liable for taxation
- is not limited by the continuing existence of its members, and
- can sue and be sued.

The liability of the company is limited. The shareholders risk only their respective contribution of capital, and not their personal assets (as in the two previous legal structures).

Under incorporation the company must lodge a memorandum of association, which outlines the objectives of the company, and the articles of association, which are the rules for running the company. Companies may be incorporated as either proprietary companies or public companies. The key difference is that proprietary companies cannot offer their shares to the public, as do public companies. Proprietary companies are often referred to as private companies, since transfer of shares is restricted.

Many people going into business believe that, by incorporating, they will be able to protect their family home and other assets in the event of the business failing. This protection is often destroyed by the presence of a director's guarantee, which allows the creditor (which could be the bank) to have access to the assets should the business fail. The protection that proprietary companies have traditionally provided for directors has been reduced significantly as courts are daily demanding that directors become more personally responsible for their companies' activities.

There are two main methods of forming (or incorporating) a company.

1 *Start from scratch* — This involves working through the Australian Securities Commission (ASC), usually with your advisers, whereby you

- select, reserve and register a business name
- write a suitable memorandum and articles of association
- lodge all documentation with the ASC
- appoint directors
- obtain your certificate of incorporation and Australian company number (ACN).

This process takes time and requires professional support.

2 *Buy a shelf company* — A shelf company is a ready-made structure that is waiting 'on the shelf' for you or anyone else to purchase. They are readily available from accountants, solicitors and businesses that specialise is selling shelf companies. Shelf companies usually require changes in the company name (or registration of a business name) and amendments to the memorandum and articles of association, as well as the lodgement of other documents with the ASC.

Trusts

A trust, unlike a proprietary limited company, is not a separate legal entity. It is a legal structure used to maximise the financial advantages of being in business, such as the distribution of income, taxation and protection against creditors. A trust offers to a family business many advantages that cannot be gained under the three legal forms already discussed.

In simple terms, a trust is a structure wherein title to a business is given to a trustee in order to:

- hold property
- run the business
- distribute the income to the beneficiaries and abide by the trust deed.

A trustee can be a sole trader, or a partnership, or a company, but a trading trust usually has a company as trustee — for obvious reasons.

The two main types of trust are discretionary trusts and unit trusts. Trusts are not a simple structure and you should seek professional advice from your accountant and/or solicitor if you are considering this possibility. Trusts are also subject to close taxation scrutiny, so if you are forming a trust make sure you have the best professional advice.

Other business structures

The other types of legal structures mentioned earlier are not usually used in small business.

The one exception is the co-operative, which is growing in popularity in areas such as craft work, primary industry, business programmes for the unemployed, and management buy-outs by employees. A co-operative is a legal structure which:

- has been incorporated

- is not a company
- has common and equal ownership by all employees with one share each
- has equal decision-making ability, with one vote per member, and
- distribution of all profits to the members.

Information about other legal forms is available from your accountant or solicitor if required.

Which structure should you use?

The legal structure you select for your business will depend on a host of different factors, such as:

- the size of the business
- the number of people involved
- the type of business
- taxation considerations
- the need for finance
- the availability of finance
- establishment costs
- location
- the exposure to risk
- the type of customers
- the need for additional skills
- your own personal preference.

Decisions on the business structure should be made after consultation with professionals such as your accountant and your solicitor. These experts should give their recommendations to you and you should then make the decision. It is also important to remember that the structure you choose can usually be altered to allow you and your business to adapt to a changing environment.

To help you decide on a business structure (in consultation with your advisers), the main legal forms are summarised in Table 12.3 on page 218.

Clearly there is no universal answer to the question 'What business structure should I choose?' Whatever structure you and your advisers decide on, remember that it *should be reviewed as your business grows and develops, and as legislation changes*.

THE BUSINESS NAME

When looking at the way your proposed business should be organised, one of the first considerations is usually to ask the question:

'What name shall we use?'

To the new starter this question is often so important that it takes precedence over many other key issues such as location, licences, capital raising or financial forecasting. The business name is a decision that all people can discuss and make contributions to; but often people do not fully realise:

- why a business name is important
- how it is registered, or
- the legal requirements of a business name.

The importance of a business name

A business name is important because it can help to:

- create an image for the new business
- aid recall for customers and potential customers (it is easier to remember a name like 'The Toronto Teahouse' than remember all the names of the owners)
- tell customers and potential customers what your business is all about (eg 'Lord Muck' is a business that cleans domestic grease traps and its motto, incidentally, is 'Service with a smell')
- give your business respectability
- give your business a common name to avoid possible conflict between owners, and
- make your business different from all other businesses.

Registering the business name

If the name you select is your own name then there is no need to register that name. It is your given name and you have every legal right to use it. If, however, you add to that name or select another name, then that new name has to be registered. Amanda Jones, for example, could operate a computer service trading as Amanda Jones. However, if she wanted to trade as Amanda Jones Computing Services then that name would have to be registered. A common approach for people like Amanda is to trade under her own name and display her occupation or services separately, but adjoining her name on business cards, stationery and signs.

Amanda Jones

Computing Services

4 Hope Street	Tel/Fax
MAINTOWN	449 9234

FIGURE 12.1 Business card

To register a business name:

1 Call in at your state government office (the Department of Consumer Affairs in New South Wales) and check to see that your proposed name has not been already registered or would not be confused with an existing registered name, or would not be considered offensive. You have to make this call in person as the Consumer Affairs staff cannot advise you by telephone.

2 Fill out an application form for registration of your business name and lodge it with a fee ($75 for three years in most states). The form contains the necessary instructions and requires details of:
   - the business name requested
   - the nature of the proposed business
   - the business address
   - the proposed commencement date, and
   - the names and addresses of applicants.

3 The actual issue of your business name is now a very rapid service due to the use of on-line terminal facilities by the Consumer Affairs branch offices.

Legal requirements of a business name

When a business name is registered, it is important to know of the following legal requirements:

- The *certificate* must be displayed in a prominent position at the place of business — usually near the door. The *registered name* must be displayed in a prominent position outside every location where business is conducted under that name.
- The name must be used on all stationery such as letterheads, invoices, statements, orders and receipts.
- Any changes to the original application must be communicated to the Department of Consumer Affairs immediately and the appropriate fees paid.
- The registration is for three years in most states and territories (except Queensland). At the end of the three years a renewal notice will be sent to the holders of the registered name.
- Registration is for the state of lodgement only. The use of a registered name is permitted in other states if the owner of that name is conducting business in those states. One business-name registration will suffice.
- Certain names are prohibited and will not be listed. A comprehensive guide to these restrictions is printed on the application forms. Each state has its own list of unsuitable names.
- Entries of your business name in Australian telephone directories will not be accepted unless proof of registration of your business name can be given.

- If the business name is absolutely essential to the business, then the name should be registered as a trade mark with the Patents, Trade Marks and Designs Office. This will give federal protection to your name which will, should conflict arise, override the state protection of business-name registration.
- A company may trade using its ACN as a business name.

INSURANCE

You may wonder what insurance has to do with legal issues. The connection is simple: an insurance policy is a legal contract. Some insurance policies are compulsory by law and every business person should have some protection from any legal actions that could be taken against them.

In earlier chapters we have seen the high risk associated with running a small business. Insurance is one way of providing financial protection against a real risk of loss — but once again, where do you start?

There are two main types of insurance to be considered by small business operators, ie compulsory insurances and desirable insurances.

Compulsory insurances

Worker's compensation — for all business operators who employ staff
Motor vehicle compulsory third party — for all business operators who use motor vehicles in their businesses
Superannuation — for all employees (except those listed on page 198)

Other insurances

Personal disability (sickness and accident)
Partnership
Key person
Professional indemnity
Product liability
Public risk/public liability
Fire
Plate glass
Documents
Stock
Water damage
Loss of profits
Burglary
Cash
Goods in transit
Machinery
Motor vehicle (comprehensive)
Tenant liability

And so the list goes on. It is not necessary to take out all of these types of insurance, but you should be aware that they are available. Your key question should be 'What insurance should I carry?' To assist you in answering this question, let us look at a brief explanation of the types of insurance listed above.

Worker's compensation

Australian employers are held responsible for any work-related sickness, injury or death to their employees. Employees may be permanent, full-time, part-time or casual — but they all have to be covered by worker's compensation insurance. Also, it is important to remember that if you have a proprietary limited company, you and your fellow directors are employees of the company and therefore must be covered by worker's compensation insurance. The law is clear — all employees must be covered by this insurance.

It is in this area that the law is often broken or ignored, and small business owners are tempted to pay cash in hand and ignore worker's compensation insurance due to friendship, cost factors, or too much trouble with paperwork. If a friend or person employed by you is seriously injured at your place of work, or going to or from work, and is not covered by this insurance, how will you feel — and how will you pay — particularly if the injury is such as to prevent that person from ever working again?

Worker's compensation insurance can be expensive to buy — and rates will differ from state to state and from industry to industry. The rates vary according to the likely risk of injury. Whatever the cost, always remember that it can be a lot more expensive if you don't have the insurance at all.

Motor vehicle compulsory third party

This insurance is compulsory as it covers the risk of injury or death to third parties, ie people other than the driver and the insured. It does *not* cover damage to the vehicle being driven. It is often referred to as 'Green Slip' insurance.

Superannuation

It is possible to insure against the loss of income when a person or an employee retires. In July 1992 the federal government introduced the Superannuation Guarantee to reduce the future reliance of the Australian population on age pensions. All employers are now compelled to provide a minimum level of superannuation cover for their employees. These payments — made quarterly to a complying superannuation fund — are currently running at 3% of each employee's base salary. They are programmed to rise to around 8%–9% by the turn of the century. There are a few exemptions to this scheme, ie employees receiving less than $450 per month, employees under 18 working less than 30 hours per week, employees aged 65 and over and domestic employees working less than 30 hours per week. There are booklets available on the Superannuation Guarantee from your local branch of the Australian Taxation Office or you can phone The Superannuation Guarantee Hotline on 13 1020 (Australia-wide). The hotline is available for the cost of a local call.

Non-compulsory superannuation is highly advisable for small business operators and this may be arranged through:

- insurance policies paying a lump sum or periodic payments upon retirement; or
- superannuation funds, managed either by insurance companies or by one's own incorporated company.

In the areas of superannuation and retirement planning, it is strongly recommended that thorough professional advice be obtained as many factors have to be considered. These include:

- taxation
- legal restraints and requirements such as trust deeds contributions, legal structure, etc, and
- the laws covering superannuation.

Personal disability (sickness and accident)

Sole traders and partnerships without employees do not have to take out worker's compensation insurance since sole traders and partners are not employees, unlike directors in a company. Instead of worker's compensation, they are advised to consider sickness and accident insurance — often called disability insurance. This insurance is designed to allow the owners to pay for replacement staff should they (the owners) be unable to work through sickness or injury. Try to imagine what would happen to your proposed (or existing) business if sickness or injury prevented you from working for, say, three months.

Partnership

It is wise for all partners to consider insurance on one another's lives. While no one likes to think of the death of their partner (who is usually a good friend as well), this insurance is a precaution that must be considered, as a sudden death has *often* meant that a business had to be sold to pay out the deceased partner's share. The purpose of this type of insurance is to give the surviving partner protection against the demands of the deceased partner's estate. Premiums are paid by the business as part of its normal operating expenses.

Key person

The business you are proposing or operating will probably revolve around the skills of a key person who is critical to the survival or prosperity of the business. Such people are difficult or costly to replace when they die or are incapacitated; a chef in a restaurant or a top salesperson in a retail operation are good examples. Key person insurance is designed to cover the business in such situations.

Professional indemnity

There is a growing trend for legal action to be taken against professional advisers for losses incurred as a result of following their advice. This insurance is not cheap, but it could be critical for people who work as consultants or who set themselves up as experts. In the past, many advisers issued disclaimers, believing that such statements would transfer the onus of responsibility from them to their clients. A series of legal challenges has changed this view on disclaimers.

Product liability

Under Australian consumer legislation, manufacturers *and* distributors can be held responsible for damage and injury caused to the customer by products made or sold through the business.

Public risk/public liability

This insurance is designed to cover a business against compensation claims for personal injury or death, and property damages to third parties. It would include common accidents — for example, a customer slipping on a wet or worn floor, a shelf collapsing, or any injury to a person while they are on your premises.

Public liability claims often take years to be settled, and it is strongly advised that cover of at least $5 million to $10 million be considered for this type of insurance. Product liability is becoming more important as producers now have to prove that their product was *not* responsible for any damage claimed.

Fire

Fire insurance is usually a general policy covering the destruction of your premises and assets by fire and other disasters such as floods and storms.

Fire policies should be examined carefully to evaluate:

- the areas covered or the types of risk accepted by the insurer (earthquakes, riots, rainwater damage or lightning)
- the exclusions of the policy (or types of risk not accepted)
- the value of the policy (replacement value as against depreciation value)
- special cases, such as flammable liquids stored on the premises, and

- add-ons, such as debris removal.

Note that many types of risk may not be covered by your fire policy. Some of these are:

1 Plate glass

Even though the business may be on rented premises, you could be required by the landlord to take out plate glass insurance. Plate glass windows are like car windscreens — easily broken and expensive to replace. If the windows have signwriting or burglar alarms, these facts should be noted when you take out the policy.

2 Documents

Your documentation may or may not be covered by your fire policy. The nature of the business, together with its size, will be critical to the cost of replacing the documents should they be lost.

3 Stock

The policy will stipulate a value for the stock covered. It is important to know the level of your stock and the expected fluctuations in this level. You should also check whether your policy covers stock on consignment and also property owned by clients. Consider the case in which a business making and repairing boat canopies and covers had a fire causing total loss. Would the seat covers and canopies owned by clients and awaiting repair be covered by the policy?

4 Water damage

This insurance covers loss due not to the fire but to water damage from sprinklers, fire hoses, or even leaks in the roof and walls.

Loss of profits

You might have the business insured against fire and be fully compensated in the event of the destruction of your premises. However, while the premises are being rebuilt expenses such as rent, loan repayments, wages, periodic payments and so on still have to be met. This policy should enable you to survive until you are able to trade again.

Burglary

This policy is designed to protect you from loss or theft of stock and other assets on your premises. Care should be taken to understand exactly what is covered by this type of policy, which deals with loss through forced entry and any resulting damage such as broken windows, doors and locks. Also check to see whether this policy covers you for loss of a client's property stolen while it is on your premises.

Cash

As we have seen, cash is the lifeblood of any business and should be protected whether it is:

- on the premises
- in transit
- at home, or
- handled by staff.

1 Cash on the premises

Insurance against loss of cash on the premises usually means insurance against armed hold-up. In the event of an armed hold-up, it is wise to remember that no amount of money is worth the cost of a life or a limb, so if you are unfortunate enough to be held up, do as they say — don't try to be a hero. If you are covered by your policy (that is, within the limits of the money you said you would have on the premises) and you can prove the exact amount you have lost, you will have no trouble recovering it all from the insurance company.

(Author's note: I was personally held up by a man with a sawn-off .22 calibre rifle. When the police caught this man and recovered the rifle they found it fully loaded. Fortunately he did not panic and pull the trigger, as did the person who shot a fellow shop-owner and left him a quadriplegic.)

2 Cash in transit

This is a favourite target for robbers. Money has to be carried to and from banks and often in vehicles as the business person moves from job to job. The key to protection, apart from insurance, is to use your common sense. Selecting different times to go to the bank, not carrying bank bags as a walking advertisement to would-be thieves, and not counting money at the till in full view of the public are all sensible precautions.

3 Cash at home

Many small business people take their day's takings home for safety, or to count or prepare the banking paperwork for the next day. If the insurance company has not been made aware of this practice and the home is burgled and money stolen, they will usually neither accept responsibility nor pay for the loss.

4 Staff losses

When a small business person runs the risk of losing large amounts of money through embezzlement or misappropriation by staff, a fidelity insurance cover should be taken out. Such a policy should be carefully discussed with your insurer.

Goods in transit

This type of policy covers materials being transported to and from the place of business by road, rail and/or air. In the case of an export business, separate cover should be sought, especially if the goods are carried by sea.

Machinery

Machinery is prone to breakdowns and these breakdowns can be insured against. When looking at breakdown or repair policies remember that stock can be spoiled or destroyed — especially in refrigerated areas. Check to see that your policy covers such a loss. Insurance can also be taken out on electronic machinery, including computers and the re-entering of lost data and programmes.

Motor vehicles

There are two non-compulsory motor vehicle policies to be considered:

1 Comprehensive motor vehicle insurance

This is for the vehicle itself (including theft) and for damage to other people's property as a result of an accident with the vehicle.

2 Third party property damage only

This covers only the damage to other people's property resulting from an accident caused by your vehicle. It does not cover damage to your own vehicle.

Tenant liability

This insurance is designed to cover you as a tenant from damage resulting from negligent actions by you or your staff. Your landlord will normally carry insurance on the premises you are renting, but if it can be proven that the negligence was yours, the onus will be on you to recoup the damage. An example of this would be if you (or your staff) left a heater on overnight which caused the building to burn down. *The growth of litigation against business owners makes it critical that you protect yourself against loss through claims that can or could be covered by insurance*

The policies included in this brief summary are *not*, by any means, a complete list of all the risks which should be insured against. This summary is simply designed as a lay person's introduction to the ever-changing insurance cover available to small business operators.

Which insurance policies do you need?

You will be taking out insurance for one of two reasons — either because:

1 it is compulsory by law, or because
2 you want to cover yourself and your business against financial loss.

As you will probably not be able to afford all the insurance you need, you must decide which risks you consider should be covered first. To help you decide this, insurance companies offer package deals (for example, a retail package for shopkeepers). These packages should include all the key policies and are designed to be tailored to the needs of the individual business. They are now being written in 'simple English' to explain to the lay person the coverage and limitations of the policies. As a general rule: the best advice to any small business is to list the key risks facing the business, consider the cost of covering those risks, and then consider the cost of *not* covering those same risks.

Insurance checklist

The checklist in Table 12.1 has been provided to assist you in your decision regarding insurance cover that you should be purchasing. As stated above, most insurance companies are offering policies which seek to provide cover for the most common forms of loss. These packages all differ and the following checklist is a means of helping you evaluate these packages and decide on the completeness or otherwise of the cover they provide for your business. It would be nice to be able to take out cover against *all* risks, but you must value the benefits of insurance against the cost. In doing so, remember that there are some insurance risks that you *cannot* afford to take.

In discussing the insurance checklist with your advisers, you might ask them about:

- replacement cost versus book value, and their recommendations
- under-insurance and your business
- the availability of cover notes and no-claim bonuses
- the merits of payments by instalments versus single payments.

After all this has been discussed, ask them to give you a cover proposal that is tailored for *your* business and *your* budget.

TABLE 12.1 Insurance checklist for small business

Please tick any areas you consider relevant			
ITEM	✓	**ITEM**	✓
Yourself		**Your premises** (cont)	
Your superannuation		Loss of rental income	
Your life cover		Glass	
Your disability		— internal	
Your personal accident		— external	
		— signs/alarms	
Your partners		— damage to stock	
Partnership insurance		— illuminated signs	
Life cover		— specified items	
Superannuation		— temporary shuttering	
Disability			
Personal accident		**Are you covered if damage is caused by**	
		Fire	
Your fellow directors		Earthquake	
Life insurance		Explosion	
Superannuation		Riots	
Key person		Water — falling	
Professional indemnity		Water — rising (eg floods)	
		Lightning	
Your staff		Impact — vehicles	
Superannuation		Impact — other	
Worker's compensation		Product failures	
Key person		Negligence	
Employee dishonesty			
Tenant liability		**Your assets**	
Professional indemnity		Plant & equipment	
Rehabilitation		Motor vehicle	
Travel insurance		— compulsory	
Trauma counselling		— other	
Your premises		Stock (NB insurance ceiling)	
(Loss, destruction or damage)		Stock in transit	
Buildings		Consignment stock	
Stock (your own)		Client's stock	
Stock (under your control)		Machinery breakdown	
Plant & equipment		— spoilt stock	
Tenant liability		— accidental damage	
Your car park		— fusion	
Lease liabilities		— repairs	
Public risk		Electronic equipment	
Relocation		— loss of records	
Demolition of damaged property		— increased working costs due to breakdown	
Removal of debris			
Replacement of records			
Consultants' fees (eg architect)		— virus damage and restoration	
Temporary repairs/ protection		— loss of income	
		Intellectual property	

(continued over)

TABLE 12.1 cont

Please tick any areas you consider relevant			
ITEM	✓	**ITEM**	✓
Your assets (cont) Cash — on premises — in transit — in locked safe — at home — in custody of staff — theft — burglary — employee dishonesty Business interruption — loss of profits — restoration costs		**Your assets** (cont) — increased operation costs — loss of rental income Customers and/or general public — public risk — product liability — professional indemnity — contractual liability — liability under your lease	
Comments		**Comments**	

How should you buy insurance?

As a small business owner you should not be backward in seeking advice. You should check with other small business people and professionals, such as your accountant, solicitor or bank manager, for the names of reputable insurance companies, insurance agents (representatives of insurance companies) and insurance brokers (independent professionals who shop around for the best insurance package). Having established a short list, you should telephone at least three agents or brokers and get them to come and see you at your place of business or your home. (If they won't come to you, what type of service can you expect if you sign up?)

When they come to see you, let them know that you are seeing other agents or brokers, and do not sign until you have considered all proposals.

This approach should give you:

- at least three quotes
- a cross-check on each agent or broker
- the best price-cum-benefits deal (the cheapest policy is not always the best for you), and
- a greater awareness of the policies you will need.

Remember that insurance policies vary greatly and rarely are two policies from different companies identical. Use the insurance checklist as a discussion point with each agent or broker.

When you have approached and listened to at least three experts, remember that the final decision is yours and not theirs — it is your business and your money.

After you have bought the insurance, don't be frightened to ask for service and advice. If your broker or agent will not visit you or help you with claims and other matters — go elsewhere. Do not fall into the trap of initially selecting one insurance agent or broker and then renewing each year without seeing what else is offering. It will pay financially to shop around each time you buy insurance, and in most cases a good agent or broker will produce the best deal.

Insurance conclusion

The main points made in this part of the chapter are:

- Insurance is a way of providing financial protection against a real risk of loss.
- Three insurance covers are compulsory for small business: worker's compensation, motor vehicle third party and superannuation.
- Many types of insurance cover are available to you, and there is no standard list of policies for every new business.
- Discuss your particular needs with at least three brokers or agents before you buy any insurance. (Make full use of your insurance checklist.)
- The decision on how you insure is yours! You have to tailor *your* needs to *your* business and especially to *your* budget.

LEGAL CHECKLIST FOR SMALL BUSINESS

So far in this chapter we have looked at the different types of business structures available to small business, at business names and at insurance. The next step is to look at a legal checklist which should be examined by all potential small business owners. This checklist is a self-help organiser designed to show the areas that will probably need legal consideration.

TABLE 12.2 Legal checklist for small business

Item	Authority	Yes	No
Location			
Is it possible to operate as a home industry or home occupation?	Local council		
Is the area zoned for			
shops	Local council		
factories	Local council		
offices	Local council		
other commercial	Local council		
Are there any plans to change this zoning?	Local council		
Which local government regulations apply?			
development applications	Local council		
building permits	Local council		
height restrictions	Local council		
parking requirements	Local council		
landscaping	Local council		
signs	Local council		
structural alterations	Local council		
other	Local council		
Shops			
Do I require any			
shop licences	Local State Small Business Agency		
health regulations	Local council		
trading hours	State Department of Industrial Relations		
fire regulations	Fire brigade		
licences for			
— cigarettes	State government		
— milk	State government		
— smallgoods and fast food	Local council		
— postage stamps	Australia Post		
— recorded music	Australian Performing Arts Association		
business name	State Corporate/Consumer Affairs		
company name	Australian Securities Commission		
company number	Australian Securities Commission		
waste water	State sewerage authority		
electricity and gas	State municipal authority		
environment protection	State environment and planning		
lifts/escalators	State Department of Industrial Relations		

TABLE 12.2 cont

Item	Authority	Yes	No
Shops (cont)			
flammable liquids	State Department of Industrial Relations		
scales, weights and measures	State Consumer Affairs		
award rates	State Department of Industrial Relations		
lay-by sales	State Consumer Affairs		
drugs	Department of Health		
poisons	Department of Health		
second-hand dealers	Court of Petty Sessions		
lease agreements	Solicitor and some state and federal government departments		
Factories			
Do I require any			
landscaping	Local council		
boilers	State Department of Industrial Relations		
flammable liquids/explosives	State Department of Industrial Relations		
safety	State Department of Industrial Relations		
waste disposal	State pollution board State sewerage authority		
scaffolding/lifts, etc	State Department of Industrial Relations		
signs	Local council		
roadside signs	Local council and government roads department		
employees' safety	State Department of Industrial Relations		
apprentices	State apprentice committee		
fire prevention	Local fire department		
electricity	Local electricity authority		
gas	Local gas authority		
weights and measures	State Consumer Affairs		
lease agreements	Solicitor and some state and federal government departments		
award rates	State Department of Industrial Relations		
business name	State Corporate Affairs Office		
licences	State Small Business Agency		
Insurance			
See insurance checklist in Table 12.1	Insurance agent/broker		

TABLE 12.2 cont

Item	Authority	Yes	No
Key licences			
Do I require licences for			
boat handling			
building			
export			
firearms			
hawker			
importing			
investment adviser			
liquor sales			
market stalls	Refer Small Business Agency/ Business Licence Information Service		
milk vendors			
mobile vendor's stand			
money lending			
motor vehicle			
my factory			
my office			
my own trade			
my shop			
plant operators			
real estate			
restaurants			
taxi operators			
tour operators			
Taxation			
What must I do regarding			
capital gains tax			
company tax			
fringe benefits tax			
income tax			
land tax	Accountant/financial adviser and Australian Taxation Office		
payroll tax			
prescribed payments tax			
provisional tax			
sales tax			
stamp duty			
superannuation levy			
tax file number			
training guarantee			
Staff			
What records must I keep and which departments must I contact?			
wage book/time sheets			
tax payments			
employment declarations	Accountant/financial adviser and Australian Taxation Office		
tax file numbers			
relevant awards			
annual and long service leave records			

TABLE 12.2 cont

Item	Authority	Yes	No
Protection What are the laws on:			
patents	Patents, Trade Marks and Designs Office		
registered design	Patents, Trade Marks and Designs Office		
copyright	Australian Copyright Council		
trade marks	Patents, Trade Marks and Designs Office		

This list is designed simply to start you thinking about legal issues related to your starting in business. Due to name changes of government departments and individual state preferences, general titles for various government departments have been used in the checklist. Your best source of detailed information on your proposed business is your own state small business advisory service. This organisation will have highly qualified staff who can assist people wanting to go into business or people already in business.

The services available in New South Wales are representative of the services available from the small business agencies or corporations in each state. They include:

Advisory

- Free confidential counselling services by qualified staff in all areas of business management.
- Provision of impartial and professional information in the areas of marketing, finance, planning, restructuring, loan applications, etc.
- Referrals to industry and other business sources of information.

First base

- Assistance to people going into business for the first time. This includes access to library information, publications, self-help computer terminals and general information on licences, business information, trade associations, etc.

Advocacy services

- Provision of staff and a mechanism to mediate in disputes in small business involving the applicant and other businesses, government departments, landlords, suppliers, etc.

Business expansion

- The provision of independent professional advice or help, often on a subsidised consultancy basis. The Business Expansion Scheme guidelines, pertaining to both proposed and existing business ventures, are available at the relevant offices.

Training

- The provision of training workshops in such areas as:
  - —going into business for the first time
  - —buying a business
  - —becoming a franchise
  - —financial planning
  - —franchising
  - —women in business
  - —marketing, etc.

The addresses of the small business head offices throughout Australia are shown below.

Small business offices —all states of Australia

Small Business Development Corporation
5th Floor, Queen Adelaide Place
545 Queen Street
BRISBANE 4000
Telephone: (07) 834 6789
Fax 5th Floor: (07) 832 3827
Fax Ground Floor: (07) 832 1221

Department of Industries and Development
Harbourview Plaza
Cnr McMinn and Bennett Streets
DARWIN 0800
Telephone: (089) 89 4295/19 3111
Fax: (089) 89 4382

Small Business Corporation of South Australia
74 South Terrace
ADELAIDE 5000
Telephone: (08) 212 5344
Fax: (08) 231 2742

Small Business Development Corporation
NZI Securities House
553 Hay Street
PERTH 6000
Telephone: (09) 325 3388
Fax: (09) 325 3981

Small Business Development Corporation
100 Exhibition Street
MELBOURNE 3000
Telephone: (03) 655 3300
Fax: (03) 650 2832

Small business offices —all states of Australia cont

Small Business Service
Tasmanian Development Authority
Lands Department Building
134 Macquarie Street
HOBART 7000
Telephone: (002) 20 6712
Fax: (002) 23 3535

Office of Industry and Development
GPO Box 158
CANBERRA 2601
Telephone: (06) 246 3071
Fax: (06) 247 3449

Small Business Council of Australia
Ring Small Business Unit on (06) 246 3071 or NSW
Representative Peter Fritz on (06) 699 8300

Office of Small Business
Department of Business and Regional Development

Head Office
Level 3, 1 Fitzwilliam Street
PARRAMATTA NSW 2150
PO Box 242, PARRAMATTA 2124
Telephone: (02) 895 0555
Fax: (02) 635 6859
NSW toll free 008 45 1511

492 David Street
ALBURY 2640
Telephone: (060) 41 3222
Fax: (060) 21 8828

85 Faulkner Street
ARMIDALE 2350
Telephone: (067) 73 7244
Fax: (067) 72 9954

142 Argent Street
BROKEN HILL 2280
Telephone: (080) 87 8033
Fax: (080) 88 5100

50 Wingewarra Street
DUBBO 2830
Telephone: (068) 84 2611
Fax: (068) 84 2486

40 Mann Street
GOSFORD 2250
Telephone: (043) 24 6300
Fax: (043) 24 5870

205 Auburn Street
GOULBURN 2580
Telephone: (048) 22 1277
Fax: (048) 22 1280

Office of Small Business
Department of Business and Regional Development cont

50 Victoria Street GRAFTON 2640 Telephone: (066) 43 1705 Fax: (066) 43 1405	251 Wharf Road NEWCASTLE 2300 Telephone: (049) 29 5818 Fax: (049) 26 1817
225 Lords Place ORANGE 2800 Telephone: (063) 63 1766 Fax: (063) 61 3956	Shop 4, The Port 68–70 Clarence Street PORT MACQUARIE 2444 Telephone: (065) 84 1330 Fax: (065) 84 1225
Cnr Peel and White Streets TAMWORTH 2340 Telephone: (067) 66 3155 Fax: (067) 66 4343	45–51 Morgan Street WAGGA WAGGA 2650 Telephone: (069) 21 5166 Fax: (069) 21 7439

HANDY LEGAL HINTS

This book does not attempt to give legal advice — rather it seeks to make you, the reader, aware of some of the legal aspects of small business. This awareness should help you to work more effectively with your solicitor and with the various local, state and commonwealth government departments and authorities.

Some of the questions that intending small business owners ask are:

1 How do I find a good solicitor?
2 What is entailed in buying or renting premises?
3 What does employing staff entail?
4 How does credit legislation affect me?
5 How does consumer legislation apply to my business?

1 How do I find a good solicitor?

As with any other adviser, it pays to make certain you have a good one.

There are various methods you should use:

- Create a shortlist after obtaining referrals from other small business people, your accountant and your bank manager. It might help to also check with the Law Society in your state.
- Unless there are exceptional circumstances, it is worthwhile to have a local solicitor who can give you immediate service. Refer to your telephone book.

- Be wary about having the vendor's solicitor represent you also if you are buying a business, as one solicitor cannot serve two clients, each of whom needs maximum protection.
- Make sure you can speak to the solicitor in 'your' language. Find out your solicitor's first name, fees and services offered. If he or she won't give you this information, or you are dissatisfied, *get another solicitor*. Remember that solicitors work for you — not you for them. You *employ* them to handle *your* legal affairs.

2 What is entailed in buying or renting premises?

The first advice is to work through a solicitor rather than try to do it yourself. The advantages in buying business premises are just the same as in buying a house — independence, security, prestige and freedom from rent payments. But be careful! The large cash outlay could mean poor liquidity, restricted borrowing ability and high loan repayments. It is interesting to note that many of the large retail firms are selling their real estate and leasing it back.

If you are in a situation in which you can choose between renting and buying, have your accountant look at all aspects to help you make the best decision.

If you are leasing business premises, make sure you have a lease for your own protection. This is normally drawn up by the landlord's solicitor; and you, as the tenant, are expected to pay for the cost of this service. You also have to pay your own solicitor to check the lease agreement and see that it suits your requirements. Remember that a lease is a binding legal contract and should not be taken lightly.

The key factors to look for in any lease are:

- The rent payments and any additional charges that are included. (Do you have to pay water rates, electricity, council rates (or increases in rates), shopping-centre management charges or land taxes? Is there an escalation clause in the lease? How often and in what manner can the rent be varied?)
- The terms of renewing the lease. (In the event of a dispute, what referee has been appointed for arbitration?)
- Any special conditions or clauses in the lease. (Can you sublet? Can you transfer your lease? Are you responsible for property insurance?)

Remember — the lease is for your protection as well as for the landlord. Your business continuity might only be as good as your lease.

3 What does employing staff entail?

The law relating to the employment of staff is complex, but there are a few basic pointers for small business people.

Awards — A copy of the relevant award must be on the premises and available to staff. This document will set down employment conditions, including hours of work, holidays and other leave, rates of pay and other related matters. Details of award rates are available from the state department of labour and industry, your trade association and the employees' unions.

Wages book — A wages book must be kept, showing hours worked, rates of pay, deductions and so on. (This area is fully covered in Chapter 20.)

Termination of staff — The method of termination, together with the rights of the employer and employee, are spelt out in the award. If there is any doubt about this area, consult your professional advisers and/or the appropriate commonwealth or state departments of labour.

Superannuation — You are now responsible for the payment of employee superannuation contributions.

Worker's compensation — You must cover all employees with worker's compensation insurance.

Training — If your wages bill exceeds $214 000 per annum you must demonstrate that you are complying with the Training Guarantee Scheme.

4 How does credit legislation affect me?

Credit legislation has placed very tight restrictions on the granting of credit — especially in the areas of:

- the rate of interest charged
- the instructions to borrowers
- the liability of lenders
- instructions to the lender.

If your business is involved in selling by credit you should be aware of this legislation and its ramifications and consult with your solicitor and/or accountant.

5 How does consumer legislation apply to my business?

The Trade Practices Act is aimed at protecting the Australian consumer from false and misleading claims and conduct by suppliers of goods and services. The act is well documented and does not seek to put restrictions upon fair and honest traders. Rather, it seeks to protect consumers by prohibiting unfair and deceptive practices and imposing heavy fines on offenders.

The Trade Practices Act is the Australian model for consumer protection legislation and as such, is usually identified with, and applied to, test cases with larger corporations. Each state has its own consumer protection legislation based upon the Trade Practices Act. It is the state legislation, such as the Fair Trading Act in New South Wales, that is enforced daily to regulate consumer (and business) protection. Each state has its own consumer/corporate affairs department to regulate this act which covers areas such as:

- a system of fair trading as opposed to misleading or deceptive conduct in the marketplace
- accurate and reliable information as opposed to false and misleading information
- sales techniques — so that they are fair and not misleading or one-sided
- product standards for a wide variety of goods, together with information on those goods and their safety standards
- remedies for both retailers and consumers for breaches of the Fair Trading Act
- an alternative to the courts for the settlement of disputes in areas covered by the Fair Trading Act (in New South Wales the Consumer Claims Tribunal and the Building Disputes Tribunal)
- implied conditions and warranties that are available to the consumer
- the enforcement of a fair and equitable system in areas such as credit, lay-by sales, etc.

Summary

The legal checklist and the handy hints provided here are designed to start you thinking about your obligations, restrictions and responsibilities in the eyes of the law. It is not expected that you become an expert in these matters — rather, that you have a working knowledge of your legal framework.

There are two well-used sayings about solicitors:

1 'The person who defends himself in court usually has a fool for a client.'
2 'The best thing about having a good solicitor is the knowledge that you do have one.'

Key words

contract
co-operative
insurance
insurance agent
insurance broker
lease
partnership
proprietary limited company
sole trader
structure
trust

Review exercises

1 (a) Consider the legal forms in Table 12.3 (presented overleaf). Which structure do you consider to be the most appropriate for your business?
(b) Who should help you to make this decision?

2 Complete the insurance checklist in Table 12.1 and prepare a list of insurance topics to discuss with your insurance broker or agent.

3 Complete the legal checklist in Table 12.2 to highlight the legal issues needing your consideration.

Table 12.3 Summary of main legal forms of business

Item	Sole trader	Partnership	Proprietary limited company
Number	One person	2–20 partners	2–50 shareholders
Management	Sole trader	Jointly as per partnership agreement	Directors
Life of structure	Death of sole trader Bankruptcy	Death or retirement of one partner Limitations as per partnership agreement Bankruptcy	Continuous — unless wound up by shareholders or directors Dissolution or winding up
Basic documents and legal requirements	Nil Business name (if required)	Partnership agreement — in writing if partnership to last more than one year (NSW excluded) Business name (if required)	Australian company number (ACN) Memorandum of association (objectives of the company) Articles of association (rules and regulations) Certificate of incorporation Company seal Company and business names plus ACN on all documentation
Type of taxation	Provisional tax	Provisional tax	Company tax
Liability	Unlimited	Unlimited	Limited to nominal value of shares held
Approximate cost of setting up	Cost of licences plus business name if required ($75 for three years)	Partnership agreement (up to $200 as a guide) Business name, if required Plus cost of licences	Starting from scratch — approx $600 plus professional fees Shelf company — approx $1000 Trusts — depends on complexity Cost of licences
Legal status	Owner and business are the same	Partners and the business are the same	Shareholders are legally separate from the business
Advantages	Easy to set up Inexpensive Few regulations Independence Few government regulations All profits to sole trader Easy to close Total privacy	Relatively easy to start Low cost Additional capital More expertise Few government regulations Possible tax advantages (Chapter 22) Shared risk Someone to talk to Non-disclosure of profits to public	Limited liability Separate legal entity Additional capital Organised control Shares transferable Possible tax advantages (Chapter 22) Ability to control authority of shareholders through type of shares issued
Disadvantages	Unlimited liability Few tax concessions Possible lack of capital No one to talk to Lack of continuity Provisional tax	Unlimited liability Each partner equally and jointly responsible Provisional tax Possible problems with partners (Question: 'Who is the boss?') Lack of continuity	Cost of establishment Government regulations (incl returns) Possible taxation disadvantages (Chapter 22) Responsibilities of directors Charter restrictions Disclosure
Typical examples	Very small businesses and home occupations, eg crafts, smaller retail businesses One-person operations, eg electrical repairs, lawn mowing, secretarial services	Husband-wife teams especially service person with partner at home, corner store etc New businesses which will change to companies as growth occurs	Larger firms Businesses subject to high risk, eg engineering consultants Firms dealing with governments and contractors etc

CHAPTER 13

Financing your business

When you have completed your feasibility study, or business plan, you might find that some additional finance is required to achieve your objectives within the time frame you have chosen. In this chapter we look at various sources of finance for your business. When you have read it, you will have an understanding of the:

- various types of finance
- differences between the types of finance
- sources of finance
- costs of finance, and
- preparation of a submission for external finance.

Even with all the help available, you could find that the finance you need is either unavailable or too costly. If this happens, then you will need to review your objectives.

One factor, often overlooked but well worth considering, is the time frame you have chosen. Before resetting the level of achievement in your objectives, you could start by considering the time you have set in which to reach them. You might find that, by extending the time, the required finance is reduced and your chance of obtaining it increased. Also, the lower finance-servicing costs might enable you to develop a 'track record' of profitability and financial management which could make it easier to obtain finance at a future time.

By extending your time targets, you might then be able to achieve your objectives in two or more stages. Finance required for each stage would be less than the original, unobtainable amount. Your risk and hence stress levels would be lower; and, by showing that you are a reliable borrower and money manager, you improve the probability of obtaining finance for later stages.

TYPES OF FINANCE

There are two basic types of finance: equity and debt. Equity finance is capital invested in the business. There is usually no provision for the money to be repaid, but there is an expectation that the investor will share in the profits of the business. Debt finance is a loan to the owner of the business. There is a legal requirement for the debt to be repaid in full, together with a specified amount of interest. Let us have a more detailed look at each of the types of finance.

Equity finance

By far the most common source of equity is the money that an owner invests in a business. Whether you are starting a new business, buying an existing one, purchasing a franchise or expanding your own business, you will need to provide at least some of the finance. Your investment is the initial Owner's Equity. Additional funds might be provided by friends or family members. If they do not want a share of the ownership of your business then these funds would be regarded as gifts or loans to you for investment in your business, and again are part of the Owner's Equity. However, if the investment is on the basis of their sharing in the ownership, then it will be necessary to structure the business to reflect this. A partnership or company structure could be chosen.

If a partnership is formed, investments by each partner are recognised in the Partnership Funds (equity of the individual partners). When a company structure is chosen, all investors become shareholders and the total investment is the Shareholders' Funds. Each investor has shares issued in their name to the value of their own investment.

Equity finance, then, is ownership finance. The major reason for investing in a business is to gain a share of the profits. Another reason might be to gain some control of the management of the business. One of the costs of equity finance from other people could be the loss of total control of your business.

> Use of external equity finance = loss of total control.

A further impact on your business is the requirement to share the profits. Unless the business is a company, profit is used to repay loan principal, reinvest in the business and pay the owner, including the owner's tax.

Where the business is a sole proprietorship (has one owner), the owner can adjust the balance between reinvestment and drawings (his or her pay) to suit his or her own personal and business objectives. A simple example of this is the retail store owner who elects to take lower drawings for a few months, and invest some more equity in additional stock for the business. More of the profits are directed to reinvestment and less to the owner's pay.

This freedom can be restricted when equity financing is used. The external investor/owner expects some return. This must be allowed for, along with the repayment of any loan principal, and the remainder can then be divided between the owner/manager and reinvestment.

Naturally, the profit should be higher if external finance is used as well as the original owner's investment so there should be a larger profit to divide between the various owners and uses. However, this is not always the situation. In slow trading times, or when the equity funding is used to purchase assets which will not become fully productive for some years, the profits might not be adequate to cover payments to the external investor/owner,tax and loan principal repayments, or provide a minimum reward for the owner/manager and funds for reinvestment.

As with all other aspects of your business, the use of equity finance should be approached carefully and the full implications studied in advance. Costs must be calculated, and their impact on cash flow in times of low profit determined. Also, you need to take into account the loss of total control of your business. If you decide after thorough analysis that equity capital is desirable, you will find the sources listed later in this chapter very valuable.

Debt finance

Most businesses face a situation at some time when additional temporary funding is necessary. This might be for a period of a few months or for several years. Borrowing, or debt, is the best way of financing these situations.

A loan is arranged by the business owner, who enters into a legal contract to repay the money borrowed (the principal) together with a predetermined borrowing charge (the interest). On loans for business purposes the interest charges are a legitimate business expense, and will have the effect of reducing profits and hence the tax payable. Two major factors to be considered when arranging debt finance are the interest rate and the term (length of time allowed for repayment) of the loan. Interest rates determine the cost of the financing, which is discussed later in this chapter. The term of the loan should be selected to suit the purpose for which the money is borrowed.

Loans are repaid from profits. It follows from this that debt finance should be used only for purposes that will increase profits. This increase must be sufficient to cover the repayment of the loan and all costs. Funds may be used to increase stock, or to purchase a new machine or some other asset. Whatever the use, you must be able to show that, by making the purchase, your profits will increase. In the case of stock, this could sell within a few months, thus generating enough profit to repay the loan in this time. If the purchase is of a machine or property it might take years to generate sufficient additional profits.

When the need is to meet a situation of only short duration, then money should be borrowed only for a short term. Additional stock is an example of a short-term need, and credit terms from suppliers, a bank overdraft or a commercial bill would be appropriate short-term financing arrangements. However, a loan for new production machinery or for property would best be arranged for a much longer term. By doing this, you can avoid taking too high a risk, while keeping the financing costs to a minimum.

> Borrow money only for as long as it takes for added profits to equal the amount borrowed.

If you try to repay the loan too quickly you might starve the business of funds needed for other purposes, or reduce your own income to an inadequate level. If the loan is spread over too long a time, the total interest paid will be higher, and you might reduce your chances of gaining further loans during this time, which could limit future opportunities for growth of your business.

A lender does not usually have any desire to play a role in the management of your business. You retain full control of the business operation. However, the lender might require regular information regarding the progress of your business. A condition of the loan might be that you provide copies of your financial statements to the lender. These will enable the lender to check that additional profits are sufficient to repay the loan as planned. They will also show whether you have entered into any other commitments that might affect the level of risk of the loan.

Differences between equity and debt financing

Each type of finance has its advantages and disadvantages. Equity finance is an investment of capital in the business. It does not usually need to be repaid, but until it is, it requires a share of the profits each year. If it is obtained from outside the business your level of control over your business might be reduced because others now have a stake in the ownership. When it is provided by the owner, the availability of funds for other uses might be limited. Also, the owner needs a higher return to compensate for the larger investment, and this requires increased profits. The cost of equity finance continues until it is repaid, or for the life of the business.

Debt finance must be repaid within a specified time. Whether sales and profits are high or low, the debt must be repaid. It has a known cost, which is a legitimate business expense. If repayments are not made on time, you might damage or lose your business. However, while this is a risk, in the meantime you at least retain full control of your own business.

Clearly the choice of appropriate finance depends on the purpose of the funding. Where the purpose is to change the entire nature of the business — for example, to increase its size by moving from owning one shop to having a chain of shops, or to franchise the operations — then equity finance would be appropriate, because the need to fund future growth would probably continue for the life of the business. Debt financing, on the other hand, is more appropriate when the purpose of the funds is for a specific asset such as stock, machinery, vehicles, etc. The choice of funding method will also be affected by availability and cost, and these are detailed below.

SOURCES OF FINANCE

While most people immediately think of banks and finance companies as sources of finance, there are many more sources than just these. Some of these sources fund only existing businesses, others are available to both existing and new businesses.

Existing businesses

Funds can often be made available from within existing businesses. These funds might be sufficient to meet all immediate needs. Even if they are not totally adequate, the effort made in searching for them and freeing them will ensure that the business is being well managed and efficiently run. Also, funds made available from within the business will reduce the amount needed to be found externally, and increase the probability of you obtaining them. Freeing up funds from within your business involves looking closely at:

- assets
- customers, and
- suppliers.

Assets

Assets include debtors, stock, pre-paid expenses, vehicles, plant and equipment, fittings and property. Each of these is a possible source of funds.

Debtors can have the use of your money for months. The total amount you have out on loan to your customers can be reduced by following them up promptly after the due date. Also, this might provide a good opportunity to review your credit terms, reducing them to 14 or 7 days for some or all of your customers.

If you are billing your customers monthly, you might be able to change the billing date to mid-month so that your account is one of the first your customers receive, and therefore pay, each month.

In some businesses, accounts are sent with the goods or services when they are delivered. By using this system, the due date for accounts to become payable is calculated from the date of delivery, rather than from the end of the month.

A further way of having debts paid more promptly is to offer an incentive such as a discount for early payment. All possible approaches should be tried, with the aim of improving the cash flow into your business.

Another way to reduce the time you wait for payment is through factoring. Factoring is a process in which debts are sold to a finance company. You send a copy of your customer invoices to the finance company, which pays you the amount, less a commission, promptly — usually within seven days. Thus, although your customers might not pay for 30 days or more, you in fact receive (most of) the cash much sooner. Because the funds made available through factoring increase as sales grow, this method is especially suited to expansion projects.

Many businesses have excessive capital tied up in stock. There are two ways in which this occurs: simply by carrying high levels of items that can be obtained from suppliers on short notice; and by having too many slow-moving items and too few fast-moving ones. Capital employed in stock can be minimised by regularly studying your stock levels and turnover rates, and reviewing your purchasing. Even when the purpose of additional funds is to increase stock, it might be possible to replace some slow-moving items with new, more popular or faster-moving lines. Your stock review should take this into account, together with current lead times (lead time is the time between order and delivery). An item-by-item stock review often reveals that changes have occurred in demand and supply patterns which you weren't aware of. These changes are opportunities to reduce stock levels of some items, and even to have 'discontinued line' sales of slow-moving items. Again, the result is a reduction of stock, and an increase in cash.

Another place where money hides in a business is in prepaid expenses. These are costs paid in advance, usually for services. Your previous financial statements will show you the total on loan to the suppliers of these services, and your record system should provide the details of each supplier (and service) prepaid. If you pay significant amounts annually (for insurance, etc), you can approach the suppliers with a view to making lower, more frequent payments rather than one annual payment. Some businesses charge a penalty cost for providing this facility, but any cost has to be compared with the cost of obtaining additional funds outside your business. Often the penalty is actually lower than the alternative costs.

Fixed assets, which include vehicles, plant and equipment, fittings and property, can also be reviewed at this time. They are often a source of a significant amount of cash. It might be possible to sell off little-used assets and hire suitable replacements as required. One small manufacturing business actually increased productivity by doing this. The owners had an expensive machine which was needed but was used only about once every two weeks. By reviewing the manufacturing methods, they found that jobs could be batched and usage compressed into one full day per month. They sold the machine and hired a replacement for ten days each year. By doing this, they had the cash from the sale available for use elsewhere in the business.

Even when the usage is much greater, it is possible to sell the asset and lease a replacement. In some cases it is even possible to sell the asset and lease the same asset. This makes cash available from the sale, but also increases the monthly cash outflow for lease payments. However, it is often a more viable alternative than retaining ownership, raising funds externally, and still having higher monthly cash outflows to repay the external funding. Either way, cash outflows are increased, but in the sale and lease-back approach funds are made available from within the business.

Customers

Customers can also be a source of business funds. Apart from the reduction of debtors discussed previously, some of your credit customers might be willing to use their bank credit cards for purchases, rather than utilise the account facility which they have with you. They still have the benefit of up to 45 days to pay for their purchases without incurring interest costs, while for you it is almost as good as a cash transaction.

If you are planning to start a new business, you might consider not offering credit to your customers, and in this way keeping funds inside your business. Also, if you have a service business, or one that supplies a product over a period of time, it is often possible to ask for a deposit, and in some situations progress payments, rather than billing after completion and waiting a further 30 to 60 days for payment. This approach not only provides a much more even cash flow, it also helps to limit bad debts, because they become apparent much earlier in the transaction process.

Suppliers

Finally, your suppliers are a possible source of funds from inside your business. Extended payment terms for your purchases or materials give you the opportunity to obtain funds from the sale of your products and use these funds to pay your suppliers. Depending on the mark-up which you apply, you need sell only 30% to 70% of the goods before sales receipts will cover your suppliers' accounts.

The longer the time between obtaining delivery and making payment, the more chance you have of achieving the required sales level and of avoiding the need for additional funding for stock. An example of this approach was provided by a ladies' clothing boutique which had built up sales to a point where an expansion of stock into new designs and sizes was considered necessary. The owner negotiated with suppliers for one order from each to be on 90-day terms. Their agreement enabled the business to expand without the injection of additional capital from the owner, and without having to arrange additional external funding.

Only after all possible avenues inside your business have been investigated and appropriate action has been taken can you be sure not only that you are seeking a minimum of additional funds, but also that your business is operating with maximum efficiency. Any additional funds must be obtained from outside your business, as must all external funds required for a new business.

Existing and new businesses

Before approaching the financial institutions for funds, it is vital that you investigate all other avenues. We have discussed possible sources inside a business, but another possibility is your family and friends. The financial institutions will be interested to know whether you have acquired all available funds from this source, and your financing costs will be kept to a minimum if you can obtain some or all funds from personal contacts. Only after exhausting all these personal avenues should you prepare to approach external sources such as banks, finance companies and investors.

Possible funding arrangements include bank bills, bank overdrafts, term loans, commercial hire purchase, leasing and venture capital. Suppliers include trading banks, finance companies, merchant banks, investment companies and private investors. Each of these offers different terms, interest rates, other costs and availability, and therefore needs to be discussed separately.

Bank commercial bills

These are a form of very short term debt finance. The amount of the bill is advanced in full, together with interest. At the end of the term, you must repay the total amount, or roll the bill over (obtain another bill for the full amount). Bank commercial bills usually provide funds for a short period of time — between 30 and 180 days. Before issuing a bill, the bank will need to satisfy itself that there is a reasonable chance of funds being available to repay the bill when it falls due. Trading figures or a detailed business plan will therefore need to accompany your application for a bank commercial bill.

Bank overdrafts

These provide an ongoing line of credit (continuous loan) by allowing a business to withdraw money from a cheque account to a predetermined level beyond the amount of money in the account. This facility is arranged with the bank and usually reviewed annually. There is normally no requirement for fixed periodical repayments, although the bank has the right to demand full repayment within 24 hours at any time. The bank charges interest on the overdrawn amount, and may also charge a fee on the unused available funds, though at a lower rate. Both of these charges are negotiable, and business owners should attempt to have them reviewed downwards at every review time.

Term loans

Term loans are available from banks and finance companies and give access to the full amount of the loan immediately. This is then repaid, with interest, by regular equal instalments over a period of time. The amount and timing of these repayments form part of the loan contract. If the length of the loan (the term) is less than one year, the loan is regarded as short-term. One to five years is medium-term, and over five years is long-term. Some long-term loans are arranged as a series of medium-term loans, in that they are reviewed periodically and the terms and conditions re-negotiated. Some form of security or collateral is generally required before a loan is approved. This might be in the form of a charge over the assets of a business, or of the owner's assets. Should the owner default on repayments, the lender has the legal right to sell the assets in part or full repayment of the loan. If the full value of the outstanding debt is not realised from the sale of assets, the borrower remains in debt for the balance. Loans can be tailored to suit specific requirements, and details of availability, amount, interest rate and term vary widely. It is usually a requirement that a business plan be submitted as part of the application for a term loan.

Commercial hire purchase

This facility is offered by finance companies, usually for the purchase of assets to be used in the generation of income for the business. The supplier or the finance company might require a deposit. The finance company advances the price of the asset less the amount of any deposit, normally in the form of a cheque made out to the supplier of the asset. This amount, together with interest, is then repaid by the purchaser in equal instalments over a period of time. The assets become the property of the purchaser at the time of the sale. Commercial hire purchase allows a business to have the use of an asset, which should produce income in excess of that required to repay the debt. Depreciation allowances can be claimed for the asset from the date on which it is bought.

Leasing

Leasing is another way in which finance companies provide access to assets without the need for a large capital outlay. Leasing only allows a business to have the use of an asset in return for regular payments based on the value of the asset. It differs from commercial hire purchase in that ownership does not transfer to the user.

At the termination of the lease agreement, the user can purchase the asset, but this cannot be arranged or agreed in advance, or the transaction might be regarded as commercial hire purchase and this would have taxation implications. Leased assets do not attract depreciation allowances for the user; however, the lease charges are an allowable expense. With some assets which have high rates of depreciation, commercial hire purchase might be preferable, especially in the early years of their life. However, leasing often has no requirement for an initial lump-sum payment, whereas commercial hire purchase might attract a deposit.

Venture capital

This can be obtained for both new and expanding businesses. Whilst the sources discussed so far are forms of debt financing, venture capital is usually equity funding. This means that a share of the ownership is sold in return for the finance.

Companies offering venture capital often impose conditions including the minimum amount of their investment, type of business, industry, geographic location and profitability. They will not consider investment in any business which does not fall within their defined boundaries. This wide range of variations prevents any general guidelines being presented here. However, a detailed listing of over 40 possible sources is provided by the development capital section of the Department of Industry Technology and Commerce, PO Box 9839, Canberra, ACT 2601. As with other forms of major financing, a full business plan will be essential before any application would be considered.

Other forms of both venture capital and debt financing might be available from private investors. Advertisements can be found in the financial press, and you can enquire through your accountant or solicitor. Before making any approach for external financing, it is essential that you prepare a thorough plan detailing all aspects of the need for, and use of, the additional funds. This should also show the cost and details of repayments or return on investment.

COSTS OF FINANCE

As with any business resource, costs are incurred to both obtain and maintain finance. These are known as initial and on-going costs. Whether you are considering debt or equity funding, it is necessary to take these costs into account, as well as the effect on the cash flow of your business. Any drain on your cash flow could result in a further capital injection becoming necessary, or alternatively indicate the need for a greater amount of initial funding.

Initial costs

Debt financing often requires loan establishment fees, valuation charges, government charges (eg stamp duties, etc) and miscellaneous costs. There is no uniform rate for many of these costs, each lending institution setting its own fees for some or all of the services involved. A recent example of the range of charges occurred when an applicant sought funds of $100 000 to purchase a business. Approaches to various lending bodies revealed charges ranging from $280 to $3500. The message from this is clear: have a good look around, and make sure you obtain an estimate of charges, preferably in writing.

Equity funding also has initial costs for legal fees, brokerage, investigation charges, and some government fees. Again, the range of costs is very wide, depending on the details of each individual arrangement. Additional initial costs may be incurred in the preparation of a detailed submission. A thorough investigation of the business, and assistance in the preparation of a business plan, might incur professional fees payable to your accountant, specialist consultants, and your solicitor. The development of a high-quality presentation could incur costs for design and production charges.

As a general guideline, it is suggested that you allow an additional 5% of the finance required, to cover initial costs.

On-going costs

Debt financing will incur interest charges for the term of the loan. These can be determined accurately before the loan commences, as lenders are required to provide full details of the total amount to be repaid. While the interest charges are business expenses, repayments of the principal amount must be made out of the profits of the business. Equity funding is not quite so simple because the costs are in the form of dividends which are paid out of after-tax profits. Whichever type of finance is selected, the first step is to estimate future profits, and then to allow for a portion of these to be used to either repay debt funding, or service equity funding. An example will help to show the steps involved in determining the costs of financing.

Example:
Consider a business that is a sole proprietorship. The owner has $100 000 equity in the business, and $50 000 invested elsewhere at 15% pa. This could be transferred to the business as additional equity, or used as collateral for a loan.

A detailed business plan shows:

1 An additional amount of $100 000 is required. (This could be for expansion, or the example could refer to the initial purchase of a business.)
2 Profits before initial financing costs, interest and tax will probably be

$75 000. It is estimated that they could be as high as $83 000, and at worst $50 000.

Assumptions:

1 Tax is at the rate of 30%.

2 Loan will be over four years at 15% pa, reducible monthly. (The average rate of interest is 8.4% of total loan each year. The average repayment of principal is 25% of total loan each year.)

3 Funding alternatives available are:
  a) 50% equity, 50% debt
  b) 100% debt.

4 Initial financing costs will be 5% of total additional funds.

Should the owner use debt and equity funding by transferring the $50 000 investment into the business and borrowing $50 000 at 15% pa, or would it be better to leave the $50 000 invested and use it as part security for full debt financing of $100 000?

Most likely Earnings = $75 000	50% equity 50% debt	100% debt
	$	$
Equity capital	50 000	—
Debt capital	50 000	100 000
Total equity and debt	100 000	100 000
Profit before financing costs, interest and tax	75 000	75 000
Less financing costs (5%)	5 000	5 000
Profit before interest and tax	70 000	70 000
Less interest (8.4%)	4 200	8 400
Profit before tax	65 800	61 600
Less tax (30%)	19 740	18 480
Profit after tax	46 060	43 120
Repayment of loan principal	12 500	25 000
Net return to owner after tax	33 560	18 120
Owner's return on equity	22.37%	18.12 %

FIGURE 13.1 Comparison of costs for the most likely situation

Best possible Earnings = $83 000	50% equity 50 % debt	100% debt
	$	$
Equity capital	50 000	—
Debt capital	50 000	100 000
Total equity and debt	100 000	100 000
Profit before financing costs, interest and tax	83 000	83 000
Less financing costs (5%)	5 000	5 000
Profit before interest and tax	78 000	78 000
Less interest (8.4%)	4 200	8 400
Profit before tax	73 800	69 600
Less tax (30%)	22 140	20 880
Profit after tax	51 660	48 720
Repayment of loan principal	12 500	25 000
Net return to owner after tax	39 160	23 720
Owner's return on equity	26.1%	23.72%

FIGURE 13.2 Comparison of costs for the best possible situation

Worst Earnings = $50 000	50% equity 50% debt	100% debt
	$	$
Equity capital	50 000	—
Debt capital	50 000	100 000
Total equity and debt	100 000	100 000
Profit before financing costs, interest and tax	50 000	50 000
Less financing costs (5%)	5 000	5 000
Profit before interest and tax	45 000	45 000
Less interest (8.4%)	4 200	8 400
Profit before tax	40 800	36 600
Less tax (30%)	12 240	10 980
Profit after tax	28 560	25 620
Repayment of loan principal	12 500	25 000
Net return to owner after tax	16 060	620
Owner's return on equity	10.7%	0.6%

FIGURE 13.3 Comparison of costs for the worst situation

The example shows that, after allowing for loan repayments, the net return on equity for the owner is likely to be higher than is currently being obtained on the invested funds. It would appear that transfer of the invested funds to the business would be the better choice. However, if profits are less than planned, as shown in Figure 13.3 — the worst scenario — the return falls below the 15% currently being earned on invested funds. The owner would need to be very confident of project figures before transferring invested funds into the business. Again, in making any decision, it is important to consider the cash flow position as well as profits.

In the worst case scenario, there is a very small safety margin when 100% debt financing is used. The total amount available to the owner for living expenses (the owner's 'wage') is much lower with debt financing, and might not be sufficient. It can be seen that a detailed study of all the financing costs provides the information needed; however, the final decision still depends on the owner's attitude towards risk-taking.

PREPARING A SUBMISSION

When you are looking for external financing, it is important to understand the different roles of the business and the owner. Business information is needed to demonstrate to the lender or investor that their money is safe, and that there will be sufficient funds for the business to service the debt, or to provide a reasonable return on their investment. The business provides some security for their capital.

> Business profits provide security for lenders' or investors' capital.

However, you, as the business manager, will be responsible for managing their money. They are therefore concerned about your reliability, experience and management ability.

> Finance is lent to (or invested with) you as a person.

Very simply, we could say, 'Banks lend money to people.' Your submission for finance must show not only that the business is a sound risk, but also that you are a competent person to manage it.

Supporting the application

Business details needed to support your application include a thorough plan for your business for the next three to five years. This must show clear goals and detailed strategies as to how you intend to achieve them.

All planned income and costs must be shown, together with projected balance sheets, and income and expenditure statements. Most importantly, a projected cash flow for the next 12 months, including leasing costs, interest and repayments of a loan, or returns on equity, must be provided. Details of the industry your business operates in, and the outlook for it in the immediate future, are valuable to support your plan, and to substantiate its credibility.

If your business has been operating for some time, historical figures will be needed to show the basis for future projections. A detailed discussion of the preparation of a business plan can be found in Chapter 14. Your plan must leave no questions unanswered. It must stand alone, because you will probably have no opportunity to answer questions or expand on any points raised in it.

In addition to your plan, you will need to provide a clear statement of the amount of finance required, and the purpose for which it is needed. Explain why you have chosen the particular form of finance, detailing the alternatives available. Show the precise amounts to be applied to various assets within your business. As with the example in Figures 13.1, 13.2 and 13.3, give a range of possible future scenarios — most likely, best and worst — explaining the operating factors that could cause variations.

Finally, support your submission with letters from customers, signed contracts, articles from the financial press or your trade association publications. These will substantiate your claims that your business is sound and operating in an industry and economic environment which indicate a successful future.

Personal details

Your personal details will need to be as thorough as those for your business. Your qualifications and experience in this business, this *type* of business, and this industry are essential. In addition, you should include any other experience in business, community or social organisations that demonstrates management ability, competence and desirable personal characteristics. The purpose of this section of your submission is to demonstrate that you have the qualifications, experience, aptitude and attitude required to take responsibility for, and manage, other people's money in a business situation. Picture yourself in the other person's place. What would you want to know about someone to whom you were considering giving your money to manage?

One approach to the preparation of this section is to imagine that your business is a subsidiary of a bank or finance company and you are applying for the position of general manager. Talk to personnel managers in large companies, or employment agencies, and ask them what they look for when selecting managers. Then show that you have what is required. You will find there are some aspects in which you are not strong. Do not hide them, otherwise the reader of your submission might think that you regard them as unimportant. Admit that you know they are necessary and explain what you plan to do about your lack of strength in them. This might include further education or other self-development, or the use of external specialists or consultants (name them), or employing a competent person on a full-time or part-time basis. Include these future actions as part of your business plan.

A simple example of this approach is in managing the taxation aspects of your business. Unless you are a qualified tax agent, it is better to refer to one when required, rather than attempt to develop the skills and knowledge yourself. This same approach can be applied to any aspect of your business where you lack all the necessary expertise. Showing that you understand what is required, and that you know when and whom to ask for help, can be a much better approach than trying to persuade someone that you know everything already. They might think that you don't fully realise how much there is to be known!

Presentation

When you have fully prepared your submission, it is time to consider its presentation. You could hand write it neatly, and photocopy it for submission with your application. However, after all the work you have put into it, it is worth ensuring that it achieves maximum impact on the reader. You can best do this by taking it to a professional word-processing service and having it set up and printed on a laser printer. You can find these services listed in the Yellow Pages under 'Secretarial and Typing Services' and 'Word Processing Services'. Have at least five copies prepared, so that you can present a potential investor or lender with multiple copies if required. If you are sending a covering letter with your submission, also have this done professionally.

The preparation and professional presentation of a thorough business plan, including your personal details, and the careful selection of the type and source of finance, will not guarantee acceptance of your submission, but it will ensure that you have done everything possible to achieve a successful result.

SUMMARY

Every business needs additional finance at some time. It might be only once, but more commonly it happens several times. The type of finance that is most appropriate depends on the need at the time. It could be the need for short-term funds to increase stock levels, or for a specific market promotion; or the need might be for long-term capital to purchase a new machine or premises, or to franchise the operation. The owner might have access to additional funds from within the business, through under-utilised assets, or through personal contacts, or might need to look outside the business.

When seeking external funds, selling a share of the ownership might be the best way to finance the need. An alternative might be to borrow funds, or to consider a combination of different types of finance. Whilst finance is rarely easy to obtain, a number of possible sources can be investigated.These include sources within the business, as well as banks, finance companies, venture capital companies, brokers, and private investors.

Costs of financing vary depending on the type and source, and if alternatives are available then costs should be compared. The cost might also persuade you that the additional finance would best be obtained some time in the future, rather than at this time.

Even though obtaining finance is rarely easy, you can ensure the best chance of success by careful and thorough preparation and presentation of a submission to the most appropriate source.

Key words

factoring
loan principal
prepaid expenses
turnover
venture capital

Review exercises

1 Briefly describe the differences between equity and debt finance.

2 Why should funds be borrowed for as long as it will take the increased profits to repay the loan?

3 What is meant by 'factoring'?

4 Where can funds possibly be freed up within a business?

5 Briefly describe the difference between a bank overdraft and a term loan.

6 How does commercial hire purchase differ from leasing?

7 Why is it necessary to give full details of the business and the owner(s) in a submission for external financing?

8 How can the inclusion of articles from the financial or trade press assist your submission for finance?

9 What is the purpose of including a detailed section about the management of your business in your submission?

3

Succeeding

Whereas the previous section of this book looked at the feasibility of going into business, this section assumes that you are already in business.

Anyone in business should be constantly asking themselves the following three questions:

- Why am I in business?
- What do I want from my business?
- What must I do to achieve my objectives?

This third section of the book is designed to help you answer these three questions. It starts with an overview of planning and provides a simple but practical approach to allow you to write your own business plan. This plan is, in reality, a combination of four separate plans, namely:

- an operational plan
- a marketing plan
- a staff plan and
- a financial plan.

To assist you in writing these plans for your own (or assumed) business, this section includes chapters on key areas such as record keeping, financial management, planning and marketing. It goes on to look at the specialised skills that are needed in the areas of retailing, production, employing staff, and time management. After an overview of taxation, this section concludes by discussing the often neglected area of owner/manager stress.

CHAPTER 14

Your business plan

Everyone plans, somewhere, some time, somehow! We all make decisions, choices, look at the future, organise and even prepare for future events. Much of this planning is very short-term, reactive and ad hoc.

In this chapter, we will be looking at planning, but the planning we will be discussing is the organised and formal planning that is critical to the success of any business. It is planning that is based upon research and fact and is organised in a methodical manner. Planning is simply deciding in advance (and that means now) what to do, how to do it, when to do it, who will do it, and which resources will be involved.

With this explanation in mind, this chapter has been divided into two parts. The first part is an overall look at small business planning in Australia, while the second part is concerned with planning your own (or assumed) business.

After working through this chapter you will be able to:

- explain the importance of planning
- discuss the role of planning in small business
- list the guidelines of small business planning
- identify the barriers to planning
- plan to be different
- write your own business plan, and finally
- rate your own planning ability.

Let us now look at the first part of this chapter — an overview of planning by small business in Australia.

PART A — AN OVERVIEW OF PLANNING

Perhaps the best starting point in looking at an overview of small business planning is to establish the guidelines that are peculiar to small business.

> Small business owners should not copy big business planning methods.

There are many reasons why planning methods which are appropriate for use in large companies are totally unsuitable in small firms. The financial circumstances of most small firms are such that they cannot possibly employ the specialised and more complex planning procedures and techniques used in many (but not all!) large firms. In those small firms where planning is carried out, it is rather different from that usually found in large corporate enterprises. Planning in successful small firms usually has the following features:

1 It has a *fairly short time horizon* (up to about two years).
2 It is *not excessively formal*, complex or detailed, although often (but not always) written.
3 It is built on quite *specific goals and objectives* rather than on the vague and unrealistic aspirations of owner/managers.
4 It is *done with help* from outside the firm (accountants, bankers, consultants), and from senior employees.
5 It is *done consistently* rather than on an *ad hoc* basis.
6 It consists of a *'master' (ie strategic) plan, and also focuses on functional areas* (such as marketing, finance, inventories, employees, production and layout).
7 It is as much *dependent on intuition and judgement* as on detailed economic and financial analysis.
8 It is *flexible*, and thereby allows the firm to:
   - *adapt* to changes in markets, technologies and economic forces, and
   - *respond* to future challenges and problems.

Small firms should have an active approach to facing change rather than just passively resigning themselves to it. This requires flexibility of attitude. Small firms may face the future in one of three ways:

- wait and see (dangerous and not recommended)
- predict and prepare, or
- make it happen (not usually possible for small firms).

Predicting and preparing to meet the challenges and exploit the opportunities from the future is the only logical response. It requires flexibility in creating and using plans.

Planning and business success

While planning does not guarantee business success, studies show that small firms in which planning is carried out consistently do better than those in which it is lacking. English (1986, p 125) offers the following comments on this:

Planning significantly increases your chances of success by focusing on five areas in which small business operators sometimes get lost:

1 *Realism. It is easy to be excessively optimistic about a new idea. Planning helps to prevent you from viewing the future in ways that the facts do not support.*

2 *The need for outside advice. Planning enables you to recognise problems that call for outside sources of information and assistance.*

3 *Recognising change. The nature of markets and consumer needs changes rapidly. Planning cannot predict change but it helps you to recognise it and to define your business strategy accordingly.*

4 *Balancing growth. Small businesses tend to either grow too fast for their capital base or too slowly to maintain cash flow. Planned growth allows you to plan your capital needs in advance and to ensure that funds are available when you need them.*

5 *Result-orientation. A detailed business plan enables you to monitor your results against an established set of goals and performance standards.*

Another study of 58 small firms in Australia reported the most important benefits gained by the 25 most successful firms as a result of planning. The findings of the study are shown in Table 14.1.

In another study of 10 570 Australian small firms, Williams (1987) found that only 988 (9.4%) had any formal (written) plans for at least two years ahead and had made them consistently and competently. Almost 54% of the 10 570 firms either planned poorly or rarely, or did not plan at all.

TABLE 14.1 Benefits gained from planning in small firms

Benefits	Percentage of firms
Most accurate forecasts	76
Ability to explore alternatives	72
More efficient resource allocation	66
Increased sales	65
Improved competitive position	64
Cost savings	52
Faster decision-making	49
Reduced feelings of uncertainty	42
More timely information	42
Overcoming cash flow problems	36
Better employee morale	31

Source: Orpen, 1985, pp 16–23

Of the 988 firms in which planning was used, 514 (52.0%) were survivors and 474 (48.0%) failed. By comparison, of the 5686 firms in which planning was rarely, poorly or never done, 2595 (45.6%) survived and 3091 (54.4%) failed. These figures show that planning significantly improves the survival ability of small firms, but does not guarantee success.

Williams also found strong links between small business success and the following management practices, which indicate the use of planning:

- breadth of the sales base (number of customers)
- use of cash budgeting
- use of time-management methods
- regular review of location suitability
- updating of technology and product knowledge
- review of sales/marketing effectiveness and business image
- use of financial information for managing, and
- overall managerial performance.

Why is planning avoided in small firms?

At least eight major reasons can be blamed for the lack of planning in Australian small firms. These are:

1 **Time pressures** Effective planning needs time away from today's problems and operations (the tyranny of the urgent). The temptation is to believe that future matters can be put off until later, yet present ones cannot!

2 **Difficulty in starting** Not knowing how to plan properly usually stops many owner/managers from starting the task.

3 **Lack of specialised knowledge** Many owner/managers lack the specialised knowledge needed to create overall plans covering all aspects of the firm's management and leading into the future.

4 **Lack of trust and openness** Committing plans to paper is resisted by owner/managers who are sensitive about 'sharing' ideas and information with others, such as employees and outsiders.

5 **Need for conceptual thinking** For practical people, thinking in concepts or about uncertainties and cause-and-effect relationships is not easy.

6 **No immediate feedback or results** Planning is a mental activity that does not usually produce immediate results. It is therefore often put off in favour of activities that do.

7 **Speed of change** Many owner/managers see planning as not worth the time and effort, because change is occurring so fast that prediction of future events, problems and opportunities, even some months ahead, is virtually impossible.

8 Cost Many small firms avoid planning because it is thought to be too costly. It does need time — but the investment is well worth it.

Studies (for instance Williams, 1987) show that serious, consistent and formal (that is, written) plans are found in only a small minority of firms. In most cases where planning does exist, it is usually

- unstructured (unsystematic and sloppy)
- irregular (not regularly done)
- fragmentary (piecemeal and incomplete)
- reactive (composed of 'If this, then that' statements), and
- given a low priority as a management task.

Most owner/managers are so preoccupied with day-to-day matters such as supervising and checking work activity (including solving dozens of problems) that they are unable and unwilling to give the future of their firm anything more than brief and casual attention. This is usually totally inadequate.

To a large extent, the pressures, crises and problems of today are a direct result of a lack of planning in the past. This vicious cycle gets so many small firms further and further into serious trouble; it can be broken only by applying time and effort today to plan for tomorrow.

All of these barriers are easily removed or overcome. Perhaps the easiest way to start is to recognise the fact that you must plan to be different.

Planning to be different

Unless a business can compete successfully in the marketplace, it will not survive!

Virtually every small firm is competing with at least one other, and most have a number of competitors or rivals. Every small firm's existence depends very much on its ability to get customers and keep them, and to increase its share of the market for the particular product or service — to become and continue to be aggressively competitive in the marketplace.

> No firm has a 'divine right' to a share of the market — it must be earned.

Sales generate profits and cash flow, thereby replenishing the firm's resources. No firm has a 'divine right' to a share in the market. Decisions to buy from Firm A or from Firm B are made only by customers and, although buying decisions are based on a variety of reasons, one fact is certain — to attract a potential buyer, make a sale and keep that buyer as a regular customer, the firm must pay close attention to its overall image. This means giving customers what they want, and in doing so providing them with better value for their money than they can get from rival firms.

Customers are becoming more and more discriminating and increasingly interested in maximising the value received for every dollar spent. In winning and keeping customers, the first consideration for a firm must therefore be to establish distinctive competence.

Distinctive competence

> What is your firm's unique/distinctive competence?

If a firm has some skill, ability, advantage or strength that others do not have, this is what makes it unique — this is its distinctive competence.

Examples are:

- a manufacturer with a superior production method
- a retailer with exclusive access to better quality merchandise
- a service firm with superior skills in providing its service
- a firm owning patent, franchise or other such contractual rights, and
- a business in a superior location.

The most common distinctive competence found in small firms is associated with the particular skills, experience and expertise of owner/managers and employees. Research in Australia by Williams (1987) shows that the owners of many small firms have no understanding of the importance of differentiation (that is, being unique and different from competitors), and are not aware of any distinctive competence in their own firms. Predictably, most of these firms are among the failures.

Having some unique feature, advantage or strength relative to rival firms is, by itself, not enough. The uniqueness must be converted into a sustainable advantage to give your firm the competitive edge it needs in order to be the leader.

Sustainable competitive advantage

Customers will not choose to buy from your firm simply because it has some distinctive competence, such as a skilled workforce or some special know-how. Customers will see value, and will be persuaded to deal with your firm, if its products or services have features which make them superior to those of your rivals in some way that influences their buying decisions. The distinctive competence must result in a competitive advantage (a quality of service which competitors cannot match, or special features of the product which persuade customers to buy). This is what attracts buyers — not the distinctive competence itself.

> A firm's success is largely determined by customer decisions.

Examples of competitive advantage are:

- lower prices (with quality equal to that available from rivals)
- quality and reliability of product or service without overpricing
- particular and useful product features
- greater range and availability of merchandise
- superior after-sales service (prompt and reliable)
- superior product knowledge (ability to give user advice)
- employee courtesy, helpfulness and service
- cleanliness and speed of service
- customer awareness of firm, products and service, and
- convenience of location.

To find out which product or service features influence buying decisions, owner/managers *must listen* to their customers. If your customers are totally indifferent to the colour of a particular item (say, a garden spade), then stocking that item in a certain colour cannot give your firm a competitive advantage, whereas features such as superior strength, reduced weight and improved style (resulting in easier use) probably can.

Having worked hard on your firm's competitive advantage, the next step is to ensure that rival firms cannot copy those features (or improve on them) and easily take away your competitive advantage. As indicated in Chapter 3, your competitive advantage might be only temporary, unless you take action to *sustain* it.

The challenge is, therefore, to look continually for new strengths, unique qualities, skills or abilities that can be converted into a *sustainable* competitive advantage. This is what can make any small firm the leader in its field, and greatly increase its chances of succeeding.

To do all this successfully requires strategic planning. In its original military use, the term *strategy* referred to gaining superiority over the enemy. In business, *strategy* relates to gaining superiority over the competitors in the struggle for customers and markets. Small firms must plan their strategies with much care, because they do not have the resources to wage long and costly struggles on all fronts.

Developing a strategy

You don't have to be brilliant to develop an effective strategy for your business. All it requires is an analytical look at your customers (actual and potential) and the way they are being serviced. Go back to basics. One signwriter saw himself as being in the story-telling business, using windows and walls as a medium. He did his homework and found out what his customers wanted — good signs, good advice, competitive service and plenty of personal help. He surveyed his competition, found their strengths (good work, but not much else) and their weaknesses (too busy, too impersonal, too rigid in their methods), and this gave him a range of goods and services that his customers wanted. His market analysis was easy. He defined the type of retailer he could serve satisfactorily and drew a map, marking out the key retail areas.

His business opportunity was obvious and his strategy was simple. He selected shops he considered needed signwriting, dropped an advertising leaflet in, and followed up with a personal visit. This visit often resulted in an immediate sale, as he was giving the retailers what they wanted: professional advice, quality signwriting, good service, reasonable prices and signs that sold. He followed up on a regular circuit, which also helped to keep out other competitors.

Another case in point is the small supermarket that adopted the motto 'competitive in price but second to none in service'. The owners were competitive in price on key lines such as sugar, coffee and soap powder but they claimed they *ran* to give service. Indeed, they did run! Whenever the check-out operator rang a bell, all staff (including the owners) ran to give price checks, open the other register, pack, or give car service. When did you last go to a supermarket where the staff ran to give service?

What will be your strategy to gain and keep your market share? Whatever it is, keep it simple — just like the washing machine repairer who gives customers a courtesy washing machine to use while theirs is being repaired in his workshop.

PART B — WRITING YOUR BUSINESS PLAN

The concept

Any business plan is simply a written answer to three questions, namely:

- Where are you now?
- Where do you want to be at a future date?
- How will you get there?

The first question — 'Where are you now?' — must be your starting point. This question seeks to provide a planning base. It looks at your business to establish such things as:

- your business idea
- your current level of sales
- your customer groups
- your products and services
- your pricing policy
- your distribution policy
- your promotional activity
- your overall operation
- your staff, and
- your finance.

To many business operators, answering the question 'Where are you now?' is a major stumbling block because they don't know where to start. To them, the planning barriers mentioned earlier make this task almost insurmountable. However, the answer is surprisingly simple — if you divide your business planning into four key areas: operational, marketing, staff and finance. As we will see in this chapter, such a division allows you to analyse your business (or assumed business) to provide your planning base.

The second question — 'Where do you want to be at a future date?' — is simply asking you to visualise your business operation at a set date in the future. This visualisation process is almost identical to the exercise of setting objectives that you were asked to do in Chapter 8. The difference, however, is that the focus is now on business objectives, instead of personal objectives.

The third question — 'How will you get there?' — asks about the steps you need to take in order to achieve the objectives you have set. These steps, or strategies, can be identified, written down and programmed.

In essence, the three questions can be shown in diagrammatic form, as shown in Figure 14.1.

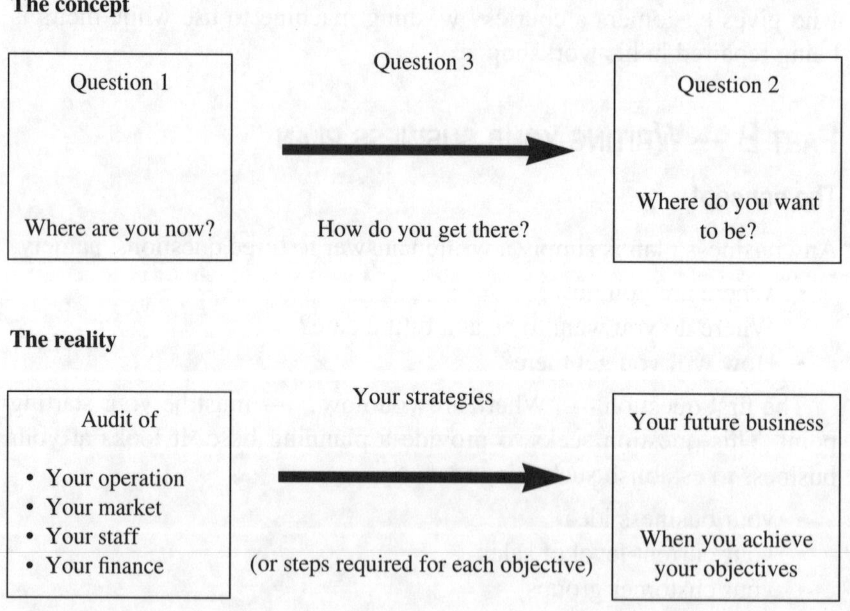

FIGURE 14.1 Three business plan questions

Let us now look at relating these three questions to your business. If you do not have a business at this stage, let us assume you have one so that you can work through this chapter.

Choose a business and imagine that it is yours. Give it a name and a location. This business has staff! It also has customers for its products and services! It has sales! It has competition and suppliers! For the sake of this exercise, your business is real — it is operating! It has to be because *you cannot write a business plan without basing it on a business.* From this point on, in this chapter the term 'your business' will mean either your actual or your assumed business.

The best way of starting to write your plan is to organise your approach and your information. To give you some idea of what you are working on, let us look at the format of your business plan. Your business plan is, in reality, drawn from four separate plans, namely:

- your operational plan
- your marketing plan
- your staff plan
- your financial plan.

A typical business plan format would link these plans together as shown in Figure 14.2.

1 Cover sheet
2 List of contents
3 Operational plan
  3.1 Introduction
  3.2 The business
  3.3 Profile(s) of principal(s)
  3.4 The information base
  3.5 Professional support
  3.6 Business objectives
4 Marketing plan
  4.1 Introduction
  4.2 The market outline
  4.3 Customers
  4.4 Competition
  4.5 Products/services
  4.6 Suppliers
  4.7 Current market activity
  4.8 Market predictions
5 Staff plan
  5.1 Introduction
  5.2 Staff outline
  5.3 Future plans
6 Financial plan
  6.1 Introduction
  6.2 Profit and loss
  6.3 Break-even
  6.4 Projected cash flow
  6.5 Future financial requirements
Appendix 1 Previous financial reports
Appendix 2 Working papers and reference material

FIGURE 14.2 List of contents for a business plan

Let us now look at the construction and contents of each section of your business plan.

Your operational plan

This plan looks at the business itself, and the way in which it will operate. The operational plan is simply a series of sections that you can write separately and then combine in the form of a plan. It should contain the following sections:

- introduction
- the business
- profile(s) of principal(s)
- the information base
- the professional support
- the business objectives.

The introduction

To start with, don't try to write your introduction first — rather, write it last. It is, after all, only a summary explaining the contents and purpose of your operational plan. Its main purpose is to prepare and organise the reader, and it should be not more than one page in length.

The business

Your description of your business requires close investigation. When describing your business it is not enough to give a quick synopsis (ie name, address and telephone number) and a general outline of your main activity. You should also be seeking to define the exact nature of the business you are in.

At a seminar I once asked a couple 'What business are you in?' Their initial answer was: 'Round fibreglass water tanks'. The couple then took time to consider their answer and recognised that:

- their tanks could hold other things besides water — other liquids, sawdust and waste materials, to name a few
- their tanks did not have to be circular or high — in fact, they would have few problems in producing tanks to any desired shape, and
- their tanks or containers did not need to have a roof.

The couple concluded that they were not in the business of making round fibreglass water tanks but rather fibreglass storage containers. This realisation widened their market potential immediately. They also saw that the demand for water tanks increased in dry periods and fell in wet periods. People relying on tank water were conscious of water storage in dry times and used water more liberally in wet times. Possible products for wet periods could be, say, fibreglass shower bases for bathrooms. This expanded product range would also give sales in the town market — an extension of their traditional rural market.

Some other people at the same seminar initially described themselves as being in the 'plant hire business'. They hired out and sold plants to business houses primarily, but noticed that whenever 'things got tough' money spent on plants was considered to be a luxury, and consequently orders were cancelled. This couple asked themselves: 'What are we really doing? Is it just hiring out plants, or is it more than that?' People who hired or bought plants didn't necessarily want the plants as such — they wanted to improve the look of their offices, houses, showrooms and so on or to create a feeling of relaxation, warmth and peace. The couple decided that the business they were really in was the business of providing an atmosphere. People consider atmosphere as an integral part of their living and working environments, whereas they often consider plant hire as a luxury.

The redefinition of this business also turned previously competitive products such as plastic plants and dried flowers into additions to their range. It also paved the way for a consulting service in their business, advising clients on how to create a particular atmosphere using their plants in a 'certain way'.

From these two examples, it can be seen that to define the nature of your business simply as

'the retail business' or
'the service business' or
'the people business'

is not enough. You must find out which customer needs you intend to satisfy — not which products you want to sell. There is a big difference here and this is covered in more detail in Chapter 17 under 'Adopt a market-oriented approach'. This concept says, in essence, that a business has to satisfy the wants and needs of customers. You don't sell products because the customers want those products (as in the above case, they didn't want the plants themselves — they wanted atmosphere); you sell those products because they help satisfy customers' needs.

Determining what customers' needs are, and identifying the products or services you will require to satisfy those needs, will help you to define what business you are in.

In this section of your business plan you should also demonstrate why your business is different — ie your distinctive competence and your competitive advantage. Consider the following two cases.

A manufacturer of photographic business cards saw that the traditional printing industry generally disliked quoting on short-run, high-quality work because of high setting-up costs. He realised that he could use the same photographic techniques himself and thus compete with the general printing industry, especially when short runs were required. This innovation gave him an unexpected share of a new market very quickly.

A Chinese restaurant started up with intense competition, but departed from tradition by installing a large viewing window into a spotless kitchen where customers could see their food being prepared. The potential customers could also see a decor of glass, and 'squeaky clean' white furniture lit with bright lights; and one of the owners serving the customers. The food was good and prices were competitive; and as a result the restaurant is full every day.

Unless you are seen to be different from, and better than, your competitors you will have trouble taking their customers and keeping them.

In summary, then, your business outline provides:

- a synopsis of the business
- a definition of the real nature of your business
- your opportunity, or the reason why you are different from your competition.

Profile(s) of the principal(s)

These profiles of you and any other principals in your business, such as your partners, are identical to the ones we discussed for the feasibility study (see page 126). If you remember, we suggested a format that included a brief outline, a highlighting of your strengths and experience, and a photograph. We also advised against writing it as a chronological résumé of your work experience since you left school. Each profile should be not more than one page in length and should be written to demonstrate skills, abilities, potential and achievements.

The information base

Any information plan must be based upon accurate information, and this comes from your record system. This section of your plan is designed to show the types of records that are kept in your business. A listing of these records also demonstrates to anyone reading your plan the managerial control you have over your business and the type of information that can be extracted from your records.

The professional support

Every business should have professional support in key areas — where specialised knowledge and skills are required. This section of your plan should list (with full contact details) professional support such as:

- your accountant
- your solicitor
- your bank manager
- your insurance person

- your business consultant, and
- any other key professionals who assist you in running your business.

The business objectives

Up to this point, all the information we have included in your operational plan has answered the question 'Where are you now?' This information is simply giving an operational overview of your business as it exists. This operational overview becomes your planning base for your future business. The process of deciding what you want your business to be doing at some point in the future begins with writing your business objectives.

In Chapter 8, we discussed the setting of objectives and said that an objective was 'a clearly defined, but measurable outcome in written form'. We also stated that there were two types of objectives — personal and business — and we went on to discuss the process of setting good personal objectives. In this chapter, however, we are concerned solely with *business objectives*, not personal ones, as we are looking at what you would like your business to be achieving at some time in the future.

Business objectives must be:

- clearly defined
- measurable
- achievable
- challenging
- brief, and
- written.

They can be either short-term (up to 12 months) or long-term (up to five years) — and a good business plan will have both. Some of the key areas usually targeted for business objectives are:

- income (eg to have sales of $500 000 during the next financial year)
- value (eg to increase the value of the business by 50% by 30 June 1996)
- liquidity (eg to increase working capital by $15 000 by the end of this financial year)
- equity (eg to increase investment by 50% by 30 June 1995)
- staff (eg to employ another salesperson by 31 November 1995)
- assets (eg to replace the existing computer with a lap-top within two months)
- efficiency (eg to increase production by 30% with existing resources by 30 June 1995)
- profitability (eg to increase net profit from 16% to 20% during the next financial year)
- market share (eg to gain a 5% share of the market by 30 June 1997)

- customers (eg to sign up XYZ company for a maintenance contract by 30 June 1995)
- size (eg to open a second store within 18 months).

Writing objectives is never easy. It takes a lot of thought, practice, discussion and persistence. (To refresh your memory of what is involved, refer to Chapter 8.)

Figure 14.3 has been developed to assist you in writing objectives for your business plan.

1 By . . /. . /. . . I will . . . .
. . . .

2 By . . /. . /. . . I will . . . .
. . . .

3 By . . /. . /. . . I will . . . .
. . . .

4 By . . /. . /. . . I will . . . .
. . . .

5 By . . /. . /. . . I will . . . .
. . . .

6 By . . /. . /. . . I will . . . .
. . . .

7 By . . /. . /. . . I will . . . .
. . . .

8 By . . /. . /. . . I will . . . .
. . . .

9 By . . /. . /. . . I will . . . .
. . . .

10 By . . /. . /. . . I will . . . .
. . . .

FIGURE 14.3 Business objectives

Once you have written your objectives, the next step is to outline your strategies to achieve these objectives, and list the steps that need to be taken. Your strategy, as we stated earlier, is simply your method or approach adopted to achieve your objectives. It will mean a course of action which can be listed as action steps. These steps are easy to determine, if you adopt an organised approach. This can be achieved using the worksheet contained in Figure 14.4 which has been designed for this purpose.

You will need a separate strategy worksheet for each of your objectives, and you will notice that each worksheet not only requires nomination of a person responsible for each step but also a time limit. It is also designed to allow you to estimate the cost of achieving each objective.

Once you have written your strategies, you have in fact answered the third question, 'How do I get there?'

Objective No .....

By / / I will ....

Outline of strategy ....

Action step	Responsibility	Date	Cost
1			
2			
3			
4			
5			
6			
7			
8			
9			
10			
		Total cost	

FIGURE 14.4 Strategy worksheet

Your marketing plan

Before you attempt to write your marketing plan, it is suggested that you read Chapter 17. This chapter, entitled 'Marketing strategy and management', explains the marketing concept, the importance of marketing to your business, and the five key decisions you need to make in your marketing plan. It explains the marketing strategy in one key question: *What* offer will *you* make to *what* market?

The emphasis must be placed on looking at your market before you look at your offer. This is the key to marketing — putting the customers first. Until you *know* who your customers are and what their real needs are, it is useless trying to sell what you *want* to sell. Customers will buy from you only when *they* believe you can satisfy their needs and/or solve their problems. You have to study your customers before you can say 'This is what they want' or 'This is the offer I will make to them.'

The offer you will be making to your customers is usually not just a single offer. Most businesses find that they have groups of customers (with common needs) rather than one unified market. This means that you will have to make group offers rather than one universal offer. The key factors you must consider in each offer are:

- the products or services you can provide
- the price you will charge
- where you can reach your customers, and
- the sort of promotion you will use.

In short, your marketing plan looks at how you intend to continue winning and keeping customers.

Let us now examine the construction and concepts of your marketing plan, namely:

- the introduction
- the market outline
- the customers
- the competition
- the products and services
- the suppliers
- the current market activity, and
- the market predictions.

The introduction

This is a summary designed to give the readers of your plan an advance insight into the contents, construction and purpose of your plan. Like the introduction to your operational plan, it should take up less than one page and be written last rather than first. It is a mechanical, rather than an analytical, part of your plan.

The market outline

How would you describe your market? Where is it, and how big is it? Perhaps the easiest way to start to describe your market is to show it on a map — outlining your market boundaries, your location, your competition, your customer base, and, if applicable, the location of your key customers. Next, try to define where your sales and your competitors' sales will come from. Your market description should be able to evaluate the overall customer base, the products/services (in very general terms) that they are demanding, and the potential sales value of these products/ services.

This section should highlight any key factors and trends that are relevant to your market. It should take into account any changes occurring in that market, since your market, like everything else, is in a constant state of change. Your ability to increase your share of the market usually depends on having recognised change and adapted faster than your competition. You should also outline any special regulatory factors affecting your market, such as legislation, trade wars, quotas, technology, etc.

This market outline is not a detailed blueprint of your market. It is simply an overview of the marketplace in which you are working. The research, demographic figures and industry studies that you use to back this market outline should be included in appendix form rather than in this section of your plan.

The customers

You have two types of customers: actual or existing customers who are or have been buying from you; and your potential customers who are buying elsewhere for a whole host of reasons. This section of your plan looks at both types of customers.

After reading Chapter 17, you should be able to divide your customers into groups or market segments. Analysis will show you how large these groups are and to which groups or segments you should give priority. This analysis should provide you with lists of actual and potential customers. The lists can be constructed from your own records, your own market research, directories (eg the telephone book) and outside reports on your market or industry. The key fact to remember is that information on your customers *is* available.

In looking at your customers, also remember the importance of the 80/20 rule (page 31), which states that 80% of your sales will come from 20% of your customers. You should in this section identify those actual or potential customers who should be regarded as key customers.

No two businesses are the same and it is not always possible to list your customers by name. If your business is targeting a mass market (eg fast food, retail, door-to-door sales, etc) then listing customers by name is often impossible or of little consequence. What is important is the measurement of your actual/potential customers by factors such as numbers, age, gender, disposable income, family size, etc. Details of these demographic factors about your target groups *are* available, and should be included in your plan.

The competition

As we discussed in Chapter 8, every business has competition. There is no law that says customers have to buy from you. They will only buy from you while you remain superior, in their eyes, to your opposition. You will have to match and beat your competition — in all areas — not just price.

This section of the plan looks at your competition. It lists:

- your actual competition right now
- your potential competition, ie those who could enter the market place quickly — for example, by extending their operations or by moving into your market area.

This list of competitors has to be more than just a list of names. It should group your competitors as main competitors and other competitors. It should provide a full evaluation of the activities of your main competitors. One way of doing this is by using a competitor report sheet similar to the one shown in Figure 14.5.

Name: ______________________ Date: ________
Location/s ______________________ Phone: ________
Fax: ________

Number of employees: ________
Main activity: ______________________
Estimated turnover: $ ______________________
Advertising: TV ☐ Radio ☐ Papers ☐ Flyers ☐ Direct Mail ☐

Presentation: Good ☐ Average ☐ Poor ☐

Comments:
Key departments: ______________________
Key suppliers: ______________________

Strengths: Weaknesses:

______________ ______________
______________ ______________
______________ ______________

Percentage of market: ______________________
Market segments by percentage:

1 ________ – % 2 ________ – % 3 ________ – %

Comments: ______________________

FIGURE 14.5 Competitor report

The information needed to complete these competitor reports should be continuously updated, and your sources should include your own knowledge, directories, suppliers and representatives, and your own and professional research. Note that you should already have marked the location of your key competitors on the map(s) you include in your plan.

If possible, it is also a good idea to show the break-up of your market share, ie that part or percentage of the market held by you and your competition. Finally, to drive home the importance of this section, remember that the only way you can gain customers is to take them away from someone else. You must know your competition!

The products and services

Which products and services should you be offering to your customers? You know, from your own records, the products and services that you are selling and you also know, from your competitor reports, which opposition products and services share the same market.

Segment / Customer ____________

KEY PRODUCT OR SERVICE	RELATED PRODUCTS OR SERVICES	COMMENTS

FIGURE 14.6 Worksheet showing related products/services

This section should include a list of the products/services you are offering to the different segments you are trying to reach. In many businesses this task is a simple process, but in others it is complex and requires a lot of thought and discussion. If your business is multi-lined eg a supermarket, choose product groups rather than individual product lines. The analysis you present in this section of the plan should show not only the product/service lines or groups that you are offering but also their relevance to your total sales. What percentage of your total sales does each product or product group represent?

The product worksheet in Figure 14.6 has been designed to assist you and your staff in planning for additional sales.

To use this worksheet, for each of your segments, sales territories or key customers:

- identify your key product and/or service sold
- ask the question 'Which related or associated products/services could I also sell to the customers (or customers in that segment or territory)?'
- write down your comments or ideas on the possible suggestions for your product range or sales opportunity.

This worksheet is an excellent control mechanism to identify sales areas that you and your staff are not fully exploiting. It is also a starting point for identifying potential new products or services.

The suppliers

Who are your suppliers? This section is to contain a list of your suppliers with their key contact details. It also shows you a list of items/products that they are supplying.

Supplier publications, such as price lists and categories, can be included in the appendix section of this plan, or they can be included in your working files. Supplier locations should also be shown on your map(s) if the location of their premises is relevant. You might also wish, in this section, to identify alternative suppliers, either in a separate list or wherever you feel appropriate.

The current market activity

Every plan has a base or a starting point. In this plan your base or starting point is simply an evaluation of where your business is right now. Your evaluation must include:

- your current level of sales,
- to your customer groups or segments,
- identifying the products or services you are offering each group/segment,
- at what price (or pricing policy),
- with what distribution method,
- through what promotional method.

This evaluation process is simply a practical application of the marketing model that is described and developed in Chapter 17. At this stage, however, in providing an overview of your business plan, we have designed a simple worksheet (see Figure 14.7) to assist you in presenting the information required for your evaluation.

	Segment 1	Segment 2	Segment 3	Segment 4	Segment 5 ....
Total sales for P/E / / $................. 100%	$................. ....%	$................. ....%	$................. ....%	$................. ....%	$................. ....%
Products & services					
Pricing policy					
Distribution policy					
Promotional methods					

FIGURE 14.7 Worksheet showing your current trading activity

The worksheet shows only five segments. If your market has more than five segments, simply expand the worksheet. In this worksheet you should:

- Identify your segments by name.
- Show your current sales level as a total figure and also as sales by each segment (in both dollars and percentages).
- List the products and services you are offering to each segment (if the space is insufficient, show the product list as an attachment).

- Identify your pricing policy to each segment, eg 'retail', or 'trade plus 10%', or 'cost plus 10%', or 'match competitors', etc.
- Spell out your distribution policy to each segment, eg 'via wholesale agents', or 'on site', or 'they come to us'. In other words, how and where does the sale take place?
- List your promotional methods used for each segment. The four promotional methods are: advertising, publicity, personal selling and sales promotion. Examples of promotional activity could be:
  —advertising — Yellow Pages, TV, radio, letterbox drops, etc
  —publicity — word of mouth
  —personal selling — sales representatives, quotations, telemarketing, etc
  —sales promotion — trade nights, contests, exhibitions, etc.

This worksheet might look daunting, BUT remember that it is based upon the marketing process described in Chapter 17. When you read and work through that chapter you will notice that this worksheet is merely an application to your business of the marketing model presented in Figure 17.8.

The market predictions

This section is designed to allow you to present your predictions of the market you are serving and the key sales and industry trends of which you are aware. It is the means by which (using the worksheet in Figure 14.6 as a base) you can realistically set your business objectives.

This section is not a large one — rather, it is a summary of all the key trends and forecasts you have made for your future trading activity (and your competitors') and for the future of the market you are serving.

Your staff plan

Your staff plan looks at how you intend to make your business operate, and it should be based upon the assumption that people are the most valuable resource of any business. For this reason it is suggested that you work through Chapter 20, entitled 'Management of employees', before attempting to write your staff plan.

Your staff plan should contain three basic parts:

- the introduction
- the staff outline
- future staff plans.

The introduction

As we stated in the preceding pages, the outline is merely a summary to brief the reader on the shape and contents of your plan. It should be short and positive and written after you have finished the other two sections of the staff plan.

The staff outline

This section should start with a statement about your staff needs *or* your intention to operate without staff. It should go on to include answers to questions such as:

- Can you operate without staff? (If you don't have staff, who will replace you if you are absent?)
- What are your staffing objectives?
- Who are your current staff?
- What does your organisational chart look like?
- How do you select and train staff?
- What are their areas of responsibility?
- What are their duties and functions?
- What are their expectations?
- Which administrative and financial record systems do you use to manage your employees?

There is no step-by-step blueprint for writing this section as your staff outline will be guided by the answers to the questions listed above.

Future staff plans

In looking at your future plans, start with your staffing objectives. What do you want, and how will you achieve your objectives? Also, you need to consider yourself and staff as people, so allow for the human element in formulating your future plans.

This section should try to answer questions such as:

- What are your staffing objectives?
- What are your requirements for holidays?
- Can you handle emergencies and your absences from work?
- What are your future staff requirements and plans?
- What effect will technology have on your staffing plans?
- What incentives are offered to employers?

Again, there is no standardised method of writing this section. Perhaps the best starting point should be to talk to your existing staff, as, after all, you should work as a team!

This forecast should not be a long and detailed report. Instead, make it a factual summary of your future staff needs as you see them, based upon your considerations of all the key factors that you can identify.

Your financial plan

This section seeks to measure, in dollar terms, the effectiveness and value of your operation, both in the past and right now, and to enable you to forecast the probable results of your future operations. You are in business to make a profit, and your financial plan will enable you to measure, control, evaluate and forecast your profitability, your financial needs and your financial viability.

Before attempting to write your own financial plan, we suggest you read and work through Chapter 15, 'Record keeping for management' and Chapter 16, 'Financial management and planning'.

The key to your financial plan is your ability to prepare forecasts and budgets.

Preparing budgets and forecasts

During the planning for your firm, it is clear that the ability to think ahead and forecast various future events and trends is a vital part of that process. For example, in assessing the likelihood of your firm reaching the sales level needed to achieve the desired profit, forecasting is used. Forecasting is aimed at trying to find out how much the firm can sell. It is not easy, but skill comes with practice and experience.

> Forecasting is 'guesstimating' the future.

A forecast is a prediction or 'best guess' about some aspect of the future. Budgets are plans expressed in numbers — usually money. These activities are future-oriented, and their purpose is to anticipate the firm's future financial situation, so that action can be taken to prevent or avoid problems or difficulties. Budgets cannot eliminate risks, but they can help to reduce their effects on the business by means of preventive action.

The existence of a well-prepared business plan, which includes financial forecasts and a set of budgets, will be widely regarded by bankers, suppliers and others as evidence that your firm is skilfully managed.

If accompanied by a good record system, budgets also allow the financial aspects of your firm to be controlled. Variations from budgeted (ie planned) costs, as measured by your firm's records, show up exactly where tighter control of costs is necessary.

There are two commonly used starting points for budgeting. One is to set your profit target, as outlined in Chapter 8. The other is to forecast the sales expected for the budget period, usually as follows:

- monthly — for the first six or 12 months, then
- quarterly — for the second year, and
- half-yearly — for the third year.

Sales forecasting requires careful assessment of the market potential for the firm's product or service, and prediction of your firm's likely share of that potential. Next, it involves predicting or estimating how much of each product line or service can be sold, and at what prices. Unit sales by unit price will give the forecast sales income. Forecasts can be made in any way desired, including:

- geographical area
- customer type
- selling department, or
- individual salesperson.

Some firms obtain a range of forecasts, from 'worst' through 'most likely' to 'best'. When your business has been operating for some time, accuracy of forecasting improves because you can use past trends, observed seasonality or variations in buying patterns and other information. For a new venture there must be some 'crystal ball gazing' involved, but this is better than not forecasting at all!

Once sales forecasts and a realistic sales budget are available, you can prepare as many other budgets as you need. These could include:

- manufacturing cost budget
- cost of goods sold budget
- profit and loss budget
- operating expenses budgets (various)
- balance sheet and funding (capital) budgets, and
- cash flow budget (in small firms, probably the most important).

Let us now look at the key sections of your financial plan, namely:

- the introduction
- profit and loss
- the break-even analysis
- cash flow projections
- future financial requirements.

The introduction

This section serves the same purpose and has the same construction as the introductions to your operational, marketing and staffing plans. Again, it should be written after the other sections of your financial plan have been completed.

Profit and loss

A profit and loss statement is often called a trading statement or an income and expenditure statement. As the name implies, it summarises a firm's trading over a period of time in order to work out the profit or loss which was achieved.

A typical format for a profit and loss statement is shown in Figure 14.8.

Profit and loss statement for the period ended 30/6/96

		$	$
Income			
	Sales		200 000
Less			
	Cost of goods sold		
	Opening stock	40 000	
	Plus purchases	125 000	
		165 000	
	Less closing stock	45 000	120 000
Gross profit			80 000
Less operating costs			
	Accountancy fees	600	
	Advertising	2 400	
	Bank charges	240	
	Depreciation	4 189	
	Electricity	1 600	
	Insurance	1 400	
	Interest	2 049	
	Miscellaneous	122	
	Printing & stationery	800	
	Rent	15 800	
	Repairs & maintenance	600	
	Telephone	1 000	
	Vehicle expenses	2 200	
	Wages & salaries	17 000	
	Total expenses		50 000
Net profit			30 000

FIGURE 14.8 Typical profit and loss statement

This report is based upon summaries of income and expenditure over the period under review. An explanation of how to prepare such a report is given in Chapter 15. It is not enough to look at what has happened over the last financial period: you must also look at the results you expect to achieve from your future trading.

Many firms prepare budgeted profit-and-loss statements with each receipt and expense item budgeted on a monthly basis. Such reports *might* be misleading, and care should be taken in interpreting them. It should be remembered that profit and loss reports are designed to evaluate your trading at the end of a period, not continuously throughout that period.

Two reports that will give you the management control that you need are your break-even analysis and your cash flow projections.

The break-even analysis

An estimate of your expected business costs is necessary for deciding on how much you need to sell. Break-even is the level of sales that equals the total of all costs, ie the point at which there is a neither profit nor loss.

You should understand what happens to costs when the level of business activity (as measured by sales) changes. In most cases, as sales increase so do costs. However, the picture is not as simple as it seems at first.

The procedure for showing the relationship between volume (sales level), costs and profit is briefly as follows:

1 **Estimate your likely costs**. Across any firm's usual range of activity there are two major types of cost: fixed and variable.

- Fixed costs are those that remain the same despite changes in sales volume. These include rent, rates, interest on loans, insurance premiums and depreciation of assets. These costs are fixed so long as the firm's existing capacity is not increased — for example, by moving to larger premises.
- Variable costs are those that change in direct proportion to changes in business activity: if sales increase by 10% so do variable costs. Examples are: purchasing, most wages, sales commission, vehicle running costs and advertising.

2 **Calculate the break-even point**. The following estimates have been made for a small firm's first year in business:

- sales $160 000
- fixed costs $59 800
- variable costs $75 200
- total costs $135 000
- net profit before tax $25 000.

Calculate the percentage of variable costs ($75 200) over sales ($160 000). This is 47%, and means that, out of every sales dollar, 47¢ are used to cover variable costs, while 53¢ must cover fixed costs and make a profit. The 53¢ point is called the 'contribution margin'. The break-even level of sales is calculated by the formula:

S = FC/C where S = sales at break-even
FC = fixed costs
C = contribution margin.

In this example, S = $59 800/0.53 = $112 830

At this sales level, all costs are covered and there is no profit.

Sales (at break-even point):	$112 830
less variable costs (47%)	53 030
Contribution margin:	59 800
less fixed costs:	59 800
Profit	Nil

This analysis can be shown by graph, as in Figure 14.9.

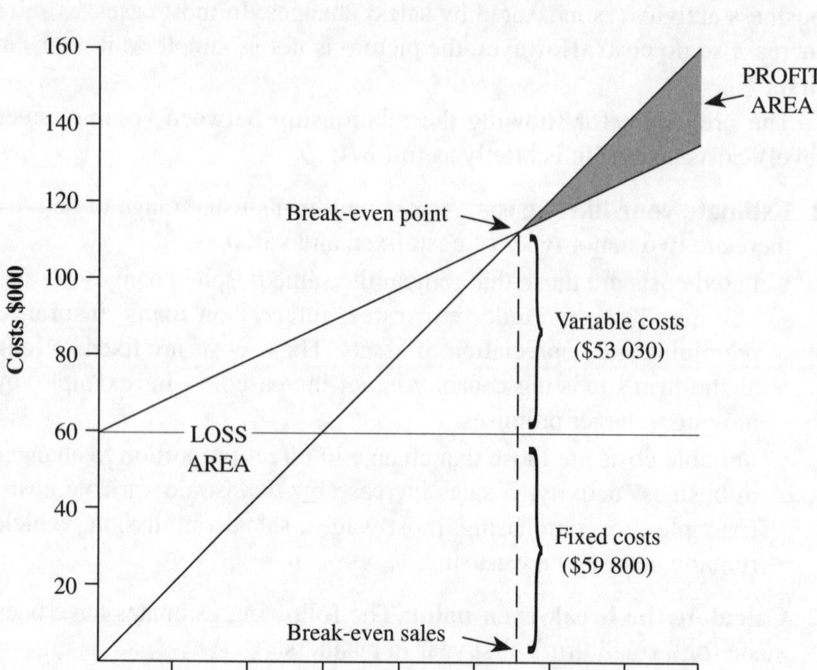

FIGURE 14.9 Break-even analysis

From this analysis, and assuming the estimated costs are reasonably accurate, the expected sales volume ($160 000) will quite easily exceed the break-even sales figure ($112 830). However, if fixed costs were higher (say, $79 000) and variable costs were $56 000 (total costs still $135 000), the firm would need sales of $121 538 to break even.

To understand this procedure better, try to answer questions such as:

- What sales level is needed to reach a certain profit figure? (To get a profit of $25 000, sales of $160 000 will be needed. Use S = (FC + profit)/C)
- At a certain sales level, how much profit can be expected?
- What contribution margin comes from each product or service? Which should be promoted, and which dropped?
- What mix of products will be most profitable?
- How would a 10% drop in sales volume affect profit?
- How will changes to selling prices affect sales and profits?
- If we expand and thereby increase fixed costs, how will this affect profits?
- How will costs be affected if sales are increased?
- How can we best improve profitability?
- What price should be charged for each product?
- Should we make or buy?

Break-even analysis (often known as cost-volume-profit analysis) is a most useful technique for helping to answer many questions that arise in running a business. Mostly, owner/managers guess or use rule-of-thumb in making decisions, a dangerous practice if it gives the wrong answers. Be different, and start using break-even analysis to assist you in making your key management decisions.

Cash flow projections

Budgeting for profit is not the same thing as budgeting for cash flow, just as cash and profits are not the same. It cannot be assumed that growing sales volume will result in more cash being available in your firm. In fact, sales growth can very likely lead to cash shortages unless there is sound financial management.

> Cash flow is the lifeblood of every business.

The cash budget is often said to be the most important of all the budgets for a small firm, given that cash is the lifeblood of small firms. A cash budget is a projection, for the budgeted period, of your firm's cash receipts, cash payments and the resulting cash surpluses or deficits. All cash transactions must be included, but non-cash items are not. A vital aspect of cash budgeting is the timing of receipts and payments, because a firm's cash situation can change in several days from having plenty to being unable to meet its commitments eg because of payroll, rent, insurance payments, loan repayments, etc. The key parts of your cash flow projection are:

1 Cash receipts. Cash can be received from:
   - funding — capital (equity) from owner(s), loans (debt) from banks and other sources
   - trading activities — cash sales (cash received immediately), commissions received, credit sales (cash collected later from debtors)
   - non-trading activities — investment income such as interest and rent, disposal of fixed assets.

   To budget cash receipts from trading it is necessary first to forecast credit sales, and second to predict when these debts will be received (eg 75% in the month after sales, 20% in the second month, 5% in the third month.) With a new business this will be a 'guesstimate', but for existing firms, patterns of debtors' payments should be available from your records.

2 Cash payments. Included in the cash budget would be all payments, namely:
   - trading activities — all purchase payments and expenses

YEAR 19___

	JANUARY		FEBRUARY		MARCH		APRIL		...	NOVEMBER		DECEMBER		YEAR TOTAL	
	Budget	Actual	Budget	Actual	Budget	Actual	Budget	Actual	...al	Budget	Actual	Budget	Actual	Budget	Actual
Opening balance															
Receipts: Cash sales Debtors Capital Loans Other															
Total receipts															
Total cash available															
Running costs: Accountancy fees Advertising Bank charges Cleaning Electricity Insurance Interest Miscellaneous Printing, postage & stationery Rent Repairs & maintenance Telephone Vehicle expenses Wages & salaries Other outgoings: Purchases Drawings (including tax) Loan repayments Additional assets															
Total payments															
End-of-month balance															

FIGURE 14.10 Typical cash flow projection sheet

- non-trading activities — payment of taxes, purchases of fixed assets (eg new vehicle)
- funding — dividends and drawings paid to owner(s), interest on, and repayment of, loans.

3 Items which will not be included in a cash budget (but which will appear in other budgets) are discounts allowed and received, bad debts and depreciation of assets. All are non-cash transactions.

4 Starting with the current cash balance(s), add all forecast cash receipts for the first month, deduct all forecast cash payments for that month, obtain the cash balance at the end of the first month and carry it forward as the opening balance for the second month. Repeat this for each month or quarter. Alongside each month's 'budget' column there should be an 'actual' column to allow for easy comparisons. In many firms the budget figures are entered in pencil (unless a computer is used), so that adjustments to future periods can be made easily once actual cash flows are recorded. Figure 14.10 shows a typical cash flow projection sheet.

The extraction of information for this cash flow projection can be simplified if you use a worksheet similar to the one shown in Figure 14.11. This worksheet is designed to assist you to collate your information into a single line total. It can be used for all headings shown in your cash flow projection, eg:

- your sales, which could be a collation of product sales, or segment sales, or perhaps sales projections for existing products/services plus expected sales for new products/services
- your vehicle expenses, which can be shown as a total of all costs relating to your vehicles
- your anticipated drawings, including your holiday requirements, tax payments, normal drawings, etc
- all your separate insurance payments covering all aspects of your business.

Your worksheet not only summarises the value of each item but it also shows when each receipt can be expected or when each payment is due. The worksheet also allows you to estimate some items as a simple percentage of sales, rather than as a set dollar figure. Examples of this could be purchases (with a known mark-up) or budgeted items such as wages. The percentages used are often based on previous profit and loss reports and are adjusted to current expectations.

Worksheet: ______ Period: / / to / / Sheet No ____ of ____

ITEM	JUL	AUG	SEP	OCT	NOV	DEC	JAN	FEB	MAR	APR	MAY	JUN	TOTAL
TOTAL													

FIGURE 14.11 Cash flow worksheet

Your future financial requirements

Your cash flow projections will allow you to know, in advance, the expected level of your bank balances. Your projection will show you when you will need extra cash or when you will have surplus cash. Should you be in the happy position of expecting to have surplus cash in your account(s) you have the opportunity to plan for future investment, or re-direction of that surplus. It is, however, more often the case that the projection will forecast a cash shortage rather than a cash surplus.

Note and identify the causes of cash shortages. One of the major purposes of cash budgeting is to identify the amount and timing of likely cash shortages. Two things follow. If cash shortages are due to excessive spending this can be remedied. If the firm has a genuine need for extra funding, financing arrangements can be made before the shortages actually occur. Such forward planning will undoubtedly make it easier to obtain funding, both short-term and longer-term.

This section of your plan should include:

- the details of anticipated shortages (or surpluses)
- the reasons for the shortages (or surpluses)
- the options open to you to rectify (or capitalise on) the situation
- your decision, and
- action to be taken.

Your appendices

This section is designed to support your plan with detail that would otherwise distract the reader from the theme of your plan. The process of placing your working papers in a separate part of your plan is a logical one. It allows readers (and that includes you) to check, whenever required, on key areas through easy access to supporting material and working papers. The inclusion of working papers also makes your tasks easier next time you want to update your plan.

It is common practice to include previous financial reports as your first appendix. The other appendices will be for such things as working papers, reference material, competitors, publications, trade reports, maps, surveys, council minutes, newspaper clippings, certificates, etc. Your appendix section is simply a separate filing system for information on your plan.

Information for your plan

Where do you obtain all the data to allow you to write your plan?

The information you need to write your plan is available — if you know where to look. Much of it will come from you own background experience and records and also from data you can gain by

- visiting competitors
- talking to relevant people

- attending workshops, seminars and courses
- asking other small business people
- joining small business groups and associations, and
- talking to the previous owner(s) if you are buying a business.

Never be afraid to ask questions or to ask for help. At the very worst, people can only say 'No!' but most people are only too happy to assist when approached correctly. If you don't know where to start, ask one of your professional advisers to point you in the right direction. Once you have made the first step in researching your business, the rest seems to follow naturally.

When you are doing your own research, remember a few key rules:

- Check your facts and if you don't know, find out — the information is available somewhere.
- Use your professional advisers — for input and also to check your proposals.
- Be practical — don't try to be 100 per cent accurate when in many cases a guide is sufficient.

A research directory, showing sources of information and help available, is included for your assistance in the appendix of this book.

Perhaps now you can understand the saying

> Most businesses don't plan to fail — they simply fail to plan!

Writing your plan

Only two points will have to be considered before you write your own plan. The first is the purpose of your plan.

Your business plan is a management tool designed to help you reach your objectives and to help your business survive and grow. It should allow you to:

- measure your progress towards your objectives
- control your business
- adjust to changes in the marketplace, and
- assist you to manage your business.

The plan is not a project that is prepared once and then put away for safe keeping. It is an ongoing activity, and should be continually updated with fresh information. Objectives should be constantly revised and your working plans should be used daily.

Your plan can also be used to help your business in other ways. If you are seeking loan funds from a bank or other financial institution, a good business plan supporting your loan application is essential. A business plan can also be used to sell your business to:

- prospective partners or others interested in investing in your business
- suppliers, especially when you are trying to persuade them that you are a potential outlet
- clients and potential clients, to whom the business plan is a professional way of getting your message across.

It can also act as a support for tenders, submissions or applications, and for prospective buyers of your business.

The remaining point to consider is the way in which you present your plan. The plan is your key to success and your presentation is vital. It is suggested that you:

- Have it word-processed or typed. This makes for easier reading and presents the document in a more official manner, giving it extra credibility.
- Place it in a folder. Folders are not expensive and they both package your plan and protect it from the effects of constant handling.
- Write your plan following the guidelines we have discussed in this chapter.

As with your feasibility study (see Chapter 8), your business plan is written by you and is for you. If you are presenting the plan to anyone else, you will probably wish to remove any confidential sections.

Summary

In this chapter we have looked at planning in two ways — firstly as an overview, and then as a blueprint for writing your own business plan.

The overview painted a picture of how successful firms planned and it looked at the barriers that prevented many firms from proper planning. It also examined the benefits of planning, especially the ability to compete successfully in the marketplace.

The second part of the chapter assumed that you had an actual business and it presented a blueprint for writing your own business plan, based upon three key questions:

- Where are you now?
- Where do you want to be at a future date?
- How will you get there?

It was shown that the answers to these three questions will give you your own business plan, as they provide:

- your starting point
- your objectives and
- your strategies.

The plan should be written in the following four separate parts or sub-plans:

- an operational plan
- a marketing plan
- a staff plan and
- a financial plan.

The chapter went on to examine each of these four plans, and in doing so provided a blueprint to assist you in writing your own business plan. In providing you with this blueprint it assumes that before you attempt to write your own plan, you will read the remaining chapters in *Section 3, Succeeding*.

KEY WORDS

break-even point
budget
cash flow (or liquidity)
competitive advantage
distinctive competence
equity
financial viability
forecast
goals
objectives
planning
segment
strategy
time horizon
working plan

REVIEW EXERCISES

1 What is planning?

2 Give eight reasons why planning is avoided in many small firms.

3 What is meant by distinctive competence?

4 A business plan is based on the answers to which three questions?

5 A business plan is, in reality, four separate plans. What are those four plans?

6 Outline a format for writing a business plan.

7 List six criteria for good business objectives.

8 What are the five key decisions you must make in your marketing approach?

9 On what assumption about people is your staff plan based?

10 What is meant by the term 'break-even'?

11 What is the most important budget for a small business?

12 Using your own or assumed business as a base, write your own business plan by following the guidelines listed in this chapter.

Self-Assessment Exercises

How good is your business planning?

If you have an existing business and wish to rate your planning, you are invited to complete the following questionnaire.

To what extent is your firm involved in planning? Please indicate (by checking the appropriate box for each item) the extent to which each of the following planning activities is part of your firm's regular practices. The boxes are headed as follows:

N = never
R = rarely
O = occasionally
S = sometimes
F = frequently
A = always

	A	F	S	O	R	N
1 Estimating the sales income you expect to earn						
A for the next year	☐	☐	☐	☐	☐	☐
B for the next two years	☐	☐	☐	☐	☐	☐
2 Calculating your firm's break-even sales and/or production volume	☐	☐	☐	☐	☐	☐
3 Comparing sales results with sales quotas and budgets	☐	☐	☐	☐	☐	☐
4 Preparing the following budgets/projections/forecasts						
A for the next year						
(a) cash flow	☐	☐	☐	☐	☐	☐
(b) net profit (income)	☐	☐	☐	☐	☐	☐
(c) plant/equipment (asset) needs	☐	☐	☐	☐	☐	☐
(d) staffing needs	☐	☐	☐	☐	☐	☐
(e) funding (ie borrowing) needs	☐	☐	☐	☐	☐	☐
(f) taxation payments	☐	☐	☐	☐	☐	☐
B for the next two years						
(a) cash flow	☐	☐	☐	☐	☐	☐
(b) net profit (income)	☐	☐	☐	☐	☐	☐

	A	F	S	O	R	N
(c) plant/equipment (asset) needs	☐	☐	☐	☐	☐	☐
(d) staffing needs	☐	☐	☐	☐	☐	☐
(e) funding (ie borrowing) needs	☐	☐	☐	☐	☐	☐
5 Estimating future inflation rates						
A for the next year	☐	☐	☐	☐	☐	☐
B for the next two years	☐	☐	☐	☐	☐	☐
6 Reviewing your firm's image/ reputation	☐	☐	☐	☐	☐	☐
7 Setting and using sales targets (weekly, monthly, quarterly or annually)						
A for the next year	☐	☐	☐	☐	☐	☐
B for the next two years	☐	☐	☐	☐	☐	☐
8 Planning major schemes/ideas to promote sales and/or profits						
A for the next year	☐	☐	☐	☐	☐	☐
B for the next two years	☐	☐	☐	☐	☐	☐
9 Setting employee productivity (ie performance) standards and reviewing results	☐	☐	☐	☐	☐	☐
10 Estimating inventory (including materials and supplies) needs						
A for the next year	☐	☐	☐	☐	☐	☐
B for the next two years	☐	☐	☐	☐	☐	☐
11 Reviewing the sales performance of each major product line or service to enable changes to be made	☐	☐	☐	☐	☐	☐
12 Conducting market surveys to assess future changes in products/services						
A for the next year	☐	☐	☐	☐	☐	☐
B for the next two years	☐	☐	☐	☐	☐	☐
13 Checking whether funds will be available for borrowing from potential lenders, if needed	☐	☐	☐	☐	☐	☐

	A	F	S	O	R	N
14 Calculating percentage profit on sales of each major product line or service	☐	☐	☐	☐	☐	☐
15 Measuring						
A overall stock turnover rate	☐	☐	☐	☐	☐	☐
B accounts receivable collection rate (or aging of accounts receivable)	☐	☐	☐	☐	☐	☐
16 Collecting and analysing data about your major competitors (eg prices, quality, sales, services, and other activities which may affect your sales)	☐	☐	☐	☐	☐	☐
17 Reviewing the cost/benefits of your firm's present location	☐	☐	☐	☐	☐	☐
18 Using inventory records and re-order methods to reduce cost of holding and buying stock, materials or supplies	☐	☐	☐	☐	☐	☐
19 Analysing all groups of expenses to ensure they are in line with expense budgets	☐	☐	☐	☐	☐	☐
20 Reviewing purchasing practices — checking availability of materials and stock	☐	☐	☐	☐	☐	☐
21 Reviewing and adjusting prices (eg by analysing demand, competition and costs)	☐	☐	☐	☐	☐	☐
22 Developing plans to minimise the firm's (or your personal) tax obligation	☐	☐	☐	☐	☐	☐
23 Assessing customer satisfaction with your firm as a place to do business	☐	☐	☐	☐	☐	☐
24 Forecasting future business and economic conditions in your general market area, and assessing their likely impact on your sales						
A for the next year	☐	☐	☐	☐	☐	☐
B for the next two years	☐	☐	☐	☐	☐	☐
25 Searching for new processes, methods and/or technologies to improve your business	☐	☐	☐	☐	☐	☐

	A	F	S	O	R	N
26 Reviewing staff conditions, including wages	☐	☐	☐	☐	☐	☐
27 Reviewing storage and space needs	☐	☐	☐	☐	☐	☐
28 Planning to cope with employee resignations, retirements, training needs, promotions, etc	☐	☐	☐	☐	☐	☐
29 Reviewing overall efficiency of major suppliers (quality, delivery time, cost)	☐	☐	☐	☐	☐	☐
30 Attending management and/or technical training courses relevant to your business	☐	☐	☐	☐	☐	☐
31 Seeking advice from external experts (eg accountants, bankers, consultants, friends in business or any others)	☐	☐	☐	☐	☐	☐
32 Identifying your firm's particular strengths and weaknesses	☐	☐	☐	☐	☐	☐

Scoring method

Always = 6, F = 5, S = 4, O = 3, R = 2, Never = 1

Add each of your 50 scores, between one and six in each case. The maximum is 300, the minimum is 50. The average score is 146. The standard deviation is 37 — about two-thirds of scores will fall between 183 (146 plus 37) and 109 (146 less 37). Scores less than 109 indicate a serious lack of any planning; scores above 183 suggest good planning.

Poor planning	Average	Good	Excellent
50 75 100	125 150 175	200 225	250 275 300

References

English, JW 1986, *How to Organise and Operate a Small Business in Australia*, 3rd edn, Allen & Unwin, Sydney

Orpen, C 1985, 'The effects of long-range planning on small business performance: A further examination', *Journal of Small Business Management*, vol 23, no 1, January, pp 16–23

Williams, A J 1987, *The Characteristics and Performance of Small Business in Australia (1983 to 1985): A Study of the Characteristics of Small Australian Business Ventures and their Owner/Managers and a Longitudinal Investigation of their Economic Performance*, monograph, University of Newcastle

CHAPTER 15

Record keeping for management

Records give you vital information about your business. Ideally, everything you do in your business should be recorded, so that you can look back later and review past events. With this information, you can tell how your business is going, make better decisions and plan for the future. Records are vital for planning and control of your business.

After reading and working through this chapter, you should be able to:

- explain why business records should be kept
- design a suitable record system for your business, and
- prepare an income and expenditure statement and balance sheet.

WHY KEEP RECORDS?

A complete set of records will help you determine:

- how much cash you have available at any time
- who owes you money, how much, and for how long
- which accounts you need to pay
- current costs of goods and services
- ways to keep costs under control
- effect of sales promotions
- when you should apply for a loan, and how much you will need
- what your business is worth, if you were to sell it
- when you can afford new plant and equipment
- seasonal patterns (busy times of the day, days of the week, months of the year)
- your profit
- staff performance, bonuses, commissions, etc, and
- when to plan for expansion.

At various times, you have to tell other people about your business. This is sometimes a legal requirement. It is also necessary if, for example, you are applying for a loan or other credit finance. As well, your insurance company might require evidence of business activity, value of stock and other assets, and wages paid, before effecting insurance or settling a claim.

These same records will give you all the information you need to satisfy the demands of:

- the taxation office
- other government departments
- insurance companies
- your accountant and solicitor
- bank managers
- finance companies
- suppliers, and
- prospective purchasers of your business.

To be useful as a business resource, your record system must be able to produce information that is:

- appropriate to the user's needs
- understandable to the user
- concise yet meaningful
- accurate (within reason)
- economically produced, and
- up to date.

Most of your records will be of money, but a lot of other information is worth noting, such as details about customers, suppliers, competitors, business contacts, advertising, staff, time and even the weather! Keeping a record of all this results in a large amount of data. The only way to make the data useful for management decisions is to summarise them. Which ones to add together, how often to add them, what headings to use, where to keep original pieces of paper — all these factors and more — determine the best record system for your business.

YOUR RECORD SYSTEM

The purpose of a record system is to record data and at the same time provide a method for building a series of summaries of the records. It must do this in such a way as to allow a path to be found back through the summaries to the source of each item of data. This provides a basis for checking the data used in the figures presented in summary form. It also allows for the detection and correction of any errors which are made.

> A record system is a way of summarising entries while providing a trail back to the source documents.

If you bear in mind that most record systems use **books**, you will have a handy way of remembering the following rules of thumb:

Bank — put all money, in and out, through your bank account.

Obvious — leave a clear trail from source documents through all records.

Organise — make sure the who, what, when, why and where of all parts of your system are clearly defined.

Keep it simple — complexity creates confusion.

Separate business and private finances.

MONEY RECORDS

Money plays a critical part in any business. The rates at which it flows into, and out of, your business determine whether or not it is a growing, healthy and successful concern. The timing and amounts of cash flows in and out determine whether your business will survive.

Proper planning and control of money are essential. An adequate record system, carefully maintained, is vital for control today and planning tomorrow. Keeping records is easy, but it does take time and money. However, once you have understood the reason for keeping accurate, detailed records, you will recognise that the time and cost are well worthwhile. Some people feel that they are not up to such a task; but this is usually because they believe that a good record system has to be complex. Some systems *are*, but this happens only in large or very diverse businesses.

> The best record system is the simplest one that gives you the information you need.

As a small business person, you might need no more than the following for your whole money record system:

- an analysis book
- some index cards for account customers and suppliers
- a pad of invoice/statements
- a receipt book
- a cheque book and bank deposit book
- letterhead paper with trading name
- a pad of general-purpose vouchers, and
- a set procedure.

Some space is also needed to file paperwork until you are ready to copy the data from it and also after you finish processing it. Legally you may be obliged to keep the originals for at least seven years, in case there is a need to refer to them. Once the information from the originals has been transferred accurately to your record system, it can be summarised. It is this summary that you refer to first when managing your business.

THE MONEY RECORD SYSTEM

This system is a simple process of four or five steps. Every transaction, whether buying, selling, borrowing or repaying, needs to be recorded. This is done on source documents. Figures from these are then gathered together into a book of original entries (journals). Once recorded, they are added together and summarised. Totals are taken and either entered in other books (ledgers), or used directly in a statement or report of some sort. Figure 15.1 shows this flow.

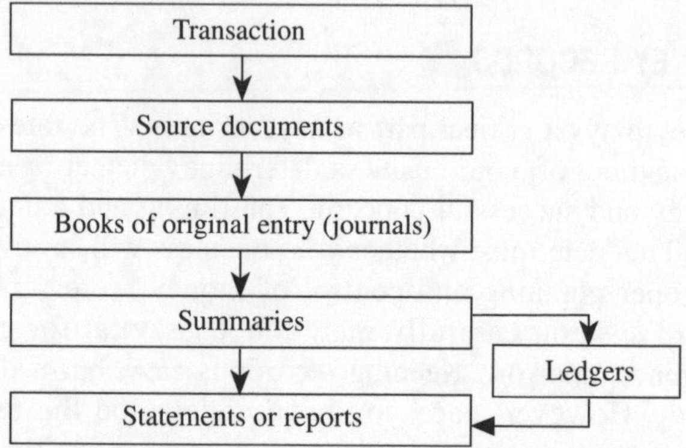

FIGURE 15.1 The money record system

Step 1: Source documents

As the name suggests, these are the starting point. There might be an **order form**, which your customer sends to you for a sale, or which you send to your supplier for a purchase. This form is not always used, especially in the case of retail sales, but where it is used it should show the:

- order number and date
- name, address and telephone number of the purchaser
- type and quantity of goods or service required
- any special delivery instructions, and
- signature of the person authorising the expenditure.

Next, there might be a **delivery docket**. This is included with the goods when they are delivered. Often the customer is asked to sign one copy of this, as proof of receipt of the goods. A delivery docket shows the:

- date
- docket number
- name, address and telephone number of the supplier
- name, address and telephone number of the purchaser
- order number
- type and quantity of goods delivered, and
- signature of the person receiving the goods.

Always check goods received against those shown on the delivery docket before signing it.

Usually an **invoice** will be sent to the purchaser. This source document includes the price of goods and services provided. Information on an invoice includes the:

- date
- invoice number
- name, address and telephone number of the supplier
- name, address and telephone number of the purchaser
- order number
- delivery docket number
- type and quantity of goods and services
- unit price and total for each item
- any special payment or discount arrangements, and
- total price of the purchase.

Always check the invoice against your order: quantaites and prices quoted, against goods received and prices charged.

An invoice may be followed later by a **statement of account**, which displays the:

- date of the statement
- opening balance
- money received since the previous statement
- date of the invoice(s) since the previous statement
- invoice number(s)
- amount owing for each invoice
- total amount owing, and
- any special payment and discount arrangements.

Delivery docket, invoice and statement can be combined in one form.

This not only saves paper and handling, but also often results in quicker payment of accounts by your customers.

Another source document is a **credit note**, which is used when goods are returned to the suppliers, for damaged goods or for other allowances. If this is not a frequent occurrence, an invoice form can be used, with the word 'Invoice' crossed out and 'Credit' written in its place.

A simple **receipt** for payment is also a source document. It should show the:

- date
- receipt number
- name and address of the supplier
- name of the purchaser

- brief description of the goods and services (for example 'tyres' or 'painting')
- amount of payment, and
- signature of the person accepting payment.

Vouchers are source documents which record small purchases (from petty cash, for instance). They show the:

- date
- voucher number (sometimes this is omitted)
- brief details of the goods and services
- amount
- signature of the person authorising the purchase, and
- signature of the person claiming reimbursement.

Many small businesses use a letterhead for their order form and receipt, and have combined delivery docket/invoice/statement forms printed if many of their sales are to account customers. A pad of general-purpose vouchers is kept and used for small purchases. If you have a cash register, it will issue receipts for customers. So you can keep your system very simple: you may need only letterheads, invoice/statements and vouchers.

Cheque butts show the date, the amount and brief details of the payee and a reason for the cheque. Some business people have caused themselves a lot of extra work by not keeping careful note of all these details. It pays to always complete the butt whenever a cheque is written.

Deposit slip butts, or copies, are the only record you have of money you pay into your account. All the important details of this money should be recorded on your copy of the deposit slip.

Summary

Every transaction should be recorded on at least one source document. You might not need to have all the source documents detailed in this step. Alternatively, you might need other source documents that have not been mentioned here. Each source document must contain a reference number which can be used to identify that document as the record of a particular transaction.

Step 2: Books of original entry

These are often known as **journals**, **cash books** or **analysis books**. Figures, and other details from the source documents, are transferred to these books. When you enter the figures, you can put them under various headings. These headings tell you what the money was spent on, or where it came from. To start with, you will need a series of columns on the paper, each one headed with an item, such as expenses (electricity, rent and so on) or income (cash sales, etc). When a figure from the source document is entered it is shown in the appropriate column.

DATE		DESCRIPTION	REF	INCOME		EXPENSES					
				Cash sales	Other	Bank charges	Electricity	Rent	Wages	Car	Total
1995 APRIL		Brought forward		15000 00	2900 00	68 75	822 40	11700 00	9250 84		
	19	L. and D. Lord 18/4 to 17/5	511					1300 00			1300 00
		Cash sales		400 00							
	20	Elec. Board 1/1 to 31/3	512				210 08				210 08

FIGURE 15.2 Cash book

Enter your figures each day. Spending a few minutes each day while your memory is fresh is much better than waiting till later, when you will need to struggle to remember the details.

Enter in numerical order the records of cheques you have written, so that it will be easy to find the details later.

It is a good idea to clip all invoices from one supplier together during a month, and pay them in one batch at the end of the month. Also, enter in numerical order records of those invoices you send to your customers.

Totals

At the end of each week or month you can add up the columns and find the total outlay for each expense item in that time. If you also keep a running total of these figures, you will have a record for the year to date. Arrange with your bank to provide a monthly statement. Check your details and totals against the bank statement each month. Adjustments can be made where necessary, and the totals ruled off when you are satisfied that they are correct. In this way, you will ensure that your figures are never more than one month out of date. This will help when you are searching for errors, because you need to work back through figures only for the current month. It will also mean that you are up to date with what is happening in your business.

> Before checking or totalling your cash book you must reconcile your bank statement.

A **bank reconciliation** is necessary to update the bank statement. It is very rare to find the same figures on the bank statement, in your cash book, and for your actual cash situation. It is vital that all figures be brought into line, so that you know exactly how much cash you have. Some cheques which you have written and posted will not have been presented to your bank by the date on which your statement was prepared. Because of this, you do not have as much money as the statement shows. Sometimes, the deposits you have recorded might not be the same as those shown on your statement. A last-minute deposit might not have been included, or a cheque you deposited might have been returned.

A bank reconciliation starts with the balance shown on the statement. You can then:

1 add any unrecorded deposits, and
2 subtract from it the total of unpresented cheques, and any dishonoured deposited cheques.

This gives you a true figure for your bank balance at the closing date.

Once you have completed the bank reconciliation, you will probably need to add some transactions to your cash book. Some payments, such as bank charges, government taxes and duties, are deducted from your account by the bank without your having written a cheque. Because there is no cheque, and no invoice or other source document, you will not have recorded these transactions in your cash book yet. When you have entered them, all entries on the bank statement and in your cash book can be cross-checked to ensure that all have been entered, and that this has been done correctly. Note that, for these transactions, your bank statement is a source document.

Month			
Balance on statement			$........
Add Outstanding deposits:			
	Date	Amount	
		....	
		....	
	Total		$........
		Sub total	$.......
Less Unpresented cheques:			
	Cheque no.	Amount	
	....	....	
	....	....	
	....	....	
	....	....	
	Total		$........
		Adjusted balance	$........

FIGURE 15.3 Bank reconciliation statement

Check the cash book totals

At this stage, total cash as shown in your cash book should match the corrected balance from your bank reconciliation statement. If it does not, then a search must be made to find the error. If you cannot find it fairly quickly, put the records to one side and do something else. If you continue, you might find that you are making the same mistake over and over again. Come back to it after a few hours and restart the checking process. If you still cannot find it, have someone else check the figures.

Rule the cash book off only after all figures can be verified and totals balanced.

Summary

Section 2 has detailed the keeping of a cash book, and the procedure to prepare summaries and verify your cash position. The records guide in Figure 15.4 provides a useful checklist. (Remember that you might not use all these records in your business.) A more detailed explanation of this process can be found in *Record Keeping for Your Own Business*, (second edition) by the same authors, published by Thomas Nelson Australia.

DAILY	Cash receipts
	Debtor receipts
	Invoicing
	Invoice costing
	Quote register
	Sales journal
	Till sheets
	Cash book
	Daily bank balances
	Wages book
WEEKLY	Wages book
MONTHLY	Wages summary
	Group tax return
	Debtors — end of month
	Sales tax
	Cash receipts
	Cash book
	Bank reconciliation
	Expense summary
	Creditors list
	Petty cash
QUARTERLY	Stocktake
	Accounting reports
YEARLY	Accounting reports
	Group certificates
	Stocktake

FIGURE 15.4 Records guide
Source: S Stephens

Step 3: The final summary statements

The steps detailed in Figure 15.4 are taken daily, weekly or monthly. Final summary statements are prepared as required, usually less frequently than this. Two statements must be prepared: the income statement and the balance sheet.

Income statements

An income statement summarises all the income and expense totals for a period. The period of time must be shown as part of the heading. Your income statement gives you your profit figure for the period. In fact, it gives you two profit figures, gross profit and net profit.

Gross profit is the difference between your sales to your customers (income) and the amount you paid for the goods (cost of goods sold).

> Gross profit = income minus cost of goods sold

Gross profit is the money your business has available to pay all expenses, to buy new equipment, to repay loans, and to pay you for your work.

Net profit is what you have left after you deduct all expenses.

> Net profit = gross profit minus expenses

The money you keep comes from the net profit. Part of this is your pay packet, so obviously it is very important to you, and you should know how to calculate it.

Total income

Start with your sales income for the period. This includes cash and credit sales, less returns, allowances, and so on.

Any other income the business receives would be added to the sales, to give total income. However, to keep it simple, we will assume that the only income is from sales.

Income		
Net sales	$	_ _ _ _ _ _ _ _ _
Total	$	________

FIGURE 15.5 Calculating total income

Cost of goods sold (COGS)

The next step is to calculate the cost of goods sold and subtract it from income to determine your gross profit. There are three ways of calculating COGS, depending on the nature of your business. In a retail business, goods are purchased for the purpose of resale, and COGS is the cost of these goods. Manufacturers buy materials and pay labour and other costs to produce their finished goods. COGS is the total of these costs. For service businesses, COGS is the cost of labour to provide the service, plus any other costs directly associated with the service provision.

The calculation of COGS for each of these types of business will now be considered in more detail.

Retail COGS

To calculate how much you paid for the goods you have sold, you must take into account the stock that you had at the start of the period, how much you have purchased since and how much you have left now.

Value of goods (at cost) at start of period (opening stock)	\$_________
Add purchases during period (from cash book 'purchases')	\$_________
Total available for sale	\$_________
Less value of goods (at cost) at end of period (closing stock)	\$_________
Cost of goods sold (COGS)	\$_________

FIGURE 15.6 Calculating COGS for a retail business

Manufacturing COGS

In making products, you need to pay for materials and labour. These are the 'direct costs'. The cost of goods sold is the cost of materials and labour used in production. Only the costs that are actually incurred in the production process are included.

Direct material costs are calculated from the quantity and value of materials used, as shown in Figure 15.7.

Direct labour costs are calculated from time spent on manufacture.

Direct labour

Time required to make 1 item ..... hours

× no. of items manufactured $_________

× labour cost per hour $_________

Direct labour $_________

Materials are those items that are components of the product.

Direct materials

Cost of material in 1 item $_________

× no. of items manufactured $_________

Direct materials $_________

Other costs (manufacturing overheads) are the costs that are essential to the manufacturing process, and include electricity used for lighting and machines, rent of factory space, etc. They do not include office wages or other costs associated with operating the business (advertising, accountant's fees, etc.)

Manufacturing overheads

Item 1 $_________

Item 2 $_________

.

.

.

Manufacturing overheads $_________

Cost of goods sold

Direct labour (from above) $_________

Direct materials (from above) $_________

Manufacturing overheads (from above) $_________

Cost of goods sold $_________

FIGURE 15.7 Calculating COGS for a manufacturing business

Some other costs may need to be included in the calculation of manufacturing COGS. Check your figures with your accountant.

Service COGS

Costs of providing a service consist of direct labour, materials, and possibly some overheads.

Direct labour costs are calculated from time spent on clients' work (paid time).

Direct labour
Time spent on clients' work .... hours
× labour cost per hour $________
Direct labour $________

Materials are the cost of items provided to your clients as a component of the service (eg replacement parts in a repair business, paper in a secretarial service, etc). Records of these costs are kept under the heading of Materials in your record books.

Materials (from your records) $________

Other costs (service overheads) include other costs that are essential to the provision of the service. Examples are telephone calls to order parts in a repair business, repair of a printer in a secretarial service, costs of travelling to customers in a lawn-moving service. They do not include general operating expenses such as office rent, advertising, etc. Details of service overheads should be kept separately in your records, so they can be identified easily.

Service overheads
Item 1 $________
Item 2 $________
·
·
·
Service overheads $________

Cost of goods sold
Direct labour $________
Materials $________
Service overheads $________

COGS $________

FIGURE 15.8 Calculating COGS for a service business

Gross profit

Once you have worked out your COGS, you can calculate your gross profit. Whatever your type of business, your income statement now looks like this:

Income
Net sales $________
Total $________
Less COGS $________
Gross profit $________

FIGURE 15.9 Calculating gross profit

Net profit

Remembering that net profit is gross profit less expense, and given the gross profit you have just calculated, all that is required is to subtract your business expenses. Totals for each of these can be found in the cash book. Each item is listed, together with the total expenses for the period.

Expenses	
Accountant's fees	$_________
Advertising	$_________
Bank charges	$_________
Depreciation (see page 293)	$_________
.	
.	
.	
Wages and salaries	$_________
Total expenses	$_________

Your complete income statement now looks like this:

Income	
Net sales	$_________
Total	$_________
Less COGS	$_________
Gross profit	$_________
Less expenses	$_________
Net profit	$_________

FIGURE 15.10 Calculating net profit

Balance sheet

The second summary document is the balance sheet. It shows what your business owns and what it owes at a specified date. The date must be shown as part of the heading. What your business owns and owes changes with every transaction. Your balance sheet is like a flashlight photograph taken at one instant in time. It is accurate only for that instant. This is why the date is so important — the situation has changed from the day before. Iit will change again by the next day. Note that your balance sheet refers to your *business*, not to *you*.

Keep business and owner's finances separate.

Things that a business owns are called **assets**. Assets are grouped into those that change often (at least within 12 months), which are called **current assets**, and those that the business will own for more than a year, which are called **fixed assets**. A third group is made up of other valuable assets which you cannot see or touch. These are the **intangible assets**, and include goodwill, set-up costs (for new businesses), patents and copyrights.

Current assets include cash, stock (or materials), accounts receivable (debtors) and pre-paid expenses.

Fixed assets are vehicles, plant and equipment, fixtures and furnishings, and land and buildings. For some of these, the value is reduced each year to allow for their loss of productive efficiency. The amount by which they are reduced is the **accumulated depreciation**. Allowable rates of depreciation are provided by the Australian Taxation Office. Depreciation is calculated for each year that the asset is owned by your business. Accumulated depreciation is the total depreciation since purchase of the asset. Accumulated depreciation is subtracted from the original cost, and the new figure is the book value, or written down value.

Book value = cost of asset minus accumulated depreciation

Some assets are expected to last longer than others. As an example, carpets have a longer life expectancy than computers. This is reflected in the depreciation rate, which varies for different assets. Depreciation can be calculated in several ways. Methods of calculation, and the corresponding depreciation rates, are provided by the Australian Taxation Office.

Your accountant will help you determine the amount of depreciation to allow for each fixed asset item that the business owns. A depreciaiton schedule will be included in you business financial statements prepared by your accountant.

Intangible assets, by their very nature, are difficult to put a value on. However, they are assets of the business and must be assigned a value.

Goodwill

The most common intangible asset is goodwill. There is a lot of misunderstanding about goodwill. Many methods of calculating its current value have been proposed, but there is no universally accepted method. It is usually shown at the value it had when the presnet owner bought the business.

Goodwill = value of business minus net value of other assets

Value of your business

The value of your business seems clear, until we look at it more closely. It depends on how many people want to buy it, how keen someone else is to own it, and how reluctant the owner is to sell it. If you have ever sold a car by taking it to various dealers and advertising it yourself, you will know how the 'value' of your car can vary. The situation is similar with a business — except that the range of 'values' is much greater.

There are two ways of estimating the value of your business:

1 consult a business broker
2 look at the 'businesses for sale' column in the classified advertisement section of your capital city newspaper.

A business broker will be able to give you a fairly accurate valuation. However, you might need to produce your trading figures and other operating details, which you might be reluctant to reveal if you are not seriously interested in selling your business.

The 'businesses for sale' advertisements provide a rough guide to the value of many types of business. If you look at advertisements for businesses like yours, you can calculate the relationship between turnover, net profit and price (value). For example, if your business is a coffee lounge, you might find that *on average* the price of a coffee lounge business is equivalent to about 20 weeks' turnover. You know what your weekly turnover is, so you can multiply it by 20 to gain a rough idea of the value of your business.

Patents, copyrights and other legal protection

Other intangible assets include various forms of legal protection for your product. The value of this protection depends on how difficult it is for someone else to produce something similar — or even better. Your product might be the only one of its kind today, but by next year there might be 20 similar ones. In this case, your patent value would change suddenly from one year to the next. In calculating the value of legal protection, it is necessary to determine how much of your business profit depends upon that protection. How much business would you lose if your protection was cancelled? What is your profit from that part of your business? How long can you expect to generate profits from it? The answers to these questions will help you estimate the value of legal protection in your intangible assets.

Your list of assets shows everything that the business owns as in Figure 15.11.

	$	$	$
CURRENT ASSETS			
Cash	------		
Debtors	------		
Stock (or materials)	------		
Total current assets			------
NON-CURRENT ASSETS			
FIXED ASSETS			
Vehicle cost	------		
Less depreciation	------	------	
Plant & equip. cost	------		
Less depreciation	------	------	
Total fixed assets			------
INTANGIBLE ASSETS			
Goodwill, patents, etc	------		
Total intangible assets			------
TOTAL ASSETS			

FIGURE 15.11 Balance sheet, showing list of assets

Because the business started with nothing of its own, it must have obtained money from somewhere to buy all these things. Some money it borrowed from banks, finance companies and other sources, and the rest it 'borrowed' from the owner(s), as their original investment. Once the business has started trading, it may also 'borrow' money from trade suppliers, through accounts which it has with them. The amount it has 'borrowed' from the owner(s) is also increased by any profits made and any additional investment. The total of these represents what the business *owes*, and it must be equal to what it *owns*. Money 'borrowed' from the owner is shown as **owners' equity**. All other debts are termed **liabilities**. They are grouped into:

1 debts due to be repaid during the next 12 months (current liabilities), and
2 debts due to be repaid after 12 months (non-current liabilities).

Current liabilities include bank overdraft, short-term loans, accounts payable (creditors) and accrued expenses.

Non-current liabilities cover long-term loans.

The list of what a business owes looks like this:

	$	$
CURRENT LIABILITIES		
Trade creditors	----------	
Bank overdraft	----------	
Short-term loans	----------	
Total current liabilities		----------
NON-CURRENT LIABILITIES		
Long-term loans	----------	
Total non-current liabilities		----------
TOTAL LIABILITIES		______
OWNERS' EQUITY		
Opening equity	----------	
Add net profit	----------	
Less drawings	----------	
Total equity		______
TOTAL LIABILITIES AND EQUITY		======

FIGURE 15.12 Balance sheet, showing liabilities and equity

From Figure 15.12 you will see that profits are added to owners' equity. This is because the business does not earn money for itself, but only for the owner. So any money earned through profit is 'owed' to the owner. Naturally, any money taken out of the business by the owner is regarded as part repayment of the owners' equity, and this reduces the amount 'owed' by the business of the owner.

Because the business must have 'borrowed' all the money needed to buy the things it owns, then the total of what it owns must always equal the total of what it 'owes'.

This is why a list of assets, liabilities and owners' equity is termed a balance sheet. It balances what the business 'owns' against what it 'owes'.

Owns = owes
Total assets = total liabilities + owners' equity

In the next chapter, these summary documents (balance sheet and income statement) will be studied to see how you can use them to help manage your business.

Summary

Every transaction must be recorded. The totals and summaries of these individual records are used initially to manage your business. A record-keeping system is required which provides the details of transactions and appropriate summaries which you need to manage your business. Recording of transactions is best done daily, with summaries made each week or month and each year. Transactions should be recorded in such a way that the summaries produced can be used both for management and as items in other summary documents or reports. A balance sheet and income statement are the final summaries at the end of a period of time (usually one year). Both of these are 'historic' — they show the financial state of the business at some time in the past (balance sheet), and how it got there (income statement). Full details of the settin up and operation of a record system are included in *Record Keeping for Your Own Business*, (second edition) by the same authors, published by Thomas Nelson Australia.

Key words

bank reconciliation	gross profit
creditor	net profit
debtor	petty cash
depreciation	source documents

Review exercises

1 Why should you keep records of your business?
2 What is the purpose of a record system?
3 List the steps in a money record system.
4 Describe the source documents used in a money record system.
5 What is a book of original entry, and what information does it show?
6 Why do you need a bank reconciliation statement?
7 What is the difference between gross profit and net profit?
8 What is COGS, and how is it calculated?
9 Why is an income statement useful?
10 What information is shown on a balance sheet?

CHAPTER 16

Financial management and planning

In the previous chapter, we saw how the figures from source documents are gathered together and summarised. At the end, we had just two reports: an income statement and a balance sheet. Together these show where the business was at the date of the balance sheet, and how it got there over the period of the income statement. They are historic reports, in that they look back at what happened in the business some time in the past.

This chapter shows you how to use these historic reports as a basis for looking ahead and planning the future of your business, as well as managing its operation. It is this planning and management which will enable you to achieve your objectives. The reports which you have produced are a vital tool in setting and reaching your business goals.

When you have worked through this chapter, you should be able to:

- identify and calculate trends and ratios from financial results
- set sound financial objectives, and prepare budgets to achieve them
- prepare a projected cash flow statement for your business
- calculate variances and use them in the control of your business, and
- explain the benefits and costs of using a computer in your business.

TRENDS

All the figures which appear on the summary reports are important in your planning and management. However, they represent the past, and the future might look very different. The first step is to see what the future will look like if nothing new happens and everything just goes on as it has in the past. This means finding trends in past figures for each of the items and projecting them forward. An easy way to see these trends is to draw a graph of the figures.

Graphs

Graphs are simply a picture of the changes which have occurred. When a time base is used, the picture is one of changes over time. To do this, all that you need is some graph paper, a pencil and your summary reports for the past years.

With the long edge of the graph paper towards you, mark the major divisions along the long edge with the years for which you have results. Start with the earliest year on the left, at the first major division line from the edge. Next, select one result to look at — say, sales. Starting from the lower edge, mark each major division on the left edge of the paper with a series of round numbers (1000, 2000, 3000; or 5000, 10 000, 15 000; or 100 000, 200 000, 300 000). Check that your sales for each year are between the lowest number and the highest number on the paper. As an example, we will graph the following yearly sales:

1987	12 000
1988	17 000
1989	19 000
1990	24 000
1991	27 000
1992	31 000

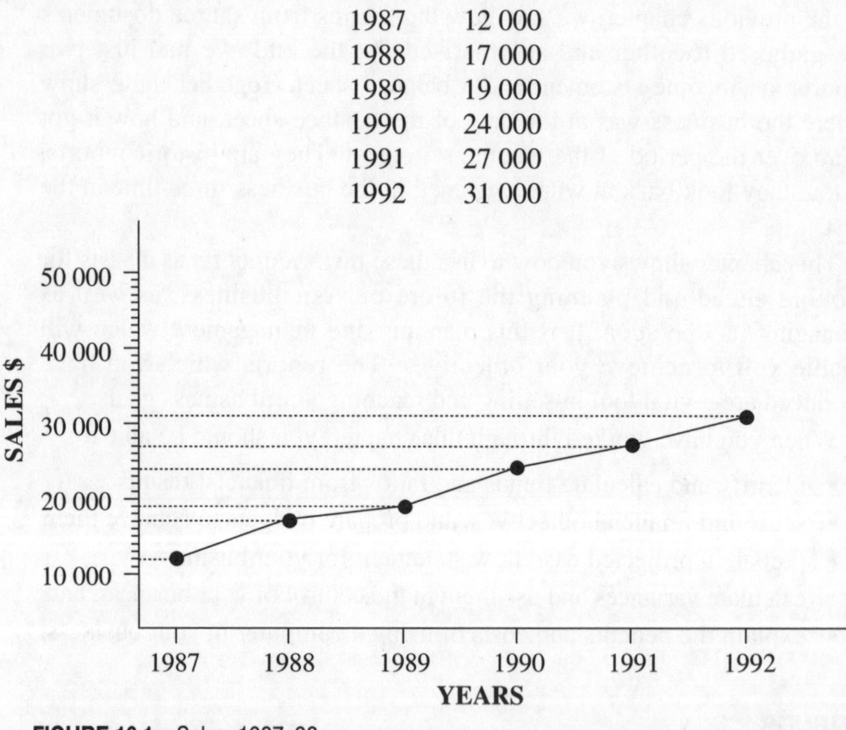

FIGURE 16.1 Sales, 1987–92

In this example, sales records range from 12 000 to 31 000, so they are all between the lowest (10 000) and the highest (50 000).

Each minor division on the graph paper is an equal part of the gap between major divisions. In the example above, if there were ten minor divisions, each would be one-tenth of the gap. The gap is 10 000, so each minor division is 1000. Taking the sales figure for the first year, mark it on the scale on the left edge. Follow the line it is on across the page to a point directly above the first year number (that is, until you reach the first major division line). Mark a small cross at this point. Take the sales figure for the next year, mark it on the left scale, follow the line across to the second major division (above the number of the second year) and mark a cross at this point. Repeat this for each year. You will have a series of crosses marked across the page, one above each year number. Starting at the left, draw a line from each cross to the one next to it. You now have a graph of sales over a period of time.

By repeating the process for items other than sales, you will have a pictorial record of how different items have varied over time. Just by looking at these, it might become clear that while some have increased steadily, others have decreased or remained constant. This shows how a trend emerges.

Measuring trends

It is often very useful to measure the trend. This can be done by drawing a straight line through your graph. Draw the line so that it has roughly the same number of points above the lines as below it, and so that the points are at about equal distances from it. You will find this easy if you use a clear plastic ruler, so you can see all the points while adjusting the position of the line. This is a trend line. Values along it will change by the same amount each year. So you can say that sales (or whatever) increase by $3440 each year on average. These last words are important because a trend is only an *average* rate of change, and the actual changes might be higher or lower than the trend (average) figure.

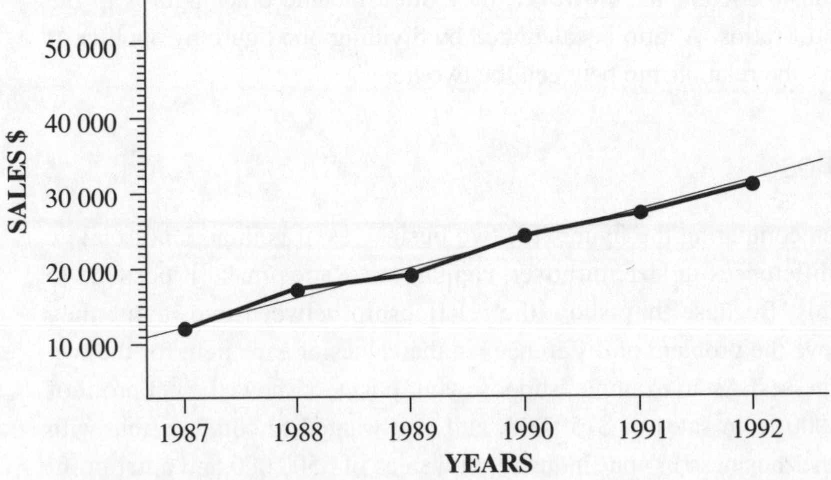

FIGURE 16.2 Sales trend, 1987–92

Projecting trends

Once you have drawn a trend line, it can be projected into the future. Do this simply by extending it on your graph. Mark the numbers of future years on the scale along the lower edge. Then mark a point on the line where it crosses the major division line for any year. It will be on a line leading to the scale on the left edge. Follow the line to the scale and read off the value. This represents the approximate value for that future year of the item you have graphed.

Deciding what to change

Projecting trend lines to forecast the future assumes that things will keep on going into the future the same way they have in the past. This might not be true, and certainly will not be true if you decide to make changes. You can determine the changes that need to be made by comparing forecast figures with your desired results — ie where you are aiming. These aiming points form part of your objectives. They might have come from your own plans or from the results of other businesses in your industry. Many trade associations and professional bodies have industry comparison figures. Others are published by universities from their research findings and are available in libraries or government departments associated with small business. These external references are also valuable tools for assessing whether your objectives are realistic and achievable. It is worthwhile preparing graphs and trend lines for all the items you have included in your objectives (eg sales, net profit etc). In many instances these published figures are for items you have included in your summary documents. However, they often include other figures in the form of ratios. A ratio is calculated by dividing one figure by another. It shows the relationship between the two items.

RATIOS

When comparing the figures for two businesses, it is important to allow for differences in size, turnover, capital, etc. Ratios make it possible to do this. Because they show the relationship between two items, they remove the problem of differences in the values of each item for the two businesses. As an example, suppose your business showed a net profit of $30 000 from sales of $150 000, and you wanted to compare this with another business in your industry with sales of $500 000 and a net profit of $75 000. This can be done by comparing the relationship between net profit and sales. In your business, dividing the profit of $30 000 by sales of $150 000 results in a relationship of 0.2 or 20%. In the other business, the same relationship is 0.15 or 15%. So even though the profit was higher in the other business, your efficiency and profitability are higher. Ratios have been developed which indicate the health (or *profitability*), and the survival (or *liquidity*) of businesses.

Profitability ratios

Sales profitability = net profit divided by sales
The answer is multiplied by 100 and shown as a percentage.
Example: Net profit = $ 30 000
Sales = $150 000
Sales profitability = 30 000 divided by 150 000 = 0.2
0.2 x 100 = 20%

This indicates the overall efficiency of the management. It shows the proportion of the sales income that remains as net profit.

Return on assets = net profit divided by total assets
This is also usually multiplied by 100 and shown as a percentage. It indicates the efficiency with which management has utilised all the capital invested in the business.

Often only fixed assets are used in this calculation, since these include the plant and equipment and so on used to generate profits. It is then called *return on fixed assets*.

Return on equity = net profit divided by owners' equity
This is shown as a percentage. It shows you the 'interest rate' on your investment in the business.

Gross margin = gross profit divided by sales, as a percentage
This shows the proportion of sales income that is retained as gross profit after deducting cost of goods sold. It indicates the appropriateness of pricing policies in terms of the direct costs involved with providing goods or services.

Efficiency ratio = individual expense items divided by sales
Each is shown as a percentage. This shows the proportion of sales income that is spent on each item of expense and indicates cost control efficiency.

Expense ratio = individual expense items divided by total expenses
Each is shown as a percentage. This shows the relative cost of each item of expense and indicates the items that need to be controlled more closely.

Liquidity ratios

Quick liquidity ratio = (current assets minus stock) divided by current liabilities
Usually shown as a number, and not as a percentage, it indicates the availability of immediate cash resources to cover current debts (current liabilities).

Current ratio = current assets divided by current liabilities
This is usually shown as a number, and not as a percentage. It indicates

the availability of cash during the next 12 months to pay liabilities falling due in that period.

Stock turnover = COGS divided by average stock
This is shown as the number of times stock is turned over or sold.
Note: Average stock = (opening stock + closing stock) divided by 2
This ratio indicates the efficiency of stock management.

Debt/equity ratio = external debts divided by owners' equity
This is shown as a number and indicates the efficiency of financial management. It shows the relative degrees of risk borne by external investors (creditors, banks, etc) and the owner(s).

Average collection period = accounts receivable debtors divided by total credit sales.
This is multiplied by 360, and the answer expressed as a number of days. It indicates the efficiency of credit management.

Each of these ratios is valuable in indicating one aspect of the management of your business. They can be used to decide which part of the operation, if any, might need attention by the owner or manager. This is done by calculating the ratios for your business and comparing the results with your previous figures, with your objectives and plans, and with other businesses in your industry. When all the ratios are considered, they indicate the profitability, efficiency and liquidity of your business. They are useful as a basis for determining the strategies that are most important at a particular time. By using the trends of results and ratios, you can identify where changes are necessary and desirable.

Planning Change

Your initial trend figures are forecasts. We need now to use these to develop objectives and budgets. When you have compared the ratios for your business with those of previous years and those of other businesses in your industry, you can determine new values to aim for in the future. These new values become your financial objectives. You can now work back from this set of ratios and calculate the figures which must appear on your next income statement and balance sheet to achieve these ratios. Included in these calculated projected figures will be cost of goods sold and total expenses. Using these, you can start your detailed planning of operating strategies. The overall cost figures will be separated into the individual item costs. You now have your budgets for the coming year. By also planning the timing of payments you can prepare a cash flow statement.

Budgets

Budgets show each individual item, including sales and expenses, from your income statement, and the asset and liability items from your balance sheet. The planned value for each of these items is entered on a monthly basis. One way to do this is to list all the items down the left-hand side of a page, and to enter the monthly values in 12 columns across the page. It is useful to have a 'total' column at the end, to show annual totals for each item.

This method is made more valuable if each monthly column is divided into two. One column to be used for the plan figure, and the other for the actual result. In some businesses a third column is used for the difference between plan and actual. This is headed 'variance'. It is a very useful figure for management control.

Variances

Each month, actual figures for each item are entered, and the variance calculated and entered. The major variances can be analysed to determine the basic cause of the difference between plan and actual results. It is important that this analysis is done thoroughly. Just to determine that the difference was due to, say, sales being higher or lower than planned is not enough. The real question becomes: 'Why were sales up (or down)?' By looking in depth at each major variance, your knowledge and understanding of your business will increase. This will result in your making better decisions as a manager. As this process is continued your decisions, and your business, will steadily improve.

Budgets can be prepared for specific activities such as advertising or sales promotions, and the results of these combined into the overall budget.

In the previous chapter the need for 'trails' leading back to source documents was discussed. Similar rules apply with budgets. Any figure included in activity budgets or summary budgets needs to be supported by the details of how it was determined. Even if a figure is assumed, this fact should be recorded. The reasons for this become clear when you are analysing the variances. As you retrace your steps to find the reason for a variance, you might need to check right back to the original figures you used. If you find that your assumptions were not correct, you can improve them next time. Again it can be seen that the planning and control process leads to continual improvement.

Cash flow

As well as planning the income, expenses and balance sheet figures, it is important to plan to have sufficient money in the bank each month. However, it might be necessary to keep some money from one month to cover expenses for the next month, or later in the year. So what you really need to know is how much money is required in the bank each month for the coming year. This is planned through a **projected cash flow statement**, often referred to simply as a **cash flow**. You prepare a cash flow by taking each month in turn for the next year and listing the total cash that you expect will flow into, and out of, your business.

Cash flows into your business mainly from sales. It is important that only those sales for which cash is received either as full price, or deposit, are included. Only the amount of *cash* to be received is recorded.

Cash flows out of your business to buy stock, pay expenses, buy new equipment and other assets, and repay loans. Some is also drawn out by you for your living expenses and private use. So the next step is to look through your list of expenses and purchases, as shown in the budget, and determine which accounts you will get each month. Show the payments in the months when you plan to pay them. Next, include any new assets that you plan to buy in the next year. Show the cash payments in the months in which you plan to spend the money. If you are planning to take out a loan to buy the assets, show the cash outlay for the deposit. Add the new loan repayments to your existing ones, and show the total repayments each month.

Finally, list the amounts of cash you will draw from the business for your own use, including living costs and taxation payments. When these are added up for each month, they will show the total outflow of cash.

	JAN	FEB	MAR	APR	MAY	JUNE	JULY	DEC
Opening balance								
Inflow								
Sales								
Other								
Total available								
Outflow								
Accounting fees								
Advertising								
Bank charges								
Stock purchases								
Wages and salaries								
Purchase of assets								
Loan repayments								
Owners' drawings								
Total outflow								
Closing balance								

FIGURE 16.3 Cash flow statement

Preparing a cash flow statement

To prepare a cash flow statement, follow three steps:

1 Starting with the first month, add the inflow to the opening balance. This shows the total cash available for that month.
2 Subtract from this the total outflow to obtain the closing balance for the first month. This amount is also the opening balance for the second month.
3 Repeat this procedure for each month in turn. The closing balance for one month always becomes the opening balance for the next month.

For some months you could have a negative closing balance. This means you might have to readjust your payment schedules, or discuss with your bank the availability of an overdraft for the months when it is needed.

You now have a soundly-based planning and control system. You know that the result you have planned will mean that your objectives will be achieved. Analysis of actual figures against plans each month will ensure that any necessary corrective measures can be taken quickly. Even more important, your abilities as a manager will improve each month. This will be reflected in your continual achievement of challenging objectives and the successful growth of your business.

Financial statements provide the basis for planning and control of your business. No business proceeds exactly according to plan. By identifying where the variances have occurred, and why they occured, you are in a position to manage change. This might mean alterations to plans, to objectives, or to the way in which you are running your business. The end result of this repetitive process is an improvement in your planning, control and management abilities. Naturally, some of the work involved, such as adding up columns of figures, is very mechanical. This work is necessary, but does not contribute greatly to your growth as a manager. Use of a computer can reduce this 'hack work' to a minimum, allowing you more time for analysis and decision-making. Many other advantages can be gained from the use of a computer in a small business.

Computers in small business

One of the most common questions asked by operators of small businesses is: 'Would a computer help me?' The answer is 'Yes!' Because small business operators today need to be cleverer, and do more in less time, a computer is now a necessity. All the financial activities detailed in this chapter and the previous one can be handled more efficiently, and more accurately, with a computer. With an appropriate business computer system, the figure work involved in calculation and comparison of results, ratios and trends can be done quickly and accurately. Often basic data needs to be entered only once. Rapid production of management reports showing results and variances against plans enables the business operator to start immediately on the meaningful work of variance analysis.

This speeds up the process of improving your management abilities and your business.

Most business programs also generate invoices for you to send to your account customers. Information about customer accounts is readily available. This enables you to find out quickly such things as which customers owe you the most, and which customers are slow payers. This helps maintain a healthy cash flow by allowing early contact with account customers. Credit sales are a way of lending money to your customers at no interest. At the same time, you are probably borrowing money at commercial rates. Fast payment by your customers means less borrowing by your business.

A computer is also very useful in the planning process, since various alternative ideas can be compared quickly in terms of the effect they will have on profits, cash flow and your objectives.

A business computer system includes:

- hardware
- software
- peripherals
- data
- staff, and
- procedures.

Hardware is the computer itself — the 'black box' and the keyboard. It usually includes storage devices such as disks.

Software is the range of programs used to link what comes out to what goes in.

Peripherals are the additional items you need to utilise all the features of a computer. They include the monitor (screen) and printer. Also included are the devices for connecting one computer to another, either directly or through telephone lines.

Data comprise the figures and words which are entered using the keyboard.

Staff are needed to operate the system. Additional training might be necessary — or even extra staff. Award wages might vary if computer operation is added to an employee's duties.

Procedures are written descriptions of what needs to be done, when, how and by whom. They should also include instructions on emergency actions.

All of these depend upon:

- the application (what you want the computer to do)
- available programs (software), and
- future expansion.

Specify the application

Before choosing a computer, it is essential that you decide exactly what you want to do with it. What data will you use? What reports do you want? Who will use it? When you have identified the applications for your computer, now and in the future, the next step is to find programs that will do all these tasks.

Find the software

In many cases, 'package' software purchased from a reliable computer-software supplier will be adequate. In some instances, software designed for your industry will be necessary. Many industry packages are available, and your trade or professional association will be able to help you with information about them.

In a few cases, it might be necessary to have a program specially written to suit your business. This can be arranged through computer consultants and analyst programmers.

Select the computer

Only after these two steps, specifying the application and finding the software, should you look for a computer. When you have identified existing and future applications, and located the appropriate software, then it is time to select a computer to run this software. Many people have bought a computer, then tried to find programs to suit their business. Finally, to their horror, they realise that no suitable software is available for the particular computer. The money and time spent to this stage is largely non-productive, and they are forced to eith do nly part of the work, or sell the computer and start again.

All software can be run on a computer, but no single computer can run all software.

A wide range of computers is available. Selecting the best one for your business requires at least some very basic knowledge of the terms used in the computer industry. Some good introductory courses are available which would help you gain this knowledge. You will find these courses very valuable not only to help you select a computer but also when you come to use it. Reference to a computer consultant can also save you expensive mistakes.

Cost-benefit analysis

We have seen that benefits can be gained from using a computer in your business. There are also costs — not only in the initial purchase, but also in operating and maintaining your computer. It is vital that you identify and calculate the dollar value of both the benefits and the costs. This should be done for a three-year period. Compare different sizes and types of computers and peripherals. Only when you are sure that the benefits exceed the costs should you proceed to install a computer system.

Each application is different and must be studied separately. A consultant will do this for you — but it will involve some cost, even if the advice is to wait some time before using a computer system. It is strongly recommended that you take advantage of the courses, seminars and workshops that are available to help you look closely at your own needs. The knowledge you gain will benefit you as long as you are in business.

Alternatives to buying

There are ways to utilise a computer without buying or leasing your own. These include:

- computer bureaus, and
- time-sharing.

Computer bureaus use your data and provide you with the reports, invoices and other documents you need. However, you lose direct control over the processing and confidentiality of your data.

Time-sharing allows you access to a large computer for a relatively low initial cost. You maintain control of the data input, but there might be restrictions on your times of access.

SUMMARY

Financial management and planning form part of an ongoing, cyclical process. Historical records from one period are analysed and ratios calculated. Trends are also computed, and forecasts developed. The figures for your business are then compared with those of previous years, and with those of other businesses in the same industry. Financial objectives are determined, based on the information generated in the forecasts and comparisons. Projected financial statements reflecting these objectives are then prepared. Detailed budgets and cash flows complete the planning part of the cycle. Monthly actual results and computed variances provide the basis for cost control. Management decisions flow from an analysis of the variances each month. Objectives and plans can be reviewed and revised, based on the actual results and variance analysis.

The management and planning cycle involves many numerical records and calculations. These can be performed most efficiently by using a computer. In considering the purchase of a computer, it is essential to identify the applications first, then to locate suitable software. Only after these two steps have been completed should a computer be selected from the range available.

Key words

budget
cash flow
efficiency
liquidity
ratio
trend

Review exercises

1 What is a 'trend'?
2 How can you use ratios to help manage your business?
3 What is variance analysis, and how does it help you to improve your management ability?
4 Why is a cash flow important in planning?
5 What benefits does a computer offer to small business owners?
6 What is the difference between budgets, cash flows, and forecasts?
7 How can you determine whether your financial objectives are realistic and achievable?
8 Why is it important to choose a computer only after defining the application and finding suitable software?
9 Describe the financial management and planning cycle.
10 Why are profitability and liquidity both essential for a small business?

CHAPTER 17

Marketing strategy and management

Many small business people avoid talking about marketing because

- they are frightened by the term *marketing*
- they do not understand what marketing really is
- they do not want any additional costs (ie they can't afford it), or
- they think they are not big enough to worry about marketing.

Marketing, as you will see in this chapter, does not need to be complicated or expensive, but it has to be practised if your business is to survive. Marketing is simply *applying common sense in order to make dollars and cents* in your business.

After working through this chapter you should be able to:

- adopt a market-oriented approach in the management of your business
- explain what marketing is
- identify the five key decisions required in your marketing approach, and
- make these five key decisions as you write your marketing plan.

ADOPT A MARKET-ORIENTED APPROACH

Every small business should aim at making a profit by matching up supply and demand for its products and/or services.

Demand is the willingness of customers to buy goods and services.

Supply is the process of organising the availability of goods and services for sale either through:

- manufacture
- buying those goods for resale, or
- organising others to have those goods and services ready for resale.

When a business looks at matching up supply and demand, the critical question is: What should you consider first — supply or demand? Too many businesses start with supply and simply assume that, because

- supply is organised, and
- they know that their products or services are good, therefore
- demand will automatically follow, and
- all their products and services will sell.

This cannot be assumed, as many small (and large) businesses have found out to their cost.

> People don't *have* to buy your goods or services and unless they really need them they *won't* buy them.

In fact, they do not have to buy from you at all! The trick is to find out what people want — what do they need or think they need. Once you know this, look at supplying the products and services they want — don't do it the other way round. If you want to succeed *you must look at demand first*, not supply. This is known as being market-oriented. People who persist in placing the emphasis on supply are seen as being sales-oriented.

If you adopt a market-oriented approach, then sales and profit should result, as you will be giving the customers what *they* want. However, if you adopt a sales-oriented approach, sales and profit will be much more difficult to achieve, as you will be concentrating on what *you* want — not what the customers want.

It is not enough to discover what the market wants and to produce the goods and services necessary to satisfy those needs and wants. We live in a world of continuous change. Technology, competition, fashion, legislation and other key factors are never static. Your customers and their needs are also constantly changing. To survive you must be able to recognise change and adapt your operation profitably to the new conditions.

The three rules for a market-oriented approach are therefore:

1 *Discover* what the market wants.
2 *Have* the right products or services.
3 *Be adaptable* to change.

WHAT IS MARKETING?

Adopting a market-oriented approach, as we have just seen, means adopting a philosophy that sales (and profit) will follow if we give customers what *they* want rather than what *we* think they want. *The process of putting this philosophy into practice is marketing*. Marketing is not just selling, or advertising, or promotion. It is much more than these; it is organising your business in such a way that you:

- can identify your potential customers
- can identify their needs
- can provide products or services to suit their needs

- are able to tell your customers about yourself and what you offer
- are able to persuade them to buy
- can make them happy that they have bought, and
- will make a profit.

Consider, as an example, that a circus is coming to your town or suburb. Not everyone will want to come, but the circus will need to advertise. A simple way to do this is with a poster saying:

This sign would have a much greater effect if it were put on the side of the elephant and the elephant paraded through town.

The association of the sign with the elephant will immediately appeal to potential circus customers, and will be telling those potential customers about the circus.

Now, consider what would happen if the elephant 'just happened' to wander onto the local council garden, and it 'just happened' that a television camera was there to record the incident favourably for the evening news.

The television publicity would greatly enhance the sale of tickets and the expected profitability of the circus. The whole process would not have 'just happened'. It would have been a planned marketing exercise which brought together supply and demand. The whole purpose of the exercise was to make a profit for the circus.

Marketing, then, can be described as:

> A planned process to bring together, in the most effective way, buyers (demand) and sellers (supply) at a profit.

Perhaps the best way to gain an understanding of marketing is to look at the construction of the actual word. The word *marketing* can be broken down into two words:

where:

- the word *market* obviously refers to the bringing together of buyers and sellers, and
- the word *ting* should remind you of the noise the cash register makes when a sale is completed. No sale is completed until the money is paid — and you are in business to make a profit.

To apply this definition to your business, you only have to recognise the fact that *you* are the 'seller', and the 'buyers' are your customers and your potential customers. Your cannot sell to everyone, as many people can't buy (they don't have the money) and many people are not interested in you or your products. Your marketing strategy is simply to identify those people who are or could be interested, find out what they want, and then plan to successfully offer it to them at a profit.

In other words, your marketing strategy can be found in the question: 'Which offer do you make to which customers?'

Let us now look at the main decisions you will have to make to work out your marketing strategy.

THE FIVE KEY MARKETING DECISIONS

1 Which customers?

At the start of this chapter it was pointed out that you should look at the customers first. In working out your market strategy ('Which offer do I make to which customers?') always look at your customers and their needs first.

What is a customer?

It is generally assumed that everyone knows what a customer is, ie someone who buys your goods or services. Closer examination, however, soon tells us that the definition of a customer should be more than this. It should include your existing customers and also your potential customers, including also the purchasers of competing products and/or services. In other words, anyone who has a need and a want for the products or services you offer, or for the benefit of those products or services, is a customer.

Customers must have a need or a want for your product or service.

While many people have a want or a need for your product or service, not all of them have the ability to pay. Unless a customer can pay you — either now or later, it is senseless to supply them.

Customers must have the ability to pay.

In every sale there is always an ultimate decision-maker who says, 'Yes, I will buy that product or service'. If you are selling, it is suggested that you identify the person who either makes the decision or influences the decision-maker. It is a waste of time trying to sell to someone who wants the product, is capable of paying, but has not the ability either to make the decision to buy or to influence the decision-maker. As an example, consider a public servant who needs a new computer. The public servant has the need, the government has the ability to pay, but that particular employee cannot say 'Yes' on behalf of the government department. To sell *that* computer for use by *that* employee you would have to identify the actual decision-maker or purchasing officer.

A customer must have the ability to decide or the ability to influence the decision-maker.

The final point to consider is that the customer must like you, or more correctly, they must not dislike you. People will not buy from sellers or organisations they dislike, regardless of the reason for their dislike. This emotional rather than logical barrier to selling is often forgotten, but it is critical when considering your customers. Your image, or the way other people see you, should be a positive one. If this is not possible, a neutral image will suffice, but a negative image will kill sales faster than any other reason.

The customer has to have a good image of the seller.

In summary, therefore, a customer is not simply a person or organisation who purchases your goods or services. A customer is anyone who has:

- a need or a want for your goods or services
- the ability to pay
- the ability to decide or to influence the decision-maker, and
- a good image of you.

Don't waste your time trying to sell to anyone who does not have all four factors.

Which customers do you approach?

Your customers or potential customers can be divided into very distinct groups or segments. These groups or segments may be defined or identified as customers within each group, all having some common factor. For example, they might:

- all be in the same geographic area
- be in different areas but in the same industry
- be in different industries or user groups
- all be in the same age, sex, socio-economic, religious, political or cultural grouping

- all read the same newspapers or magazines, or
- have some common interest or activity.

This process of grouping your customers will give you your market segments. A segment can be defined as any group that can be reached with one offer. This offer is simply the message or the invitation that the seller wishes to transmit. The means of getting the message across to the group could be a television commercial or a newspaper advertisement or a road-side sign or even a letterbox drop.

As an example, a company manufacturing industrial soaps and chemicals might decide that it has the following market segments for its products.

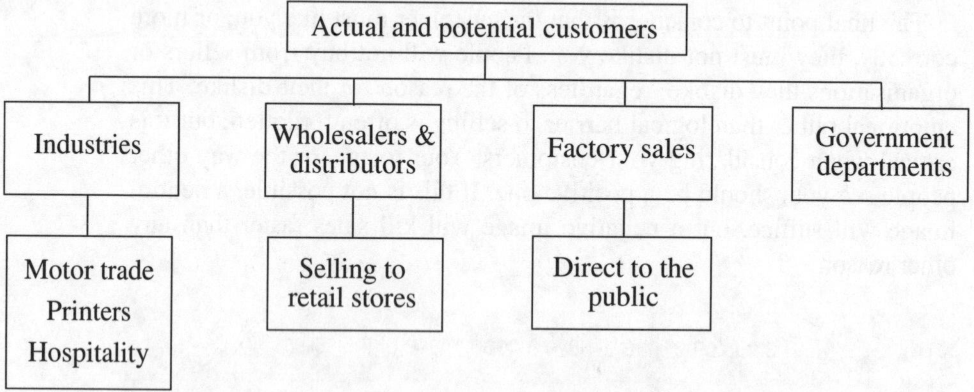

FIGURE 17.1 Market segmentation — XYZ Soap Company

Each segment has a common factor, which might be:

- usage of products
- location
- type of distribution
- common interest, or
- central buying decisions.

It is important to remember that, when you segment a market, you should be able to measure the segments — ie by numbers, dollar amounts, names, or units. This measurement does not have to be statistically exact, but it is useless to segment a market if you cannot measure the segments in some way.

Once you have identified the segments, the next step is to make the first of the key marketing decisions, by asking yourself

'Which segment do I approach?'

To answer this question, remember the 80/20 rule which states that 80% of your sales come from 20% of your customers or 20% of your products.

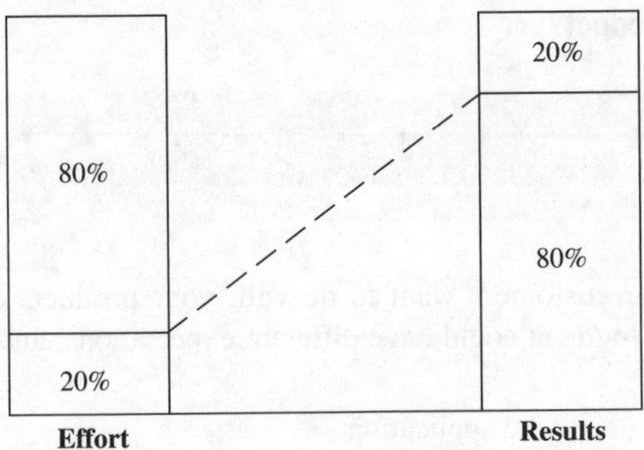

FIGURE 17.2 Pareto or the 80/20 rule

In other words, which segment is going to give you the greatest return?

Also, consider which segment would be easiest to approach with your existing resources, and what additional resources would be necessary to reach the other segments. It *might* be possible to reach all of them, but each one has different needs and to satisfy these needs you might have to offer different products or services. The offer made to each segment has to be tailor-made.

Your first marketing decision is to select the customers you wish to approach.

Your offer

You have now identified your main segments and nominated which key segments you will approach first. Your next step is to research each of the segments and decide on the particular offer you will make to *each* segment.

The offer you make has four key factors. You have to decide, segment by segment:

Which **P**roduct?

at

What **P**rice?

from

Which **P**lace?

with

What **P**romotion?

These four variables — often referred to as 'the four Ps' — are your **marketing mix**, that is, your tailor-made offer to your selected segment.

2 Which product?

> Your second marketing decision is:
> 'Which product or service will I offer this segment?'

What do your customers want to do with your products or services? Each market segment could have different expectations, and you should be looking at:

- product or service application
- product range
- quality
- packaging
- unit size
- guarantees or warranties, and
- benefits to customers.

In the case of the soap and chemical manufacturer, the products offered to industry segments would be vastly different from those offered to retail outlets. There would be differences in packing sizes, packaging and instructions to users, just to name a few. The products being offered to government departments would not be the same products offered to the public at the factory, even though the basic soaps or chemicals could be identical.

In deciding which product or service you should offer to your segments, always be aware of what your competitors are offering. Do not just copy them — you must be different in some way.

As well as being aware of your competitors' products, you should be looking closely at the demand for your own products. Demand *will* change over time, and each product has its own lifecycle.

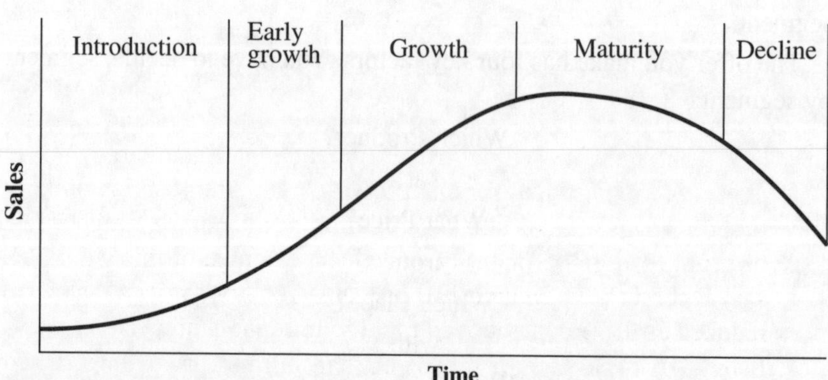

FIGURE 17.3 Product lifecycle

Demand will be slow in the introduction stage, increasing rapidly through the growth stages, then steadying through maturity before an inevitable decline. The length and shape of each stage can be expected to vary quite dramatically from product to product. If your products are in their mature or declining stages you should be looking at the introduction of new products.

3 What price?

> Your third marketing decision is:
> 'What price will I charge to customers in this segment?'

Having identified the product or service required for your market segment, the next key decision to be made is: 'What price to charge?'

Price can be seen as a direct result of the interaction of supply and demand. If your customers are faced with a saturation of identical products (for example, petrol, refrigerators or cigarettes) then there is little room for you to wander from the marketplace price. However, if you have a product which is substantially different or rare, price will react accordingly.

In setting your price, remember:

- You are in business to make a dollar — and part of your price is the *profit contribution*. Don't throw profit away by charging a price lower than is necessary. Continually ask yourself the question: 'What if I were to put my price up by *x%* — how many customers would I lose?' It is surprising how often small business operators throw profit away simply because they never consider putting prices up.
- Demand for products and supply of products will both vary as neither is fixed. Therefore, be prepared to make price adjustments as *variations in supply and demand* occur.
- You should be aware of your *product's lifecycle*. If your product is in the introduction or early growth stages, you are taking a higher risk than someone selling proven products and you can therefore expect premium prices for that product. In the introduction or early growth stages there is still the opportunity to achieve a higher rate of profit than in the maturity stage. (An example of this would be, say, Rubik's cube, which had high introductory prices that were reduced as the product moved rapidly through its lifecycle.)
- It may be necessary to set lower than normal prices in order to achieve *short-term objectives* such as:
  —gaining a market share
  —clearing stocks
  —eliminating competition

—matching competition
—discouraging competition
—generating cash flow.

Whatever price you set, remember that you are in the business to make a profit. Setting a price is not easy, and it is not a once-only decision. *Price setting is a continuous process* that should be based upon accurate research, good management planning and control, and an ability to read the marketplace. An accountant might be able to advise you on the prices you should be charging, but in the end it is your decision.

4 Which place?

Your fourth marketing decision is:
'What is the best way of getting my goods and services to the customer in this segment?'

The term 'place' refers to the place where the exchange between buyers and sellers occurs. In simple language, deciding on the place means finding the best way to get your goods and services into your customers' hands. It is your method of distribution.

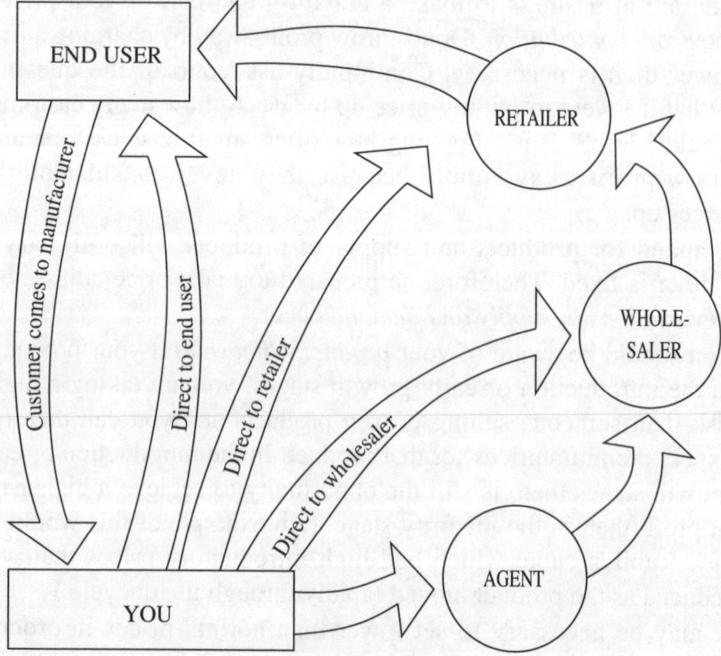

FIGURE 17.4 Methods of distribution

You should be asking yourself:

- How do I reach my market segment?
- What do they want?
- Do they want to come to me (as in a retail operation) or do they expect me to come to them (as in a catering business)?

If they are expecting to come to you, where should you locate? Location for a retail outlet is critical, particularly when competition is strong. If the customers expect you to come to them (as in many service businesses), your location is less than critical.

Many small business people are reluctant to use agents, wholesalers and other distributors because they believe that they will be losing revenue by employing a middle person. However, you should do your sums carefully to see which channel of distribution will maximise your profits.

A toy manufacturer spent her time equally between making toys and selling them to retailers and end users. Due to stock limitations, sales were severely restricted as she could not produce quickly enough. After considering the problem, she decided to employ an agent to do the selling, thus freeing herself to concentrate solely on producing the toys. This led to much higher sales and, more importantly, higher profits.

5 What promotion?

Promotion can be described as an exercise in communication. You need to communicate with your potential or existing customers to tell them of the goods and services you have to offer.

> Your fifth marketing decision is:
> 'What is the best way of promoting my goods and services to this segment?'

Earlier in this chapter, we said that you cannot sell to everyone and that you should be identifying market segments; that is, groups that can be reached with one offer. There is no universal way of telling every segment about the products and services being offered to it. The main tools for communicating your offer to the selected segments are:

- advertising
- publicity
- personal selling, and
- sales promotion.

The way you use them to relay your offer to your market segment is called your *promotional mix* (or, if you prefer, your communication mix).

Let us look at the four promotional tools.

Advertising

This is the *paid* presentation and promotion of ideas, products or services by an identified sponsor. Advertising is non-personal and a one-way means of communication. The main questions you should ask about your advertising are:

- Why?
- Who?
- What?
- When?
- Where?
- How?

> The first question to be asked is:
> 'Why am I advertising?' If you don't know why, don't advertise.

All advertising should have an objective. It is pointless to advertise just for the sake of advertising, so *why* do you want to advertise and what is your objective? The clearer your objective, the more effective your advertising.

It is also pointless trying to sell everyone everything. You cannot do it — especially in one advertisement. Once you have decided on your objective you have to establish your target group — that is, *who* you are trying to reach. Which segment(s) have you selected? This decision will influence the answers to the remaining questions.

What you are promoting or presenting in your advertisement should be clearly identified. Is it your products, your price, yourself, your company, your company's record, or maybe even your future plans?

The decision about *when* you should advertise depends upon two factors:

- your reasons for advertising — what you are trying to achieve
- the nature of your target segment. Work out the best time to reach it. Look at the time of the day, or perhaps the time of the week, the season, or even the year that will have the greatest impact.

When faced with the problem of *where* to advertise, once again you should look at the characteristics of your market segment and see which medium will have the capacity to reach that group. Some of the avenues for advertising are shown in Table 17.1.

TABLE 17.1 Means of advertising

Mode	Type of advertising	Comments
Visual	Newspapers — metropolitan — country — local — non-English — specialised Newspaper supplements	'The more you tell The more you sell' plus large circulation and multiple readership
	Magazines and journals	Repeat exposure
	Directories — telephone — trade — other	Fast information direct to potential customers
	Brochures	Selective, fast and effective
	Letterbox drops (junk mail)	Can be low-cost, fast and efficient
Audio	Radio — AM — FM	Has a sense of urgency
Audio-visual	Television Theatres and drive-ins	Credibility and reach Captive audience
Outdoor	Bus seats Billboards Buildings Outdoor signs	Continued reinforcement through exposure
Personal	On own products Uniforms	Fashionable and cost-effective
	Direct mail	Pre-screened target Personalised
Mobile	Vehicles — own — taxis — public transport super buses — other, eg planes, blimps	Efficient Continued exposure to wide audience
Community	Sponsorship — sporting bodies — local events	Identifies local involvement

This list is not meant to be exhaustive as it seeks to identify only the more popular means of advertising.

The question of *how* to advertise has thousands of answers, and probably all of them are correct. However, there are three main ways of constructing your advertising:

- use an advertising agency
- rely on other people
- do it yourself.

Using an advertising agency is the ideal method, and the professional approach. By using such a service correctly you will be able to interlock your entire promotion and have it reflect the specialised skills of the agency. However, your type of business, your stage of business development, and especially your advertising budget might preclude the use of an agency.

Relying on other people to construct your advertisement is a common approach in small business but it is not always recommended. Many small business operators will simply delegate the job back to the newspaper or the printer for a variety of reasons, including 'I don't know how to write an ad!' This delegation can be dangerous and often brings about a poorer result.

If you are writing the advertisement yourself, remember a few key guidelines:

- Don't try to be too creative. Make sure your advertisement will comply with the 'AIDCA' rule:
  —Attract **Attention**. You want prospects or potential customers to read, hear or see your advertisement. To do this your headline or opening words have to be compelling or the total advertisement is wasted. The prospect will be asking the question: 'What's in it for me?' The headline or opening statement has to start to answer this question immediately.
  —Create an **Interest**. There has to be a motivation for the prospect to continue reading/listening to the advertisement. The advertisement should develop the theme of the headline or opening to deter the prospect from losing interest.
  —Build a **Desire**. The interest of prospects should be developed by the advertisement to the point where they believe they *must have* the product or service being advertised.
  —Create **Conviction**. The prospects will find numerous reasons why they cannot follow the directions of the advertiser. By giving the prospect sufficient information to remove doubts, substantiate claims, provide endorsements, etc, the advertisement will overcome the prospect's objections.
  —Bring about **Action**. Many advertisements fail to tell the prospect what to do, ie they fail to close. Your advertisement should direct the prospect to act in a definitive manner, eg 'Ring now!' Advertisements might even include an inducement or a penalty to prompt prospects into action.
- Use short words and don't talk down to the audience.
- Choose your headline carefully. Be brief. Personalise the message and use key words — eg *your*, *free*, *now*, *guarantee*, *bonus*, etc.
- Make sure you summarise — and bring 'urgency' into the message.

- In print advertisements, don't cover the whole space with words. In newspaper advertisements, allow at least 25% of white space and consider using photographs or illustrations, especially of people.
- Seek *advice* from experts such as media people, media organisations and consultants. One key contact is:

  The Newspaper Advertising Bureau of Australia
  77 Berry Street
  North Sydney NSW 2060
  Telephone (02) 955 1044

  This bureau is a non-profit research and marketing organisation and has produced some excellent publications on advertising techniques and principles.

Publicity

This is any *unpaid* presentation or promotion which develops or enhances the demand for the ideas, products or services of an organisation. The two main forms of publicity are:

- word of mouth
- the mass media.

Of these two forms, **word of mouth** is considered to be the more effective. Word of mouth is simply a direct personal recommendation of you, your products or services or your organisation, given with the conviction of a satisfied customer.

> The best way of promoting you, your products or services, or your organisation, is by word of mouth.

Mass media is a general term which covers television, radio, newspapers, magazines, etc. There are two ways of promoting you and your business through the mass media. The first is by paying for your messages (eg advertising) while the other is publicity, which is unpaid.

There are several ways of approaching the media to obtain publicity. They can be contacted by telephone or fax, visited personally or even invited to visit you or your organisation. Regardless of which way you contact them, be organised and have your story prepared in the format they are familiar with, ie a media release.

The key rules for using a media release are:

- Select the media that you believe will be interested in your story.
- Organise your facts in writing. Tell your story in a concise form which explains who, what, when, where, and how.
- As in the guidelines for advertising, check that your story meets the requirements of the AIDCA rule.
- Provide a headline for your story — no more than five to six words in length.

- Type your story, remembering to use:
  - —double spacing
  - —wide margins (about 4 cm) on both left- and right-hand sides of the text
  - —short paragraphs
  - —letterhead if possible
  - —one side of the page only.
- Use the heading 'Media Release' at the top of your story.
- Keep your story short, ie a maximum of one page of typed copy.
- Don't assume — use lay person's terms and make your story easily understood.
- Support your story with figures and photographs (black and white for non-colour publications). Do not be frightened to give quotes, estimates, forecasts, predictions, etc — but make certain your facts are correct.
- Provide access to further details by including contact names, addresses and telephone numbers — both business and after hours.
- Hand-deliver your media release and try to reach the reporter you believe could be interested in your story.

The key to obtaining publicity in the media is to understand that such organisations survive by selling advertising space (television, radio and print); and that they sell that space to advertisers who are interested in reaching the viewing, listening or reading audience.

This audience has selected their media because they want to be informed, interested, entertained or even distracted. As long as the media satisfies their interests or needs they will keep viewing, listening or reading. While they are using the media they are also exposed to the advertising. The media, in seeking to maximise their audience, are always looking for stories that their audience will be interested in. This is the key! To have your story covered, look at the audience of the media and tailor your story to suit its interests. If you can present your story as news or as a human-interest story then you have every chance. If, however, the media suspect that you are being commercial, begging for free time, or asking a favour, they will simply not be interested. All you have to do is select your story and write a press release for each media organisation you wish to approach.

Finally, remember that publicity is unpaid — that is, free. Unlike advertising, which must be paid for, you cannot control the placing or appearance of your story. It is a numbers game — but it is also rewarding, effective and fun.

Personal selling

This is any oral presentation to one or more potential customers with the objective of making a sale. Unlike advertising and publicity, this is a two-way exercise and is highly personal. To be successful with your personal selling:

- Set your objectives so that you know exactly what you are trying to achieve.
- Do your research on your potential customers, your products and services, your competitors and your approach.
- Be organised. Look at the image you are presenting: check your dress and your approach and enhance your credibility with tools such as brochures, samples and your 'brag book'.
- Remember the AIDCA rule (attention, interest, desire, conviction, action).

The best way to approach selling is to make sure that you are customer-focused, ie concentrating on the customer and their needs and wants, and helping them to find solutions to their problems.

The actual art of selling can be broken down into seven basic steps, which are shown in Figure 17.5.

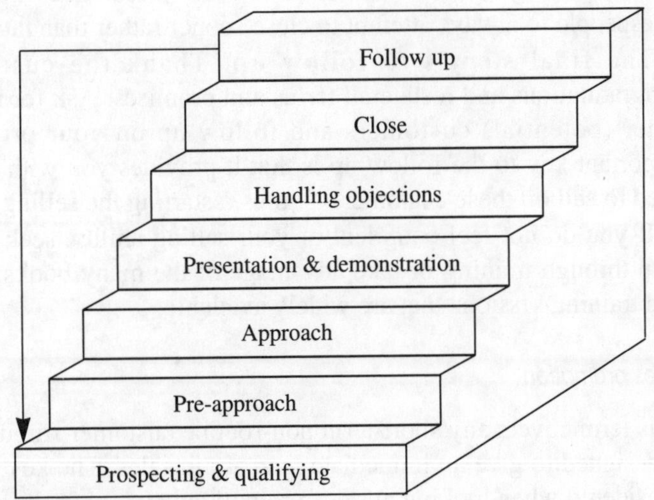

FIGURE 17.5 The seven steps of selling

The **prospecting and qualifying** step is a research step designed to maximise your selling effort. It allows you to concentrate on potential customers rather than trying to sell to everyone. It is a sorting-out process which leaves you with a list of prospects.

In the **pre-approach**, details of individual prospects are investigated. The seller tries to find as much information as possible about the potential customer. Research on the prospect will show the best method of approach — the prospect's needs, interests, likes and dislikes, and the prospect's company rules. In simple terms, it seeks to provide the seller with the best possible approach to the potential client.

The **approach** is the physical act of approaching the client, based upon the research in the previous step. If the prospect is new, an introduction by a mutual party is a great advantage. With the approach, the seller must be completely prepared and have all selling aids, etc, in order.

The **presentation and demonstration** are the 'sales pitch', where the product or service is demonstrated and explained. The emphasis should be on the benefits rather than the technical details. Once the salesperson feels that the prospect has absorbed the concept being presented, a 'trial close' should be attempted in an attempt to get the prospect to say 'Yes'.

If the prospect raises doubts, hesitations or **objections**, the salesperson should seek to overcome these reservations by discovering what the real objection to buying is, and then removing it. Very often it is merely that more information is required, or that the prospect wants further reassurance, ie that he or she is making the right decision.

The next step is **the close** — a step ignored by approximately two thirds of all salespeople in Australia. The close is simply asking for the sale, ie getting the customer to say 'Yes!' Most sales trainers advise salespeople to always attempt to close sooner rather than later.

The final step is to **follow up**. Thank the customer, give congratulations and restate all terms and promises. Ask for references of other (potential) customers and follow up on your promises. One important key to the follow up is that it provides you with the data you need to call on these customers — thus restarting the selling process.

If you do not feel confident of your selling ability, seek professional help through training or take advantage of the many books, kits, videos and training sessions that are widely available.

Sales promotion

This term covers any short-term non-routine customer stimulation which is designed to give an immediate increase in sales. The key factors to be considered when looking at sales promotion are:

1. It is short term. A sales promotion campaign will usually be less than three months in length and rarely longer than six.
2. It is a break from the normal selling approach, being designed to create maximum consumer interest and invite publicity.
3. It is designed to increase sales immediately. This can be done by targeting new users, aiming at repeat sales or boosting stock held by resellers.
4. Sales promotion can be actively directed at all levels of sales, eg:
   - your own salesforce
   - agents

- wholesalers
- distributors
- retailers
- final consumers.

Typical examples of sales promotion activity include:

- displays
- shows
- exhibitions
- handouts
- stickers
- gimmicks
- tastings
- special events
- demonstrations
- samples
- discounts
- guest appearances
- premiums
- contests
- sweepstakes
- bonus stock
- coupons
- gifts
- point-of-purchase material such as dump bins, stands, feature sales, brochures, etc.

Sales promotion can perhaps be seen as the catalyst of the marketing mix. It is often the focal point which brings together the advertising, publicity and personal selling activities of a firm or organisation. It seeks to induce the buyer to act *now* rather than *later*.

The composition of your promotional mix

The four avenues of promotion (or communication) — advertising, publicity, personal selling and sales promotion — should not be seen as being mutually exclusive. Rather, they are four separate but interrelated activities that must be present in any promotional plan.

Advertising allows for awareness, the creation of demand, the building of an image. Sales promotion seeks to get the buyer to act immediately. Publicity via word of mouth or the mass media helps build the desired image of the organisation and backs up the advertising and sales promotion activities. Personal selling is the process of getting the customer to say 'Yes.'

All four activities are necessary but the ratio of the importance of each activity will vary from industry to industry, and firm to firm. There is no standard or ideal mix, however, as each market needs a tailored approach.

In Figure 17.6, the promotional mixes of three businesses have been illustrated.

With the retail store, the promotional mix is leaning heavily on advertising and sales promotion, backed up with personal selling and publicity (mainly word of mouth).

The electronics manufacturer, selling to end users, is facing severe competition and relies heavily on personal selling.

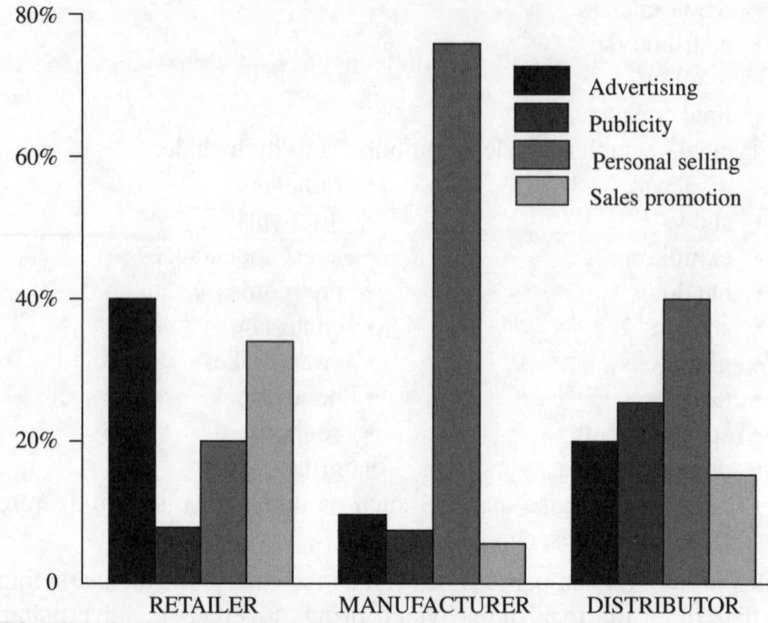

FIGURE 17.6 A typical promotional mix for three types of business

The computer distributor has a more even mix, with a high need for advertising support, a good public image, a strong sales team and a constant need to induce customers to buy now.

The activities of the mix support one another. Sales promotions need to be advertised; advertising needs credibility; personal selling is assisted by sales promotion, advertising and publicity; and the cycle goes on and on.

In designing your promotional mix, what emphasis will *you* need to reach your target segments?

Planning your promotion

We have just seen that the four avenues of communication — advertising, publicity, personal selling and sales promotion — should not be seen as being mutually exclusive. Indeed, in considering any promotion, a plan should be drawn up to bring these promotional avenues together in the most effective way.

The plan should be:

- objective
- accurate
- assertive
- innovative
- co-ordinated, and
- controlled.

Objective

You should have a definite goal for your plan. Who are you trying to reach and what are you trying to tell them? If you are not clear in this area, your chances of a successful campaign will be greatly reduced.

Accurate

Before you make any decisions on how to communicate, be sure of your facts and figures. Who are you trying to reach, what do they want, and which is the best way to reach them? Are you offering what the customer wants?

A country motel set about increasing its occupancy rate by offering seven-day bus tours based at the motel and covering a host of local attractions. The offer was made to organisations right throughout the state by means of selected media, directories, personal selling and brochures at tourist centres. Despite all this, few people took up the offer. Investigation showed that the offer was based upon party bookings of 45 people — a large group to bring together for seven days. The size of the groups was determined solely by the size of the bus being used. A smaller bus was quickly substituted and the tours became very popular.

Assertive

The plan should be result-oriented and to achieve this you need to be assertive. Do not be frightened to promote yourself and your strengths, and never lose an opportunity to do so. Your approach should be bold and original rather than a carbon copy of your competitor's plan.

Innovative

Try to find the most effective way of reaching your market segment. A hairdressing-salon owner recognised the fact that her Chinese background was a drawcard for many of her customers. To promote her business the hairdresser organised the distribution of simple photocopied handbills in Chinese through a Chinese restaurant several kilometres away. This approach was far more successful than the traditional media advertising or letterbox drops.

Co-ordinated

Your promotional or communication mix should be co-ordinated to gain maximum results. A standard logo, for instance, should appear in all visual materials. Through consistent advertising, many firms can be identified simply by, for example, the design of their wrapping paper or bags, or by a stylised logo, or even a symbol. To achieve this, the common element (the logo or design symbol) should be prominently and consistently used. A printing business, run by an energetic couple with a good sense of humour, employed the slogan: 'Magic — today . . . miracles 2 days!' to promote their fast service. To drive home the point, they adopted a magician as a type of logo and featured him on all their stationery — especially their business cards. When they produce an order for a client they enclose in the delivery a 'with compliments' slip which also features the magician.

FIGURE 17.7 Examples of a co-ordinated approach

The effect of this co-ordinated approach is not only a display of professionalism, but also an invitation to their clients to use word-of-mouth publicity, as most clients want to show their friends both the business card and the compliments slip.

Controlled

Your promotional activities should be planned, and part of the plan is to see whether or not you are reaching your objectives. You should be looking at such points as:

- Are you reaching your target segment?
- Is your message correct?
- Is your message effective?
- Are you within your promotional budget?
- Does your plan need adjustment?

You should be talking to your customers, asking them how they heard about you, why they are buying from you, and what they like and dislike. Monitor your sales and review each promotional campaign carefully. Don't be afraid to make changes if your plan is not working. If it is working — stick to it!

SUMMARY

At the beginning of this chapter we talked about the importance of a market-oriented approach and then we defined marketing and also marketing strategy. We stated that any marketing approach needed to consider five key variables:

1 which customers to approach
2 with which product
3 at what price
4 from which place
5 with what promotion.

These five variables can be seen in the form of a model as shown in Figure 17.8.

To demonstrate the effectiveness of this model consider, as an example, a couple who started out making garden gnomes as a hobby. This couple developed a high-quality garden gnome — each one with its own personality created by the individual hand-painting of facial features, clothes and so on. The first attempt to sell these gnomes was through selected garages at a competitive price (approximately $20). Sales soon outstripped supply as each gnome took at least six hours just to paint — and obviously at $20 each they sold immediately. Without realising what they were doing, the couple had adopted a sales-oriented approach — concentrating on the product they wanted to sell, without reference to marketing. The result of this was that they could not make any profit; indeed, if labour costs were to be included, they were making a loss.

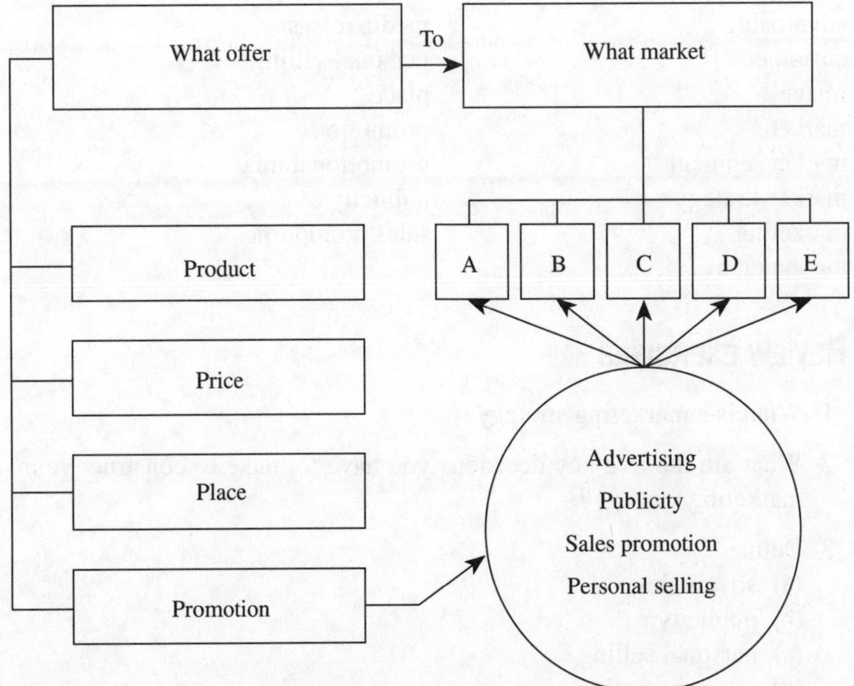

FIGURE 17.8 The marketing model

The couple had to make the five key decisions. In looking at their customers they realised that they really had two major segments: a market for garden gnomes, and a market for quality statuettes of 'little people'.

If they decided that they were in the business of making and selling garden gnomes, then they could identify their customers as people who would pay $20 for gnomes, and these people could be reached through service stations with very little promotion. The only promotion needed would be, say, a stand to display the gnomes and a sign to draw attention to the gnomes and their selling price. However, the product would have to be modified from the original high-quality concept to one of lower quality which was consistent with competitive products and within the budget of the $20 price tag.

If the couple, decided, on the other hand, that they were in the business of making and selling 'little people', then their customers would be entirely different. They would pay at least $60 to $70 for the product because of its high quality and individual nature. But these people would not be reached through service stations. Likely places of exchange would be, say, gift shops or craft galleries, and promotion would need to be more extensive and detailed than that required for service stations.

Marketing, therefore, is not something you leave to chance. It is a planned process, based on the customer, to make *you* a profit.

Key words

advertising
customer
image
market
market segment
market strategy
marketing
mass media
media release
personal selling
place
promotion
promotional mix
publicity
sales promotion

Review exercises

1 What is a marketing strategy?

2 What are the five key decisions you have to make to construct your marketing strategy?

3 Define
(a) advertising
(b) publicity
(c) personal selling
(d) sales promotion.

4 Explain the AIDCA rule.

5 What is the most effective method of promotion?

6 List the seven steps in the selling process.

7 Give six examples of sales promotion activities.

8 List six characteristics of a promotional plan.

9 Using research sources listed in the appendix, together with your own information, identify and quantify the market segments for your actual or proposed business.

10 Consult Table 17.1 — Means of advertising. Which advertising avenues have you selected for your actual or assumed business? Why did you select these avenues? What other avenues could you consider?

11 Assume you are about to either:
(a) open a new office
(b) start a new business, or
(c) celebrate your fifth year in business.
Construct an appropriate media release (for the option you have selected) using the media release guidelines discussed earlier in this chapter.

CHAPTER 18

Retailing

Contrary to what many people believe, retailing is a science, not just an easy way of going into business. Retailing is an area in which only those who know what they are doing really make money. It is a highly competitive and constantly changing industry.

If you are considering going into business or already have a retail operation, ask yourself:

'Why is retailing different from other forms of business?'

Among the answers you find there should be two key facts:

- The customers normally have to come to you, rather than the other way around.
- You usually have only a brief encounter with the customer in retailing, unlike in other forms of business. It is therefore critical that you know how to reach your customers, how to make them want to buy, and how to make them come back.

After reading this chapter you should be able to:

- plan for profits in your retail operation
- ensure that you have an adequate supply of new and repeat customers
- recognise early warning signs of problems in your retailing business, and
- establish control systems to protect yourself and your business.

PLANNING FOR PROFITS

Retailing, put simply, is the process of making it easier for people to buy goods and services. Successful or continuing retailing relies on making a profit by managing this process. If you do not make a profit (and retailing is not immune from loss-making), you won't be in business for long.

Basically, there are two types of retailing:

1 the provision of goods, (eg through supermarkets, pet suppliers, greengrocers, clothes shops, etc) which are purchased for resale — at a profit, of course

2 the provision of services, eg hairdressing, appliance repairs, travel agencies, or dry cleaning, to name a few.

It is recognised that there are other types of retailers, such as stall holders, mobile 'shops', hawkers or mail order businesses. This chapter, however, will be primarily concerned with the two basic types.

Retailers make their profit by buying goods (and services) and selling them for a higher price to their customers. The amount that is added to the cost is called mark-up. *A mark-up is simply the dollar value or percentage that is added to the cost price to give a selling price.* This gives us Rule Number 1 which states:

RULE 1 Cost price + mark-up = selling price

This rule applies regardless of whether you are talking about an individual item being sold or about total sales value over a period.

Retailers in Australia, however, often talk about:

- their margin
- their margin of gross profit
- their gross profit margin
- their gross profit, or (simply)
- their profit.

Whenever they do so, they are talking about that part of their selling price (or sales) that is left after they have deducted the actual cost of the goods or services. This gives us Rule Number 2, which states:

RULE 2 Selling price = cost price + margin

A margin can be defined as that part of the selling price, expressed as either dollars or a percentage, which represents profit. Consider an example in which an item is bought for \$15 (cost price) and is sold for \$20 (selling price). The difference of \$5 is both the mark-up (or amount added to cost) and the margin (or margin of profit).

Cost price
(\$15)

+

Mark-up (\$5) / Margin (\$5)

=

Selling price
(\$20)

If you are talking about mark-ups and margins in dollar terms only, a mark-up must always be equal to a margin. It is only when mark-ups and margins are expressed as percentages that some people become confused. This confusion can be avoided by remembering that:

- *mark-ups should always be related to cost price*
- *margins should always be related to selling price.*

In our example our mark-up percentage can be calculated as:

$$\frac{\text{Mark-up (\$)}}{\text{Cost price (\$)}} \times \frac{100}{1}$$

$$= \frac{\$5}{\$15} \times \frac{100}{1}$$

$$= 33.3\%$$

Our margin can be calculated as:

$$\frac{\text{Margin (\$)}}{\text{Selling price (\$)}} \times \frac{100}{1}$$

$$= \frac{\$5}{\$20} \times \frac{100}{1}$$

$$= 25\%$$

Thus, while our mark-up ($5) and margin ($5) are expressed in dollars, there is no difference. But if mark-up and margin are expressed as a percentage, they must be different.

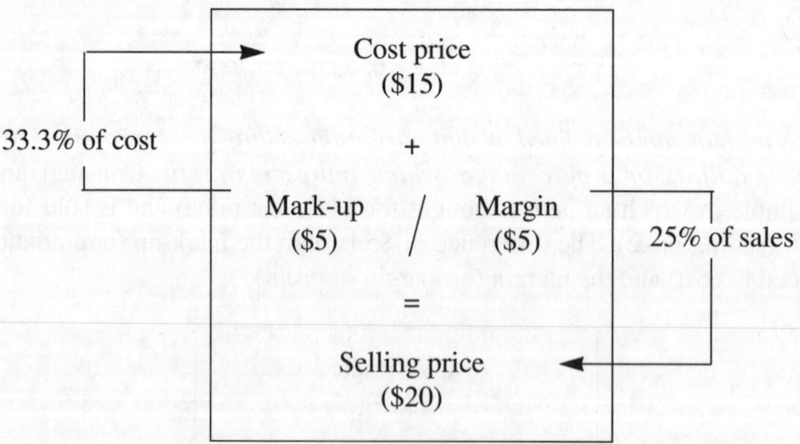

Thus we have Rule Number 3, which states:

RULE 3 Mark-up equals margin in dollar terms
but
does not equal margin in percentage terms

By definition, a mark-up percentage will always be greater than a margin percentage. Retailers instinctively recognise this and also the fact that there is a constant relationship between mark-up percentages and margin percentages. This relationship, if expressed in the form of fractions rather than decimals, becomes very clear, for example:

Mark-up shown as a fraction of cost price	Margin shown as a fraction of selling price
1	1/2
1/2	1/3
1/3	1/4
1/4	1/5
1/5	1/6
1/6	1/7
1/7	1/8
1/8	1/9
1/9	1/10
1/10	1/11

FIGURE 18.1 Mark-up and margins expressed as fractions

In checking this table against the example we looked at earlier, it can be seen that the mark-up of 33.3% (or 1/3) is the same as a margin of 25% (or 1/4).

At this stage, try completing the table in Figure 18.2 to see whether or not you understand the relationship between mark-up and margins. Remember your three basic rules, ie:

1 Cost Price + Mark-up = Selling Price
2 Selling Price = Cost Price + Margin
3 Mark-up ($) = Margin ($) but Mark-up (%) does *not* equal Margin (%)

(The answer appears in the solution section at the end of this book.)

While it is easy to see the relationship using fractions, we tend to talk and think in decimals. Decimals, in simple language, are only fractions worked out: 1/10 is 1 divided by 10 which gives an answer of 0.1. By converting the fractions into decimals we can produce the table in Figure 18.3. This table is really a mental tool or a 'ready reckoner' to assist you in your retail decisions.

Cost price + mark-up as a fraction of cost	=	Selling price	=	Cost price + margin as a fraction of sales
$100 + (1) $100	=	$200	=	$100 + (1/2) $100
$100 + (1/2) $......	=	$....	=	$100 + (1/3) $.....
$100 + (1/3) $......	=	$....	=	$100 + (1/4) $.....
$100 + (1/4) $......	=	$....	=	$100 + (1/5) $.....
$100 + (1/5) $......	=	$....	=	$100 + (1/6) $.....
$100 + (1/6) $......	=	$....	=	$100 + (1/7) $.....
$100 + (1/7) $......	=	$....	=	$100 + (1/8) $.....
$100 + (1/8) $......	=	$....	=	$100 + (1/9) $.....
$100 + (1/9) $......	=	$....	=	$100 + (1/10) $.....

FIGURE 18.2 Understanding mark-ups and margins

Mark-up as a percentage of cost price	Margin as a percentage of selling price	Mark-up as a percentage of cost price	Margin as a percentage of selling price
5.00	4.76	85.00	45.95
10.00	9.09	90.00	47.37
12.50	11.11	95.00	48.72
15.00	13.04	100.00	50.00
17.50	14.89	125.00	55.56
20.00	16.67	150.00	60.00
25.00	20.00	175.00	63.64
30.00	23.08	200.00	66.67
33.33	25.00	225.00	69.23
35.00	25.93	250.00	71.43
40.00	28.57	275.00	73.33
45.00	31.03	300.00	75.00
50.00	33.33	400.00	80.00
55.00	35.48	500.00	83.33
60.00	37.50	600.00	85.71
65.00	39.39	700.00	87.50
70.00	41.18	800.00	88.89
75.00	42.86	900.00	90.00
80.00	44.44	1000.00	90.90

FIGURE 18.3 Your pricing ready reckoner

While the table in Figure 18.3 demonstrates the relationship between mark-up and margins, it also drives home the point that it is almost impossible to get a margin of 100%.

A set of exercises is included at the end of this chapter to test your understanding of the practical application of mark-up and margins.

As a retailer you will probably be selling a range of products. It is usual to have varying mark-ups (and therefore margins) for different products or service lines, so care should be taken that your main selling lines are those with your highest margins. It is only through planning and control that you can ensure that your sales will provide enough gross profit to make your venture worthwhile.

Ensuring your supply of customers

Unless your shop is heavily geared to the holiday trade or passing traffic, your customers will probably consist of regular clientele and a fairly stable proportion of floating clientele. However, each year about 12.5% of your regular customers will probably be lost due to natural aging, death or a change in residential address or employment. It is critical, therefore, that you continually work to reach new customers.

Customer loyalty is not as strong as it was many years ago. Customers are now much more mobile and far better informed (through the media) about competitive activity and competitors' offers. The changing socio-economic environment is also making price a dominant factor in deciding where to buy. In fact, you could almost say that customer loyalty does *not* exist today.

Retailers, therefore, cannot become complacent and must plan to:

- keep existing customers
- replace lost customers, and
- find additional customers

if they are to survive and grow.

To keep existing customers you must find out what they want and be able to satisfy them. This means that you and your staff must talk to your customers and listen to what they have to say. They will tell you what they want and think, and it might not always be what you expect or want to hear.

You should also keep a regular watch on your competition. This can be done by:

- talking to them
- talking to representatives, and
- by visiting competitors' shops (personally, or using staff or your friends).

You should also try to see your shop in the same way as your customers see it. Too few retailers walk outside their shops, turn around and look — just to see what impression is given to the public. Is it clean? Is it neat? Does it reflect the image you are trying to promote?

The best way to influence new customers is by word of mouth from existing customers who recommend you to their friends and colleagues. It does not hurt to say to your regular customers: 'Please tell your friends about us . . .'; but to be able to do this you need to have your shop in order.

The most efficient way of reaching new customers is to plan your promotion. This plan should aim at an ongoing programme of advertising (and publicity) that will let your potential customers:

- know that you exist
- know where you are
- know how to get to you
- know what you have to offer, and
- be drawn to your store.

This plan should follow through to ensure that, once inside your store, the potential customer will be helped by personal selling (you and your staff) and by point-of-sale material and layout to:

- see what you are offering
- find what they want
- make a decision to buy
- be happy with that decision, and
- pay you.

One of the main points to remember about keeping existing customers or gaining new ones is:

> Make it easy for people to buy: don't make it hard for people to buy.

Your layout should be designed with this principle in mind. As well as the points on layout covered in Chapter 11, remember:

- Customers don't have to shop with you.
- Customers often need only one barrier or obstacle to send them elsewhere.
- Dump bins *do* sell.
- Plan for impulse sales.
- Treat customers as special people.
- Plan your shelves — the top and bottom shelves are usually the slowest sellers.
- Have good point-of-sale material.
- Where possible, avoid handwritten tickets unless you are skilled in this area, or unless they fit your image.
- Try to keep shelves below eye height (except wall shelves). This opens up your store visually and makes it easier for customers to shop.
- Have your departments well signposted.
- Keep your shop clean and tidy.

One final point about customers — remember to give every customer a smile.

> Smiles cost nothing, are contagious, and are your best guarantee of repeat sales.

RECOGNISING EARLY WARNING SIGNS

Retailing, by its very nature, leaves you very little time to stand back and look at your total operation. You should plan to make time, and know what to look for. As a general rule you should be looking for warning signs such as:

- significant changes in the demand for your goods or services
- cash flow shortages
- a drop in employee morale
- changes in competitors' activities
- changes in suppliers' attitudes, or
- an increase in customer complaints.

Changes in demand for your goods and services can be picked up from general observation, but more likely will be detected from stock cards, order books, your stock control system or maybe even your suppliers. If you find stock is not moving as fast as it was previously or your stock is slower than the industry average — then you should be seriously looking at your products and finding out why the slow-down has occurred. If your products suddenly start to sell at a much faster rate, then perhaps you have under-priced your stock or missed a recent cost price increase.

Almost every retailer can claim to be short of money, but when the cash flow starts to really dry up you should look at such things as:

Credit control — Are you allowing too much credit or not collecting your money as you should?

Theft — This may be from the cash register or from the shelves. (Remember that not all theft is by customers.)

Pricing policy — Are you selling too cheaply?

Stock control — Has the level of your stock risen above your required holdings?

Too-rapid expansion — Has the cost of sudden growth been too great a drain on your cash availability?

Running costs (wages, rent, electricity, etc) — Have they become too high?

Invoice costs (purchase costs) — Have they risen faster than your selling price?

Remember to check every invoice.

Employee morale is perhaps the best barometer of the health of your business. If things are going well, employee morale usually follows suit. If you find your employees are not staying, arriving late, taking 'sickies' or generally are not happy, you need to find out what is wrong — quickly!

Your competitors are also watching the industry and customers' demands and patterns. If your customers suddenly move into new areas or change their habits, find out why. To be able to see this change in competitor activity you need to keep a regular watch on your competition.

If your suppliers become reluctant to supply you or show a marked change in attitude, look for possible new competition, or at your track record, or at the suppliers themselves for the reason.

Finally, the fastest indicator that you have problems is your customer complaint level. You will always have complaints, no matter how good you are, but if there are increased signs of dissatisfaction such as returns, refusals to pay, passive complaints (they stop coming into your store) or vocal abuse, then you have a major problem somewhere. Make sure you investigate these complaints and report back to the customer where appropriate.

ESTABLISHING CONTROL SYSTEMS

Most of the early warning signs we have just discussed come from simple retail control systems, such as:

Daily customer counts — This figure is often available from the cash register readout. In some stores an hourly record could also be desirable to identify peak periods and allow for staffing requirements.

Average sales per customer — By dividing total daily sales by the customer count we gain an average customer purchase figure, which should be keeping pace over time with inflation at least. Both daily customer counts and average sales per customer should be kept in a special record book so that trends can be seen quickly. Remember, however, that daily figures are guides only; don't panic if sales for today are not as good as sales for, say, the same day last year.

Sales by product group — This breakdown is invaluable and can usually be taken straight from the cash register detail roll.

Stocktakes — Many retailers avoid stocktakes because they involve too much time and effort. Regular stocktakes will tell you whether you are increasing your overall stock or not, and by how much. They will also tell you whether you have a shrinkage problem — that is, losses from theft.

Stock cards — Every retailer should keep stock cards in some form.They will show slow-moving lines, excessive stock holdings, and areas where stocks held are not sufficient to meet demand. Stock cards will also help you meet seasonal fluctuations in demand. Examples of two types of stock card are shown here. Figure 18.4 is designed for fast-moving lines such as soft drinks, confectionery, cigarettes or groceries, where reordering is frequent. Another type of stock card is shown in Figure 18.5. This card is designed to hold more information to assist the retailer in reordering.

Colour-coded price tickets — This is a simple way of recording the time of purchase to allow the retailer easy visual control of stock. Price tickets, marked with a highlighter pen, can be colour-coded for, say, each month or each quarter.

Loan register for merchandise on loan — Staff often want to borrow stock for greater product knowledge (in record stores or computer stores, for example). Have a simple register of stock borrowed and returned, and set a *written policy* on staff loans.

Cash register control sheets — These sheets are controls designed to protect not only the retailer but also the register operators. Regular cash register checks should be conducted in all stores, at different times and on different days. This will enable track records to be built up by all check-out operators. A simple cash register control sheet is shown in Figure 18.6.

Cash flow projections — Most retail stores are subject to major seasonal fluctuations caused by Christmas, summer, winter, school holidays, and so on, and cash flow planning is essential. (This area is well covered in Chapter 16.)

Competitor activity — A simple, pre-planned, written roster of scheduled visits to be made to competitors' stores should be drawn up. Unless a special time is put aside for these visits they will probably not be made.

With any control system, make sure that your staff are fully trained and know the importance of following the procedures you have established.

STOCK GUIDE

Supplier ____________________ Telephone ____________________

Contact ____________________ Order frequency ____________________

ITEM		DATE							
	Min / Max	In Stock / Order	In Stock / Order	In Stock / Order	In Stock / Order	In Stock / Order	In Stock / Order	In Stock / Order	In Stock / Order

FIGURE 18.4 Stock card for fast-selling items

ARTICLE						COST	UNITS OF	STOCK MAX		STOCK MIN	
DATE	TO OR FROM	NO.	IN	OUT	BALANCE	DATE	TO OR FROM	NO.	IN	OUT	BALANCE

FIGURE 18.5 Stock card showing detailed information

Front

CASH COUNT		CHANGE DRAWER	REGISTER no 1	REGISTER no 2	TOTAL
CHEQUES					
CREDIT CARDS					
$ 100		-	-	-	-
$ 50		-	-	-	-
$ 20		-	-	-	-
$ 10		-	-	-	-
$ 5		-	-	-	-
$ 2		-	-	-	-
$ 1		-	-	-	-
50¢					
20¢					
10¢					
5¢					
TOTAL					
- FLOATS					
THIS FLOAT					
ADD PREVIOUS PICK-UPS	1				
	2				
	3				
	4				
BANKING					

Back

DATE ____________

ITEM	REGISTER no 1	REGISTER no 2	TOTAL
NAME OF OPERATOR			
LATEST Z READ			
LESS PREVIOUS Z READ			
= GROSS SALES			
LESS CREDIT CARDS			
LESS REFUNDS			
LESS VOIDS			
LESS WAGES (NET)			
LESS PETTY CASH			
LESS CASH PURCHASE			
= NET CASH			
LESS BANKING			
= UNDERS → OR OVERS →			

AFFIX Z READS
VOIDS
DOCKETS, ETC
IN THIS SPACE

FIGURE 18.6 Cash register control sheet

Handy hints for retailers

To help you manage your store, the following handy hints are listed for your consideration.

Your buying

- If you put in a new line, make sure you delete a slow one.
- Don't let the representative make the order out for you.
- Check all deliveries and invoices.
- Watch bulk-buying offers.
- Check payment terms.
- Don't rely on one supplier only.
- Keep good stock cards.
- If possible, order at the start of the month — not the end — to gain a crash flow advantage.
- Return damaged stock.
- Ask suppliers for promotional material and displays.

Your cash registers

- Have regular cash register checks.
- Let the operator check the float and count the drawer.
- All voids must be sighted and signed by you or your nominee.
- Don't make cash purchases from the till.
- Don't count your till takings in public view.
- Never ring up with the drawer open.
- Lock your register if you have to leave it unattended.
- Have regular pick-ups from your cash register.

Your premises

- Register with the local police as a key-holder (the person who holds keys to your premises).
- Change your locks regularly.
- Have two locks on your front door.
- Have a security light.
- Keep your premises clean.
- Check to see whether your windows need security grilles or bars.

Your staff

- Build a staff team — treat each member as somebody special.
- Don't let staff ring up their own purchases.
- Have regular staff meetings to gain feedback and build teamwork.
- Delegate.
- Know your staff.
- Train your staff continually.

Your security

- Acknowledge every person entering your store — thus telling them that you are aware that they are present.
- Watch for sudden crowding or unusual distractions.
- Ensure that all your stock is visible from your action point; if necessary, install mirrors.
- Install a burglar alarm.
- Know the law regarding apprehension of shoplifters.
- Train your staff in security.
- Keep high-priced lines under glass or out of reach.
- Keep a list of emergency numbers in plain view near your telephone.

Finally

Join associations relevant to your business, eg:

- The Retail Traders Association
- The Food and Liquor Retailers Association
- The Hairdressing Association
- The Australian Booksellers Association.

If you don't know your association's contact details, ask your government small business office.

SUMMARY

In this chapter we have seen that retailing is more than just an easy way of making money. Customers are fickle and do not have to shop in your store.

You have to manage your operation so that:

- you satisfy your customers
- you gain new customers
- you can pick up warning signs of trouble, and
- you can establish control systems to help your store survive, grow and make money.

KEY WORDS

competitor
cost price
customer
margin
mark-up
merchandise
retailer
selling price

Review exercises

1 What is retailing?

2 To demonstrate the difference between mark-ups and margins, complete the pricing exercise in Figure 18.2.

3 Try to answer the following questions using the formula:

Cost price % of cost + Mark-up / Margin = % of Sales selling price

You can also refer to your ready reckoner in Figure 18.3.

(a) You are selling shirts for $30 with a gross profit margin of 50%.

What is your mark-up? $______; ______%

What is your cost price? $______

What is your margin? $______

(b) You are selling brooms. You buy them for $16 and add 25% to sell them.

What is your selling price? $______

What is your mark-up? $______; ______%

What is your margin? $______; ______%

(c) You buy tool kits for $90 and want to sell them and make a profit of $60.

What is your selling price? $______

What is your mark-up? $______; ______%

What is your margin? $______; ______%

(d) You mark up by 50% and want to sell shirts for $45.

What price must you buy them for? $______

(e) Your competition is selling gloves for $36, and you know that they always want a profit of 66.7%.

What is their cost price? $______

What is their mark-up? $______; ______%

What is their margin? $______; ______%

(f) You sell shoes for $90 and they have a profit margin of 50%.

What is your cost price? $______

What is your mark-up? $______; ______%

What is your margin? $______; ______%

(g) You buy seat covers for $20 each and want a profit margin of $30.

What is your mark-up? %______

What selling price would you charge on a pair of seat covers?

$______

4 Identify the six early warning signs of trouble in your retail business.

5 Using the 'Handy hints for retailers' in this chapter, create an action list for your business.

CHAPTER 19

Production management

Production is a factor in all types of small business. It involves creating the business's output. In Chapter 8 we discussed customer needs and wants. Your business must meet these needs if it is to be successful. All the factors which make up the way in which you meet these needs represent the output of your business. This could include prompt reliable service, high-quality products, value for money, etc. To achieve each of these requires creative effort on the part of the business owner, and this creative effort is the production function. Like all other aspects of your business, the production function needs to be managed — that is, planned and controlled.

After reading this chapter, you should be able to:

- define the factors of the production function in your business
- identify the measures of performance
- determine the costs and benefits of various levels of performance
- set standards and production objectives, and
- plan and control the production function.

THE PRODUCTION FUNCTION

Production is a creative process. This means bringing together all the necessary resources to create the desired output. Resources have been traditionally categorised as materials, machinery, staff and money. In order to study the production process in your business, let us discuss each of these in some detail.

Materials

These are items which are consumed during the production process. In a manufacturing business it is easy to recognise and measure materials. If the products are clothes or furniture, for instance, the materials used are quite obvious. However, if the output is a service, the materials might not be as easy to identify. Items such as toner in the laser printer of a desktop publisher, or carry bags used by a retailer as part of the overall service provided, are materials used in production. You can see from these examples why it is necessary to look broadly at the production process and regard it as the creative effort required to meet customer needs.

Production is the creative effort required to meet your customers' needs.

Materials are obtained from **suppliers**. In planning and controlling your production, you must determine that suitable materials are available — when required and at an appropriate cost. This demands a knowledge of sources, quality, and costs.

It is important to identify a range of suppliers. If you know of only one supplier, your business becomes dependent on that supplier. Any production or delivery problems suffered by your supplier can result in a serious loss of profit, or even failure of your business.

Your business is only as safe as your suppliers.

It is a good idea to keep a record of possible suppliers, including their names, phone numbers and comments about the quality, price and range of their products, as well as the time usually taken from the placing of an order to delivery. Such records enable you to find a suitable supplier quickly to meet any special needs you might have (eg an urgent order, unusual material, different quality, etc). A simple card system is all that is required, although if you have a computer, a special database can be created.

Provision must be made to **store** materials. Production costs will be reduced if materials are stored as close as practicable to where they will be used. This saves time, and hence money. The storage facilities must ensure that materials are protected and their quality maintained until they are used (eg keeping photocopy paper dry). Space is needed to store materials before they are used. In some businesses, transport might also be needed to move materials from storage to the machines (eg steel fabrication).

Quality control of materials needs to be carried out before acceptance from a supplier. To avoid disputes over quality, a clear, detailed quality specification should be included with your order. Acceptance tests must be carried out in accordance with this specification. If the quality is shown by your tests to be below that specified, you can discuss the shortfall with your supplier and negotiate a mutually satisfactory solution.

The first step, then, is the preparation of quality specifications. These must include all aspects of the material which could affect the quality of your finished product, or the efficiency of your production processes. To do this, you need a thorough knowledge of materials. If you do not have this knowledge, it is possible to discuss your requirements with a number of suppliers, or with others in your industry, perhaps through your industry association. In this way, you can learn enough to prepare a suitable specification. It then remains to implement appropriate testing procedures. Again, information about these can be obtained from external specialists.

It can be seen that materials management requires planning and control of supplies, storage, quality and cost. All these factors must be considered in relation to the production process itself.

Machinery

This includes all the equipment needed in the production process, whether manual (eg shears used by a landscape gardener), engine powered (eg a cement mixer), gas, electric or electronic. All machinery requires maintenance, and every item is subject to breakdown. Breakdowns result in a loss of production time, and disruption of production schedules. The need to reschedule production puts additional time demands on you. Preventive maintenance can reduce the frequency and severity of breakdowns, and thus increase productivity. Any machine with moving parts should be scheduled for regular maintenance, including cleaning, lubrication, adjustment, and a thorough inspection. One mistake made by many business owners is to not carry out maintenance at the due time, even though they have prepared a detailed schedule. This is false economy, because subsequent breakdowns will be more frequent and more costly in terms of both time and money.

Preventive maintenance reduces costs.

By planning ahead, it is usually possible to schedule maintenance when a machine is idle, at night, or at weekends when the business is closed.

Machines without moving parts (eg electronic cash registers) do not usually require the same type of preventive maintenance. However, breakdown of these can be just as disruptive and costly. It might be possible to minimise these costs by arranging with a repairer for the supply of a replacement while repairs are made. Alternatively, you might be able to make arrangements with other business people to share machines at crisis times.

The owner of a secretarial-service business organised a network of businesses with similar equipment, and they agreed to make their computers, printers, etc available to each other in the event of breakdowns. This involved working overnight on occasions when all were busy during the day, but at least production was still able to continue.

Another approach is the use of service agreements. Service agreements or contracts are available for most types of electronic equipment. Under the terms of these agreements, a repairer contracts to provide a specified level of service. This could be at your premises or it could require you to send the machine to the repairer. An annual fee is charged, which is dependent upon the terms of the agreement. The cost of a maintenance agreement should be compared with the cost of time lost due to a breakdown. This will indicate whether a maintenance agreement is appropriate for your business.

When purchasing machines, a balance might be required between highly specialised and more general-purpose machines. Usually the specialised machines are faster and often more accurate. General-purpose machines are more flexible, and can process a wider range of jobs. Selection of the most appropriate machine begins with a thorough investigation of the type of work you are doing now in your business, and the future developments you have planned in terms of sales, market segments, customers and products. All of these will have an impact on the most suitable machine. (This again demonstrates the need for a thorough business plan, as discussed in Chapter 14.)

Apart from the capital cost of a machine, other costs associated with machine selection might include increased insurance premiums, and operating costs. In addition, the selection might affect staff requirements, calling for specific skills. This could involve additional training, or might cause scheduling problems due to the lack of availability of suitable operators.

Staff

This is the third group of production resources. Production staff need specific skills, which must be identified before the selection process begins. In a retail business, for example, one output is customer service. Before selecting staff, the skills required to generate customer service must be identified. In all businesses, the required skills should be listed and arranged in order of importance. This enables you to rank applicants for positions according to abilities relevant to your particular business. In some situations the measurement of skills levels is very difficult during an interview. In these cases it can be valuable to have a period of probation, during which a person's abilities can be evaluated on the job. When this technique is used, it is vital to have a clearly defined way of assessing performance. New employees must be made aware of the assessment methods and criteria.

Even with the best available selection techniques, the development of staff will be an ongoing need. Some people will have initial weaknesses which need to be overcome. But, more importantly, your business will be changing, and this will require new skills, or a higher level of some skills, in both you and your staff. A staff development plan is essential to enable you to achieve your objectives.

Whether you are planning to introduce a new machine, or a new service or retail product, your staff must be prepared for it before you make the move. The best time to make the change might well be determined by how long it takes you to develop your staff.

> Production planning must include planning for the development of you and your staff.

Many avenues are available for staff development, including formal courses through TAFE colleges or private providers, and on-the-job schemes, or combinations of these. Like any other business activity, these should be planned. This means setting clear objectives and selecting appropriate strategies to achieve them.

Motivation of staff

This vital factor in ensuring efficient production is covered in more detail in Chapter 20.

All aspects of staffing involve costs, of both time and money. For your business to be successful, you must decide how much needs to be spent, and what is the best way to apply it. The costs themselves are an essential ingredient in success; trying to avoid them will reduce efficiency and may even result in failure of your business.

> Training and development costs are essential for success.

Money

As we have seen, money is another factor of production. It is required for materials, machines and staff. There is never sufficient to do all the things you want to do when you want to do them. In this way it becomes the main limitation on both objectives and strategies.

After the initial production objectives have been set, all costs involved must be identified and accurately estimated. It is unlikely that all objectives will be achievable within the time frame you have specified. One common approach to solving this problem is to assign priorities to the production objectives. However, this can be done successfully only by taking into account all of the business objectives. Production objectives must be related to marketing, finance, and personnel objectives for the whole business. This requires a clear understanding of where your business is directed, as discussed in Chapter 14 (which details the preparation of a business plan).

> Financial resources must be sufficient to enable all your business objectives to be achieved.

Thus, not only production, but all objectives must be assigned priorities. When this has been done, you can begin to implement the strategies required to achieve your production objectives, within the limits of available financial resources. As the strategies are implemented, it is then essential to monitor and control activities and results.

Production Planning and Control

Day-to-day operations require jobs be scheduled so that the required materials, machines and skills are available when and where they are needed. Also, to maintain productivity, machines and people need to be productively employed for the maximum number of available hours.

Small manufacturing businesses usually have either *continuous production* or *jobbing production*. Continuous production is the manufacture of standardised products. Jobbing is the production of specialised products to meet individual customer orders. Planning and control methods which are suitable for one type of production might not be at all appropriate for the other.

Continuous production

Planning and control techniques for continuous production are aimed at the development of 'steps' of equal duration. When each operation in the manufacturing process takes equal time, then flow through the plant will be steady. Very little paperwork is required. The need for control actions is indicated very quickly by an over-supply of work at one station and a lack of work at subsequent ones. The major source of problems is the need for specialised machines and operators. A machine breakdown causes delays, not only in that process but also in all the steps that follow. Use of an alternative machine, even on a temporary basis, might be difficult to arrange because of its specialised nature.

Similarly, absenteeism might cause greater difficulties because of each person's particular knowledge or skills. Job rotation might be a worthwhile investment — not only in terms of staff morale and interest but also as a type of insurance against major delays. After a work stoppage, it is difficult to make up for lost time and regain the planned schedule in any way other than by working additional hours. This is because each step takes the same time, which is the minimum practical time, and the final step produces finished products at this rate. To produce more, it is necessary to work longer hours.

Jobbing production

Jobbing, or batch, production has more flexibility than continuous production and is more common in small business. Usually the machines are multi-functional and the operators multi-skilled. In the event of machine breakdown, or operator absenteeism, it is often possible to make alternative arrangements for production to continue. The most likely sources of delays in the jobbing situation are shortages of materials, tools and fixtures, or a customer's change of mind. Detailed planning can minimise delays caused by materials or tools, but customer-related delays cannot be fully controlled. Clear specifications of what the customer orders, and what you will supply, are an essential starting point. Even where this is done, changes can still be required, with resulting delays to that job and possibly to other jobs needing the same machines or operators. Gantt charts are a simple and easily used method of production planning that is suitable for jobbing plants. They show the planned workload for each machine and operator, and also the progress on each job. The effect of variations due to delays can be viewed in conjunction with all other existing and planned jobs.

There is more paperwork associated with jobbing production than with continuous production. Records should be kept of materials and times spent on each job, the development and use of special tools and equipment, scheduling time and quality control checks. Planned and actual figures should be recorded for each item of cost, so that a comparison can be made later. In this way, control can be exercised, and planning and budgeting can be continually improved.

Scheduling techniques

In continuous production, as we have seen, each operation has equal duration. When this is achieved, the production line is said to be 'balanced'. Scheduling of continuous production is centred on this need to balance the line. Data needed to do this can be obtained from a detailed analysis of all the tasks required to manufacture one product. The use of standard times for each task enables them to be grouped into separate operations, so that each operation has the same duration.

> Scheduling of continuous production is based on an analysis of the tasks.

The introduction of new machines, methods and work practices causes changes to the times of some of the tasks, and the line must be re-balanced. Workplace layout and the design of individual work centres must be kept under continuous review as changes are made to tasks. Industrial engineers specialise in this field, and reference to a competent consultant can bring major savings in production costs for continuous production.

Almost every product is different. If your product is a service, you will know that every customer is different, and you might find the scheduling techniques used in jobbing production appropriate in your business to reduce costs and increase productivity. Whatever your business, the first step is to define a measure of productivity. It might be the number of jobs completed in a set period of time (or number of customers served, or number of paid hours spent on clients' work), together with the costs involved. The major factors affecting productivity are the machines and skills used. Scheduling techniques for jobbing production concentrate on matching machines and skills to the job.

Scheduling of batch production is based on the allocation of skills and machines to jobs.

When the jobs are complex and require a number of different machines, processes and skills, scheduling for maximum productivity requires the use of charts or computer analysis. Specialised training is needed to develop adequate scheduling skills. If you do not already have these skills, you could obtain them through a recognised institution, or alternatively, the employment of an industrial engineer, either as a staff member or consultant.

For simpler jobbing situations, where the machines and skills are fewer, simple wall charts are adequate. These show the available machines and skills, and allocation of tasks is planned to ensure that the resources required are available when needed for each job. The simplest form of scheduling for jobbing processes is the staff roster.

Every manager does some type of scheduling, even if it is only for their own time. The use of a planning chart can help to organise resources so that tasks are completed in order of priority. Planning charts are not used only for manufacturing businesses.

Most small businesses can use planning charts to improve efficiency.

One hidden benefit of planning charts is that they focus a manager's attention on objectives and strategies, thus enabling him or her to find the best way of managing the business.

Because planning charts are visual, they also provide a convenient basis for control. Any delays in reaching planned progress can be seen at an early stage. Early recognition enables immediate action to be taken, and thus avoids major crises later. Progress of each job should be assessed frequently and compared with the planned schedule. In many businesses, the manager does this at the end of each day's production. Any problems that become apparent can be dealt with, and if revised schedules are needed they can be prepared, ready for implementation at the start of the next day.

Planning charts are also control tools.

As each job is completed, an analysis can be made of the actual times, skills and machines used. This information will be valuable in the future, when a similar job is scheduled. Records should be kept showing the job details, with planned and actual resources used. Any comments regarding reasons for variances (eg machine breakdown) should be included in the records.

Summary

The production function is the creative effort required to generate the output of a business. All small businesses, in meeting their customers' needs, create some form of output. Resources required in the production process include materials, machines, staff and money. Each resource needs to be managed to ensure that it is available when needed, and that efficiency and productivity are maximised. The resource-management techniques used in manufacturing are also valuable in other industries. Methods of planning and controlling the production process are available for both continuous and jobbing (batch) production. These techniques are also widely applicable. While specialised techniques are used for various factors of the process, the whole business must be kept in focus, and an integrated approach to planning used which considers not only the factors of production but also the interrelation of the production function with all other functions of the business.

Key words

batch production
continuous production
jobbing production
maintenance agreement
preventive maintenance
resource

Review exercises

1 What are the main differences between continuous and jobbing production?

2 List the main factors of production.

3 Explain why all small businesses have some form of production function.

4 How does preventive maintenance improve productivity?

5 Which factors are the major considerations in scheduling:
(a) continuous production?
(b) jobbing production?

6 Explain why records should be kept showing details of a number of available suppliers of materials.

7 List the factors that could affect your decision on whether to enter into a maintenance agreement for your machines.

8 Why is continuing training and development of production staff essential?

9 How can you plan the allocation of financial resources to the production function in your business?

10 What steps can you take to overcome a lack of production-planning and scheduling skills in your business?

CHAPTER 20

Management of employees

People are the most valuable resource in any business. This is especially the case in small business, because fewer people are involved than in large corporations. Any objectives set should ensure that conditions are created and maintained to provide profitable and efficient use of this major resource. Special attention must therefore be given to those aspects of management which affect the people in the business. This is best achieved by treating staff as human beings and being concerned about their total work environment.

After reading this chapter, you should be able to:

- plan ways to involve your staff in the operation of your business
- adopt a procedure for hiring staff which will ensure that you obtain the best people available
- implement strategies to develop and retain high-quality staff
- take appropriate action to minimise stress when dismissing staff.

Legal issues are not discussed in this chapter. They have been outlined in Chapter 12.

THE STAFFING PLAN

As with the management of all other resources, a plan is essential for managing human resources. This task is more complex than when the resources are physical (eg finance). Intangible factors such as human dignity and personal ambition need to be considered, together with a range of moral and ethical issues. Your plan must take these into account. The first step in developing a staffing plan is to set objectives.

Setting objectives

Your objectives could include:

- number of staff
- turnover of staff
- type of person employed
- pay and conditions

- development of staff, and
- results.

Wherever possible, staff should be involved in the objective-setting process. They often have good ideas and a different way of looking at the business, both of which can help you to set better objectives. Also, when staff contribute to the setting of goals, they are usually more committed to the achievement of those goals.

A set of clear, measurable objectives will enable you to determine the progress of your business. Good staffing objectives will provide staff with clear guidelines and allow them to see for themselves how well they are succeeding. In this respect objectives are often of more value than are duties statements or job descriptions. This is because the goal remains fairly constant, while details of the work to be done frequently change, often causing problems. However, objectives that have been set in co-operation with the staff provide clear goals, making the *details* of the job less critical. Your management becomes more concerned with guidance, and less with issuing instructions. This makes for a happier and more efficient workplace.

Your staff's continued contribution to the objective-setting process depends on their knowing that you will also be committed to helping them achieve the desired results. This requires your looking at the overall business objectives to identify new methods, technologies, products and markets in which your business will need to be involved.

Training and development objectives for your staff are essential. Your staff will need to be prepared for future changes. Such objectives are likely to indicate a need not only for additional skills or knowledge but also for information about the changes and the impact these could have on their work. All this preparation needs to be completed before the changes are introduced. Training and development take time. To ensure that you can have the necessary preparation completed in time for the introduction of any planned changes, you might need to look at your business objectives two years ahead.

Staffing the changes means changing the staff.

The price of not planning

Typical examples of the penalty for lack of preparation can be found in many businesses where new machines are unused or under-utilised because the staff can't or won't operate them. A typist who is suddenly given a new word-processor in place of a typewriter will not be prepared for the change, and cannot be blamed for treating the new equipment as an electronic typewriter. Much of the initial capital outlay and many of the cost-saving benefits will thus be lost. Loss is due to lack of planning by the manager. It could have been avoided by looking ahead and incorporating staff development in the equipment purchase strategy. If the typist had been trained to use the word-processor as soon as it was installed, productivity and staff motivation would have been higher and the business more efficient.

Formulating strategies

Similar benefits are gained if staff are involved in the formulation of strategies. Asking them for their ideas on how their objectives can best be achieved will benefit your business in two ways:

- it will give you ideas you might not have thought of yourself, and
- it will boost the morale, motivation and commitment of your staff.

This can go a long way towards ensuring that the objectives will be achieved.

Enthusiastic staff will make your managerial tasks easier and more rewarding. Again, this needs real two-way communication and commitment. You must be prepared to accept and implement employees' ideas, even though you might disagree with them. If everything is always done the way you want, your staff will quickly cease putting any effort into giving you their ideas. You will lose the benefit of valuable opinions, and staff management will become more difficult and less effective. In one business, absenteeism was traced to this source. When staff ideas began to be implemented, absenteeism decreased dramatically.

In formulating any strategies which affect your staff (and most do!), it pays to seek their active involvement from the start. Ask them how they feel about your idea, and what they think is the best way to approach its implementation. If objections are raised, consider these carefully, and discuss with your people whether the objections outweigh the benefits to them. The benefits might include easier work, or gaining additional skills, greater responsibility and improved self-esteem. Many people do not identify such benefits, just as you might not have been aware initially of some of their objections. Open discussion of these issues will result in both better strategies and smoother implementation of them. In fact, it is worth emphasising again that implementation of your strategies (that is, getting anything to happen) depends on your staff. It requires them having the appropriate skills, knowledge and abilities available when they are needed.

> Your staff make your ideas a reality.

TAKING ON STAFF

Staff management begins at the time when you decide that you need additional people in your business. At this time the characteristics of your 'ideal' employee need to be specified. These details should include all aspects of the person you seek — knowledge, experience, personality and any special factors you feel are important.

Writing all these down is best spread over a period of about a week. Draft a list on the first day, then review it for a few minutes each day after that. At the end of a week you will have a clear idea of the person who would best suit your business.

Finding prospects

Pick out the main points and include them in your advertisement for staff. Make a complete list of these points for use in interviews. It is very helpful if this list also shows how you are planning to get the information you need. If this entails asking questions, plan them in advance and check to ensure that applicants' answers will give you the information you want. Talk to your existing employees about the type of person they would like. Again, include on your list questions to get this information

If you are planning to use an agency to make the initial selection, it would be to your advantage to discuss your needs fully with them before any advertising is done. They might already have a file of suitable applicants, and this could save advertising expense. Also, it will ensure that your needs are fully understood, which will minimise any wastage of time when you begin your interviews.

Interviewing

Best results are gained from interviews held in a fairly relaxed atmosphere. It is not easy to achieve just the right amount of informality. After all, you are involved in a major investment decision. Applicants know they are being judged in a number of ways, so they also are a bit tense.

If you are too abrupt, you might frighten away an excellent prospect. Too much informality, on the other hand, can detract from the seriousness of the matter and lead to an unwise choice.

One way to achieve a good balance is to be relaxed yourself and get the applicants to talk about themselves. It's the one area in which the other person is sure they know more than you do, so they feel confident in talking about it. Also, it's one area you need to learn about, so you're going to have to be a good listener.

Make sure that you ask each applicant the questions you have prepared, so you can compare responses later. Also, it is important that each applicant be given equal opportunity to express themselves and explain the benefits that they can bring to your business. Some states have laws governing equal employment opportunity, and it is illegal to discriminate against applicants on various grounds. It would be advisable to become familiar with these laws before conducting any interviews.

To avoid misunderstandings, it is essential that working hours, pay rates and other conditions be clearly specified in the interview.

Selection

After all the interviews, responses to your questions can be compared. From this, you can choose the three or four applicants who best meet your criteria. A detailed review of their applications and your interview notes will help you to choose the most suitable applicant. It is often a good idea to arrange for informal contact between each applicant and the existing staff. You can gain more information about each applicant this way, and this could help you make the best choice.

Notification

Giving the news to the successful applicant is pleasant and easy. However, when this has been done, all other applicants must be advised that they were unsuccessful. This should be done promptly. It is not only courteous; it is also good policy, because it will help to build your reputation and improve the image of your business.

Induction

Before a new employee starts, draw up an action plan for their induction. Give some thought to the initial introduction and any basic training required. All businesses are different, and your new employee needs to know how your business operates. Some friendly guidance and careful direction on the first day will help ensure that your new starter becomes effective as soon as possible. If additional training is needed through some outside organisation, raise this matter with your new employee during the first week. Details could be left for a while, but the requirement needs to be aired early. Once it has been agreed to, a suitable course can be selected.

Evaluation

Friendly guidance during the first few weeks will ensure that your new staff member quickly comes to recognise the main features of your business. This will help them to make a valuable contribution to the setting of objectives and the forming of strategies and plans. All of this makes your task of evaluating their performance much easier. Once they have a set of objectives to work towards, you can concentrate on finding ways to help them to achieve these objectives. Working *with* staff is the best way to manage. Regular reviews of their progress towards goals they have helped set will minimise the need for constant close supervision.

> Praise loudly in public. Criticise quietly in private.

We all tend to feel hurt when we are criticised, no matter how justly it was deserved. After criticising an employee, take a little time to rebuild their morale. This can be done by mentioning good aspects of their work, personality or attitude. Let them know that you are not criticising their entire performance, just part of it.

Termination

Sometimes, even with all the help you can offer, a particular employee is revealed to be just not suited to the job. When it is necessary to terminate their services, there is one golden rule:

> Say as little as possible.

Have your accountant calculate the payment due on termination. Speak to the person privately and let them know that their services are no longer required. Thank them for their work to date. Tell them that they will be leaving on a particular day at a specified time, and where and when they will be paid.

Stop!

Many employers feel that they need to discuss reasons, express sympathy, or just talk because they are nervous and embarrassed. This will not help, and can cause problems. Dismissals are never pleasant, but are least unpleasant when handled calmly, politely and briefly.

Administration

Staff records

As with all other aspects of your business, some record keeping is necessary. This should be as simple as possible. Details to be recorded include:

- name
- address
- phone number
- next of kin
- date of birth
- date employed
- position
- award rates of pay and dates of implementation of changes
- space for comments
- annual leave, sick leave or other leave taken, and
- date terminated.

Often a simple staff card system is all that is necessary.

Figure 20.1 shows an example of a staff record card. Each employee should know what is recorded on their staff card.

Front

FULL NAME

ADDRESS

POSTCODE

PHONE

NEXT OF KIN

DATE OF BIRTH

FILE NUMBER

DATE EMPLOYED	POSITION/AWARD CLASSIFICATION	RATE

COMMENTS

DATE TERMINATED

Back

ANNUAL LEAVE					SICK LEAVE				
Date	Details	Due	Taken	Bal	Date	Details	Due	Taken	Bal

FIGURE 20.1 Staff record card

Taxation

It is a legal requirement that you keep a wages book. Suitable books can be purchased from business office supply firms, stationers, and even some newsagents. These books are ruled ready to use, including headings and columns. They often have instructions in them, but the column headings are self-explanatory. Each employee must be given the opportunity to complete a general exemption form. You can obtain these forms from the Australian Taxation Office or any post office. Each form has detailed instructions on it. Information on the general exemption form will determine the amount of tax you must deduct from your employee's pay. See Chapter 22 for more details

Income tax

Tax payable on income is specified by the Australian Taxation Office. You can obtain copies of 'Weekly Rates of Income Tax Instalments' from your region's taxation office or your local post office. These forms show the amount of tax applicable to every level of weekly pay. You must forward to the Australian Taxation Office the tax you have deducted from your employees' wages. This can be done using the tax stamp method or group certificates. It is worth contacting the Australian Taxation Office to obtain details of both these methods. You can then select the one that best suits you and your business.

Fringe benefits tax

A wide range of employee benefits is subject to this tax. Advice from the Australian Taxation Office is readily available. It is vital that you are familiar with the requirements for this tax, as penalties are severe — in terms of both fines and the time that will be needed to calculate and substantiate it later.

Advice

Taxation laws and regulations are subject to major changes. At the same time, the penalties and costs of non-compliance are severe. You should keep in close contact with your accountant to ensure that your records and actions meet the requirements of the Australian Taxation Office.

KEEPING GOOD STAFF

Earlier in this chapter, we mentioned the importance of treating employees as human beings. This means applying particular management skills to the fields of employee relations, communication and motivation.

Employee relations

Just as you have personal objectives, so too do your employees. They might not set them out as clearly as you do, but that doesn't mean they don't have them. However, your business does not play as large a part in their goals as it does in yours. You cannot expect your staff to care as much about your business as you do because they will allow other facets of their life outside work to affect their concentration at times. Treating them as human beings means recognising and accepting their different goals and levels of commitment. After all, you have employed them for their skills and talents — you have not leased an entire person as you might a piece of equipment.

People like to feel good. This might seem quite obvious, but do you really know what makes people feel good about their work? In the 1960s psychologist Abraham Maslow studied this question. He found that five major 'levels of need' are at work in employer–employee relations:

1 survival
2 security
3 a sense of belonging
4 esteem
5 self-actualisation (reaching full potential).

These 'levels of need' apply to everybody and are arranged like the steps on a ladder. Each need level must be addressed before we start on the next. Until we are reasonably sure we can survive, we do not address our need for security. When we are confident of survival and security, then we look for a sense of belonging, and so on up the ladder. Each day, in various aspects of our lives, we are at different levels on this ladder, always trying to reach the top rung. Your employees are doing the same.

To achieve full self-actualisation at work, and the self-fulfilment it brings, staff must feel a low degree of threat to their survival and security. They must also feel that they belong to their work group, and that they are respected at work. You have an impact on all of these factors, through the way you run your business. While providing leadership, in both direction and efficiency, you need to be guide, instructor and coach of your business team. At the same time, each individual employee needs to feel safe, secure, respected and appreciated. And they need to be confident that they will feel this way into the future. This requires ongoing development not only of *their* skills, knowledge and abilities but also of *yours*. Remember: people are the most valuable asset in your business. Managing them is therefore the most important part of your work. If you need additional skills in this area, make the gaining of them a part of your own objectives.

> Managing people is the most important part of your work.

This is one area in which the use of consultants is valuable for special projects but is not appropriate for daily operations. You must develop these skills yourself. An essential part of both developing and applying these skills involves communicating with your staff.

Communication

Possibly the major key to working *with* your staff lies in *communication*. Because your business is small, you should be able to communicate closely with your staff. This can help you to identify their needs, including why they want to work for you. Recognising and taking account of what they want, and where they are going, will help keep their morale high.

At the same time, you would be well advised to keep them informed of your plans for the business. We have suggested that you involve your staff in setting objectives. This brings with it the responsibility for you to keep them informed of progress towards achieving those objectives. When you plan to make changes in your business, explain to your staff the reason for the changes. They will appreciate this, and often make constructive suggestions.

The more you understand human behaviour, the better equipped you will be to manage the working environment of your staff. Many seminars, courses and workshops are available on the topic of human relations, and some time spent at these will pay dividends by reducing both your staffing costs and problems.

Employment of friends or relatives as members of your staff should be approached very carefully. While this arrangement can be very successful in some instances, there are also many in which it can prove disastrous for the business. Lines of communication tend to get blurred when friends or relatives must take on the role of superior and subordinate while at work.

Most of the points mentioned so far require listening, recognition and acceptance — relatively passive processes. A more active approach is necessary in the management area of staff motivation.

Motivation

Everyone in your business is doing their best to achieve their goals. By planning your employees' work, training and development, you can work together with them to achieve progress towards your objectives as well as theirs.

Each employee is an individual and every business is different. Motivating your employees requires a plan that recognises these differences. To develop such a plan, you must first identify the differences. Where is each person on the 'needs level ladder'? What does he or she need to achieve self-fulfilment at work? In answering these questions, you will find ways to help your staff and, in helping them, to help yourself. We have stressed the need for communication, both talking and listening. This is the basis of motivation. *Talk* to your staff about your dreams, your objectives, your strategies, where they belong in these, and how well they are doing their work. *Listen* to your staff about their needs, their dreams, their ideas, their problems, and how well they feel you are doing your job.

After talking and listening comes the doing. Change your employees' work to make it more interesting for them but not so much as to unsettle them. Implement their ideas. If their ideas don't work out, at least you have all tried, and perhaps everybody has learnt from it. If their ideas do work out, give them the recognition they deserve. Recognise not only their ideas but also their contribution to the success of these ideas.

Talking, listening, doing: together these activities build a powerful team of committed employees. Their satisfaction will be obvious, not only to you but, more importantly, to your customers. Treating your staff as human beings takes courage, skill and commitment. The benefits are worth it.

Summary

Your staff are your business's most valuable asset, and so managing this asset is, not surprisingly, the most important part of managing your business. Doing so requires a range of skills. Every step along the way is critical — from finding and selecting the best people, to training, developing and retaining them. Even termination is critical, because of the effect it can have on you and on those who stay. The basic guidelines are to treat your staff as human beings, to realise that they want to feel good about their work, and to build a powerful team of committed employees. Although apparently simple, applying the guidelines demands your courage, commitment, in-depth knowledge and a wide range of skills. Your employees form an integral part of your objectives and strategies. You need to involve them in every step of the way. And you need them to make it all happen.

Key words

communication	levels of need
effective	self-actualisation
esteem	sense of belonging

REVIEW EXERCISES

1 Why should employees be involved in setting objectives?

2 What steps should you take when preparing to hire staff?

3 How can you ensure that a new employee becomes effective in the shortest possible time?

4 What approach should you adopt when dismissing an employee?

5 Describe the benefits to you of discussing business strategies with your employees.

6 List the five levels of need developed by Maslow.

7 Why is managing your employees the most important part of managing your business?

8 What is the basis of motivating your staff?

9 Explain the benefits of staff motivation.

10 List the qualities you need in order to manage your staff effectively.

CHAPTER 21

Time management

In Chapter 3 we saw that time is an important resource available to every manager. As a business resource, it must be managed properly to increase its value to the firm. Better use (that is, more efficient and more effective use) of time is a skill that produces many benefits, including cost savings, greater job satisfaction, reduced stress and improved productivity.

The objectives of this chapter are to:

- help you understand the importance of time management
- make you aware of the major time-wasters that prevent most people from achieving job satisfaction, and
- enable you to develop a simple method of improving your own use of time.

> Time is a unique resource.

In most firms, small and large, managers and workers in general pay little attention to the basics of time management, thereby wasting much valuable time — and, therefore, money. Like the air we breathe, time is usually ignored until we run short of it. It is an invisible resource, and most small business operators find it the hardest one to manage.

EFFICIENCY AND EFFECTIVENESS

In managing the use of time (and any other resource) two measures apply:

- efficiency, and
- effectiveness.

Efficiency is concerned with methods. It means getting more done each hour, day or week (which results in decreased costs for the same amount of work, or more work done at the same cost).

Effectiveness is concerned with results. It means doing the jobs that are most important. This requires planning and setting priorities in the use of work time.

> Good time management doesn't just mean getting more done in your available time.

In improving their time management, owner/managers must be concerned with both efficiency and effectiveness. To focus only on efficiency (activity) and ignore effectiveness (results) might mean doing the wrong things in less time!

WHAT IS TIME?

Time is a resource available to every person. A resource is something we have to use to achieve our goals or objectives. However, time is unique — it is different from all other resources.

The following characteristics of time are of particular relevance to the small business manager:

1 Each of us has the same amount of time as every other person. None of us has any more or less than anyone else.
2 Time cannot be stored up for use in the future. It must be used as it comes.
3 Time is totally inelastic — it cannot be expanded or contracted to suit personal wishes.
4 It cannot be stopped or reversed. Destroying the alarm clock at 5 am does not stop the flow of time, or put off the time when we should start work.
5 Time cannot be replaced — an hour or day wasted is gone forever.

Author and management consultant Peter Drucker (1967, pp 26–27) has described time's unique qualities with these words:

one cannot rent, hire, buy or otherwise obtain more time. The supply of time is totally inelastic. No matter how high the demand, the supply will not go up. There is no price for it . . . Moreover, time is totally perishable and cannot be stored. Yesterday's time is gone forever and will never come back. Time is, therefore, always in exceedingly short supply. Time is totally irreplaceable . . . There is no substitute for time. Everything requires time. It is the one truly universal condition. All work takes place in time and uses up time. Yet most people take for granted this unique, irreplaceable, and necessary resource.

> The moving finger writes; and, having writ,
> Moves on: nor all your piety nor wit
> Shall lure it back to cancel half a line,
> Nor all your tears wash out a word of it.
>
> 'Rubaiyat of Omar Khayyam'

According to time management consultant Alan Lakein (1973, p 11), 'Time is life. It is irreversible and irreplaceable. To waste your time is to waste your life, but to master your time is to master your life and make the most of it.'

The importance of time management to managers is well summed up by Drucker (1967, p 53): 'Time is the scarcest resource; and unless it is managed, nothing else can be managed.'

Time is a finite space into which each one of us must fit all we wish to achieve in life. So often we say 'I don't have enough time', whereas the fact is that we do not *use* our time as well as others, and we therefore think we *have* less of it.

> Better time management takes planning and self-discipline.

Most of us know someone who can get far more done than we can in the same time (by greater efficiency), and get the right things done in that time (that is, be more effective), which gives them much greater satisfaction in their work and in life generally. For many people, time difficulties control their lives — time is a source of continual worry! Inability to complete jobs in the time allowed, facing deadlines, and carrying heavy workloads are a major source of stress for many workers. For many people, time is the master of their lives — a tyrant! Improved time management can reduce stress, increase job satisfaction and enhance our sense of achievement.

MAJOR TIME-WASTERS

All of us fall into bad habits which result in much time being wasted every day. Keeping a record of how we use the 24 hours we have will prove the point. One survey (by Williams) of 40 people of different ages, of both sexes, and from quite different backgrounds and occupations found that their typical daily use of time over three weeks was as shown in Table 21.1

TABLE 21.1 Average daily use of time (work days)

Activity	Time spent
Sleeping	7 hours 15 minutes
Meals	1 hour 15 minutes
Travelling	1 hour 15 minutes
Work and/or study	7 hours 45 minutes
Social/other activities	1 hour 45 minutes
Total identified time use	19 hours 15 minutes

These figures show that the 40 people were unable to say how they 'filled in' (used?) an average of nearly five hours every day. This 'wasted' time totals about 25 hours in a working week — more than three working days. It is also quite likely that some of the work or study time was not used well — constituting even more time wasted!

In his book *The Time Trap*, R A Mackenzie reports some studies on the major time-wasters of different groups of managers. Some time-wasters are mentioned by all groups (Mackenzie, 1972, pp 4–5).

Another management expert, Humble (1980, p 26), listed the major time problems of 900 managers in nine countries in order of importance as follows:

1 **Telephone interruptions** — in addition to an excessive number of calls, many conversations tend to be long-winded. Difficulties also occur in placing outgoing calls.
2 **Meetings** — many are unnecessary, too long, and/or badly run.
3 **Unexpected visitors** — too many people, colleagues and others, drop in without prior notice or appointment.
4 **Poor delegation** — work that could be done by subordinates is often delegated poorly or not at all.
5 **Crises** — unexpected problems can disrupt or cancel planned work schedules.

Some time-wasters are due to personal deficiencies in management and other skills, and others are due to problems that affect many people in the same firm.

What are your main time-wasters?

The following list of 20 major time-wasters has been obtained from a study (by Williams) of the work habits of many thousands of small business owner/managers in Australia, and their senior employees. Some brief suggestions are provided on how the problems might be solved or avoided.

Time-wasters in small firms

1 Telephone interruptions, delays and complications. Contact Telecom for help with using better telephone techniques.

2 Meetings — too many and poorly run. Time wasted with meetings and committees can be reduced by asking: 'Why?' 'When?' 'Who?' and 'Where?' for every meeting. Meetings must have a purpose, and be planned (that is, have an agenda), start and finish on time, and be kept on track. They are best held just before lunch or in the late afternoon.

3 Lack of objectives, task priorities and daily action plans (no clear job descriptions or procedures coupled with lack of co-operation and teamwork, leading to confusion, mistakes and duplicated effort). Take time to plan. Planning needs time, but it saves more than it uses and it gets better results.

According to Mackenzie (1972, p 42) planning saves time, as shown below. More time spent in planning means less time needed for the job overall.

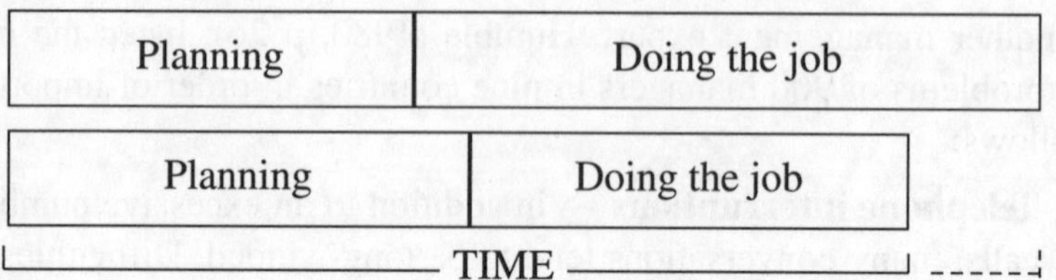

People who work without setting priorities, and hence without daily action lists, tend to spend time in amounts inversely related to the importance of their tasks (Parkinson's Second Law). They spend 80% of their time achieving only 20% of the results.

4 Succumbing to the tyranny of the urgent. This means that tasks calling for instant action (such as answering the telephone) get done at the expense of more important and usually less urgent tasks. The endless pressures of the 'here and now' are a major concern to most managers, and cause stress.

5 Ineffective delegation (being swamped in routine, detail and 'administrivia', often through a compulsive 'need' to control and supervise everything). Managers with this problem should experiment with:

- Management by exception — letting the employee do the job delegated unless some specified problem occurs. (Beware of upward (or reverse) delegation caused by saying: 'Do nothing without checking with me' or 'Leave this problem with me'.)
- Selective neglect — ignoring some tasks. (If the wrong task — an important one — is ignored, someone will telephone, write or call in person.)

6 Accumulating 'trivial' jobs — having pride in one's own indispensability. Parkinson's Law says: 'Work tends to expand to fill up the time available.' This applies if you are always willing to add to your workload.

7 Too much work to do in the time available. If possible, eliminate some tasks, and delegate others.

8 Confused responsibility and authority. Set up job descriptions and give employees the authority they need to go with their responsibilities. In this way, jobs get finished and reverse delegation is avoided.

9 Drop-in visitors. An 'open-door' policy need not mean your door is literally open all day, implying that you welcome anyone (and everyone!) to drop in. Be frank and firm with time-wasters. Ask: 'Is there anything else you need?' or arrange for your secretary to call you. Don't invite the unwelcome visitor to sit. Body language can work well — stand up and move towards the door, or go on working.

10 Not planning for some unavailability. This time can be used for thinking — namely planning! This is called *discretionary* time in which important work is done, in contrast with *response* time in which managers respond to the demands of other people. This is discussed more fully in a later section of this chapter.

11 Leaving tasks unfinished (a source of stress). This can happen for various reasons, but should be avoided. Where possible, tasks should be worked at until finished. Jobs that are too large to finish in one go should be cut up into logical bits tackled this way.

12 Lack of personal organisation. ('A cluttered desk is the result of a disorganised mind.') Get advice on office management and better systems for dealing with paperwork. Make every effort to handle each piece of paper only once!

13 Being spread too thinly across too many tasks — from lack of planning and setting of priorities to failing to concentrate effort on the few critical tasks (see points 6 and 7).

14 Failure to say 'No!' and mean it, when the willing worker is being unfairly loaded with more work and responsibility. Some owner/managers are unable to turn down work from customers, even when it cannot be completed by the due date. It is often better to say 'No' than accept more work, make promises and then fail to deliver.

15 Indecision and procrastination. If you frequently put off making decisions and taking action, you are probably losing time and opportunities and increasing pressure on yourself. These habits usually develop out of a fear of making mistakes. Is a wrong decision better or worse than no decision?

16 Working hard, but not seeing the distinction between activity and results (being busy is not necessarily getting results). Being very busy can be a sign of insecurity. Many people who have a need to keep busy have lost direction — they have no objectives.

17 Lack of self-discipline (not being able to settle down to, and concentrate on, the one task until it is completed). People who lack self-discipline also tend to ignore advice about the need to plan before starting work on some task.

18 Accepting upward (or reverse) delegation. Do not encourage employees to depend too heavily on you for answers. When delegating, avoid insisting that the employee 'do nothing without checking with me first'. When delegating a job, make sure the worker is told where and how to find the information needed to complete it (see point 5).

19 Inadequate support staff, and therefore no way to delegate.

20 Faulty communication (working without enough accurate information and instruction, or with sloppy and congested information systems and too much paperwork). Use of concise and clear language improves understanding of instructions, and saves time.

Other time-wasters found in small firms include the following:

- Making snap decisions (taking action without proper thought, leading to more mistakes which take time to correct).
- Poor health or motivation (working more slowly), and physical weariness from working longer and harder (not smarter).
- Over-use of memory (not having visible reminders of tasks). You cannot do what you cannot remember. Large wall-charts or a daily action list pinned up can give you a visible reminder of the work priorities for the day or week.
- Setting and trying to work to unrealistic deadlines, which create stress and reduce work quantity and quality. (Murphy's First Law: 'Nothing is as simple as it seems.' Murphy's Second Law: 'Everything takes longer than you think.')
- Inability to end conversations and visits. Acting firmly but courteously to end time-wasting is a valuable skill to develop.
- Having to 'carry' incompetent employees/subordinates (thereby needing to remedy many mistakes and poor-quality work).
- Disruptive (for example, noisy) work space.
- *Reacting* to emergencies rather than anticipating them. If you prevent emergencies (by means such as maintaining equipment) you can avoid costly and time-consuming breakdowns. (Murphy's Third Law: 'If something can go wrong, it will!')
- Failing to distinguish between symptoms and causes of problems, thereby wasting time by working only on the symptoms and not the real problems.
- Not combining activities (for example, having working lunches).
- Not trying out new methods (such as the dictaphone) or learning new skills (such as speed reading).

Improving your time management

All managers who are aware of the need to improve their time management, and thereby become more efficient and effective in their work, can succeed by following seven basic steps. Although the steps are obvious and logical, it is first necessary to remember two things:

1 Replacing bad habits with good ones needs *planning*, *self-discipline*, and *greater assertiveness*.

2 There are limits to how far one person can improve his or her time management at work, because of the effects of other workers' methods. Results are better when all members of a firm are involved in improving their time management.

Step 1

Be serious about improving your time management. Because old habits are hard to break, and better results are gained when all members of the firm take part, there is little to be gained unless all concerned are serious about the need to make more efficient and more effective use of work time. A bonus scheme for improved efficiency could encourage greater enthusiasm and participation.

Improved time management leads to greater job satisfaction.

Step 2

Find out how you use your time. Keep a time log for about three normal working weeks, listing every activity each day in, say, 15-minute blocks. At the end of that time, summarise how you spent your available time and show the results as percentages — for example, telephone: 20%, making sales 42%, checking on jobs being done 38%.

Step 3

Establish a list of work priorities. This means deciding *what* must be done each day, week, or month as a matter of utmost importance for reaching your goals and those of the business! For most people, about five or six priority tasks are enough.

There are several possible ways of doing this. Lakein (1973, pp 28–29) recommends the ABC priority method:

- 'A'-rated jobs are those of highest value
- 'B' tasks have medium value, and
- 'C' jobs are those of low value.

Another method is to rank all tasks by their importance (their contribution to goals, or their results) and by their urgency. By adding or multiplying these rankings, you arrive at overall priorities.

Unless you make some effort to set priorities and work to them in planning the best use of your daily, weekly and monthly work time you, like most people, will tend to work on the easy (and less important) jobs first, and put off starting the harder tasks (the so-called 'Allen's First Principle of Operating Priority').

To the owner/manager of a small firm, survival of that firm must be the ultimate objective of, and have top priority in, all decisions and actions — and use of time.

What are your key priorities?

Step 4

Compare the time log (Step 2) with your priorities list (Step 3). You will be rather unusual if your use of work time fits your priorities list. It is more likely that you spend much of your time doing things that are not important — that is, you follow the '80/20 rule' (see Figure 3.1) which states that most people spend the greater part of their time in achieving few of the results.

Step 5

Identify your main time-wasters. This means noting which unimportant and less-important activities are taking large parts of your time.

Step 6

Sort your time-wasters into two groups, and take appropriate action:

- *eliminate* those that do little or nothing to help you reach personal/business goals
- *delegate* tasks which need to be done, but which are not important enough to be allowed to intrude into your time. If some task consumes a lot of time and does little or nothing to achieve the firm's goals — and its survival — delegate it.

Step 7

Repeat these steps in about six months, and persevere.

TIME MANAGEMENT AND BUSINESS SUCCESS

Efficient and effective use of the most precious resource available is essential for success in business. Success comes from doing the essentials well, and there is probably no more essential task for any small business owner/manager than planning the future of the firm, and setting priorities (see Chapter 8).

Good planning requires thinking — not thinking in small doses, piecemeal and *ad hoc*, but thinking in periods of time long enough to develop ideas properly, and consider as many aspects and consequences as possible. You will not get much uninterrupted blocks of time for concentrated thinking and planning unless you believe in the need for 'planned unavailability', and insist on getting it.

This need is based on the fact that, in any work day, there are two types of time.

Response time (also known as 'contact', or 'available' time) is the part of the day when you are available to deal with problems, handle enquires and complaints, make and take telephone calls, run or attend meetings, speak with and work alongside employees, and 101 other things — in all cases responding to the demands of others for your available time, effort, ideas and knowledge. If these demands consume the whole day every day, you might soon develop a severe case of stress from the constant and varying pressures. Furthermore, you will have neither time nor energy to turn to 'more important' matters.

Discretionary time (also called 'controlled' but *not* 'free' time) is what all owner/managers need in suitable blocks, during which they are *not available* to others, except in clearly specified emergencies (say, if the building is on fire). Sometimes known as 'quiet' time, this is to be used at your discretion, but is intended for thinking, planning for the future, or working on major tasks that need unbroken lumps of time.

Williams (1991, p 147) has reported that less than one-quarter of 10 570 Australian small firms studied were rated as 'excellent' or 'good' in their time management methods. Thirty per cent made no use or poor to rare use of such methods, and another 27% were assessed as 'below average'. This study showed that firms in which time management methods were used had a better chance of surviving.

SUMMARY

There is no easy way to improve your time management. It might require that you change habits of a lifetime, and there are always plenty of 'reasons' why 'it won't work' for you! While it might seem that none of us has enough time to do all the things we wish to do, in fact, most of us know people who *are* able to so control the use of their time that they not only get more done every day but also do the things that are of major importance to them. Their work is a much more satisfying experience because of this. Becoming a better manager of your time is only as hard as breaking old habits — it requires self-discipline!

The basis of better time management is setting priorities (by planning) for the more efficient and effective use of our time, and identifying major time-wasters that must be either eliminated or delegated. Improved time management can improve job satisfaction, overall work productivity and business success. Evidence of good time management is having enough discretionary time to use for doing the really important things.

KEY WORDS

discretionary time	response time
effectiveness	time
efficiency	time log
important	time-wasters
priorities	urgent

SELF-ASSESSMENT EXERCISE

How well do you manage your time?

Answer each of these questions by ticking one of the three boxes.

	Yes	Sometimes	No
1 Are your instructions clear and understandable?	☐	☐	☐
2 Do you try to discourage visitors when you are very busy?	☐	☐	☐
3 Do you plan in advance what you want to do or to have done by others?	☐	☐	☐
4 Do you plan in advance who will do what?	☐	☐	☐
5 Do you keep meetings to a minimum?	☐	☐	☐
6 Do you use a daily work plan or schedule?	☐	☐	☐
7 Do you act to stop employees wasting time?	☐	☐	☐
8 Do you make decisions quickly?	☐	☐	☐
9 Do you have enough staff to get the work done?	☐	☐	☐
10 Do you set a good example by arriving on time, completing your work on time, and not being absent without good reason?	☐	☐	☐
11 Do you break up big jobs into manageable bits?	☐	☐	☐
12 Do you separate important tasks from those that are urgent?	☐	☐	☐
13 Do you insist on having some uninterrupted time every day or so?	☐	☐	☐
14 Do you look for short cuts to save time?	☐	☐	☐
15 Do you say 'No' to some demands made on you?	☐	☐	☐
16 Is everything needed to complete a job arranged and ready before the job is started?	☐	☐	☐

	Yes	Sometimes	No
17 Are your staff properly trained and competent?	☐	☐	☐
18 Is all your equipment in good order?	☐	☐	☐
19 Do you run short meetings?	☐	☐	☐
20 Do you group similar tasks to be done together?	☐	☐	☐
21 If you get stuck on a tough problem, do you leave it and come back to it when refreshed?	☐	☐	☐
22 Do you insist that all work be done properly and on time, and refuse to allow poor quality workmanship?	☐	☐	☐
23 Do you insist that all equipment be kept in its right place to avoid delays and losses?	☐	☐	☐
24 Do you work on important tasks during your best working hours, eg early in the day?	☐	☐	☐
25 Do you delegate work and then leave the employee alone to get it done?	☐	☐	☐
26 Are you willing to accept suggestions and advice from people working for you?	☐	☐	☐
27 Do you avoid accumulating more and more jobs?	☐	☐	☐
28 Is your work space kept neat and tidy?	☐	☐	☐
29 Are you a decisive person?	☐	☐	☐
30 Do you have good health?	☐	☐	☐
31 Do you set realistic deadlines for your work?	☐	☐	☐
32 Do you have a good memory?	☐	☐	☐

Scoring method

Yes = 3; Sometimes = 2; No = 1

Total score ☐

Very poorly	Below average	About average	Above average	Very well
20	40	50 60	80	

References

Drucker, P 1967, *The Effective Executive*, Pan Books, London

Humble, J 1980, 'Time Management: Separating the Myths and the Realities', *Management Review*, October, pp 25–8, 49–53

Lakein, A 1973, *How to get Control of your Time and your Life*, New American Library, Signet Books, New York

Mackenzie, R A 1972, *Time Trap*, AMACOM

Williams, A J 1991, 'Small business survival: The role of formal education, management training and advisory services', *Small Business Review* 1990–1991, Bureau of Industry Economics, Small Business Research Unit, Australian Government Publishing Service, Canberra, pp 43–82

CHAPTER 22

Taxation

No topic arouses more interest, and is more confusing, for people in small business than that of taxation. New laws and regulations, and an endless stream of court judgements, combine to create a climate of continual change, and the detailed requirements of every business are different. This chapter provides a broad overview of the major types of taxation. After reading it, you should be able to discuss with your accountant the implications for you and your business of the various types of taxation.

Taxes are payable to both federal and state governments. State taxes are generally an allowable business expense when calculating the assessable income for federal taxes. While federal taxation legislation is uniform across Australia, state taxes vary from state to state.

Federal taxes

The following information about federal taxes has been taken from publications of the Taxpayer Assistance Group of the Australian Taxation Office (ATO). The Commonwealth of Australia holds the copyright, and it is reproduced by permission.

The tax laws are complex and undergo frequent changes. This information is intended only as a guide; you should discuss all these matters in detail with your accountant.

Keeping tax records

By law, any books of accounts, records or documents relating to the preparation of an income tax return for an individual or a business must be retained for a period of at least five years. Records relating to fringe benefits tax must be kept for seven years.

Under Australian tax law, a person carrying on a business must keep records that document and explain all transactions. These records include any documents that are relevant for the purpose of ascertaining the person's income and expenditure. The records must be written in English.

If you are selected for a taxation audit, your business records will be required. These records could include the following documents:

- journals
- ledgers
- invoices
- job sheets
- stock sheets
- debtors listing
- creditors listing
- cash books
- quote books
- receipts
- cheque butts
- wages books
- loan agreements
- lease agreements
- general journal
- accountant's working papers
- minutes of directors' meetings
- bank statements
- personal financial records
- building society books
- credit union books
- all passbooks and deposit books
- cheque butts
- bank statements
- full details of payments to sub-contractors, including name and address of each sub-contractor and amounts paid.

This list is not exhaustive and other documentation might be required. The time taken to complete an audit depends on the adequacy of your records and availability of information. If disagreements occur, you must prove your explanations or your claims will be disallowed.

Not all receipts are accepted by the Tax Office as proof of your deductions. To be valid for tax purposes, a receipt must show:

- the date of the receipt
- the date of the expense
- the name of the supplier
- the amount, and
- a description of what you bought.

Receipts must be in English unless you made the payment in a non-English-speaking country. If you spent the money overseas, the receipt must show the currency it is in.

Not all cash-register documents meet these requirements — you might need to ask for a separate receipt. Credit-card vouchers are generally accepted as long as the supplier shows enough details to describe the goods or services purchased.

For some expenses it is not possible to get a receipt. In such cases, you can keep a diary to prove your claims. This diary will prove your expenses if each one is no more than $10 and the total is no more than $200, or it was unreasonable to expect to get a receipt. Each expense entry in the diary must contain all the details that would be required of a valid receipt, and you must sign each entry.

Paying tax

Tax may be paid by mail or in person at a Tax Office. Some payments may be made at post offices and agencies as a result of an agreement between the Tax Office and Australia Post. This service, called ATO Billpay, is similar to that used by many members of the community to pay a range of public utility accounts such as Telecom, gas and electricity.

The main benefits of the Billpay service are:

- no fee is charged
- there are 4400 Australia Post outlets across Australia
- a receipt is provided
- the date of payment is recorded on the taxpayer's account, and
- post office agencies which have extended trading hours provide extra flexibility for taxpayers.

ATO Billpay can be used to make the following payments:

- PAYE group tax
- income tax
- child support, and
- sales tax.

Care should be taken to use the correct stationery for each type of payment.

Tax file number

A tax file number (TFN) is a unique number issued for each taxpayer by the Tax Office. As a small business, you will need to obtain a TFN as explained below.

If your business has savings accounts or investments that earn more than $120 a year in interest you may choose to quote its TFN to avoid having tax deducted from that interest at 48.25% (the highest marginal tax rate plus Medicare levy). The $120 threshold applies only to bank, building society and credit union accounts.

Your role in TFN

As an employer, you are required to collect from each employee an employment declaration which might or might not include a TFN. If an employee has not quoted their TFN on their employment declaration, you must deduct tax at 48.25% (the top marginal rate plus Medicare levy). If your employee has shown on the employment declaration that an application for, or inquiry about, a TFN has been made, you must then give the employee 28 days to provide you with the number before deducting tax at 48.25%. During these 28 days you should deduct tax as if the number had been quoted. An employer does *not* have the right to withhold payment of an employee's wages on the basis that they do not have a TFN, and a prospective employee should not be discriminated against when applying for a job just because they do not have a TFN.

You must record your employees' TFNs. Under the Privacy Act you are required to:

- use them only for tax-related purposes
- keep them secure
- restrict access to authorised staff only, and
- disclose them only in accordance with the tax laws.

Registration

To register for a TFN, individuals and organisations must complete an appropriate application/enquiry form. For individuals, these are available from the Tax Office, from post offices or through a registered tax agent.

If you are applying for a TFN for the first time, you will need to provide proof of your identity, as explained on the form. If you already have a TFN but cannot find it, fill in the form and your TFN will be posted to you. You will not be required to prove your identity. Partnerships and companies require their own TFNs; application forms are available from the Tax Office or through a registered tax agent.

Income tax

Personal income tax

Income tax is that part of your personal income which you are required to pay to the federal government, and which is used by the government to meet its expenses in running the country.

The formula for calculating your taxable income is:

> Assessable income minus allowable deductions = taxable income

Deductions are expenses that are incurred by you in gaining or producing assessable income. Expenses that are private, domestic or capital in nature are generally not tax deductible. Some examples of expenses that can be allowable deductions from personal income are tools, car expenses and protective clothing.

The formula for calculating your tax payable is:

> Gross tax on taxable income minus tax instalment deductions, rebates and other credits = tax payable

Gross tax on taxable income is calculated at marginal tax rates. The *Tax Pack* has details of the current rates.

Once your personal tax has been calculated, you will be given credit for any tax paid during the year under PAYE, Prescribed Payments System or provisional tax system. The formula for calculating the net amount payable is:

Tax payable + Medicare levy = net amount payable

Your role in income tax

You need to keep records relating to income, deductions and rebates as you receive them during the year. Without these records, you will find it difficult to complete your tax return.

For your personal income tax, you fill in the Form I tax return. The information you show in your tax return allows your tax to be calculated. If you fill in your tax return incorrectly you may be subject to a penalty.

If you have paid too much tax, you will get a refund of the overpayment.

Partnerships

If you are a partner in a partnership that is carrying on a business, all income earned by the partnership and deductions claimed for expenses incurred in earning that income must be shown in a partnership return (Form P). Deductions are allowed for expenses such as salaries and wages paid to employees (other than partners), rent of business premises, depreciation, and car expenses.

A partnership is not required to pay tax on its income as such. Each partner must include the whole of their individual share of the net partnership profit or loss (which is calculated according to the terms of the partnership agreement) in their personal tax return (Form I). If there is a profit, the individual share is included in the partner's assessable income. If there is a loss, the individual share is allowable as a deduction against the partner's other assessable income.

Companies

Companies, like individuals, pay tax on their taxable income, which is the income earned less any allowable deductions. Deductions are the expenses in running the company, such as wages, cost of stock, rent, bad debts and previous year losses. Tax is calculated at 39% of the taxable income.

The tax owing may be reduced by any credits (such as tax deducted from payments to the company under the Prescribed Payments System) and rebates (reductions in tax for some items, such as dividends paid by other companies). Depending on how much tax is to be paid, the company is required to pay the tax in one or two instalments. Usually companies pay most of their income tax (85% of the previous year's tax) in July and the balance in March, but they can opt to pay the full amount in December. If the tax for last year is more than will be due for this year, the company may send the Tax Office an estimate of the tax due.

Primary producers

Primary producers face particular difficulties in their business. The tax laws therefore have special provisions to assist them, including:

- income averaging
- three-year write-off for the cost of conserving or conveying water
- special provision for double wool clips
- Income Equalisation Deposit Scheme, by which income from good years is deferred to bad years
- outright deduction for soil conservation, including erection of fences to prevent soil degradation
- insurance recoveries for livestock and timber losses, and profit on forced disposal or compulsory destruction of livestock may be spread over five years
- installation of a telephone line is deductible over ten years
- capital expenditure on timber access roads and timber mill buildings is deductible over 25 years and there is a special deduction for timber depletion.

You should check that you meet the Tax Office's definition of 'carrying on a business of primary production'. Factors which they consider include:

- the size or scale of the activities
- whether the activities are profitable; if not, whether the taxpayer genuinely believes the activities will be profitable, and that belief is a reasonable one
- whether the activities are carried on in the same manner as that type of activity is ordinarily carried on
- whether there is repetition and regularity in the activities
- whether the activities are carried on in a business-like, systematic manner
- whether a 'significant commercial purpose or character' can be ascribed to the activities, or whether they may be more properly described as a hobby or recreation
- the purpose and intention for which the activities are being undertaken.

Other factors which may be taken into consideration include the location of the property, the type of produce grown, the livestock maintained on the property, and the acreage of land used.

The Tax Office does not make a decision on primary production status until you have lodged your tax return for that particular year of income. If you aren't certain you are carrying on a business of primary production, show your primary production business income and expenses on your income tax return and include a request for a Section 169A(2) ruling. This will include full details of your current and future activities. It is advisable to apply for a ruling the first time you lodge a return with primary production income, or if you have a major change in your primary production activities.

Income averaging applies automatically to primary producers. Income averaging means you receive a tax rebate in years when your taxable income is greater than your average income and pay complementary tax when your taxable income is less than your average income. You may opt out of the averaging system by notifying the Tax Office in writing, but once you have done so you cannot opt in again.

Primary producers who employ labour need to deduct PAYE tax from employees' wages. Special schedules for calculating tax instalments for shearers and seasonal workers in the horticultural industry are available from the Tax Office.

Capital gains tax

Income tax is charged on gains made on the sale of assets acquired after 19 September 1985. Special rules apply to the way the gain is worked out, and the tax paid is called capital gains tax (CGT).

You show the capital gain or loss in your individual, trust or company return, depending on how the asset was owned.

Assets include real estate (including land), some motor vehicles, the goodwill of a business, leases, shares in companies, options to acquire shares, units in unit trusts, some antiques, works of art, jewellery and collectables. This list does not cover all the assets subject to CGT. However, most motor vehicles and a family home are generally not subject to CGT.

Your business may be subject to CGT even on an asset it didn't buy, or on an asset it didn't actually sell. If you are selling or giving away an asset, or if your asset is lost or destroyed, you should contact the Tax Office to check if CGT will apply.

Your role in CGT

The records relating to a business asset (receipts and other details) should be kept for five years after the disposal of the asset. You need to record:

- the date on which the asset was acquired
- amounts of expenditure for purchase and capital improvements
- when you sold it, and
- how much you sold it for.

Rules for calculating capital gain are explained in the *Tax Pack* and in the *Capital Gains Tax* booklets. Basically, the capital gain is the difference between the purchase price and the resale price. There may be adjustments for the incidental costs of buying and selling the asset, for the capital costs of improvements, for some current expenses, and for inflation.

If you made a loss on selling an asset, this can only be used to reduce a capital gain and not your other business income. If not used in the current year, it can be used in future years.

You should show the capital gain in your business tax return. If there is any tax payable, you will be advised on your notice of assessment. If you made a capital loss, it must still be shown in your tax return.

Registration

There is no need to register for CGT. You simply declare any capital gains as part of your firm's taxable income for the relevant financial year. All details will be shown in the tax return.

Pay-as-you-earn tax

The pay-as-you-earn (PAYE) system is the method by which salary and wage earners pay their tax and Medicare levy by instalments deducted from their pay. The employer makes the deductions, and pays them directly to the Tax Office. At the end of the financial year the employer gives each employee a group certificate which shows how much the employee earned during the year and how much tax was deducted. Deductions may also be made by means of tax stamps; consult your accountant to find out which method suits your business.

Your role in PAYE

As an employer, you need to ask each employee to fill in an employment declaration. These forms are available from post offices and the Tax Office. One copy is sent to the Tax Office and one is kept for your records.

You deduct tax from the salary or wage of each employee according to the information on the employment declaration. The Tax Office publishes schedules which tell you how much tax to take out. Schedules for weekly, fortnightly and monthly pay periods are available from any post office or the Tax Office.

The tax which you deduct from your employees' wages must be sent to the Tax Office by the seventh day of the next month. If you deduct less than $10 000 in tax from your employees each year, you may pay quarterly.

At the end of the financial year, you must give each employee a group certificate, by 14 July. If an employee leaves during the year, you should issue the group certificate to them within a week of their leaving. A reconciliation statement and copies of the group certificates must be sent to the Tax Office by 14 August each year.

Registration

If you wish to use the group tax system, you will need to complete an Application for Registration as a Group Employer. This form is available from any Tax Office. You will be notified of a group number, which you will need to use in all dealings with the Tax Office about PAYE.

Provisional tax

Provisional tax is a method of paying personal income tax by making provision for the current year's tax. The system is for people who earn more than $999 per year of non-salary or non-wage income, and thus applies to most sole traders and partners. Companies do not pay this tax. The income may be from investments, business, primary production, distribution from a trust or any other source not covered by the PAYE system. Additionally, provisional tax is payable if you receive salary or wage income from which sufficient PAYE deductions were not made.

Many people call provisional tax 'next year's tax' although this is not true. Provisional tax is paid in the year in which you earn the income. People whose provisional tax payable was more than $8000 in the previous year must pay their tax in quarterly instalments.

Your role in provisional tax

From your tax return, the Tax Office determines whether your are subject to provisional tax. If you are, you will be informed on your notice of assessment.

Provisional tax is based on your income in the previous year. It is calculated by taking your previous year's income, and increasing it by a percentage (currently set at 8%). Provisional tax is calculated on this increased income, and then reduced by any credits to which you are entitled.

Provisional tax due is shown as a debit on your notice of assessment. The provisional tax you pay during the year will show up as a credit on your next assessment notice.

Registration

You do not need to register for provisional tax. If you are required to pay it, you will be sent an assessment notice which includes your provisional tax liability on it.

If you believe that the Tax Office's estimate of your income is too high, you can lodge a Variation of Provisional Tax form to make your own estimate. However, if your estimate of your income is too low you may be subject to a penalty.

Prescribed Payments System

The Prescribed Payments System (PPS) is a way of paying tax for many people who work and earn money under a written, verbal or implied contract. If you employ contractors, or your business is concerned with provision of contract services to others, a knowledge of your responsibilities under PPS is essential.

PPS applies particularly to people working under contract in any of the following industries:

- building and construction
- joinery and cabinet-making
- architectural services
- cleaning industry
- engineering services
- motor-vehicle repair industry
- survey services
- road transport industry
- professional building and construction services.

If your business makes contract payments to a person for the transportation of goods on a regular and exclusive basis, you may also have tax obligations under PPS. For further information about your obligations, contact your local branch of the Tax Office.

Receiving contract payments

As a **payee** under PPS, at the start of work with each payer, you may give each payer a completed payee declaration. If you do not do so, the payer is required to deduct tax at the top rate (currently 48.25%) from payments made to you, unless you have obtained an exemption (discussed later). If you do complete a payee declaration, tax is deducted at the rate of 20% from payments, or at a lesser rate if you hold a deduction variation or deduction exemption certificate and complete its details on the payee declaration.

At the end of each financial year each payer is required to give you the original copy of a completed PPS payment summary. This records all the payments made to you and tax deducted by the payer during the financial year. Payment advices are available if you require a receipt as confirmation of a payment made by a payer. The use of this form is at the payer's option. If you wish to have a rate of tax higher than the prescribed or varied rate deducted from payments, you may notify the payer in writing.

Making contract payments

As a **payer** under PPS you must register with the Tax Office by sending in a paying authority notification.

When a contractor gives you a payee declaration, you must complete the payer section and send the form to the Tax Office within 28 days.

You must deduct tax at the appropriate rate from payments to the contractor, and maintain a record of gross payments and tax deductions made during a financial year, completing a separate PPS payment summary for each payee.

Each month you must send to the Tax Office a payment for the amount of tax deducted for the previous month, together with a completed remittance advice.

At the end of the financial year, you must give each payee their payment summary by 14 July. A reconciliation statement and copies of the payment summaries must be sent to the Tax Office by 14 August each year.

Exemptions

Contractors may apply to the Tax Office for a reporting exemption approval number. A payee who has such a number is not required to provide a payee declaration, and the payer is not required to deduct tax or record payments while the exemption is in force.

Fringe benefits tax

Generally, any benefit provided by an employer to an employee in place of salary or wages is considered to be a taxable fringe benefit. Fringe benefits commonly involve the use of motor vehicles. However, there are also many other types of taxable fringe benefits. The different types are:

- cars available for private use
- loans with low or no interest
- payment or reimbursement of employee expenses
- property, such as land, electricity, clothing or insurance policies, provided free or at a discount
- housing or accommodation provided free or at a reduced rate
- board (meals) provided free
- airline transport provided at a discount for employees in the airline or travel industry
- some entertainment expenses
- living-away-from-home allowance.

Fringe benefits tax (FBT) is paid by the employer who provides the benefit. The value of each fringe benefit is calculated according to certain rules. More information is available from the Tax Office or your accountant.

Your role in FBT

FBT payers must keep sufficient records so that their FBT can be accurately assessed. The records required depend on the types of benefits provided. The booklet *Fringe Benefits Tax — A Guide for Employers* gives details of the records required. All FBT records must be kept for a minimum of seven years.

If you have never paid FBT, or your previous year's liability was less than $3000, you need only make one payment for the year — when you lodge your annual FBT return in April.

If you paid FBT in the previous year and your liability was $3000 or more, you will need to pay FBT in four instalments throughout the year. These instalments should be paid by the following dates:

- 1st instalment — 28 July
- 2nd instalment — 28 October
- 3rd instalment — 28 January
- 4th instalment — 28 April.

The first three instalments each amount to one-quarter of your previous year's liability. The Tax Office will send you a reminder notice a few weeks before these payments are due. If you don't receive this reminder, you must still pay the instalment by the due date. The fourth and final instalment should be paid by 28 April when you lodge your annual FBT return. The amount to be paid will equal the total amount of tax payable for the year as assessed on your return, minus the instalments already paid.

If you estimate that your FBT liability for the current year will be less than it was last year, you may send a written explanation of your estimate to the Tax Office and pay the lower amount. If you underestimate your FBT liability, you may be subject to a penalty.

Registration

You should register as soon as you begin providing fringe benefits. You will not need to make your first payment until you lodge your first FBT return the following April. The Tax Office will send you the appropriate forms.

Sales tax

Sales tax is a tax that is generally charged on the wholesale value of goods. It is charged on goods which are produced in or imported into Australia, unless they are specifically exempt from the tax.

Sales tax is generally payable when the goods are sold by a manufacturer or wholesaler to a retailer. However, sales tax is also paid where goods are leased, imported by retailers for sale, imported by a consumer for private use, given away for promotional purposes, used as samples, used in the repair of other goods, or transferred to stock for retail sale by a manufacturer.

Your role in sales tax

Manufacturers and wholesale merchants of taxable goods must register as explained below.

Retailers pay sales tax on goods when they purchase them. They have no further liability when they sell the goods by retail. Importers who are neither manufacturers nor wholesale merchants pay sales tax to the Collector of Customs when the goods enter the country.

To calculate the tax payable, consult the sales tax schedules that list the various rates of tax. You must collect the appropriate amount of tax from your customers. Show sales tax as a separate item on each invoice when goods are sold by wholesale.

You should send your payment, accompanied by a sales tax return, to the Tax Office by the 21st day of the next month or quarter. Quarterly payment is available to taxpayers with an annual sales-tax liability of less than $51 200. If no sales are made during a month or quarter, send a sales tax return marked 'No sales'.

Registration

If you are a manufacturer or wholesale merchant (even if the goods are from overseas) you must register with the Tax Office for sales tax. You must register within 28 days of becoming a manufacturer or wholesale merchant; penalties may apply for non-compliance.

Your requirement to register may be dispensed with if your business deals entirely in the manufacture or wholesale of goods exempt from sales tax.

Also, if you are a small manufacturer (ie your annual value of sales of all goods is less than $50 000, or your tax payable is less than $1000 per annum) your registration requirement may be dispensed with, and the goods which you manufacture will be exempt from sales tax. However, you must still pay sales tax on raw materials and machinery used in the manufacture of those goods, unless the goods are exempt in their own right.

To register for sales tax you will need to complete an Application for Sales Tax Registration, available from any Tax Office. A sales-tax registration number will be issued to you, and you should use it in all correspondence to the Tax Office about sales tax.

The Child Support Scheme

As an employer, you may be required to deduct child support from an employee's wages. The Child Support Scheme commenced in June 1988 for the benefit and support of children whose parents separate. It is administered by the Child Support Agency.

The Child Support Agency was set up as part of the Tax Office because of its experience and resources in revenue collection. The Agency collects the child support or maintenance from the liable parent (the payer) either directly or through the auto-withholding system, which is where employers participate in the scheme.

Your role in the Child Support Scheme

If the Child Support Agency writes to you because you are the employer of someone who is liable to pay child support by the auto-withholding system, you must make the deductions and send them to the Agency.

Under the Child Support (Registration and Collection) Act 1988 you are required to:

- deduct the child support amount specified
- advise your employee in writing how much you deduct or do not deduct from their salary or wage each pay period
- pay the deducted amounts to the Agency by the seventh day of the month following the month in which the deductions were made (as for PAYE deductions)
- advise the Agency of any variations to the amounts deducted and the reasons for such variations, and of any business changes
- protect the privacy of your employee by restricting access to the child support information to authorised staff, keeping it secure, and using it only for child support purposes.

It is illegal to discriminate against any employee or potential employee because of their child support or maintenance obligations.

While the person is your employee, you must take instructions about the deductions only from the Agency. Do not follow directions from the employee, their solicitor or any other person purporting to be acting on the employee's behalf.

Child support deductions are not taxation amounts, so they should not be shown on a group certificate.

Registration

You do not need to do anything unless you are asked in writing by the Child Support Agency. If you are contacted by the Agency you will be sent an employer package about what to do.

Training Guarantee

The Training Guarantee came into being in 1990 as a result of the federal government's concern about the low level of industry training in Australia. The development of workplace skills is vital to the improvement of productivity and to the ability of Australian industry to compete on the international market. The Training Guarantee (Administration) Act 1990 aims to improve the efforts of employers who spend too little on training.

Your role in the Training Guarantee

The legislation requires employers whose annual national payroll is more than a set amount to spend at least 1% of that payroll on training related to employment. The payroll threshold for 1992–93 was $222 000.

If employers do not spend the minimum amount on training for the year, they must pay the shortfall, using a shortfall statement form, to the Tax Office by 30 September of that year. An income tax deduction is now allowable for the payment of the shortfall amount. The money received is used to fund additional training.

Employers should keep in mind three criteria to make sure the training they are considering is eligible under the scheme:

1 The sole or principal object of the training programme must be to develop, maintain or improve the employment-related skills of employees or other people.
2 The programme must not have significant recreational activities or objectives which are not related to employment.
3 The programme must be structured: that is, before it begins, the employer must identify the skills, knowledge or competencies to be acquired by the participants, how the skills will be imparted to these people, and the expected outcomes and productivity gains.

The training programme then needs to be approved by a person who knows the subject and has some training background. A suitable person would have at least three years' experience in designing or providing training, or have attended a train-the-trainer course of two or three days.

The costs incurred by the employer in preparing the training courses can be claimed as expenditure under the Training Guarantee. This also includes salary or wages of the participants during training, spending on travel, accommodation, meals and childcare to enable training, course fees for training and payments made solely to enable someone else to provide training.

Employers who receive a government subsidy for training, or any other sort of subsidy or reimbursement for any of their training expenditure, must deduct those receipts to work out their net eligible training expenditure. Only the employer's net expenditure counts.

There is a special deeming provision to give employers a minimum net expenditure for apprentices and for Australian Traineeship System trainees, if the employer so chooses. Employers don't have to deduct subsidies or reimbursements from the deemed amount.

You need to keep records that show your annual national payroll, as well as the net eligible training expenditure for that year. In addition, records need to show:

- who designed or approved the training programmes, and their qualifications or experience
- what skills, knowledge or competencies were identified, before the programme began, as the skills to be acquired by the participants
- the means of imparting the skills, knowledge or competencies, and
- the expected outcomes or productivity gains.

You can keep these records in any form you choose, as long as they are in English. In fact, your income tax or PAYE records may already show some of the information required for Training Guarantee purposes.

Registration

There is no registration of employers, trainers, or people who design or approve training, for the Training Guarantee. If you need help in deciding what is eligible training, you can consult the Tax Office or a registered industry-training agent.

Valuing stock

If you operate a business, the tax laws say that you must record the value of all trading stock you have on hand at:

- the beginning of the year of income (generally 1 July), and
- the end of the year of income (generally 30 June).

This is so that you can work out whether or not you have a taxable income for the year. The best way to work out the value of your stock on hand is to count it. This is called stocktaking (see Chapter 18).

Except for the first year you are in business, the value of your stock at the beginning of the year will be the same as its value at the end of the previous year. If the value of the stock at the end of the year is more than it was at the beginning of the year, you must include the difference as part of your assessable income when you lodge your business tax return. If the value of the stock at the end of the year is less than it was at the beginning of the year, your assessable income will be reduced by the difference.

What is trading stock?

'Trading stock' includes anything produced, manufactured, acquired or purchased for manufacture, sale or exchange. Things that are commercially regarded as trading stock generally fall within that definition for tax purposes as well. This includes livestock (except for animals used as beasts of burden and animals used to work in a non-primary-production business). It excludes standing or growing crops, timber or fruit while still attached to the tree; they become trading stock only when they are picked or harvested. It also excludes stocks of spare parts for doing repairs or maintenance; these become a deduction from your assessable income when they are used.

Video cassettes owned by a video lending library do not count as trading stock because they are used to earn income by hire or rental, not for manufacture, sale or exchange. Likewise, consumable aids to manufacture such as cleaning or bleaching agents, sandpaper etc are not considered to be trading stock.

If you are not sure what to include, ask your tax adviser or your local Tax Office for advice.

How do I value trading stock?

There are three methods for valuing trading stock (livestock is dealt with below.) Chapter 15 gives more details.

Cost price The cost price includes all costs connected with bringing the stock into existence. The cost price of finished goods, for example, should include such things as freight, customs duties and delivery charges, as well as the actual purchase price. For manufactured goods and work in progress, all fixed and variable costs associated with the production, eg power, rent, rates and all other overheads, should be included in the cost price.

Market selling value This is the current or normal selling value of the stock. This amount does not take into account a reduced value where you are forced to sell for some reason.

Replacement price This is the price of an identical replacement item on the last day of the year of income.

You can change the method you use to calculate the value of trading stock every year, and you can use different methods for different items of stock. However, the value of your stock at the beginning of each financial year must be the same as the value of the stock at the end of the previous year.

How do I value livestock?

You have two options when working out the value of livestock: cost price or market selling value, as explained above. The same valuation method must be applied to all of your livestock, but there are special provisions for valuing breeding horses of either sex.

When should I stocktake?

You should stocktake on the last day of the financial year (30 June), or as close as practical to it. If it is impractical for you to count your income over the standard year, ie 1 July to 30 June, you can ask the Commissioner of Taxation to substitute dates more convenient to you. This is called a substituted year of income.

STATE TAXES

Because each state and territory determines the nature and level of taxes independently, it is important that the following descriptions be regarded as guidelines only. Full details of current taxes can be obtained from the relevant office in each capital city. Addresses of these offices are listed at the end of this chapter.

Bank account debits tax

Bank account debits tax is a charge on banks for debits to customers' accounts. The amount charged depends on the dollar value of the debit. Charges are usually passed on by banks to their customers. Details of the rates of tax, dollar values to which they apply, and the amount to be collected from customers' accounts can be obtained from your bank.

Your role in bank account debits tax

You should ensure that you have sufficient funds in your bank account to cover this tax, which is taken out of your account by the bank, usually each month. The amounts charged are shown on the statement of account you receive from your bank. Include the total bank account debits tax paid each year in your business expenses.

Registration

You do not need to register for this tax. Your bank calculates the amount payable on your transactions each month and subtracts this amount from your account.

Land tax

Land tax obligations and assessment are very complex. If you have any ownership rights over land which is used, in whole or in part, for commercial or industrial purposes, it is essential that you determine your liability for this tax.

Land tax generally applies to land for which the value exceeds a certain amount, and which is used for commercial or industrial purposes. There are many uses which are exempt or for which concessions apply. Values are determined by government valuers but owners can apply for concessions based on the nature of usage or restrictions on the usage.

Your role in land tax

Contact your tax agent or the state revenue office to determine your liability. Addresses of the state offices are listed at the end of this chapter.

Registration

If you have a liability to pay land tax, you register by lodging an initial return.

Payroll tax

Payroll tax is that proportion of the payroll of large employers which must be paid to the state or territory government. Payroll may include wages, salaries, commissions, bonuses, directors' fees, fringe benefits and some contract payments. Allowances paid to employees may also be included if they exceed prescribed threshold levels.

Your role in payroll tax

Contact your tax agent or your state revenue office to determine your liability. Even though your business may be very small, there exists in some states a system of 'grouping'. Under this system, your business may be considered part of the business of your major customer. In this way, even very small businesses can have a payroll tax liability. It is your responsibility to determine your liability.

You must record all payments to your employees, showing the exact nature, purpose and amount of payments. Each month you must calculate the payroll tax payable, and lodge a return within seven days with your state revenue office.

Registration

Immediately your wages exceed the prescribed threshold, you must register with your state revenue office. Registration is usually required within seven days. Forms for this purpose are available from the state revenue office, which will also provide all necessary payroll tax return forms.

SUMMARY

As a small business person, you have several duties and responsibilities in the area of taxation. These include both the payment of a range of taxes on behalf of your own business, and the collection and despatch of other taxes to the Australian Taxation Office. Details of your specific taxation requirements can be best determined through discussions with a competent, reputable and experienced taxation adviser. Before you seek this advice, it is recommended that you obtain and study the relevant literature available from state and federal taxation offices.

KEY WORDS

bank account debits tax	payroll tax
capital gains tax	Prescribed Payments System
Child Support Scheme	provisional tax
deductions	sales tax
fringe benefits tax	stocktake
income tax	tax file number
land tax	trading stock
PAYE	Training Guarantee

Review exercises

1 For how long must you retain business records and account books?

2 Does a small business with a sole proprietor pay income tax?

3 If you employ people, when must you send the PAYE tax deductions you have collected to the Tax Office?

4 What is provisional tax?

5 Which industries are subject to the Prescribed Payments System?

6 When do you need to register for fringe benefits tax?

7 Are you liable for capital gains tax on assets which you didn't pay for, or didn't actually sell?

8 Do retailers need to collect or pay sales tax?

9 Does the Taxation Office require you to do a stocktake?

10 How do you know when to start deducting child support payments from an employee's wages?

Further information

The Australian Taxation Office has issued the following publications.

- *Record Retention — A guide for businesses*
- *Record Retention — A guide for individuals carrying on a business*
- *Record Retention — A guide for companies*
- *Record Retention — A guide for partnerships*
- *Record Retention — A guide for electronically stored information*
- *Tax Rules for Savings Accounts and Investments*
- *Provisional Tax — Including Quarterly Provisional Tax 1991–92*
- *PPS and Payers*
- *PPS and Payees*
- *PPS and Tax Exempt Organisations and Businesses in Non-prescribed Industries*
- *PPS and Householders*
- *PPS and Ownerbuilders*
- *Fringe Benefits Tax — Does it apply to you?*
- *Capital Gains Tax — How it affects you*
- *Capital Gains Tax — What records you need to keep*
- *Capital Gains Tax — How do you work it out?*
- *Capital Gains Tax and Your Home*
- *Capital Gains Tax and the Assets of a Deceased Estate*
- *Capital Gains Tax and Investments in Shares and Unit Trusts*
- *Stocktakes for Primary Producers and Small Business*
- *The Child Support Scheme — A guide for parents who have separated*
- *The Child Support Scheme — A guide for employers*

- *The Training Guarantee — Your questions answered*
- *Swing into Action and Prosper in the Business Jungle*
- *Training Guarantee — It's easy to comply*
- *Training Providers for the Training Guarantee Legislation*

If you wish to phone or visit your local branch of the Australian Taxation Office, addresses and telephone numbers can be found in the *Tax Pack* or in the Commonwealth Government section at the front of the telephone directory.

Contacts for matters concerning state and territory taxes are as follows:

New South Wales
Office of State Revenue
132 Marsden Road
Parramatta NSW 2151
(02) 689 6200

Queensland
Office of State Revenue
202 Adelaide Street
Brisbane Qld 4000
(07) 227 7111 (land tax)
(07) 227 8903 (payroll tax)
(07) 227 6851 (stamp duties)

South Australia
State Taxation Office
Torrens Building
Victoria Square East
Adelaide SA 5100
(08) 226 2987

Tasmania
State Revenue Office
15 Victoria Street
Hobart Tas 7000
(002) 338 011

Victoria
State Taxation Office
436 Lonsdale Street
Melbourne Vic 3000
(03) 603 9480 (payroll tax)
(03) 603 9312 (land tax)
(03) 603 9000 (enquiries)

Western Australia
State Taxation Department
Central Government Buildings
20 Barrack Street
Perth WA 6000
(09) 323 1444

Australian Capital Territory
ACT Revenue Office
Cnr London Circuit and Akuna Street
Civic Square ACT 2608
(06) 207 0083

CHAPTER 23

Owner/manager stress

As we move through life, each of us must learn to deal with the demands that many situations, events and people make on us. Some of us handle these demands quite well, while others cannot cope and suffer greatly as a consequence. Those who face inordinately heavy, important and ongoing demands can suffer devastating effects on their mental and physical health. These effects are known as stress. In our day-to-day living, some stress is inevitable.

Stress is caused by two related things:

- the amount, type and variety of pressures we face, and
- how well we handle those pressures.

Work problems can be a major source of stress. When this source is added to the social, family, marital and financial sources of stress affecting so many people, it is hardly surprising that some specialists consider stress to have reached 'epidemic' proportions.

From careful study of this chapter, you should be able to:

- understand what stress is and how it affects your work and your health
- identify the major sources of stress in owning and managing a small firm, and
- manage stress to increase your chances of succeeding.

Most medical experts now believe that stress is closely linked with many serious illnesses, and in fact *causes* some of them.

WHAT IS STRESS?

People experience stress when they respond in some way to pressures and demands called stressors. These responses can be psychological (mental and emotional) or physiological (bodily), and both very often occur together.

> Stress is the result of a person's inability to cope with problems and difficulties. This can prevent success.

It is usual to think of stress as negative — for example, the frustration and anxiety we would feel if we were unable to solve a problem at work on which the winning of a major sales contract depended. This is the *distress* side of stress, which is associated with fear, anger, frustration, anxiety, uncertainty, pressure, conflict, tension, or emotional distress.

> Every person needs some stress to be able to perform at or near top level when necessary.

However, psychologists generally agree that much of our positive behaviour is caused by pressures and demands. The reminder that we owe someone money imposes a deadline which prompts us to take the required action, especially if there is a severe penalty for late or non-payment. Knowing that the foreman will check the work we do, or that we might get a bonus for good work, will usually cause better and/or more work to be done. This suggests that we do our work better when there is *some* pressure, and therefore some stress is not necessarily bad for us. Up to a point our work improves as more pressure is applied, but once that pressure reaches the level where we cannot do better, it begins to create excessive stress, and then our performance will not improve — in fact it is likely to worsen (see Figure 23.1). Some people cope with problems and pressure better than others, and there are many reasons for this, including personality.

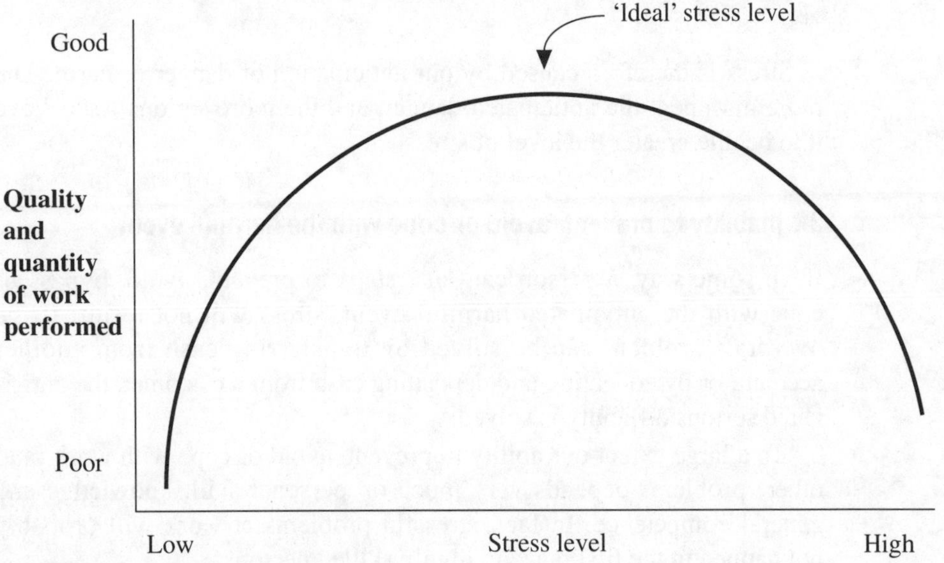

FIGURE 23.1 Stress and performance

Causes of stress

There is more to becoming stressed than just facing pressures and problems. For stress to occur several other factors need to be present.

1 Awareness of a problem

A problematical situation cannot cause stress unless the person in it is aware of it. Being heavily overdrawn at the bank can cause stress only if the bank notifies the customer of that fact.

2 Real or imagined threat of danger or harm

Being aware of some problem or situation is not enough. For stress to result, the person must either realise that it will cause harm, danger or serious difficulty, or think that it might. Whether or not the problem really is harmful does not matter. If it is thought to be, that can lead to stress. Surgery generally cures rather than kills, yet most of us are fearful of it. Being overdrawn at the bank, of itself, might not cause stress, but being advised by the bank that cheques will not be paid (which in turn will have suppliers refusing to deliver — a very real threat to a small business) is likely to do so.

> A problem, awareness of it, threat of harm, and inability to cope with, avert or avoid a threat all cause stress.

Stress is therefore caused by our anticipation of danger or harm. The more imminent the anticipated danger, and the more serious we believe it to be, the greater the level of stress.

3 Inability to prevent, avoid or cope with the harmful event

If, in some way, a person can take steps to prevent, avoid, bypass or cope with the anticipated harmful event, stress will not result. If the overdraft problem can be solved by transferring cash from another account, or by collecting and depositing cash from a customer, the anticipated serious difficulty is solved.

To a large extent our ability to prevent, avoid or cope with work (and other) problems depends very much on personal skill, knowledge and general competence. In fact, stressful problems at work will probably not happen in the first place to highly skilled persons.

Incompetence

4 Serious consequences from not preventing, avoiding or coping with the problem

If the consequences of not being able to prevent, avoid or cope with the harmful event are serious, more stress will result. If there is no hope of the bank agreeing to a higher overdraft limit and cheques will be dishonoured, the matter is more serious, and therefore more stressful.

If we can deal with stressors as they arise, our general stress level will remain much the same. However, if we cannot cope with problems, our reactions (physical, mental and emotional) tend to continue, even after each problem or threat has passed. Unless this 'vicious cycle' is stopped, we might become increasingly stressed, even when faced with minor problems (see Figure 23.2).

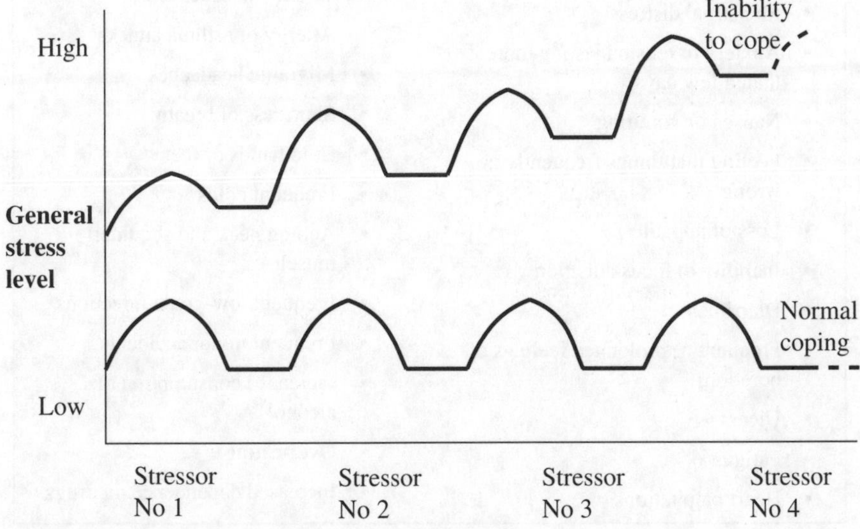

FIGURE 23.2 Coping and not coping with stressors
Source: adapted from Miller, Ross and Cohen, 1985, p 37

Effects of stress

Each of us differs in our ability to cope with, and work under, stressful conditions. If we suffer high levels of stress for long periods of time at or near our personal tolerance level, we usually develop physiological as well as psychological symptoms.

Stress effects differ from one person to another.

Among the better known physiological symptoms and reactions indicating distress are: cardiovascular problems (high blood pressure, hypertension, rapid heartbeat, coronary diseases); increased perspiration; faster breathing rate; higher body temperature; gastro-intestinal ailments (ulcers, indigestion); headaches; fatigue; insomnia; vision difficulties; asthma; problems with muscular co-ordination and many more. Most of these bodily upsets are linked with stress reactions in the nervous and hormonal systems, and they are therefore called *psychosomatic* ailments (psycho = mind; somatic = body).

Each person must learn to read their stress warning signals.

- Feeling unable to slow down and relax
- Indigestion
- Explosive anger in response to minor irritation
- Menstrual distress
- Anxiety or tension lasting more than a few days
- Nausea or vomiting
- Feeling that things frequently go wrong
- Loss of appetite
- Inability to focus attention
- Diarrhoea
- Frequent or prolonged feelings of boredom
- Ulcers
- Fatigue
- Heart palpitations
- Sexual problems
- Constipation
- Sleep disturbances
- Lower-back pain
- Tension headaches
- Allergy or asthma attacks
- Migraine headaches
- Shortness of breath
- Cold hands or feet
- Frequent colds
- Aching neck and shoulder muscles
- Frequent low-grade infections
- Frequent minor accidents
- Increased consumption of alcohol
- Over-eating
- Increased dependence on drugs

FIGURE 23.3 Stress warning signals
Source: Miller, Ross and Cohen, 1985, p 10

A highly stressed person will usually have mental and emotional problems as well as (and usually before) some bodily upsets. These can include: fear and anxiety; depression; anger; irritability; difficulty in concentrating, thinking and making decisions; apathy; frustration; rigidity of attitudes; and a strong need to be largely or totally concerned with the cause of the stress, and therefore unable or unwilling to do other things properly — often called 'tunnel vision'. It is important that we can recognise our body's distress signals. The more common among these are shown in Figure 23.3.

It is not hard to imagine how problems such as those listed, especially those affecting bodily skills, can lead to work accidents, which are a huge cost to industry. Also, mental stress is a major cause of staff turnover, absenteeism, reduced productivity and general job dissatisfaction.

- Ability to carry out jobs efficiently
- Ability to take responsibility
- Ability to work under authority, rules, difficulties and limits
- Reasonable sense of independence and self-reliance
- Ability to adapt to changes
- Reliability
- Sense of belonging
- Tolerance of others
- Ability to show friendliness and love
- Ability to take recreation, relax and sleep
- Sense of humour and fulfilment
- Self-direction
- Tolerance of frustration

FIGURE 23.4 Signs of successfully coping with stress and strain
Source: Miller, Ross and Cohen, 1985, p 78

STRESS AND OWNER/MANAGERS

Job stress occurs when people cannot cope with the many and varied demands of their work — when they are 'out of their depth', so to speak. Stress is therefore less likely to occur in people who are skilled and competent in doing their work — because they are more able to do the job efficiently and effectively.

Whereas some employees get promoted by others to positions above their level of competence, owner/managers of small firms self-select themselves into that work role. Many of them suffer badly from stress because they can't handle the job (and they become aware of that fact), the fear of failing is very real, the results from doing so are usually serious, and they cannot get out of the situation without losing money and self-respect.

The role of the small business owner/manager is a fertile source of stress for many. As you will have gathered from earlier chapters, the skills and areas of competence needed for successfully starting and managing a new small business are many and varied. Because these skills are rare, many owner/managers become subject to much stress from being unable to cope. As a result, and as the failure figures show, their firms have severe difficulties, especially in the early months.

Some of the main characteristics of small firm management, which can lead to stress, are:

- task complexity
- role ambiguity
- work overload
- role conflict
- fear of failure
- supervising the work of others
- boundary-spanning problems
- the 'wrong' reasons for entering small business.

1 Task complexity

The process of getting started in a small firm, and of keeping the venture going, especially during the most dangerous early months, is difficult and complicated, full of uncertainty, and obviously risky. For people who lack the necessary skills and experience, and who will not seek help, these difficulties are even more serious. Having to learn and master a wide range of skills 'on the run' puts great pressure on such people and they usually suffer stress.

In a partnership or private company the skill, knowledge and experience of one partner or shareholder/manager often (but not always) makes up for a lack on the part of the other(s). This cannot be the case with a sole trader business, and sole owners are more likely to suffer stress.

2 Role ambiguity

A major source of stress, role ambiguity occurs when people cannot do their work because they do not know what to do or how to do it. Trying to cope with uncertainty and their own lack of know-how affects most people, some more seriously than others because some have less tolerance of ambiguity.

Anyone who takes on a hard job without proper experience and training, and without the skills and knowledge needed for doing that job, will face role ambiguity. This situation certainly applies to many people who start their own firms. When this happens they lose self-confidence and self-respect, and experience a sense of futility and frustration, which are all part of stress.

3 Work overload

During the first few months in a new business, when funds are not usually available to hire all the help needed, owner/managers commonly work very long hours because there is so much to do. Time is a scarce resource and the inability to get work done in the time available creates stress for most people. Work overload and stress are increased if business and management skills are lacking, because work will take longer to complete. Many owner/managers who cannot or will not delegate some of their work to reliable employees might suffer from stress due to work overload for several years.

> A major source of stress is poor time management.

The advantage to an owner/manager in being able to share a heavy workload with a partner or fellow director is clear.

4 Role conflict

When ownership and management of a small business create heavy workloads, and demand long hours and much close attention, owner/managers are faced with role conflict which forces them to choose between spending time at work or with family and in recreation.

Being pulled in two different directions may lead to indecision and internal conflict. The greater the lack of experience and skill of the owner/manager, the greater the need for time and effort — to learn what to do (often by trial and error) and to correct mistakes made in starting and running the firm. This increases work overload and is likely to create more role conflict.

5 Fear of failure

Because owner/managers have more than a job at risk, many have an unhealthy (but quite understandable) fear of failing, which can cause stress. This fear can be fed by insensitive criticism from others when errors are made. There are always plenty of spectators and cynics for every new business venture.

6 Supervising the work of others

Many people find it difficult and stressful to supervise the work of others. Working as a manager before starting one's own business is probably the best way to gain experience in managing others. Research by Williams (1991) shows that, among small firms in Australia, 53% of owner/managers have had less than two years' work experience in management, including 26% who have had no such experience. Of those who reported having at least two years' work experience in management, 37% had no managerial experience in the same trade, occupation or profession as their business, and only 15% had reached upper or top levels in management.

It is clear that the great majority of owner/managers have had little or no experience in supervising other workers before starting in business, and therefore the hiring of employees is often resisted until it is absolutely necessary — another source of work overload for owner/managers! Trying to avoid stress from one direction can often create it in another.

7 Boundary-spanning problems

Owner/managers are faced with another problem — that of dealing with unpredictable demands and pressures from customers, suppliers, government departments and others outside the firm, and converting these into orders and instructions to employees inside the firm. They must, in effect, span the boundary between the firm and the world outside. For example, customer requirements about delivery dates, quality of products and service all put pressure on owner/managers who, in turn, must do likewise with their employees. This might be rejected by employees who might not wish to work overtime to meet customer-imposed deadlines. Owner/managers are thereby squeezed from both directions.

It is obvious that owner/managers must be able to 'keep peace', both with their employees and with important outsiders on whom the firm's success could depend, such as customers.

Further problems are caused when pressures and demands from customers are conflicting (for instance, several jobs to finish by the same date), or when difficulties with others lead to uncertainty and confusion (inability of a major supplier to deliver on time, for example). For the firm to survive, owner/managers must be able to negotiate, bargain, deal with and solve such problems and, at the same time, keep their employees busy. This 'balancing act' can be very stressful.

8 The 'wrong' reasons for entering small business

As stated above, starting a new business venture can be very stressful. For those who get into small business ownership for the 'wrong' reasons, additional stress is likely. Many decide to enter business ownership as a last resort, having quit or been 'sacked' from their previous job (often in very unhappy — and stressful — circumstances), and not wanting to be unemployed.

If the driving force behind the decision to get into one's own business is desperation, conflict, personal disagreement or frustrated career plans, then extra tension, worry and stress will make the task even harder.

Stress and Small Business Failure

In several Australian studies of the effects of owner/manger stress on small business performance (in fact, survival or failure), Williams has concluded that stress has a very important influence.

> Stress is a major factor in the failure rate of small firms.

In a study of 250 small firms, of the 125 which had 'below average' performance, 76% had highly stressed owner/managers; of the 'above average' performers, only 28% had owner/managers with high stress levels (Williams, 1985). From a much larger study (of 10 570 small firms and 22 034 owner/managers) over 12 years, Williams (1991) had similar results: whether or not small firms survived or failed was very much related to the levels of stress among the owner/managers of those firms. As shown in Figure 23.5, of those firms whose owners reported that their work had been badly affected by high stress levels, only one in five survived and 80% failed. In contrast, of the firms whose owners reported 'low' or 'very low' stress, three-quarters survived.

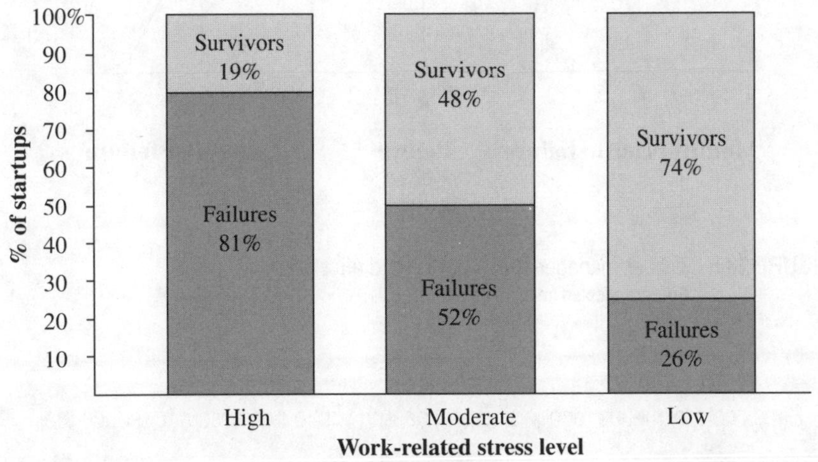

FIGURE 23.5 Owner/manager stress and business survival (as percentages of startups which fail or survive)
Source: adapted from Williams, 1987, p 272

To find out whether small business failure might be a result of high stress levels, or a cause of stress in owner/managers, Williams (1985) measured owner/manager stress levels before and after failure. The results are shown in Figure 23.6.

As can be seen in Figure 23.6, average stress levels increased steadily before failure (as owner/managers became more aware of the danger signs, and of the increasingly unavoidable threat of failing) and then decreased after the actual failure. On average, stress levels before failure were found to be much higher than stress levels after failure. From this evidence it seems certain that owner/manager stress is more likely to be a cause of business failure (through poor management) than a result of such failure.

Owner/manager stress is associated with (and is likely to be a major cause of) small business failure. Stress is much higher in those owner/managers who are seriously lacking in business or management skills, knowledge, general expertise in starting and running a small firm, and entrepreneurial drive.

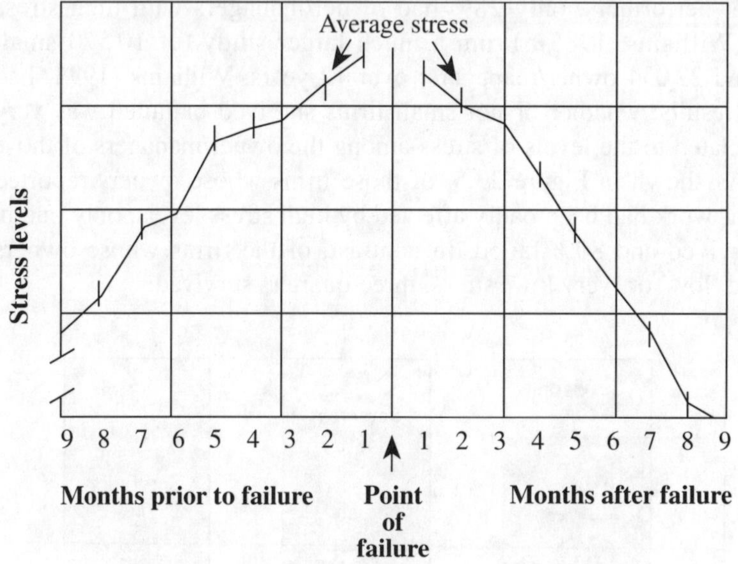

FIGURE 23.6 Owner/manager stress before and after failure
Source: adapted from Williams, 1985, p 21.

> Stress control means recognising and dealing with our stressors to reduce their impact on our lives.

From what we know about the major sources of stress in small firms, and how they affect the work performance of owner/managers, such people should take steps, before committing money to a new business, to:

- assess their personal suitability for business ownership
- prepare properly for the startup
- gain the skills required for the trade or business of the firm and in management and business ownership, and
- acquire business knowledge.

There are five groups of stressors:
- those we can avoid
- those we can change
- those we contribute to
- those we create ourselves
- those we cannot avoid.

Source: adapted from Miller, Ross and Cohen, 1985, p 76

STRESS IN SMALL AND LARGE FIRMS

It seems reasonable to assume that people who suffer from work-related stress probably do not enjoy their work very much. In other words, people whose work does not cause them frustration, tension, pressure, or other forms of emotional distress are very likely to report that they are satisfied with their jobs.

Is job satisfaction in owner/managers and employees of small firms higher than for employees of large enterprises? Williams (1986) has found that job satisfaction levels in smaller firms in Australia are much higher than in large businesses, and this is so at all levels in those firms (see Figure 23.7).

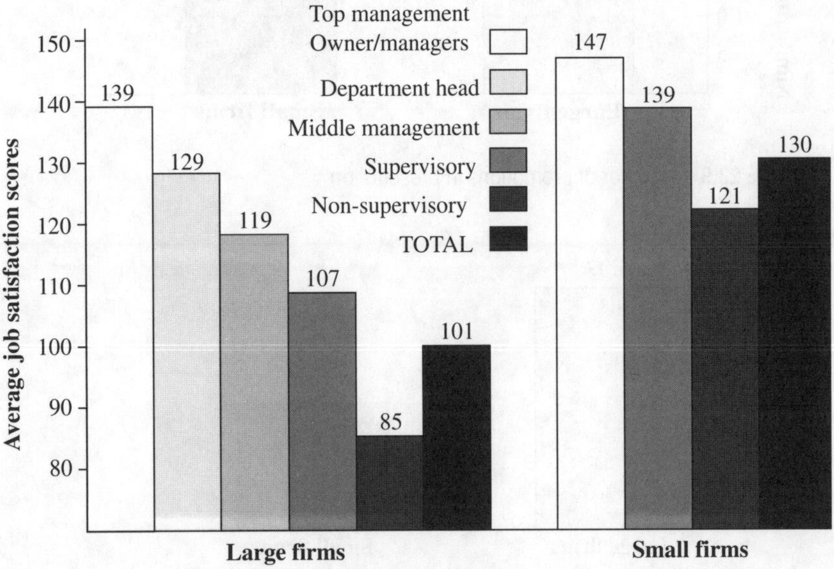

FIGURE 23.7 Job satisfaction in large and small firms
Source: adapted from Williams, 1986, p 34

As further evidence that workers and owners in small firms are generally more satisfied with their jobs, Figures 23.8, 23.9 and 23.10 compare small and large firms by:

- length of service of workers in the present firm (Figure 23.8)
- number of promotions in the present firm (Figure 23.9), and
- number of days absent from work during the past six months (Figure 23.10).

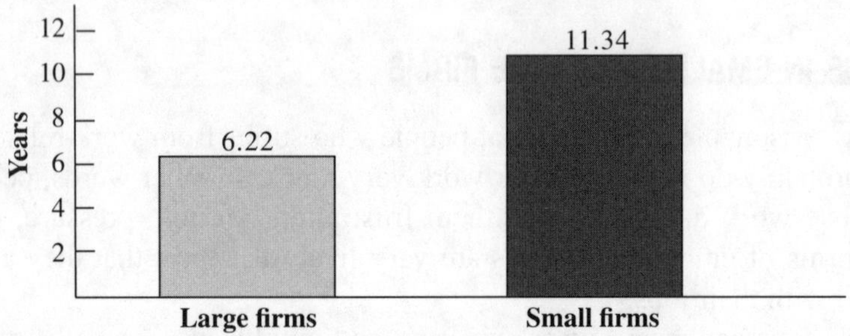

FIGURE 23.8 Length of service (years) in present firm

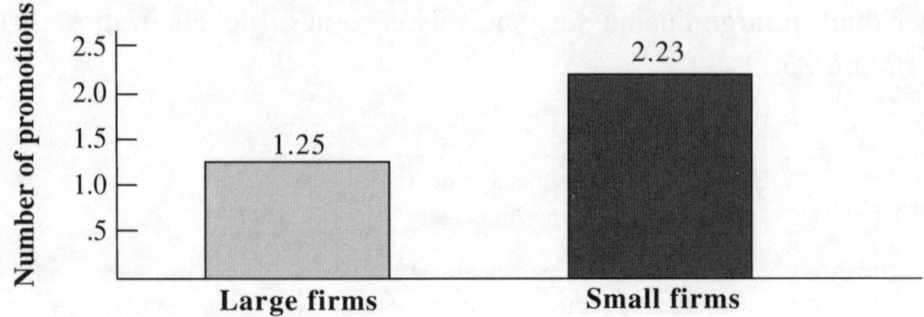

FIGURE 23.9 Number of promotions in present firm

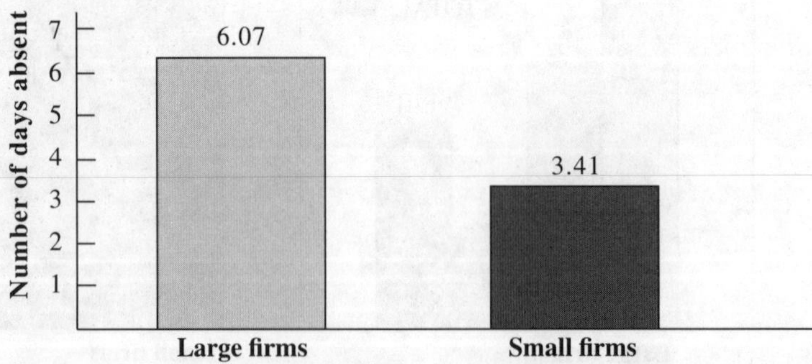

FIGURE 23.10 Number of days absent during past six months

Source: Figures 23.8–23.10 adapted from Williams, 1986, pp 33–4

Summary

Stress is very common in places of work, and is known to seriously affect owner/managers of small firms, particularly those who are unable to cope with the many pressures and demands of that work. Stress is the result of not being able to handle pressures and problems, and knowing that the consequences of this are serious. While some pressure is probably desirable, a high level of stress can cause health problems, and it can greatly reduce work performance.

Owner/managers need to be fully equipped to undertake the complex and difficult task of owning and running their business. Unless they have the right experience, skills, knowledge and drive and can provide technical, managerial and entrepreneurial inputs, owner/managers will be hard pressed to cope with the many, complex and varied demands on them. This can cause stress, which will further reduce their ability to give the business strong and skilled leadership. Unless this cycle is broken, the firm can only go downhill.

Key words

physiological
psychological
psychosomatic illness
stress
stressors

Self-assessment exercises

Personality and stress

People whose behaviour is described as type-A are 'aggressive, competitive, impatient, hostile to frustration, and possess a strong sense of time urgency' compared to type-Bs who 'are exactly the opposite; they are rarely harried, able to relax without feeling guilty, and work without agitation' (Gmelch, 1982, p 17). Type-A people are more likely to have high blood pressure and high cholesterol levels, and therefore will probably suffer stress-related illnesses.

Do you show type-A or type-B behaviour?

Answer the following questions by indicating what most often applies to you. There are no right or wrong answers.

	Yes	Sometimes	No
1 Do you feel compelled to do most things in a hurry?	☐	☐	☐
2 Are you usually the first one to finish a meal?	☐	☐	☐
3 Is it difficult for you to relax, even for a few hours?	☐	☐	☐

	Yes	Sometimes	No
4 Do you hate to wait in line at a restaurant, a bank or a shop?	☐	☐	☐
5 Do you frequently try to do several things at once?	☐	☐	☐
6 Are you generally dissatisfied with what you have accomplished in life?	☐	☐	☐
7 Do you enjoy competition and feel you always have to win?	☐	☐	☐
8 When other people speak slowly do you find yourself trying to rush them along by finishing the sentence for them?	☐	☐	☐
9 Do you become impatient when someone does the job slowly?	☐	☐	☐
10 When engaged in conversation do you usually feel compelled to tell others about your own interests?	☐	☐	☐
11 Do you become irritated when something is not done exactly right?	☐	☐	☐
12 Do you rush through your tasks to get them done as quickly as possible?	☐	☐	☐
13 Do you feel you are constantly under pressure to get more done?	☐	☐	☐
14 In the past few years, have you taken less than your allotted holiday time?	☐	☐	☐
15 While listening to other people, do you usually find your mind wandering to other tasks and subjects?	☐	☐	☐
16 When you meet aggressive people, do you usually feel compelled to compete with them?	☐	☐	☐
17 Do you tend to talk quickly?	☐	☐	☐
18 Are you too busy with your job to have time for hobbies and outside activities?	☐	☐	☐
19 Do you seek and need recognition from your boss and peers?	☐	☐	☐
20 Do you take pride in working best ‘under pressure’?	☐	☐	☐

Scoring method

Yes = 2; Sometimes = 1; No = 0

Add the scores for your 20 answers and place an X in a corresponding position in the table below. A score of 30 or more suggests you are an extreme type-A person; a score below 10 shows you are an extreme type-B person. For most successful (and non-stressed) owner/managers a score between 16 and 28 can be expected.

40 36 32	28 24 20 16 12	8 4 0
Extreme		Extreme
type-A	type-B	

Source: adapted from Gmelch, 1982, pp 99–100

Measuring stress in small business owner/managers

This part of the self-assessment exercise measures your ability to cope with the difficulties and pressures of being in your own business. There are no right or wrong answers. The results will be more useful to you if you answer honestly and without trying to disguise the truth.

For each question, tick the box that gives the 'best' answer. The box headings are as follows:

N = Never
R = Rarely
O = Occasionally
S = Sometimes
F = Frequently
A = Always

	A	F	S	O	R	N
1 Are there times when you have seriouslythought you would be happier as an employee?	☐	☐	☐	☐	☐	☐
2 Do you find that owning and running your own firm gives your life more meaning, purpose and enjoyment?	☐	☐	☐	☐	☐	☐
3 Does making important decisions worry you?	☐	☐	☐	☐	☐	☐
4 Are you ever tempted to sell out and quit?	☐	☐	☐	☐	☐	☐
5 Do you become anxious and worried when things do not seem to be going right?	☐	☐	☐	☐	☐	☐

	A	F	S	O	R	N
6 Do you ever really doubt your own ability to succeed in business?	☐	☐	☐	☐	☐	☐
7 Do you get more personal satisfaction as an owner than you did as an employee?	☐	☐	☐	☐	☐	☐
8 Do your business duties ever cause any stress or problems between you and your spouse and/or family?	☐	☐	☐	☐	☐	☐
9 Does the fact that you are very much responsible to others (eg employees, customers, creditors, bank and — maybe — partners) worry you at all?	☐	☐	☐	☐	☐	☐
10 Do you find that running your own business takes up time that you would like to spend with your family and/or friends and/or in leisure activities?	☐	☐	☐	☐	☐	☐
11 Do you ever wish that you had taken more time and advice in getting ready to start and run your own business?	☐	☐	☐	☐	☐	☐
12 Are you ever faced with and worried by problems that you find very hard to solve?	☐	☐	☐	☐	☐	☐
13 Do business responsibilities and problems ever have any effect on your heath?	☐	☐	☐	☐	☐	☐
14 Despite the problems, do you find that owning and running your own business gives you a greater challenge than working as an employee?	☐	☐	☐	☐	☐	☐
15 Are you enthusiastic and excited about your business and its chances of success?	☐	☐	☐	☐	☐	☐
16 Do you find that business problems and crises can upset you (eg make you lose your temper or get frustrated) at work?	☐	☐	☐	☐	☐	☐
17 Do you feel you have the full support of your spouse/family/friends, and their help when needed (ie are they willing to make sacrifices too)?	☐	☐	☐	☐	☐	☐

		A	F	S	O	R	N
18	Do you ever regret or become anxious about having invested money in a business that could fail?	☐	☐	☐	☐	☐	☐
19	Do you find that you have to work very long hours just to keep the business going?	☐	☐	☐	☐	☐	☐
20	Do long days and heavy pressure cause you to be mentally and physically tired at the end of each day?	☐	☐	☐	☐	☐	☐
21	Do you feel confident about leaving the business in the hands of either (say) a partner or a senior employee, and taking a holiday for at least a week?	☐	☐	☐	☐	☐	☐
22	Does it worry you when any of your employees makes a decision without first checking with you?	☐	☐	☐	☐	☐	☐
23	Do you have to spend so much time dealing with immediate (ie urgent) problems that you don't have enough time for planning and thinking about more important matters?	☐	☐	☐	☐	☐	☐
24	How often can you find time to plan ahead for (say) the next year, or longer?	☐	☐	☐	☐	☐	☐
25	How often are you faced with the fact that you are ignorant or weak in some important area of managing your business?	☐	☐	☐	☐	☐	☐
26	Do you ever seriously regret not having the security of a regular and certain income as an employee?	☐	☐	☐	☐	☐	☐
27	Do you ever get worried that your business might grow bigger, making you personally unable to handle the increased work and responsibility?	☐	☐	☐	☐	☐	☐
28	Do you find it hard to delegate authority to your employees and let them make their own decisions on important matters?	☐	☐	☐	☐	☐	☐
29	Do you ever find that you want to put off making important decisions because you are worried about making the wrong ones?	☐	☐	☐	☐	☐	☐

	A	F	S	O	R	N
30 Do you ever become frustrated (angry or worried) when employees do not seem to be as loyal and hard-working as you wish?	☐	☐	☐	☐	☐	☐
31 Do you ever find that you are working less efficiently than you know you can and should (ie spending more time than you should in doing your work)?	☐	☐	☐	☐	☐	☐
32 Do you find it annoying to have to do things in a rush, without having enough time to think about the likely effects of your actions or the advantages of other ways of doing things?	☐	☐	☐	☐	☐	☐

	Yes	Unsure	No
33 If this business were to fail, would you try again?	☐	☐	☐
34 Despite all the problems and worries, do you really enjoy owning and running your own business?	☐	☐	☐
35 If you had known then what you know now about running your own business, would you have ever started?	☐	☐	☐
36 Do you have ideas or are you making any specific plans for improving and/or expanding your business?	☐	☐	☐

Scoring method

Score

A	F	S	O	R	N
6	5	4	3	2	1

for items 1 ☐ 3 ☐ 4 ☐ 5 ☐ 6 ☐ 8 ☐ 9 ☐ 10 ☐ 11 ☐ 12 ☐ 13 ☐ 16 ☐ 18 ☐ 19 ☐ 20 ☐ 22 ☐ 23 ☐ 25 ☐ 26 ☐ 27 ☐ 28 ☐ 29 ☐ 30 ☐ 31 ☐ 32 ☐

Score

A	F	S	O	R	N
1	2	3	4	5	6

for items 2 ☐ 7 ☐ 14 ☐ 15 ☐ 17 ☐ 21 ☐ 24 ☐

Score	Yes	Unsure	No	for items 33 ☐ 34 ☐ 35 ☐ 36 ☐
	0	1	2	

Your total score ☐ out of 200

Compare your stress level with the average for 22 034 Australian small business owner/managers. The average (a score of 107) is shown by an asterisk (*). Nearly 70% of those 22 034 persons scored between 76 and 138. If you scored below 76 you might be 'under-motivated'. A score above 138 suggests you are heavily stressed and in danger of becoming unable to manage your firm effectively. You might need to get medical advice, unless you can see ways of getting rid of the stressors.

Low stress	*	High stress
30 40 50 60 70 80	90 100 * 110 120 130	140 150 160 170 180

References

Gmelch, W H 1982, *Beyond Stress to Effective Management*, Wiley, New York

Miller, L H, Ross, R N & Cohen, S I 1985, *Stress*, Bay Books, Sydney

Williams, A J 1985, 'Stress and the Entrepreneurial Role', *International Small Business Journal*, vol 3, no 4, pp 11–25

Williams, A J 1986, 'The Discretionary Component of Work: A Comparative Study of Work Discretion and Job Satisfaction in Large and Small Enterprises', in Renfrew, K M & Back, R D, *Australian Small Business and Entrepreneurial Research*, Institute of Industrial Economics, Newcastle, pp 23–42

Williams, A J 1987, *The Characteristics and Performance of Small Business in Australia (1983 to 1985): A Study of the Characteristics of Small Australian Business Ventures and their Owner/Managers, and a Longitudinal Investigation of their Economic Performance*, monograph, University of Newcastle

Williams, A J 1991, 'Small business survival: The role of formal education, management training and advisory services', *Small Business Review 1990–1991*, Bureau of Industry Economics, Small Business Research Unit, Australian Government Publishing Service, Canberra, pp 43–82

Your total score = ____ (out of 28)

[illegible]

Low scores					High scores					
[illegible]										

REFERENCES

[illegible]

[illegible]

[illegible]

[illegible]

[illegible]

[illegible]

4

Growing

Growth periods in the life of a business can be the most exciting times. They provide a feeling of achievement and the prospect of reward for all the hard work you have done. All successful businesses are growing businesses. To remain successful and survive the growth periods, the expansion must be controlled carefully. There are 'growing pains' with businesses, and it is not uncommon for the management demands at these times to exceed the abilities of the owner, or for the need for additional resources to put too great a strain on the business. In Section 4, we help you to identify in advance the additional resources needed during growth, possible pitfalls, and alternative strategies which you could use to grow. One important aspect of expansion is that it is not an isolated event. There are clear stages in the growth of a business and they are all linked. Decisions made during one expansion period will affect the timing and nature of the next growth stage. So growth is a long-term activity composed of a series of stages, each dependent on the preceding stage, and affecting the next. Some long-term planning is therefore essential, together with detailed planning and control in the short term. Good planning includes evaluating a range of activities, many of which we describe in this section. Careful study of Section 4 will help you ensure that your own business becomes increasingly successful as it grows.

CHAPTER 24

What your business needs to grow

A healthy business is a growing business. After reading this chapter, you should be able to:

- determine how to identify those factors limiting growth of your business
- plan the provision of resources to allow growth, and
- set objectives for each growth cycle of your business.

BUSINESS CYCLES

Small businesses have a lifecycle (see Figure 24.1). This means that, during their lives, they tend to follow a certain pattern of growth. The general pattern starts with a period of slow growth, and is followed by a time of fairly rapid increase of sales. Sometimes this is hard to recognise. While sales in dollar terms might continue to increase as prices rise, sales by number of units might be declining at the same time. The reason for a slowdown in sales is that some of the resources of the business are being used to their limit.

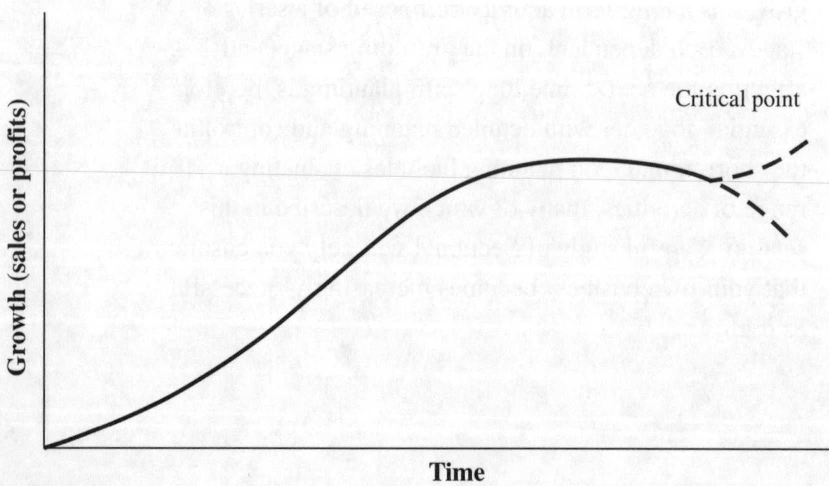

FIGURE 24.1 The business lifecycle

If no action is taken, the business will go on at much the same level, and then start a decline that will end with its sale or closure. If action is taken, the result is another growth stage, up to a certain level. Again action is needed if a static level of operation and later decline are to be avoided. It is as though the business needs an occasional meal to keep it healthy and growing.

LIMITING RESOURCES

Although the critical point shown in Figure 24.1 will occur in all businesses, the timing and cause of it will vary. Usually, though, it will occur because one or more resources are being fully utilised. The limiting resource might be:

- owner's time
- owner's knowledge or skills
- finance
- space
- equipment
- staff
- market size
- product, or
- owner's attitude.

Strong future growth depends on your taking appropriate action when it is needed. To do this, you must know exactly what the action is designed to achieve. Whatever the limiting resource in your business, it is vital to identify it accurately.

In one retail business, the shop became very crowded with stock. The owner assumed that the limiting resource was space, and moved to larger, more expensive premises. When the sales did not improve, the owner found that much of the stock comprised 'low-demand' items. Even when these were replaced with more popular items, the market was not large enough to warrant carrying that much stock. The initial decision to move premises proved very costly because the limiting resource was product, not space.

> You must know what is preventing growth before you can take appropriate action.

Sometimes a resource barrier can be overcome through better management of that resource. Let's look more closely at each of the resources, and discuss ways of overcoming limitations.

Finding more time

In many one-person businesses, such as trades or professions, the business provides a service through the owner. The service can be provided for a fixed amount of time each week. Once the owner is fully occupied, a critical point is reached. If no action is taken, the business will stay at about the same size for a while, then start to decline. However, if steps are taken to increase the availability of the specialised service, then the business will move into another growth cycle. If your business is at this stage, there are ways to increase the amount of services available. These include reducing the non-specialised work that you are doing by hiring additional staff. For example, if you are a plumber, and spend some time keeping the financial records, then you can free up more time for plumbing by hiring a bookkeeper.

When your time is the limiting resource, time management becomes vital. If your time is fully utilised in providing the specialised service that only you can give, then you might look at hiring more staff who can also provide this service. If the business cannot support two operators (which is usually the case at this point) you might investigate the use of part-time employees, or other businesses as contractors. Sometimes the business can be expanded by taking a partner who is willing to work part-time and accept a proportion of the profits. Another possibility in certain businesses is the employment of an apprentice. To ensure growth and success, every likely means of increasing the availability of services must be considered.

If your time is fully utilised in productive work, and the business cannot afford any additional staff, then you might be advised to review your pricing structure and the range of services you provide. It is strongly recommended that you seek the advice of a professional consultant at this point. Such consultation need not be expensive. Most state governments offer a consulting service, either directly, or through local advisory centres.

Overcoming knowledge and skills limitations

Where the limiting resource is the owner's knowledge or skills, this is often not easy to recognise. Also, not every owner is willing to admit that they can no longer do everything necessary.

One good way to both identify and avoid this problem is for you to attend relevant seminars and workshops run by reputable organisations. These will enable you to improve your knowledge and skills, and recognise your limitations. They will also give you the opportunity to meet specialists in various aspects of business. You will then be able to determine whether to undertake further training or to hire specialists from outside your business. If the use of external people is the most appropriate action, then the knowledge you have gained will help you make the best selection. You will also be better equipped to discuss the situation in the specialist's language and correctly interpret the specialist's advice.

Because small business is subject to rapid changes, it is essential that you maintain your knowledge of technology and techniques. Make time to read trade publications and specialist magazines which concentrate on your industry and on small business. Watch for trade fairs. These can save you a lot of time because you can see a whole range of new equipment, and talk to a number of sellers and users.

Finally, don't overlook your competitors. If you hear that someone else is willing to provide the same product or service faster or more cheaply, check it out. Either you will find new technical knowledge or skill, or you will gather some information which will help you with your marketing.

Overcoming financial limitations

This is one problem which is not as difficult to overcome as many business owners think. Before going on a search for additional funds, it is important to know where your business's existing money has been used. Your balance sheet shows this very precisely. If you don't have a balance sheet, look around your business — at machines, fittings and stock, or, if you have credit customers, at the hidden use of funds in your debtors. Make a list of the items or areas in which your money has been invested, then ask yourself whether you can free up some of these funds. Is there a machine which is not used fully? Could you sell it and hire a similar one on occasions when you need it? Even if a machine is fully utilised, you might be able to sell it and lease a replacement. If your machine is fairly new, a finance company might even buy it from you and lease it back to you. Any surplus machines or fittings, and so on, should be sold.

Stock can provide another source of funds. Reducing your inventory of goods or materials yields additional funds for the business. If you have a range of items in stock, you will need to look at each item and decide what stock level is really needed. This might mean that you pay higher prices because you are buying smaller quantities. However, if by doing this you reduce your borrowings, you will save on interest charges. So have a close look at your stock of materials, goods and parts. And, of course, having reduced your stock, ask yourself whether some of the fittings that are no longer used for storage can be sold.

Your debtors are another area in which you have invested money. You can often reduce this investment by reviewing your credit policy, and by taking stronger measures to get payments on time. Offering a discount for prompt payment can make significant funds available. Again, the cost of this could be compared with interest charges on borrowings. Basically, lending less money, for a shorter time and to fewer customers, will reduce your need for additional finance. Factoring your debtors is yet another way of reducing your need for external funds (see page 224). But again the cost of doing so must be compared with interest costs.

If, after taking all these steps, finance is still your limiting resource, you will need to obtain additional funds externally. Before approaching financial institutions, it is worth talking to your suppliers. By buying your supplies on credit, you can free up funds within your business. Be prepared to discuss your needs for extended credit with all possible suppliers, not only your regular ones. Trying all the avenues we have mentioned will not only reduce the amount you have to borrow, but will also impress lenders and increase your chances of borrowing externally. It shows that you are a good manager.

However, your chances of obtaining external finance, and of getting it for the lowest cost, are usually much better if you have a well-prepared business plan. This will identify how much finance is required, and how it will be used. Your plan will also show the increased profits from the growth. This information is very important to the people who lend money to businesses. If you plan to borrow the expansion capital, a business plan is essential. Apart from borrowing, another possibility is to form a partnership with a person who is willing to invest money for a share of the profits. This same idea can be extended to finding a number of people (or a finance company) willing to invest for a share of the profits, and forming a company. Whatever the course of action to reduce limitations on finance, in all cases a business plan will be required.

Making more space

As your business grows, space can be a limiting factor. But before embarking on a costly and time-consuming study of alternative locations, it is essential to review the utilisation of the space you already have. It is usually cheaper to move a wall or two than to move a business. Look closely at the space you have, and what it is used for. Is everything in the space essential? Could some fittings or furniture be replaced with smaller items? A different layout could increase the utilisation of existing space. And don't forget to consider *all* of the space.

A music shop avoided the need for larger premises by building a second floor inside the shop. About half the size of the existing floor, this was raised about three metres above it. The owners fitted an ornamental staircase and located all the classical music stock on the upper floor. Not only did this give them more space without moving, but their classical music customers also appreciated having a separate shopping area.

If additional space is *not* available in your existing premises, you will need to move, possibly even leaving your current market area for a new one. To compare the costs and benefits of all possible locations you will need to make a detailed study. Some government assistance might be available to offset part of the costs of this feasibility study and relocation.

Breaking the equipment barrier

Limitations on growth due to inadequate equipment are fairly rare. When they do occur, they are more often a problem of finance than of the equipment itself. Only in cases where equipment has been specially made or modified is finding a larger capacity, or more of the same, a problem. If special equipment is fully utilised and inadequate, you might be wise to review your entire process, perhaps modifying it to operate with more readily available equipment.

A recent example of this review of the entire process occurred with a small manufacturer of protective clothing. One sewing machine had been modified extensively for use on one part of the product. As demand increased, production was limited by this machine. The owner of the business started to modify another machine, but then sought advice on the whole manufacturing process. As a result, the method of manufacture was altered, and standard machines were used for all processes. The owner had no trouble obtaining equipment to allow production to be expanded.

Overcoming staffing limitations

Your business could be hampered if hours worked by staff, or staff knowledge and skills, are inadequate. Your evaluation of any such problem should begin with an assessment of how existing staff resources are being utilised. This will give you the information you need to determine if the limitation is one of time or knowledge or skills. The same remedies apply as those applicable to owner limitations. If your existing staff time is fully utilised, and this is limiting further growth, it is often a wise policy to use casual or part-time staff before employing additional full-time staff. This way, you can plan to employ more people only at those times when you need them. This will also give you a chance to see how well they work, which can help you when you are looking for full-time staff later. If the work necessitates extensive training of staff, take the opportunity to review the tasks of each person. You might find that some of the less-skilled work can be given to casual staff, leaving the existing staff with more time for the specialised tasks.

It is just as important for your staff as it is for you that their available time and knowledge be productively utilised. Ensure that each staff member is allocated work that makes the best use of their capabilities. Give them the opportunity to keep up with developments in your industry. Make available to them the magazines that you read yourself. Encourage their attendance at trade fairs and seminars.

Pushing back marketing limitations

Before taking any action to push back marketing limitations, it is vital that you identify the part of the marketing mix that is the cause of the barrier. Begin with a detailed look at your total market; this might reveal a new niche or one that is not being fully exploited. Follow up with an analysis of existing and possible future market segments. Your current promotional activities might need to be altered to reach a new, primary target-market segment. Alternatively, or additionally, your pricing policy may be your limiting factor. If your prices are too low, you could well be missing the quality-conscious market segments and your mark-up might be inadequate to provide sufficient profits for future growth. On the other hand, overly high prices can also limit the number of customers. Again, your promotion policies need to be considered. Perhaps you could strongly promote other benefits to de-emphasise price in the minds of your customers.

If your product or service has reached the limits of the market you initially defined for it, you might need to extend the geographic boundaries of your marketing area. This requires detailed studies of other marketing areas. Where possible, export possibilities should be looked at closely, and government help sought, including advice and financial incentives.

All the factors comprising your marketing mix are discussed in detail in Chapter 17. You can use this information to determine whether the market is really the underlying limitation and, if so, which factor is the primary cause.

Overcoming product limitations

The product itself can be another cause of marketing limitations. The first step in your product review is clear identification of your customers' needs and wants. These often change over time, as people move into and out of your marketing area, and as changes in technology, products and competition alter customers' needs and wants. Have a close look at all the advertising in your area, and more importantly, talk or listen to your customers.

If you have only one product or service which is successful but your customers want something different, your business's growth can be stunted. You can overcome this by introducing more products or services into your existing market area, or by identifying complementary or supplementary products that fit in well with your existing range. Again, a study of your market area in relation to the new products or services would be essential.

The owner/operator of a photocopier maintenance-and-repair service recently sought advice on a similar problem. Travelling times defined the geographic boundaries of the marketing area. By extending the product range to the servicing of other office equipment, and also to sales of new equipment, the product limitations were overcome.

If you offer a range of products you can use a similar approach. But each item must be treated separately, and items with low demand must be considered for extra promotion or for replacement with higher demand products.

Looking at owner attitude limitations

This limitation is without doubt the most difficult both to recognise and to overcome. First, you need to stand back and look at yourself. We do this every day, in a physical sense, by using a mirror, and when we want to look at our attitudes, we can use other people as our mirror. As well as our eyes, we can use our own responses to see ourselves. When somebody's behaviour makes us feel angry, envious, happy, or any other strong emotion, we can be sure that what they are doing in some way reflects our own attitudes. Become aware of how you feel when your customers or competitors do things that affect the growth of your business or theirs. Use this to identify your own attitude towards expansion of your own business.

Often an owner decides that the business is big enough. This might be because the profit is adequate, or because it is felt that all expansion opportunities have been explored. Whatever the reason, the attitude exists that effort to gain further growth is not warranted. Obviously, little can be done until either the attitude or the owner changes. Changing ownership at this point might be your best action; perhaps you would be happier if you sold your business while it is successful, and started again in a smaller way. You could then build up the new business to the same stage, and repeat the process. Each time, you would have additional capital resulting from the price difference between the current business and the new one, and you would not be continuing to operate a business that has been going into a decline and taking much of your investment with it. If your attitude is that the business is big enough now and expansion is not necessary, either you sell it, or continue to operate it until it starts to decline. Unfortunately, after the business has gone into decline, the owner usually waits until the point of failure before seeking help. Sometimes the business can be rescued, but this requires a lot of hard work — all just to get back what you used to have.

Looking ahead

When you have identified the limitation on the growth of your business, and taken action to overcome it, your business starts another cycle. The new business (and that is what you have) follows the same pattern as shown in Figure 24.1. It, too, will reach a critical point at some time in the future. When it does, you will need to take the same steps to identify and overcome the limitation. However, the nature of that next limitation will be determined to a large extent by what action you have taken this time. That is, what you do now will determine how and when your next limitation will occur. In the next chapter we will look more closely at the link between your current solution and your next limitation.

Summary

When growth of your business reaches a critical point, you need to take some action to revitalise it. The first step in deciding what to do is to find out what is likely to prevent continued growth. Probably one resource alone will be found to be fully utilised. Other resources might still be under-utilised but unable to be accessed because of the lack of availability of the limiting resource. Any one of your business resources — the owner, finance, space, equipment, staff or the market — could prevent further growth unless you act promptly. The first step is to identify correctly the limiting resource. When you know this, and take the appropriate action, your business will enter another growth cycle.

Key words

complementary products
critical point
factoring
growth cycle
limiting resource
resources
trade fair

Review exercises

1 What is the main reason for a business slowdown?

2 How can you ensure that your knowledge and skills are sufficient to make your business a success?

3 What is the first requirement when you are seeking expansion capital outside your business?

4 Which factors need to be considered to overcome market limitations?

5 List the resources of a business that could be limiting its growth.

6 Describe the steps an owner could take to increase his or her productive time.

7 How can an owner minimise the possibility of equipment becoming a limiting resource in the future?

8 Describe the steps required to identify product limitations and list possible strategies to overcome them.

9 Explain how small business owners can identify their own attitude towards expansion.

10 Why is it essential to overcome limitations to the growth of a small business?

CHAPTER 25

The growing firm: Problems and challenges

Although growth of a small firm is surely better than failure, it can bring various problems and challenges. The cliche 'grow or die' over-simplifies the complex links between a small firm's expansion and its chances of survival. Small firms generally have limited resources and this fact increases the risks associated with growth, especially if it is rapid, unplanned or becomes the goal in itself. Growth must increase the firm's survival capacity — it must not be regarded as more important than survival.

From reading this chapter you will have a better understanding of:

- the likely effects of growth on your small business
- the business lifecycle (or growth curve) and the five stages in small-firm growth
- the challenges presented by each crisis point as your business moves along its growth curve, and
- how owner/managers must be able to change their management approach as their business grows larger and more complex.

As already mentioned, small business survival depends on sound management of the five critical resources of the firm. If growth overtaxes the firm's resources, its survival might be at risk. This is not to say that growth should be avoided. On the contrary, survival often depends on steady, well-planned development that increases resources. As expressed by Cohn and Lindberg (1978, p 6):

while it is recognised that growth in sales volume does not insure survival and profitability, and can in fact be a negative factor, the price of neglecting opportunities to grow that do not involve erosion of liquidity and profitability can be very high indeed. What may be at stake is a firm's market position, and if an opportunity to improve that position is unnecessarily forgone, there can eventually be serious consequences.

Healthy growth comes from seizing opportunities that fit your growth plans.

There is no single best way for a small firm to grow. Opportunities for development will differ from one firm to another, as will each firm's ability to respond to those opportunities. Probably the most important advice for owner/managers of growing firms is: plan the method, direction, speed and all other aspects of growth; in short, control your firm's expansion. This advice suggests caution.

As small firms grow larger (employing more staff and making more sales) they also change in various ways. In particular, the role played by the owner/manager will change greatly — from one of a self-employed worker to one of a 'professional' manager. Many owner/managers cannot cope with this change from 'worker' to 'manager', and suffer much stress because they are unable to manage properly the larger and more complex firm.

As your firm grows, your work as an owner/manager will change.

One way of studying such changes and the problems they bring is to use the concept of the lifecycle. Just as plants and animals have lifecycles, starting with birth and ending with death, so, too, do products and services in terms of consumer demand. Since most small firms sell either a single product (or service), several that are closely related (for example, refrigerators and air-conditioners), or a range of similar products (such as car accessories and parts), the growth of such firms will naturally tend to follow rather closely the lifecycle of those products.

THE BUSINESS LIFECYCLE

The evolution or change process in a small business is described by the staff of United States business consultants Rohrer, Hibler and Replogle (1981, p 129) as follows:

[There is] a simple analogy between the organisation and the individual human being. Individuals are obviously growing, living organisms; so are organisations. Just as individuals have distinct personalities and a life cycle of maturational stages between birth and death, so do organisations. Like people, organisations begin with a traumatic entrance into the world, small and vulnerable, and proceed through a period of growth wherein they establish their identity and character; finally they arrive at a period of maturity. They may then drift off into organisational senility, marked perhaps by hardening of the markets.

The major stages in the lifecycle of small firms are shown in Figure 25.1. So long as a small firm survives, it will move along the growth curve, becoming larger and more complex. As it moves from one stage into the next, the nature of the firm and the problems it faces will change.

Owner/managers must recognise these changes if their firms are to survive. Too often these important changes are not noticed because owner/managers:

- are not observant enough
- are too busy
- are too close to the action (they are not able to 'see the wood for the trees')

or because most changes are gradual.

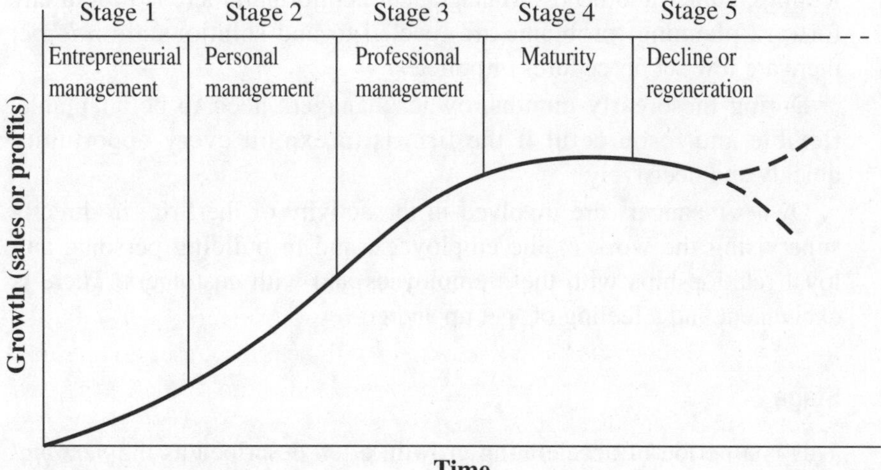

FIGURE 25.1 The business lifecycle

A firm with only two employees might be run quite effectively in a very casual, informal and flexible way, but this is not so when there are twenty or more on the payroll. Most entrepreneurial individuals are not good managers or administrators; they do not delegate well. This matters less in a firm with two employees than in one with twenty. As a firm grows larger it needs different (and probably, better) management skills and methods, and without them it could well fail.

> Each stage of growth brings its own opportunities and problems.

Let us look briefly at each of the five stages of the small business lifecycle, and at the kinds of problems likely to arise during these growth stages.

Stage 1

The first stage of small business growth is the startup, initiation or *entrepreneurial* stage — birth and infancy. As statistics on business failure show, small firms are very vulnerable during this period. The main concern is getting the firm established on a solid foundation in the face of much risk. Without doubt, the single most important task is to create a sales base of sufficient size to enable the firm to survive — an entrepreneurial challenge that entails creating a competitive advantage.

In this early period, life is very uncertain — everything is new, and resources (especially money) are usually very scarce! The new firm is usually a 'one-person show'. The owner/manager dominates all decision-making, and tends to run the business according to personal feelings, values and needs. Management is informal; there is little if any forward planning; problems are reacted to and solutions are *ad hoc*; there are few set procedures or policies.

During these early months, owner/managers need to be adaptable, flexible and resourceful if the firm is to exploit every opportunity quickly and decisively.

Owner/managers are involved in the activity of the firm, in directly supervising the work of the employees, and in building personal and loyal relationships with these employees and with customers. There is excitement and a feeling of 'get up and go'.

Stage 2

This is a period of accelerating growth, often described as the *personal management* stage. The firm now has perhaps 8 to 12 employees, including one or more senior supervisors (in specialised areas of the business) who form a management team with the owner/manager(s).

Management is still fairly informal, and in most cases the owner/manager is still the dominant force in the firm, often having a 'fatherly' influence. Quite a few small firms never get beyond this stage, especially those that are owned and run by a family. Traditions are taken seriously, and new ideas for change and improvement are received with little enthusiasm. Company loyalty and security are strong features — to owner/managers the firm is an extended family. Rocking the boat is not tolerated.

By this stage employees will have much knowledge and expertise, and the firm will probably have a reputation for a good product or service. Owner/managers and employees are likely to feel intense loyalty to, and much pride in, the product or service on which the firm was founded and built.

> Growth increases your firm's size and complexity.

The main task during this stage is to maintain and improve the firm's competitive advantage, and thereby increase its market share through growth. The most serious hurdle in doing this is the steadily increasing wish not to change what appears to be a comfortable existence. Lack of attention to what competitors are doing might hide the fact that competitive advantage is not being maintained and sales growth is starting to slip. Lack of concern about costs and efficiency might erode profits. The firm cannot respond quickly and effectively to change.

Stage 3

This later growth, or *professional management*, stage is a most difficult one for many people in small firms. It requires a serious rethinking about how the firm should be run if it is to survive. The difficulty comes from the realisation that the firm could lose the vitality of its earlier entrepreneurial stage unless a more controlled and professional approach is taken. This might necessitate a real shake-up, starting with the personal management style, which must be replaced by more businesslike, cost-conscious, profit-based and market-oriented methods.

Usually drastic and sometimes painful internal changes are called for. Some actions that must be taken to help small firms to grow and survive are: more effective planning, budgeting and control; better books and records; better utilisation of specialist managers (by more delegation and authority); shedding of unproductive staff (no matter how loyal they might be); bringing in cost-saving programmes; and having a close and critical look at the firm's distinctive competence(s) and hence its competitive advantage.

One of the real dangers associated with bringing professional management into small but growing firms is that of replacing the entrepreneurial drive (looking for and/or creating new markets and new products) of Stage 1 and early Stage 2 with a concern for greater internal efficiency. The challenge is to introduce professional management *without* robbing the firm of its entrepreneurial spirit, its vitality and its momentum. Figure 25.1 shows a clear slowdown in the rate of growth (in sales and profits) as firms move into and through the next phase, Stage 4. In most cases, the reason has been the shift from an entrepreneurial approach to one in which the major emphasis is on internal operating efficiency.

Stage 4

A firm moves into the *maturity* stage of the lifecycle when its growth rate in both profitability and sales slows down.

Growth in sales will slow down (and even decline) when the firm cannot make sales at the level previously reached. This is often referred to as 'hardening of the markets', a late-middle-age ailment similar to hardening of the arteries, and there are various reasons for it:

- actions by competitors, such as price cutting
- actions by competitors, such as selling better quality products

- market saturation, namely too many firms competing for the buyers' dollars
- changes in technology making this product or service obsolete
- changes in fashion, style and general consumer preferences
- poor location, and
- lack of attention to marketing, resulting in poor promotion or packaging, or an inferior product.

Most of these reasons for a slowdown in sales can be avoided or prevented. Entrepreneurial management (which includes good marketing) means knowing what the consumer wants and providing it. There is no excuse for any firm to try to sell out-of-date (and therefore unwanted) products or inferior services, but it happens — all too often.

All managers must realise that their product or service will not sell forever, and long before declining sales growth occurs the search for new products, new markets, or both, must begin. This means accepting the fact that change is inevitable, and taking steps to benefit from this predicted change — doing something now to make sure the firm has a future! Obviously this is a matter of planning. An active search for new products, markets or both should go on continually, and it should start while the firm is in the personal management stage (Stage 2). If done well this should help the firm avoid the more serious effects of a decline in the sales of its original product(s) or service(s).

A slowdown in profits earned can be remedied by improving cost control, by improving productivity of resources (staff in particular), increasing margins (if possible), and/or by getting sales moving again.

Stage 5

Once a firm has reached maturity it can go in either of two directions. It may *decline*, or it might enter a second entrepreneurial stage — *regeneration*.

Decline

Falling sales and profits, unless reversed, will cause serious liquidity (cash flow) problems, and lead eventually to insolvency — that is, failure. It will become harder to borrow money, suppliers will become more nervous about extending credit or will even cut off supplies without cash on delivery (COD), and creditors will start demanding immediate payment. These extra pressures will hasten the firm's decline and make its failure inevitable.

Regeneration

Although difficult, firms *can* be saved, even at this late hour, by much determination, effort and skill. There are several methods of regeneration.

One is a campaign of drastic cost-cutting, getting rid of unprofitable products or activities, selling off assets, reducing the workforce or hours worked (for instance, overtime), and/or rapidly increasing sales. This internal regeneration is not easy because cost-cutting could prevent an increase in sales — careful balancing is needed.

If a firm cannot be regenerated in this way the only choice left is to seek external help. This could entail:

- selling a share of ownership for cash
- seeking government assistance (low-interest loans, grants) or
- purchase by, or merging with, another company.

Growth curve crises

As small firms move up their growth curves they face a number of critical periods — crises for many — which must be solved if they are to survive and grow. Not all firms meet all of these crises, nor do they meet them in the same order. Some firms might even be hit by several crises at the same time.

Some growing pains are unavoidable.

The crises listed here are not the only problems faced by small firms as they grow, but they are common to most. Firms that fail in an early stage of the growth cycle will obviously not experience later crises. Failure to overcome any of these crises could be fatal for any firm.

The starting crisis

Four main mistakes destroy many new small firms before the end of Stage 1:

1 *Lack of owner/manager experience*

Management in a small firm is many-sided, particularly when specialists cannot be afforded. Lack of experience and skill (and, therefore, poor performance) in any area of management can cripple a small firm. By contrast, effective small-firm management is *well-rounded* — that is, based on experience in as many areas of business management as possible — selling, design and production, finance and accounting, and staff supervision at least. The high incidence of top salespeople, engineers or dressmakers who start their own businesses without rounded experience in management is well known to accountants working with bankruptcies.

Good management also comes from experience in *supervising other staff*, and decision-making at a fairly high level concerning major resources. The best experience in decision-making comes from being responsible for one's decisions.

Finally, experience in the *same type of business* is better than experience in a totally different type. If your work background and managerial experience have been in the service industry, you would be wise to start your own business in that industry.

2 *Lack of verified market*

You should not embark on any business venture without verifying that a real business opportunity or market niche exists. Whether a new business is being started or an existing firm is being purchased, a careful study of the likely market for the particular product or service must be carried out before any funds are invested.

3 *Inadequate records and information*

Managers need to make decisions, and good decisions are impossible without up-to-date, reliable and meaningful information. An accounting system must be planned and put in place (with help, in most cases, from a good accountant) right at the beginning of a firm's operations, to be maintained and adapted throughout the life of the business.

It is foolish to regard accounting (or bookkeeping) as a waste of money, or an expense that can be afforded only once the firm has grown larger. Certain financial facts and figures are critical in small firms — namely, margins, costs, break-even point and itemised sales figures. Many contractors have failed because their job quotes were hopelessly unrealistic — they had no records and therefore no idea of past costs; and more than one retail store has been found to be selling goods at below cost because no one bothered to check purchase prices from the invoices. Buchele (1967, p 21) quotes an investment adviser:

Before you open your doors for business, invest a few hundred dollars in having a competent public accountant set up a paperwork system that will give you adequate accounting records. If you can't afford this, you're too undercapitalised to be in business. If you don't understand the need for this, you don't have enough management experience to be starting a business.

4 *Underestimation of capital needs*

Trying to start a business with too little money invested by the owner(s) is a common failing. Most owners of new firms greatly underestimate the money and time needed to start the firm and create positive cash flow (where cash received exceeds cash payments).

Williams (1991) found that surviving small firms in Australia had taken an average of 1.5 years after startup to create positive cash flow, while those that failed had taken (on average) 4.5 years. Liquidity problems in the early period increase the already high risk of failure. Adequate equity (owners' funds) backed by borrowed money, give a new firm time — time to perfect a new product, to get a new production set-up operating efficiently, and to develop customer acceptance of the product. Time schedules slip, expenses run higher than planned — all this soon depletes an inadequate supply of capital (Buchele, 1967, p 123).

The cash crisis

Many owner/managers cannot understand how a small firm can be growing rapidly and recording good profits, and then literally expand into insolvency — or grow itself to death! The cash crisis occurs when a firm becomes unable to meet its financial commitments (pay its debts) from its cash resources without having to borrow funds to do so.

Main causes of such a crisis are:

- under-capitalisation at startup (see above)
- poor financial management
- inability to handle rapid growth.

> Uncontrolled growth can cause failure by weakening your firm's resources.

A cash crisis can be caused by under-capitalisation, but cash crises can also occur in firms that start with adequate funding. In many cases poor financial management and inability to handle rapid growth occur together. Growth (namely, increasing sales) calls for more and heavier investment in stocks, raw materials, spare parts, equipment and accounts receivable, and increased overheads — all of which necessitate more and more cash and credit. If, at the same time, there is poor financial (particularly, cash) management, the cash crisis will be worse and more likely to be fatal.

To quote Buchele (1967, p 28):

The cash crisis is rooted in the intense concentration of many small-firm operators on profits and growth. They fail to keep clearly in mind that profits and growth must be achieved while maintaining a healthy cash position.

Solutions

To avoid or remedy the cash crisis, you must take the following actions:

1 Try to control the firm's rate of growth so that demand for extra cash to finance growth is within the firm's ability to

- earn the cash
- borrow funds.

2 Budget cash flow as follows:

- From careful analysis of past records, budget (that is, forecast) cash receipts and cash payments for at least six months ahead in detail.
- Keep accurate cash records.
- Do monthly comparisons of forecast and actual cash flows and the end-of-month cash position. Differences should be noted, then:
  —steps taken to remedy problems (such as lower than forecast sales, or increased expenses), and
  —adjustments made to the following months' forecasts.

3 Manage cash properly. The purposes of good cash management are to improve the rate of cash flow and to increase the firm's useable cash resources. Cash can be seen as the lifeblood of the firm, and as such it must flow.

To improve the use of cash, the following matters need ongoing attention:

- management of inventories (stocks of goods for sale, raw materials, spare parts, supplies and partly finished goods)
- control of credit and accounts receivable
- the level of investment in fixed assets
- control of overhead expenses
- unprofitable products and services
- the level of drawings by owner(s)
- the timing of payments to creditors, and the earning of discounts
- the seasonal patterns affecting sales and cash receipts, and
- the suitability of the firm's accounting system.

Owner/managers need to be aware of ways to save cash, such as taking purchase discounts, reducing receivables, renting fixed assets or buying services (instead of tying up cash in fixed assets), keeping inventories at a minimum, avoiding volume-happy big deals that tie up capital but yield little or no contribution to overhead or profits, and trimming the product line to eliminate items that make insufficient profit or contribution to overhead (Buchele, 1967, p 33).

The delegation crisis

When the firm reaches the awkward stage where it is too large for one or two owners to run properly but still too small to afford a team of specialised managers, owner/managers must delegate some management responsibility to someone else.

Why is this a crisis? The answer lies in an understanding of the entrepreneurial personality. Most entrepreneurs have a strong wish to be independent, and are psychologically or emotionally unable to hand over to a new partner or senior employee the authority to make important decisions that might affect the firm's success. Their high level of independence means that they like to make the big decisions and be in control — delegation means losing some of this control.

This situation is a crisis in many firms because their owner/managers fear, and therefore resist, losing their independence and control over *their* firm — their 'creation'. But, as the firm grows larger, owners must delegate or they and the firm will suffer. Otherwise, work overload will lead to stress, and then mistakes will occur.

Delegation does not mean completely abandoning decision-making and control. Effective owner/managers must know what is going on in all areas of the business, but this does not mean they should do it all themselves. As the firm grows, owner/managers must become more and more managers, and less and less technicians.

Solutions

Solutions to the delegation crisis include:

- bringing in a competent, trustworthy partner
- hiring a competent, trustworthy employee who can take responsibility for, and manage, one vital area of the business, or
- merging with another firm.

In any of these steps, it is important that the new partner or employee have experience and skills that are lacking in the original owner — that they are strong where the owner is weak! This will give the firm rounder managerial expertise and must therefore improve its performance.

While all concerned must be willing and able to work together for the good of the firm, there is little point in the new partner or employee being a 'yes person'! It is important that they challenge wrong practices and be willing to shake up the firm as needed. Also, it is reasonable for the new person to expect some share in the ownership of the firm (after a trial period), forcing the original owner to accept the fact that '80% ownership of a prosperous, growing business is worth a lot more than 100% ownership of one that is stalled or declining' (Buchele, 1967, p 42).

The leadership crisis

As the firm continues to grow in size and complexity it reaches the point where a manager is needed for each functional area — production, sales, accounting/finance, and so on. Consequently the owner/manager becomes more and more a full-time manager, and must learn and use professional management skills and methods.

Being now two levels removed from the 'workplace' (the 'action'), owner/managers will be less and less able to maintain close and regular contacts with all workers, and (often regretfully) will have less time to be involved in the actual work. They now have to work through their managers, and need to improve skills in planning, thinking ahead, paper communication, co-ordination of more diverse activities, budgeting and control techniques, and leadership.

In many cases this transition — from simply delegating to others to taking a more formal leadership role — is not made easily. Delegating responsibility and authority to a team of executives is not quite the same as sharing ideas and work with one or two trusted colleagues, but it must be done. No longer is 'muddling through' good enough.

One of the more serious results of this change is that owner/managers can gradually lose touch with how the firm is going. The inevitable growth of a deadening mass of administrative detail and paperwork can sap the owner's will, physical and mental strength, and enthusiasm. As never before, detailed planning and control are vital tasks, and owner/managers must concentrate on developing and implementing better accounting, information and decision-making systems so that the whole firm and all its many activities can be melded into a more cohesive whole. Efficiency has become the all-important goal.

The most unfortunate result of all this is that owner/managers simply do not have the time or energy to be entrepreneurial, and the firm can be in real danger of losing its momentum and vitality. In many firms at this stage in their growth, efficiency of ongoing activities becomes the prime concern; people are busy and may become lulled into a false sense of security and believe that all is well. However, tomorrow is never far away, and the firm's competitive position could be in danger.

Solutions

Solving this crisis might require some or all of the following courses of action:

- striving to become a more effective leader
- studying management techniques appropriate to the situation
- seeking honest, confidential and constructive criticism
- examining your job and how you are performing it
- getting help by being involved in a business association
- keeping a time log and setting out to improve time management, and
- building a competent management team.

The finance crisis

Continued growth will inevitably create more pressure on the firm's finances. Furthermore, at some point many small firms embark on expansion programmes which, if poorly planned, can over-extend the firm's financial (and other) resources. Many small firms have been caught up in overly ambitious and costly expansion plans that often lead into new, untried and uncertain areas of business activity where lack of experience and know-how can cause costly errors and delays.

Expansion programmes must be carefully planned and in line with the firm's competitive strategy. Unless expansion is approached in this way, serious financial difficulties are likely. For vigorous growth, and significant and well-planned expansion, large investment decisions will be called for. The demand for funds will usually exceed the supply available from equity investments from the original owner(s) and from retained earnings.

Solutions

There are four possible courses of action, each with advantages and disadvantages:

- borrowing the required finance
- introducing a new partner or shareholder
- seeking equity capital from a venture capital source, and
- registering as a company and 'going public'.

Borrowing

- Borrowing must be long-term if it is being invested into fixed assets.
- Interest costs are a fixed cost which must be met from earnings.
- In times of declining and fluctuating sales and profits, heavy interest charges can cause cash flow difficulties.
- This course of action does not introduce more owners, and so allows control of the firm to be retained by its original owner(s). This might cause further delegation and leadership crises.

Introducing new partners or shareholders

- A silent partner or shareholder might provide capital without wishing to be involved in managing, or might insist on an active role in management.
- It is not easy to find and attract individuals with funds available for major investments in small firms.
- There are the usual dangers of personality clashes between new and original owners.

Venture capital investment

- Venture capital investment will provide a professional approach to investing and management, including the preparation of a business plan. Some involvement in management will usually be required.
- The cost of venture capital is often less than that of borrowed funds. The main concern is for capital gain, so the venture capitalist is interested in growth.
- Management help and guidance are usually available.

'Going public'

- 'Going public' can bring in large amounts of equity funds without the owner necessarily losing control (because shares are usually spread out among many shareholders).

- Legal and other costs can be heavy.
- Public companies are required to prepare and submit many reports and returns to corporate affairs authorities. Additional tax burdens are also likely.

The following guidelines for solving the finance crisis are offered by Buchele (1967, pp 72–74):

- Fear of losing control over the management of the firm should not be an excuse for allowing the finance crisis to fail a business with growth potential.
- Do not delay obtaining funds when they are needed.
- In most cases the advantages of obtaining venture capital make it the preferred method of funding large-scale expansion of small firms.
- Avoid heavy reliance on long-term debt — unless the firm has outstanding management expertise, a history of above-average earnings and substantial equity funds.
- Before committing the firm to any expansion funding, seek advice on the best method and source. There should be a proper balance in the firm's capital structure.

The prosperity crisis

Having avoided or survived all crises so far, and finding themselves facing a promising future, some firms get into difficulty through the illusion of 'prosperity'. There are two traps:

1 complacency
2 fast growth.

Complacency

When the firm's future looks secure, it is quite natural for owner/manager(s) to relax and settle back to enjoy the fruits of their labours. Complacency can take various forms:

- sloppy management
- owner/manager absenteeism
- delays and indecisiveness
- lack of initiative and innovation (a reluctance to make any changes such as looking for new products, for instance).

If complacency is allowed to prevail, the business will go downhill rapidly. It might lose its efficiency, thereby becoming unprofitable. It might also lose its entrepreneurial drive and thus risk its competitive advantage.

Solutions

To avoid these dangers, attention must be given to:

- sales growth (new products and/or new markets)

- production and general operating efficiency
- watching the financial and other signals
- maintaining and/or renewing competitive advantage
- avoiding 'caretaker management'.

Fast growth

As already noted, rapid growth in sales volume brings serious resource problems, unless management skills match the growth rate. A successful startup, followed by rapid growth, can sometimes delude small business owners into thinking they are high-flying business tycoons. They might become too adventurous too fast, and set off on a course of rapid and poorly planned expansion. As has been shown, such practices can lead to trouble with cash, finance and management (specifically, leadership).

All growth should fit predetermined plans. Therefore, all growth should be controlled for speed and direction. Controlled expansion allows time to measure progress; and assessing and thinking through problems is the only sure way to achieve sustained growth.

The major outcome of ill-timed, ill-directed and overly rapid growth is a serious run-down in essential resources. A high level of ambition and aggressiveness in owner/managers needs to be balanced with common sense and an awareness of fallibility.

The management succession crisis

A succession crisis can occur at any time, in the form of the death, serious injury or illness of the owner and key decision-maker. Many owner/managers are unwilling or unable to hire, train and use good managers, with the result that, if or when they become unable to carry on, the firm is left to flounder without leadership. Having the business taken over by a totally unprepared (and therefore unwilling) family member, or by one of the employees, can spell disaster.

All growth crises can be predicted and their solutions planned.

Solutions

Every owner/manager knows that the firm will inevitably be confronted with this problem, unless it fails or is sold first. If an owner/manager dies, the provisions of his or her will should indicate the steps to be taken. Normally the business will be disposed of, or carried on by someone else. In the case of a partnership or private company, the agreement or articles will outline the procedure to be followed, and usually the remaining members will continue. All businesses should have in place plans for the disposal or continuation of operations when the owner/manager is unable to carry on through death, disability or retirement.

Summary

So long as they survive, most small firms will grow larger and more complex. This growth generally follows the S-shaped curve. Over time and because of this growth from infancy to maturity, most firms experience distinct changes in their nature, and in the kinds of problems and challenges they face. The major change that all firms must be able to make is that from a small entrepreneurial venture to a more professionally managed business. This shift must be achieved without losing the entrepreneurial spirit and drive that got the firm up and moving.

As your business grows it will very likely face a number of critical growing pains — crises. Unless each of these can be solved, your business could face failure. Most of these crises are the result of the mismanagement of vital resources — people, cash, time, physical assets and information. To avoid the more serious effects of these crises, the firm's growth rate should be controlled so that resources are not stretched too far.

Key words

business growth curve
business lifecycle
delegation
entrepreneurial
leadership
maturity
professional management

Review exercises

Fill in the gaps.

1 Growth of a small firm, if not properly managed, can stop it

_ _ _ _ _ _ _ _ _ _

2 Small business growth should be _ _ _ _ _ _ _ and

_ _ _ _ _ _ _ _ _ _

3 For most small firms, sales and profit growth usually follows the

_ -shaped curve.

4 Entrepreneurial small firms usually grow to the point where they

need _ _ _ _ _ _ _ _ _ _ _ _ _ management.

5 In small enterprises in the entrepreneurial stage of the lifecycle, management is fairly _ _ _ _ _ _ _ _ _, and is commonly _ _ _ _ _ _ _ _ _ _ by the owner/manager.

6 As growing small firms are managed more professionally, a danger is that they will lose their _ and _ _ _ _ _ _ _ _ _

7 A business that has reached the stage of maturity might either _ _ _ _ _ _ _ _ or become _ _ _ _ _ _ _ _ _ _ _ _

8 The starting crisis is the result of mistakes in some or all of the following four matters:

(a) poor or non-existent _ _ _ _ _ _ _ _

(b) lack of _ _ _ _-_ _

(c) no verified _ _ _ _ _ _ _ _ _ _ _ _ _ _ _ _ _ _ (or _ _ _ _ _)

(d) being _ _ _ _ _ - _ _ _ _ _ _ _ _ _ _ _ _ at startup

9 The cash crisis is usually a result of

(a) _ _ _ _ _ -_ _ _ _ _ _ _ _ _ _ _ _ _ _ _

(b) poor _ _ _ _/_ _

(c) uncontrolled _ _ _ _ _ _

10 The prosperity crisis is caused by

(a) _ _ _ _ _ _ _ _ _ _ _ _ _ _ _ _ _ _ _

(b) _ _ _ _ _ _ _ _ _ _ _ _

REFERENCES

Buchele, R 1967, *Business Policy in Growing Firms*, Chandler Publishing Co, Scanton, Pennsylvania

Cohn, T & Lindberg, R A 1978, *Survival and Growth: Management Strategies for the Small Firm*, AMACOM & New American Library, Mentor Books, New York

Rohrer, Hibler & Replogle, Inc 1981, *The Managerial Challenge: A Psychological Approach to the Changing World of Management*, New American Library, Mentor Books, New York

Williams, A J 1991, 'Small business survival: The role of formal education, management training and advisory services', *Small Business Review 1990–1991*, Bureau of Industry Economics, Small Business Research Unit, Australian Government Publishing Service, Canberra, pp 43–82

CHAPTER 26

Ways to grow

Whenever your business reaches some limit, and you take action to overcome it, your business grows. It is the limiting resource that will determine to a large extent the way your business will grow at any time. But, as we have noted, what you do now will also affect which resource will limit your business in a few months' or years' time. A long-term plan will help you determine the best action to take now. When you plan ahead, you can foresee which resource will limit growth. An example of this is a retailer whose business is growing. Customers are starting to complain about how long it takes to get served. One solution would be to employ more staff. But what happens next? More *stock* might be needed to cater for the additional customers; this might bring about financial limitations; or more space could be required for the stock. If *finance* will become the limiting resource, a working partner could be sought. A suitable person could be found now who would bring both labour and capital into the business. Such an action would both solve the current problem and avert the next one. However, if *space* is the next likely problem, it may be better to look at relocation now, rather than employ more staff locally and then move.

Yet another possibility is to change systems or procedures. In the example, self-service facilities could be introduced. This could reduce customer waiting time by allowing sales staff to spend less time with each customer.

You can see from the example that the best action to take to overcome existing limiting factors depends on future limits as well as immediate ones.

Concentrating on short-term solutions can cause long-term problems.

Whatever action is taken, the result is the start of a new cycle of expansion for the business.

After reading this chapter, you should be able to:

- outline a long-term growth plan for your business, and
- select the most appropriate method for expanding your business.

AVENUES FOR EXPANSION

Too many small businesses grow by lurching from crisis to crisis. You can avoid this by planning the growth of your business. Planning will enable you to ensure that your business continues in line with your own objectives. In this way, you will always run your business; it will never run you. Planning growth requires that you look several years ahead, so that you can be fully prepared for each growth phase and can obtain the resources required for growth to proceed the way you want it to.

Some of the ways in which you can expand your business are by:

- simply becoming bigger
- expanding the ownership
- expanding your market
- expanding your share of the market
- expanding your product range.

Whatever you choose to do, your business will never be the same again. Each of the methods shown above will introduce new opportunities and new challenges because what you have is really a new business.

Becoming bigger

Growing bigger requires the expansion of existing resources, particularly staff and space.

More staff

Employment of more staff means that more of your money and time will be needed to manage the human resources of your business. It also means a different style of operation for your business. Some of the time you previously spent with customers will now be taken up with your staff. There will be more administration — with wages books, staff records, work and holiday rosters, and arranging replacements for absent employees. If the extra staff are full-time, then you will need to generate enough extra income to cover all the additional costs of wages, insurance, superannuation, holiday and sick pay every week. Hiring, training and development of staff all take time to plan, and time and money to implement. Building an efficient and effective team requires not only time, but also knowledge and skills related to people management. These are needed as soon as you begin to employ new staff. If you do not have them already, then you need to allow time to gain them through attending courses. You can see from this why it is so important to plan well ahead.

More space

Obtaining more space usually means moving premises. There might be ways to improve your utilisation of existing space by changing the layout, and the furniture and fittings. But when the space is fully utilised and is still inadequate, more space can be obtained only by moving. This will cost time and money, not only for the move itself, but also before and after the move.

Before moving, you will need to select an appropriate location. Gathering the information you need about possible sites in the time you have available each day could span a few months. There could then be a delay until suitable premises become available. Your planning needs to allow for both of these delays. In fact, the further ahead you can plan your change of premises, the more likely the success of your move, because you will have had a chance to research it thoroughly. Larger premises will probably cost more in rent, repairs, maintenance, power, and insurance. In addition, more capital might be required for stock, furniture, fittings and initial preparation. An early start on the planning is essential to ensure that sufficient finance is available to fund the move and the added operating costs.

Expanding ownership

When the limiting resource is finance, or the owner's knowledge and skills, one possible action is expansion of the ownership of the business. This can be done through partnership or shareholders. To utilise the shareholder option, the business must incorporate as a company. The advantages of partnerships and corporate structures are covered in Chapter 12. In both cases, the management strength of the business can be increased. However, you will need to give some of your control to other part-owners. Clearly, expanding ownership is a major change in any business — one which should not, and usually cannot, be made hastily. Deciding whether it is an appropriate strategy requires a thorough review of your personal goals, and of the business objectives. If achieving your objectives depends on owning and running your own business, then this option might not be the best for you. However, if playing a major role in the management of a bigger business fits in with your objectives, it can be appropriate.

Before sharing the ownership, you will need to be very sure about the other owners and the way in which management activities are to be divided. If any aspect is unacceptable to you, then you would be wise to seek alternative arrangements. Finding possible co-owners, getting to know them and discussing ownership and management sharing is a long process. Because it takes so long, planning for the expansion of ownership should begin at least two to three years ahead. Strategies to achieve it could include identifying prospects, researching their background and credentials, meeting with them, and negotiating mutually suitable details. An example of the consequences of insufficient planning is provided by the case of a hairdresser who expanded into a partnership as a quick way to grow. It soon became apparent that the new partner had a different view of money management, and withdrew cash from the takings each week. No record was kept of these drawings, and the business ultimately failed through the combination of insufficient funds and constant arguments between the owners.

Expanding your market

If the geographic boundaries of your market are limiting further growth you might need to increase the number of operating locations. You can do this by franchising the business, opening branches, or combining with another existing business.

Franchising

Many businesses are suitable for franchising as a way of providing facilities and additional outlets for products or services. By selling the rights to use your trading name and business operation ideas, you can recoup your establishment costs. Franchising is particularly suited to businesses that continue to supply products to be sold through the new outlets. (This is covered in greater detail in Chapter 9.)

Plans to franchise your business are best put in place when the business itself commences operation, despite the fact that this could be many years before franchising becomes a reality. Every aspect of your business must then be designed with franchising in mind, including the products, equipment, decor, layout, staff, appearance and operating procedures. Documenting your procedures alone is a long process. Firstly it requires a trial of different ways to perform activities until you find ones that are both simple and effective. These must then be written as a series of steps which can be easily understood and followed by someone who doesn't have your knowledge and experience.

Thus, while franchising is a financially rewarding and increasingly popular avenue for expansion, strategies to achieve it require that you document in detail every aspect of the operation of your business. You will need to have contracts prepared in advance, ready for checking by the franchisees' solicitors. Advice regarding these contracts should be obtained from solicitors who are experienced in this type of work, and general advice can be sought from the franchisors' association in your state. Finally, you will need to produce information brochures giving details of the business with realistic projected financial results and operating procedures. And all this must be done while you are managing your business and ensuring its growth and success!

Additional branches

Another way to expand geographic boundaries is to establish a branch of your business in a new location. This necessitates increases in stock and staff. Record keeping and management become more complex because you need to plan and control two separate businesses. You might be able to take advantage of greater quantity discounts on your purchases and there could also be cost savings on some expense items. Some businesses have found that customers in the two markets are so different that the products at each location need to be stocked in different quantities. A detailed location study would be necessary before establishing a branch. Planning for a new branch is similar to planning for more space. However, the capital required will be much greater, as will the total revenue from sales. Almost everything will double. Your time will be spent much more on administration and management, and much less on customer contact and doing those things that you did when you first entered the business. You must therefore be absolutely sure that this is what you want to do. If you enjoy administration and management then the operation of branches could satisfy your needs. However, if your satisfaction comes from the 'hands-on' side of your business, operating branches might not be an appropriate strategy for you.

Mergers

A third way to widen geographic boundaries is to combine with an existing business in another area. This approach minimises the need for a location study. The combination could be through a merger, with the two owners sharing control and benefiting jointly from cost savings. They could also combine advertising and share other resources.

A long lead-time is again important in planning and preparing for a merger. You need to be sure that the other business is not only successful now but is managed in a way that ensures future success. The other owner's objectives must not conflict with yours; they need not be identical, but both must be achievable. One way to anticipate agreement or conflict is to compare the business plans of the two businesses. The time required to research prospects, including identifying suitable businesses and watching and analysing their performance over a period of time, means that planning for a merger must commence at least three to four years ahead. The steps in the planning process are similar to those for expanding ownership.

Expanding your market share — purchase of a competitor

It might not be geographical boundaries but simply the available market that is your limiting resource: you might have too many competitors for your share of the market to be profitable. Rather than trying to buy a larger share through more aggressive promotion, you might consider buying the business of one or more of your competitors, and operating it/them as a separate branch of your business or closing it/them down.

If you continued to operate you should gain all of the existing customers — thus increasing your share of the market, as well as your operating costs.

If you closed the purchased business, customers would go to all the remaining businesses — increasing your share of the market, as well as that of your remaining competitors.

The location of all competing businesses is a major factor in such a decision. If one competitor is near you and the remainder are relatively distant, then you might gain a large proportion, if not all, of the competitors' customers. Closure of the purchased business would mean little increase in your overhead costs.

Planning for an expanded share of the market is a factor in every review of your business plan. While this would normally concentrate on the more traditional elements of marketing, the purchase of a competitor can reduce the need for ever-increasing spending on current undertakings such as advertising, etc. Keeping a close watch on the trends of your promotional costs and those of your competitors can indicate a future time when purchasing a competitor would represent the best way to expand your market share. This analysis can show that the extra spending you must do over a period of time due to the existence of your competitor will outweigh the purchase costs.

Expanding your product range

You can expand your product range by one of two means:

- increasing the number of stock lines you hold
- starting another business.

More stock lines

If your product range is limiting further growth, you could increase your range of stock or look at starting up a new and different business. Location and marketing factors will determine which is the better way to go. You might be able to find a range of products which complement your existing stock. One example of a business taking this approach was a craft shop whose owners extended their pottery range to include aromatic oils. These could be sold and used in small ornamental bottles which formed part of the existing stock range.

Before adding new product lines, you should carry out a full product audit. Product lines that are not selling should be eliminated. If no products are removed before introducing a new line, sales of all products should be studied closely during the initial sales period of the new line, as sales of the new products could reduce sales of an existing one. Deciding which line to maintain, and which to remove, will depend to some extent on the profit level of each line. Planning an expansion of product lines begins with keeping sales records for each item you now offer. Over time, the slowing down of sales of any product will indicate that it is approaching the peak of its sales. At this time, you should be ready with new products, having remained constantly aware of possible replacements for every product that you offer — using information gathered from suppliers, competitors, customers, and other markets locally or even overseas, and by remaining aware of new products through trade fairs, magazines, and your industry and business networks. Allow time to familiarise yourself with the product features and customer benefits of any new products which you introduce.

Starting another business

Where suitable complementary products cannot be found, you might look at starting, or buying, a business with totally different products. It is usually a good idea to choose one which has the same type of customers as your existing business, allowing you to utilise your knowledge of your existing customers and market. The factors mentioned earlier in relation to starting a separate branch would again apply.

SUMMARY

There are many ways to overcome limits to growth. Selection of the best way depends on the nature of the limitation, and on the likely effects of a particular choice. The options chosen will determine the direction in which your business will grow. Planning is vital to ensure that you remain in control of your business. Expansion represents a major change, and planning for it in most cases must commence well before the actual event. This long lead-time is necessary to gather information, for upgrading your skills and knowledge and that of your staff, and to gather together the resources you will need.

Before making any expansionary move, you need to ensure that the new business that will result still helps you achieve your personal objectives.

A major factor in the choice of a particular option is the attitude of the owner. An aggressive, confident, risk-taking attitude will result in the choice of a radical, innovative option.

KEY WORD

overhead costs

Review exercises

1 How can long-term planning affect decisions about immediate expansion problems?

2 Describe the ways in which a business can expand.

3 What are the advantages and disadvantages of expanding?

4 List the factors that you need to consider when planning expansion through franchising your business to others.

5 Compare planning for expansion of your market with expansion of your share of the market.

6 How can expansion affect the way you operate your business?

7 Discuss the major factors involved when expanding ownership of your business.

8 Explain the way an increase in staff can affect an owner's tasks.

9 List the activities that are necessary when you are preparing to expand your product range.

10 How can an owner's attitude affect the expansion of a business?

APPENDIX

Where to get help and information

The following checklist is designed to help you in your search for information and the avenues of assistance you will need when getting started in business.

1 Your own research

- Visit competitors.
- Go to exhibitions, displays and trade shows.
- Attend conferences.
- Enrol in small business courses (especially TAFE).
- Use your own experience.
- Talk to other small business owners.
- Join small business groups or associations (eg chambers of commerce).
- Use the research section in your capital city library.
- Talk to suppliers.

2 Your professionals

These people have the skills, interest and experience to help you, and many of them do not charge a fee. Do not regard consultation with *your* professional adviser as an expense — it is an investment.

- **Your accountant** should advise you in *all* financial matters — legal form, cost of establishing or buying, raising finance, setting up your records, taxation, financial viability and so on — and act as a monitor for the financial management of your business.
- Your **solicitor's** services are covered on page 213.
- Your **bank manager** Get to know your bank manager early and discuss your proposal before you officially request a loan.
- Your **insurance broker** or **agent** See page 205.
- **Consultants** These are professionals in private practice who provide advice, guidance, information and assistance — for a fee.
- **Government counselling** (See page 210.) These professionally trained people are there to talk to you, to listen, advise, direct and assist you with your proposal, problem or enquiry.

- **Teachers** in the areas of small business management, or the skills you need to employ in your business, can be found in colleges (eg TAFE), universities, and schools.
- **Sales representatives** have product and technical knowledge, and they should also be aware of what is happening in the industry and what your competitors are doing.
- **Media representatives** are a specialised source of help in the advertising area.

3 Government departments

Government departments are there to help you — but you have to make the approach. Remember the old adage:

> If you don't ask — you don't get!

If you don't know which government department to approach, look in the front of your local telephone directory for the Government Special Help number.

Some of the key departments to consider are:

- Australian Bureau of Statistics
- AUSTRADE
- Australian Securities Commission
- small business offices, agencies or corporations
- NIES (National Industry Extension Service)
- DITAC (Department of Industry, Technology and Commerce)
- government information offices
- departments of industry/labour/industrial relations
- Patents, Trademarks and Designs Office
- craft councils
- Department of Consumer Affairs
- Australia Post
- various development boards
- Corporate Affairs Commission
- business enterprise centres
- Australian Taxation Office
- Telecom
- local government (ie councils. Note their publications such as council minutes, regulations, meetings and discussion papers and proposals.)

4 Libraries

Librarians are trained to know what is available, help you obtain information, and direct you to further references. You can find this type of assistance at:

- state libraries (in each capital city — these libraries have a free research section to assist you)
- local libraries
- council libraries
- industry/association libraries
- mobile libraries
- educational libraries (at universities, colleges and schools)
- newspaper libraries.

Remember also to see what is available on films, cassettes and videos.

5 Specialists

Specialised, and perhaps local, help is available to clients and/or members of:

- research agencies
- research companies
- research centres
- technology centres
- trade associations
- trade unions
- credit bureaus
- suppliers
- franchisors.

6 Publications

It is surprising just how much information and assistance is available in printed form — in such resources as:

- trade journals
- magazines (such as *Business Review Weekly, Small Business and Investing*)
- banks — all major banks have a range of free publications on small business
- newspapers
- business reviews
- industry profiles (Financial Management Research Centre, Armidale, New South Wales)
- directories (telephone books, street directories, *Kompass*, year books, catalogues etc)
- government publications:
  - annual reports
  - special publications
  - reports
  - White Papers
  - submissions

- Department of Industry, Technology and Commerce (DITAC) publications, as follows:
  1 *Checklist for Starting a Business*
  2 *Sources of Finance for Small Business*
  3 *Retailing*
  4 *Importing*
  5 *Control Records — the Key to Improving Retailing Profits*
  6 *Marketing*
  7 *Buying or Selling a Small Business*
  8 *Avoiding Management Pitfalls*
  9 *Riding your Brainwave — Marketing for Inventors and Innovators*
  10 *Repair Services*
  11 *Planning for Managing Succession*
  12 *Building Trades*
  13 *Keeping Ahead in the Road Freight Business*
  14 *Evaluating a Franchise*
  15 *Finding and Managing your Employees*
  16 *Taxation*
  17 *Exporting*
  18 *Credit Management*
  19 *Starting a Restaurant*
  20 *Holiday and Travel Accommodation Businesses*
  21 *Survival and Growth in Apparel Retailing*
  22 *Presenting a Case for Finance*
  23 *Cash Flow — Cash Management*
  24 *Management for the Self-employed*
  25 *Job Costing and Estimating*
  26 *Checklist for the Small Engineering Workshop*
  27 *Advertising*
  28 *Insurance*
  29 *Selling It: a Guide to Marketing for Craftspeople*
  30 *Staying Up Front — Business Management for Long-distance Owner-drivers*
  Staying Up Front (audio cassette)
  31 *Helping your Small Business Survive and Grow*
  32 *Leasing Questions and Answers*
  33 *Small Business and the Law*
  34 *Your Own Menswear Store*
  35 *Sportsgoods Retailing*
  36 *Getting into Gifts*
  37 *Full Bottle — Managing a Retail Liquor Store*
  38 *Dictionary for Small Business Starters*
  39 *Home-based Businesses — Guidelines for Starting a Small Business at Home*
  40 *Managing a Newsagency*
  41 *Computers for Small Business*

42 *Costing and Pricing*
43 *Fast-Food Outlets*
44 *Short Cuts for Hairdressers*
45 *Bookshops*
46 *Directory of New Business Opportunities*
47 *How to Value a Small Enterprise*

Manufacturing:
1 *Business Planning for Small Manufacturers*
2 *Financial Budgeting for Small Manufacturers*
3 *Costing and Pricing for Small Manufacturers*
4 *Accounting Systems and Procedures for Small Manufacturers*
5 *Management Reports and Information for Small Manufacturers*
6 *Inventory Management and Control for Small Manufacturers*
7 *Production Planning and Control for Small Manufacturers*
8 *Total Quality Control for Small Manufacturers*
9 *Just in Time for Small Manufacturers*

Trimpac (training management packages):
Trimpac 1 Starting a Small Business
Trimpac 2 Evaluating a Small Business
Trimpac 3 Bookkeeping for Small Business (Parts 1 & 2)
Trimpac 4 Financial Budgeting in Small Business
Trimpac 5 Understanding Costs in Small Business
Trimpac 6 Marketing for Small Business (Parts 1 & 2)
Trimpac 7 Personnel Management

Films and videos (all VHS or Beta):
The Business Plan Package
Counselling Your Small Business Client Package
Free and Enterprising
On Target Marketing — Retailing and Services; Manufacturing
Plain Sailing/Firm Foundations
Having a Go
Profit and Loss
Making It
Staying Up Front

Audio cassettes:
Planning and Starting a Small Business
Planning and Starting a Small Retail Business

Hospitality training packages:
Hotel/Restaurant package
Accommodation with Restaurant package
Caravan Parks and Camping Areas package

Single module (with video)
Getting Started
Handling Finance
Sales and Marketing
Accommodation
Double modules (with video)
Restaurant Administration/Operation
Liquor Administration/Operation
The Business of Retail Trade package

These publications are available from Commonwealth government bookshops, DITAC, the Australian Government Publishing Service, or from state small business agencies, offices or corporations.

- Trademarks and Patents Office publications:
  Guide for Applicants for Designs
  Guide for Applicants for Patents
  Guide for Applicants for Trademarks

- Department of Industrial Development. This department is now defunct, but the following publications are still available from small business agencies:
  Guide to Budgeting for the Small Manufacturer
  Guide to Costing for the Small Manufacturer

Remember the golden rule: help and information are always available somewhere.

Solutions

The following are suggested solutions to the review exercises at the ends of chapters.

Chapter 1

1C 2D 3C 4C 5D 6C 7D 8A 9C 10A

Chapter 2

1 (a) changes in female values and roles
(b) more women seeking professional careers
(c) social marginality caused by working in male dominated and controlled industries

2 (a) Female small business owners tend to employ a greater proportion of female staff than either male owned or male/female owned enterprises.
(b) Ethnic proprietors employ the highest proportion of ethnic staff and family members in their small businesses.

3 (a) loss of skills caused through spending long periods of time outside the workforce
(b) the need to juggle work and domestic responsibilities
(c) encountering discrimination when applying for finance and other resources

4 (a) inability to find employment because of discrimination and hostility
(b) inability to find meaningful work due to lack of recognition of skills and qualifications

Chapter 3

1C 2D 3C 4C 5B 6A 7A 8B

Chapter 4

1 (a) money you have borrowed
(b) your other assets
(c) your health
(d) your family and friends
(e) your self-esteem

2 (a) expectations of your customers
   (b) the need for decision-making
   (c) the need for continuous planning
   (d) maintaining your desired image
   (e) staff performance
   (f) cost considerations
   (g) income protection

3 A business is run for profit, a hobby usually for enjoyment.

4 (a) responsibilities to people
   (b) responsibilities under law

Chapter 5

1D 2B 3D 4A 5B 6C 7A 8D 9D 10A

Chapter 6

Scoring instructions are provided at the end of each section of this self-assessment.

Chapter 7

Self-assessment — refer to Figure 7.1 on page 112.

Chapter 8

1 A feasibility study is a systematic analysis of the possibility of putting a business idea into practice.

2 The key parts of a feasibility study are:
   - the business idea
   - the key people
   - the market
   - the operational structure
   - financial considerations
   - recommendations
   - appendices.

3 Good objectives must be:
   (a) clearly defined
   (b) measurable
   (c) achievable
   (d) challenging
   (e) brief
   (f) written.

4 Your personal objectives should include all aspects of your life, namely:
   (a) material
   (b) physical and mental
   (c) psychological and emotional
   (d) spiritual and intangible.

5 The one business objective you should include in your feasiblity study is to have your feasibility study completed by a set date.

6 The seven steps needed to evaluate financial viability are:
   (a) Calculate your family/personal net worth.
   (b) Determine total funds available for equity investment.
   (c) Calculate your monthly living costs.
   (d) Calculate the borrowed funds needed.
   (e) Calculate profits needed.
   (f) Calculate sales level needed.
   (g) Ask if sales can be reached.

Chapter 9
1D 2B 3A 4C 5D 6C 7D 8D 9C 10B

Chapter 10
1D 2B 3A 4D 5A 6D 7D 8A 9B 10C

Chapter 11
1D 2B 3A 4B 5B 6C 7B 8D 9B 10A

Chapter 12
1 (a) Refer to Table 12.3 on page 218.
   (b) Your accountant and your solicitor.
2 Your answer will be assisted by checking the details shown on pages 203–6.
3 Refer to pages 207–10.

Chapter 13
1 Equity finance is capital invested in the business. There is usually no provision for the money to be repaid, but there is an expectation that the investor will share in the profits of the business. Debt finance is a loan to the owner of the business. There is a legal requirement for the debt to be repaid in full, together with a specified amount of interest.
2 If you try to repay the loan too quickly you might starve the business of funds for other purposes, or reduce your own income to an inadequate level. If the loan is spread over too long a time, the total interest paid will be higher, and you might reduce your chances of gaining further loans during this time, which could limit future opportunities for growth of your business.
3 Factoring is a process in which debts are sold to a finance company. You send a copy of your customer invoices to the finance company, which pays you the amount, less a commission, promptly and usually within seven days.
4 Freeing up funds from within your business involves looking closely at assets, customers and suppliers.
5 A bank overdraft provides an ongoing line of credit (continuous loan) by allowing a business to withdraw money from a cheque account to a predetermined level beyond the amount of money in the

account. Term loans are available from banks and finance companies and give access to the full amount of the loan immediately. This is then repaid, with interest, by regular equal instalments over a period of time.

6 With commercial hire purchase, ownership of the assets transfers to the purchaser immediately and a depreciation allowance can be claimed by the business. Leasing charges can be claimed in full as expenses, but no depreciation is allowed. Depending on the value and depreciation rate of the asset, there could be significant taxation advantages in one or the other of these financing methods.

7 Business profits provide security for lenders' or investors' capital. Finance is lent to (or invested with) the owner as a person.

8 These will substantiate your claims that your business is sound and operating in an industry and economic environment which indicate a successful future.

9 The purpose of this section of your submission is to demonstrate that you have the qualifications, experience, aptitude and attitude required to take responsibility for, and manage, other people's money in a business situation.

Chapter 14

1 Planning is simply deciding in advance (and that means now) what to do, how to do it, when to do it, who will do it and which resources will be involved.

2 (a) time pressures
(b) difficulties in starting
(c) lack of specialised knowledge
(d) lack of trust and openness
(e) need for conceptual thinking
(f) no immediate feedback
(g) speed of change
(h) cost

3 Distinctive competence refers to a unique feature which a firm has and its competitors do not. This feature may be converted to a competitive advantage.

4 (a) Where are you now?
(b) Where do you want to be at a future date?
(c) How will you get there?

5 (a) An operational plan
(b) A marketing plan
(c) A staff plan
(d) A finance plan

6 See page 247.

7 (a) clearly defined
(b) measurable
(c) achievable

(d) challenging
(e) brief
(f) written

8 (a) what customers to approach
(b) what products
(c) what price
(d) what place
(e) what promotion

9 The staff plan is based on the assumption that people are the most valuable resource of any business.

10 'Break-even' refers to the level of sales which equals the total of all costs, ie the point at which there is neither profit nor loss.

11 The cash flow budget.

Scoring instructions are provided at the end of the self-assessment exercise.

Chapter 15

1 Records will give you all the information you need to satisfy the demands of:
- the taxation department
- other government departments
- insurance companies
- your accountant and solicitor
- bank managers
- finance companies
- suppliers
- prospective purchasers of your business.

2 To produce information that is:
- appropriate to the user's needs
- understandable to the user
- concise yet meaningful
- accurate (within reason)
- economically produced
- up to date.

3 (a) Record transaction on source document.
(b) Copy to journal or cash book.
(c) Summarise copy to ledger (optional).
(d) Transpose totals to reports or statements.

4 See pages 282–4.

5 Journal, cash book or analysis book. It shows where money came from, or will come from, and where it has gone (bank, expenses or capital).

6 To produce an accurate record of available cash.

7 Expenses.

8 Cost of goods sold
Retail COGS = opening stock + purchases minus closing stock

Manufacturing COGS = direct labour + direct materials + manufacturing overheads.

9 It shows a summary of all income and expenses, and hence gross and net profit.

10 What the business owns and owes.

Chapter 16

1 A trend is an average rate of change.

2 Ratios can indicate which aspect of your business needs the most attention. This helps you manage because your effort is applied where it is most needed.

3 Variance analysis involves identifying the reasons for differences between planned and actual figures. This helps you develop an understanding of your business and apply your effort most effectively.

4 It indicates how much cash will be available to operate the business each month.

5 Speed, accuracy and complete sets of reports.

6 Budgets show the planned, (future) itemised income and expenditure, and the monthly trade surplus or deficit. Cash flows show only cash transactions, and planned monthly cash balances. Forecasts indicate the probable future value of an item if nothing else changes.

7 By comparing them with previous results and with industry figures, or generally accepted values.

8 Because all software can be run on a computer, but no single computer can run all software.

9 Financial management and planning is an ongoing, cyclical process. Historical records from one period are analysed and ratios calculated. Trends are also computed, and forecasts developed. The figures for your business this year are then compared with those of previous years, and with other businesses in the same industry. Financial objectives are determined, based on the information generated in the forecasts and comparisons. Projected financial statements reflecting these objectives are then prepared. Detailed budgets and cash flows complete the planning part of the cycle. Monthly actual results, and computed variances provide the basis for cost control. Management decisions flow from an analysis of the variances each month. Objectives and plans can be reviewed and revised, based on the actual results and variance analysis.

10 Profitability indicates the health of a business and the returns to the owner(s) over a period of time. Liquidity determines the probability of survival of the business.

Chapter 17

1 Deciding what offer to make to what market.

2 (a) What customers you should approach.
(b) What products/services they want.

(c) What price you should charge.
(d) What your method of distribution should be.
(e) How you tell them about yourself and your offer.

3 (a) Advertising is the paid presentation and promotion of ideas, products or services by an identified sponsor.
(b) Publicity is any unpaid presentation or promotion which develops or enhances the demand for the ideas, products or services of an organisation.
(c) Personal selling is any oral presentation to one or more potential customers with the objective of making a sale.
(d) Sales promotion is any short-term, non-routine, customer stimulation which is designed to give an immediate increase in sales.

4 Attention, interest, desire, conviction, action

5 Word of mouth (publicity).

6 Prospecting and qualifying, pre-approach, approach, presentation and demonstration, handling objections, close, follow-up.

7 Refer to the list on page 329.

8 (a) objective
(b) accurate
(c) assertive
(d) innovative
(e) co-ordinated
(f) controlled

Chapter 18

1 Retailing, put simply, is the process of making it easier for people to buy goods and services.

2

100	200	100
50	150	50
33.3	133.3	33.3
25	125	25
20	120	20
16.7	116.7	16.7
14.3	114.3	14.3
12.5	112.5	12.5
11.1	111.1	11.1

3 (a) Mark-up $15; 100% Cost price: $15 Margin: $15
(b) Selling price: $20 Mark-up: $4; 25% Margin: $4; 20%
(c) Selling price: $150 Mark-up: $60; 66.7% Margin: $60; 40%
(d) Cost price: $30
(e) Cost price: $12 Mark-up: $24; 200% Margin: $24; 66.7%
(f) Cost price: $45 Mark-up: $45; 100% Margin: $45; 50%
(g) Mark-up: 150% Selling price: $100/pair

4 (a) significant changes in customer demand
(b) cash flow shortages

(c) falling employee morale
(d) changes in competitor activity
(e) changes in supplier activity
(f) increase in customer complaints

Chapter 19

1 Continuous: standard product, special machines, repetitious tasks, specialised staff skills. Jobbing: varied output, standard machines, multi-skilled staff.
2 (a) materials
(b) machinery
(c) staff
(d) money
3 All small businesses have some form of output. Production is the creative effort required to generate that output.
4 Preventive maintenance reduces breakdowns of machines. Breakdowns that do occur are likely to be less costly to repair. Also, because they are less frequent, less management time is needed for rescheduling of production.
5 (a) analysis of tasks: actions and times required for their performance
(b) allocation of skills and machines to jobs
6 If only one supplier is known, interruption of that business, or deliveries, can cause difficulty, and even failure of your business.
7 Cost of time, and customers, lost due to breakdowns, and alternative courses of action available to overcome problems when production is interrupted.
8 To overcome initial weaknesses in new staff and to meet the changing needs of your business resulting from new technology, methods, techniques and products.
9 By considering all objectives, identifying priorities for each, and selecting those with highest priority in terms of the overall direction of your business. Then concentrating on the production objectives with the highest priority.
10 Develop your own skills and abilities through further education at a recognised institution, or employ a competent engineer on a staff or consulting basis.

Chapter 20

1 So that you can incorporate their ideas into the objectives, where appropriate, and to increase their motivation and commitment.
2 (a) write a specification
(b) attract applicants
(c) prepare questions for use in the interview
(d) check equal opportunity legislation
(e) conduct interviews
(f) provide for input from existing staff

(g) review all information
(h) select applicant
(i) notify all applicants

3 Plan and prepare their induction into your business.
4 Be prepared, calm, polite and brief.
5 New ideas, early warning of possible objections, possibility of better strategies being developed, smoother implementation, improved chance of reaching objectives.
6 Survival, security, a sense of belonging, esteem, self-actualisation.
7 Because people are the most valuable asset in your business.
8 Communication. Talking and listening to your employees.
9 The building of a powerful team of committed employees. Their satisfaction will be obvious not only to you, but more importantly, to your customers.
10 Courage, commitment, skill, knowledge, communication, caring, leadership.

Chapter 21

Scoring instructions are provided at the end of the questions for this self-assessment.

Chapter 22

1 For at least five years.
2 No. The proprietor pays income tax on the profits he or she derives from the business.
3 Each month, by the seventh day, unless total deductions for the year are less than $10 000, in which case they can be sent every three months.
4 Provisional tax is a system used to make provision for this year's tax on earnings of more than $999 on which PAYE tax has not been paid.
5 (a) building and construction
(b) joinery and cabinet making
(c) architectural services
(d) cleaning industry
(e) engineering services
(f) motor vehicle repairs
(g) surveying services
(h) road transport
(i) professional building and construction services other than architectural, engineering and surveying services
6 As soon as you begin providing benefits to your employees in place of salary or wages.
7 Yes. If you are selling or giving away an asset, or if your asset is lost or destroyed, you should contact the ATO to check whether CGT will apply.
8 Retailers pay sales tax on goods as part of the wholesale price when

they purchase them. They have no further liability when they sell the goods by retail.

9 Yes. The Income Tax Assessment Act says that you must record the value of all trading stock you have on hand at the beginning and end of each year of income.

10 You are advised in writing by the Child Support Agency which provides the only authority for these deductions.

Chapter 23

Scoring instructions are provided at the end of the questions for both parts of this self-assessment.

Chapter 24

1 The lack of one or more resources is limiting growth.

2 Attend relevant workshops, seminars and training courses, read books, and talk with other business people.

3 Ensure that all avenues for generating funds from inside your business have been fully explored (see Chapter 8) and prepare a detailed business plan (see Chapter 14).

4 You should carefully consider:
   (a) geographic size and locations
   (b) your product/service range
   (c) your customers' needs and wants.

5 Owner's time, owner's knowledge or skills, finance, space, equipment, staff, market size, product, owner's attitude.

6 Identify how time is being used now. Find others to take over non-productive activities, on a part- or full-time basis, as staff members or consultants.

7 Purchase and use only standard machines, without any modification.

8 Review customer needs and wants. Make any changes to products or product range to meet the needs of customers.

9 Become aware of the feelings aroused in them by others' behaviour.

10 Because any other action will result in future failure of the business.

Chapter 25

1 surviving

2 planned controlled

3 S

4 professional

5 informal dominated

6 entrepreneurial drive vitality

7 decline regenerated

8 (a) records
   (b) well-rounded managerial experience
   (c) market opportunity niche
   (d) under-capitalised

9 (a) under-capitalisation
(b) cash/financial management
(c) growth
10 (a) uncontrolled growth
(b) complacency

Chapter 26

1 It indicates which resource might be limiting growth or will probably limit the current growth phase.
2 Some of the ways you can expand your business are by:
- just growing bigger (more staff)
- expanding the ownership (partners, shareholders)
- expanding your market
  —franchise your business
  —start another branch
  —merge with another business
- expanding your share of the market (buy a competitor)
- expanding your product range
  — more stock lines
  —start another business.

3 Advantages are increases in your rewards — the reasons why you went into your own business. Disadvantages are increasing demands on your personal resources. However, by facing and meeting these challenges, the rewards are even greater.
4 Equipment, decor, layout, staff, appearance. Documentation of procedures. Preparation of contracts and information.
5 Market expansion usually involves new geographic locations, and requires locational analysis. Market share expansion concentrates on gaining more customers from within the existing market area.
6 New skills and knowledge will be required. More time will be spent on administration and management, and less on using the skills that were the basis of the business previously.
7 Finding prospects, obtaining details of their credentials and experience, determining their personal goals and management style, negotiating mutually suitable arrangements.
8 More administration of wage and staff records, more time spent training, motivating, supervising, and arranging rosters, etc. More time needed to plan the use of the human resources.
9 Keep records of sales of existing items. Analyse these to identify which ones are reaching the peak of their sales. Find replacement items by referring to customers, suppliers, competitors, other markets. Keep up to date with developments through trade fairs, suppliers, magazines, and business and industry networks.
10 An aggressive, confident, risk-taking attitude will result in the choice of a radical, innovative option.

Glossary

Accounts payable Money owed to creditors (suppliers of goods or services on credit) and due for payment.

Accounts receivable Money owed to a business by its customers for goods or services sold or supplied on credit.

Advertising The paid presentation and promotion of ideas, products and services by an identified sponsor.

Aesthetics Qualities relating to beauty and general attractiveness.

Aim Boundaries within which goals are to be achieved.

Assets Items of property owned by a business and what is owed to it (for instance, cash, buildings, machinery, accounts receivable, inventories and goodwill). Assets are the resources of a business.

Atmospherics Aspects of a store's physical appearance which will be aesthetically pleasing or otherwise. Lighting, colour, style of furnishing and general decor all contribute to atmospherics.

Bad debt Money owed to a business (account receivable) which cannot be collected, and is written off as such.

Bank reconciliation A process whereby the final balance shown on a bank statement is adjusted to show the current position by including pending transactions.

Bankrupt If a person or business refuses to pay a debt, a creditor may take legal action to recover it. If the debtor is declared bankrupt the assets are sold and the proceeds divided among creditors in a specified order. For a person or business to become bankrupt it is usual (but not necessary) for liabilities (debts) to exceed assets.

Batch production A process where the output is varied, being designed to meet specific customer requirements (also known as *jobbing*).

Beneficiary A person who receives a gift or benefit and, more usually, one who inherits property from the estate of a deceased person through a will.

Break-even point The level of sales (in dollars or in units) at which income and expenses are equal and there is neither profit nor loss.

Budget A statement of likely future income and expenditure (or of cash receipts and payments) indicating forecast profit or loss (or cash surplus or deficit) ie a plan expressed in numbers, usually money.

Business failure A situation in which a business ceases to operate because it is bankrupt, insolvent or unable to trade profitably, or because of any other financial difficulty. Usually, but not always, there is loss to creditors. A failure can result from the action of a creditor (leading to bankruptcy) or from a decision by the owner(s) to close the business down.

Business growth curve See *Business lifecycle*.

Business lifecycle The pattern of growth and development of a business from its birth, through various stages, to maturity and (sometimes) decline. Most lifecycles follow an S-shaped pattern.

Business plan The master plan or action blueprint for the future direction of a business. It outlines goals and objectives, strategies and various other plans.

Cash flow (liquidity) Cash received less cash paid out. Liquidity is a measure of how well a business can pay its debts from its cash flow (which can include borrowed money, if needed). Negative cash flow occurs when cash payments exceed cash receipts.

Central business district (CBD) The original business (shopping) centre of a town. Growth and expansion of the population into suburbs, and the development of suburban and regional shopping centres, has often led to deterioration of CBDs as shopping areas. Recently, many CBDs have been rebuilt and modernised.

Commitment A promise, agreement or pledge to do something. It can be an obligation (legally enforceable or otherwise) to someone else, or a promise made to oneself. Commitment also implies dedication to a cause and persistence.

Communication The process of transmitting and receiving information.

Competitive advantage An advantage which a business has over its competitors because of superior products, services or other benefits, and which persuades customers to buy from it rather than from its competitors.

Competitor Any rival person or firm offering similar goods or services to the same customers.

Complementary products Goods (or services) that increase the demand for each other, such as bread and margarine or butter, cars and petrol.

Continuous production A process in which a large number of identical products are created.

Contract A legally binding agreement between two or more parties, with penalties if either party breaches (fails to carry out) the agreement. Not every agreement is a legally enforceable contract.

Co-operative A voluntary association of persons (often employees, suppliers or customers) who have agreed to take shares in the ownership of a business venture and run it for their own mutual benefit.

Cost of goods sold (COGS) The cost of goods (stock or inventory) at the start of a financial period, plus the cost of goods purchased during that period (including cartage and such costs), less the end-of-period inventory (at cost). COGS is therefore the cost of merchandise actually sold during the financial period. Sales minus COGS = gross profit.

Cost price The total cost of buying an item of merchandise or raw material, which includes its invoice cost, any freight or cartage, insurance, import duty or any other such costs.

Creditor One to whom money is owed.

Critical point The time at which the sales growth of a business begins to slow, leading to levelling, and then decline.

Crowding The experience of being hemmed in by people or physical barriers, to the point where psychological discomfort results. People perceive crowding in different ways and react to it differently, but most will avoid it.

Current assests Cash and other assets that can be changed into cash fairly quickly (for example, accounts receivable and inventories).

Customer Someone who has a need or want for your goods/services, plus the ability to pay and the ability to make a decision, and who also has a good image of you.

Debtor One who owes money (to a creditor).

Deductions Expenses incurred in generating income. They do not usually include personal expenses or the cost of capital assets.

Delegation The allocation of work responsibilities and authority to others.

Depreciation The loss in value of fixed assets through aging, wear and tear, and obsolescence. Depreciation is a business expense.

Destination traffic Shoppers who enter a store knowing what they wish to buy and where to find it, and who therefore move as directly as possible to where the merchandise is placed.

Discretionary time Blocks of time set aside to do important work without interruption. It is time to be used at the person's discretion, rather than to be used in responding to the needs of other people. See *Response time*.

Disposable income Income available to spend as wished, after payment of taxes and other fixed obligations.

Distinctive competence A skill, ability, strength or superiority that a firm has and its competitors do not have. It is a unique feature that may be converted into a competitive advantage.

Down-time Time when a resource (usually a mechanical asset such as machinery or equipment) cannot be used because of breakdown, repairs and maintenance.

Drawings Cash or goods removed from a business by a sole trader or a partner.

Effecting insurance Taking out (that is, obtaining) an insurance policy which provides the protection needed to minimise the risk of financial loss through fire, burglary or any other insurable event.

Effectiveness Doing the right thing to achieve a goal or objective.

Efficiency Doing something with minimum use of resources (eg at the lowest cost and in the shortest time possible). A person or business can be efficient at doing the wrong things, and therefore be ineffective.

Entrepreneur An individual who can project an idea into the future and then make it happen through innovative action. Such persons are skilled at identifying and/or creating business opportunities, are forward-looking and ambitious, are action people, and are willing to take a risk that matches their ability and skill.

Entrepreneurial Having the characteristics and behaviour of an entrepreneur.

Entrepreneurial drive The motivational force to undertake entrepreneurial activities, such as starting a new business venture.

Equity An owner's financial interest in a business or a property. If a business has assets worth $100 000 and liabilities of $30 000, then owner's equity would be $70 000.

Esteem A feeling of being competent and worthy and being viewed that way by others.

Factoring A process whereby a finance company buys the debts of a business for a price less than the face value of the debts.

Family-run business A business owned and run by a husband-and-wife team and/or other members of a family.

Feasibility study A systematic analysis of the possibility of putting a business idea into practice.

Financial viability A firm's ability to survive, as judged in terms of its profitability and/or cash flow in comparison with its owner's financial needs.

Fixed assets Assets of a 'permanent' nature (such as building, vehicles, equipment, machinery, furniture and fittings) owned by a business and not intended for resale as part of normal business operations.

Forecast A prediction of the future (for instance, a sales or cash flow forecast). Most forecasts are based on extrapolating (that is, extending) from figures of past years and are adjusted for current and likely future influences.

Franchise An arrangement under which the owner of a product, service or production process (the franchisor), in return for a fee, permits a distributor (the franchisee) to sell or use that product, service or production process. Franchisors usually provide assistance in setting up and managing the franchisee's business.

Franchisee The dealer or retailer who sells a franchised product or service, or uses a production process under licence from the franchisor.

Franchisor The owner of the franchised product, service or production process who agrees to have a franchisee sell or use it in return for an agreed fee.

Goal A statement in general terms which describes a desired outcome.

Going concern A business that is still operating. A business can be bought and sold as a going concern, ie in going order.

Goodwill The value of the favourable attitudes of customers and others about a business. Goodwill is recorded as an asset only when the business is sold as a going concern. Its value is based on estimated (or forecast) future profits over and above what might be regarded as normal earnings.

Gross profit Balance available from trading, after deducting cost of goods sold, to pay all overhead costs and yield a net profit.

Growth cycle A pattern of growth followed by products and businesses. It is usually one of slow growth, rapid growth, level sales and declining sales in that order.

'High-tech' industries Industries using advanced and therefore usually complex technology in their products, services and production processes. Technology relates to the use or application of knowledge to work and production. Electronics is a 'high-tech' industry.

Image The view or perception that you and other people have of your organisation. Every business has a reputation or appearance that will either attract customers or turn them away.

Independence Being free to do what one wishes; not relying on others; being able to think and act for oneself.

Innovation To innovate is to do new (and better) things and, therefore, to bring about change. Entrepreneurs are innovative.

Insolvency A situation in which a person or business is unable to pay debts as they fall due. This is not the same thing as being declared bankrupt, but insolvency can lead to a refusal to pay a debt which, in turn, might lead to bankruptcy. Poor cash management can result in insolvency.

Insurance A contract under which the insurer, for a fee (premium), agrees to make good any financial or other loss suffered by the insured. Insurance is a way of reducing the risk of financial loss.

Insurance agent A person who acts (with authority) for an insurance company. Such a person is often an employee of the insurance company.

Insurance broker A person who arranges insurance cover and acts as a consultant, but does not represent any particular insurance company.

Inventory Stock of goods (materials or merchandise) purchased either for resale (by retailers and wholesalers) or for use in manufacturing or providing services.

Invoice Notice sent by a creditor to a debtor detailing the amount owing.

Jobbing See *Batch production.*
Journal Book of accounts showing details of transactions.

Layout The physical design and arrangement of the internal space of a shop, factory, office or other place of business, and the placement of furniture, equipment, aisles, check-outs, machinery, storage areas and advertising displays. Good layout maximises traffic (in retailing) and reduces workflow delays and costs (in manufacturing).

Leadership Showing the way by example and by going first; the ability to guide, direct or indicate the way.

Lease A contract under which one party (the lessee) agrees to rent or use property owned by the owner (the lessor). Leases are invariably in writing; they allow long-term occupancy and use of property.

Ledger Book of accounts in which summaries are kept of entries in journals.

Lessee One who leases (that is, occupies and uses) property owned by another party for a specified fee or rental.

Lessor The person who owns property and agrees to its use by another (the lessee).

Levels of need Groupings of basic human needs arranged like rungs of a ladder from survival up to self-actualisation.

Limiting resource That resource of a business that is fully utilised to produce the sales level at the critical point in its growth cycle.

Liquidity The ability of a business to pay its debts (liabilities) on or before their due date.

Loan principal Amount borrowed which must be repaid, usually with an additional (interest) charge.

Location The general placement or situation of a business. A site is the specific address of the business.

Location affinity The practice of locating similar businesses close to each other, which makes it easier for customers to make comparisons.

Location complementarity The result of locating complementary businesses near each other. Cinemas and restaurants, and greengrocers and butchers, are examples of complementary firms — customers frequently buy from one after buying from the other.

Maintenance agreement A contract between a repairer and a machine owner to provide a specified level of maintenance and repair service.

Management buy-out The purchase of a business by its managers and/or other employees. This often occurs if a firm is failing and its owner(s) are seeking to sell out.

Managerial skills Skills in efficiently and effectively dealing with (managing) the resources of the business — its people, finances, physical property, time and information. Business failure is very much associated with a lack of high-level managerial skill.

Manufacturer A business that converts raw material into finished goods for sale.

Margin The difference between cost price and selling price, expressed in dollars or as a percentage of selling price. A shortening of the terms *margin on gross profit* or *gross profit margin*.

Mark-up The amount that is added to the cost price of goods or services to give the selling price. Mark-up can be expressed in dollar value or as a percentage of cost price.

Market The actual and potential buyers of goods and services.

Market segment A measurable group of customers who have something in common and can be reached with one offer.

Market strategy The process of deciding what offer to make to what market.

Marketing A planned process aimed at discovering and satisfying customers needs at a profit.

Mass media A general term to encompass television, radio, newspapers and magazines.

Maturity A business is said to be mature when its growth (usually measured in sales and/or profits) has slowed. Unlike human beings, a business may 'take off' with further growth after a period of maturity. Many mature businesses continue to stagnate and die.

Media release A standardised method of communicating information to the media for publication or presentation. It is often called a press release.

Merchandise Goods purchased for resale, or finished goods manufactured for sale. Unsold merchandise is known as stock-on-hand or inventory.

Need levels See *Levels of need*.

Neighbourhood shopping centre A group of shops and businesses (up to about 15 or 20) serving the needs of a neighbourhood. It is smaller than a regional shopping centre.

Net profit The earnings of a business from sales (or other types of income, such as fees) less all expenses incurred in running the business. Net profit represents the owner's reward for the equity (ie risking the financial investment in the venture) and for the necessary work, time, skill and overall responsibility.

Objective A clearly defined, measurable outcome in written form.

Occupancy costs All costs relating to the rental or leasing of property. In addition to actual rental costs, other charges might include water rates, general rates, insurance, repairs and maintenance. Tenants or lessees must know exactly what occupancy costs they are to be responsible for before signing any agreement.

Operational plan See *Working plan*.

Overhead costs Operating expenses that are not directly productive.

Owner/manager A person who owns and is actively involved in running a small business venture. This includes sole proprietors, partners and shareholder directors.

Partnership An arrangement between persons carrying on business in common for the purpose of earning a profit. Each partner is a part owner of the business. The rights and duties of each partner should be clearly spelled out in a written agreement to avoid disputes about who is entitled to or responsible for what. By law, a partnership is not a separate legal entity, and all partners are personally responsible for paying the partnership debts.

Personal selling Any oral presentation to one or more potential customers for the purpose of making sales.

Petty cash A sum of money set aside and made available for small ('petty') expenditures such as stamps and small office needs. A record is needed of petty cash expenditures.

Place The point at which the exchange between buyers and sellers occurs. It can refer to an actual location or to a method of distribution.

Planning Deciding in advance (that is, now) what should be done in the future. Planning is a vital part of every manager's work. Most firms lack good planning, and suffer for it.

Policy Performance standards that are determined by management for the operation of the business.

Prepaid expenses Payments made in advance for future services.

Preventive maintenance The planned periodic inspection, cleaning, lubrication and adjustment of machines.

Priorities Those activities that are most important as means of reaching goals. Putting priorities on things means placing them in order of importance, and is essential in good management, especially time management.

Professional management A systematic (rational) approach to managing in which much care and attention is given to planning, organising, co-ordinating and controlling the resources and activities of the business. Many small firms seriously lack professional management.

Profile A short personal outline highlighting the key points or skills of an individual. It is a general picture and not just an employment history.

Promotion Communication with existing and/or potential customers.

Promotional mix The combined activities of advertising, publicity, personal selling and sales promotion used by a business to reach its target market.

Proprietary limited company An association of people who have invested share capital to form a business which the law recognises as having an existence separate from its shareholders. There can be no more than 50 shareholders and there are restrictions on the sale of shares. Each shareholder is responsible for the company's debts only to the extent of the cost of shares held. (For example, a shareholder with 100 shares of $10 each has a risk [or liability] limited to $1000.) The continuation of a company is not affected by the death or retirement of any shareholder.

Psychosomatic illness Physical health problems (such as hypertension or ulcers) associated with nervous (that is, stressful) conditions.

Publicity Any unpaid presentation which stimulates demand for the ideas, goods or services of an organisation. The two main avenues for publicity are word of mouth and the mass media.

Purchasing power A measure of the earnings and therefore the ability of people to spend money to purchase. High-income earners (for instance, professionals) are one recognised market segment, as are low-income earners.

Ratio A figure that expresses the relationship between the value of two items.

Regional shopping centre A large shopping centre, often consisting of 50 to 100 shops of a predetermined mix, serving a large area of perhaps 50 000 people.

Research The systematic and logical investigation of some matter or problem for the purpose of explaining, understanding and/or predicting.

Resources The means available to a business by which its objectives can be reached. Resources can be broadly grouped into people (labour force and customers), money, physical assets (both fixed and current), time and information.

Response time Working time allocated to deal with the demands and problems of other people. Those who are poor time managers usually spend too much of their available time responding to the needs of others, and therefore have too little discretionary time.

Responsibility Liability, answerability or accountability. A duty or obligation — either by law, or self-imposed.

Retailer A business which sells to the general public.

Risk The chance of loss or failure. Individuals differ in the level of risk they are prepared to accept.

Sales promotion Any short-term, non-routine, customer stimulation which is designed to give an immediate increase in sales.

Security (1) A state or feeling of being safe; having no fear or concern about one's well-being. (2) A guarantee of payment, made by pledging something of value to the creditor as proof of the debt.

Self-actualisation A lifestyle in which a person is utilising their full potential.

Self-fulfilment See *Self-actualisation*.

Selling price The price at which an item of merchandise is sold.

Service firm A business that earns most of its income by providing (ie selling) services of some kind.

Shopping mall A vehicle-free shopping area, providing pedestrian access to shops. Many CBDs are being converted to malls, which can take the form of a plaza, a square, a cloister or a court.

Shopping traffic Shoppers who enter a store wishing to wander and browse before buying.

Site The specific address of a business. See *Location*.

Site plan A map or plan of a building or contruction showing the key features.

Small businesses A business which is (1) managed by its owner(s) in a personalised way; (2) independent of external control; and (3) relatively small in its industry.

Sole proprietorship A business owned and operated by one person.

Sole trader See *Sole proprietorship*.

Source document The first written record of a transaction.

Staples Goods or services that are essential to most people; not luxuries. Purchases regularly made by most shoppers.

Starting from scratch Converting an idea into a business without buying a business as a going concern; creating a new business from nothing.

Strategy A step-by-step plan to achieve an objective.

Stress The effects on one's mind, body and emotions of the many, varied and persistent pressures and demands of life, when the person concerned is unable to cope.

Stressors The pressures and demands which can lead to stress.

Structure The organisational form under which a business is operated, eg sole trader, partnership, proprietary limited company, etc.

Technical skills Skills associated with work, occupation, method, technique or procedure.

Technology See *'High-tech' industries.*

Time horizon The future (the number of years) for which planning is carried out.

Time log A record kept of how working time is used; a diary.

Time-wasters Those activities that do little or nothing towards the achievement of important goals.

Trade fair Any gathering of suppliers of goods for the purpose of displaying or demonstrating them to prospective buyers.

Trading area The geographical area from which most of a firm's customers will come.

Trading stock Goods on hand intended for manufacture, sale or exchange.

Transaction An activity involving the transfer of money and/or goods and services from one person to another.

Trend The average rate of change of the value of an item relative to time or to a second item.

Trust (1) A high level of confidence in another person. (2) A legal situation in which one person (the trustee) holds and uses property for and on behalf of another (the beneficiary).

Turnover Total sales of a business during a specified period of time.

Type A personality A personality with urgent, competitive, aggressive and impatient behaviour.

Type B personality A personality with relaxed, passive and unharried behaviour.

Venture capital Funds available for investment in a business, generally in return for a share of the ownership.

Viability Capacity for independent life; ability to exist, thrive, develop and grow; possibility; workability; feasibility.

Wholesaler A business which buys from manufacturers and sells to retailers.

Working capital The funds necessary to run a business on a day-to-day basis. It is also expressed as the value of current assets minus the value of current liabilities.

Working plan A plan relating to a firm's work flow, to the use of one of the firm's resources (such as employees and information), or to an aspect of management such as control. Working plans need to be co-ordinated.

INDEX